Tears

of the

Rain

ISBN: 978-1-885270-60-3

Cover Design: Rachel Mast

Third Printing: March 2007

Printed in the USA

For more information about Christian Aid Ministries, see pages 478-479.

To order additional copies of *Tears of the Rain* please contact:

TGS International
PO Box 355
Berlin, Ohio 44610 USA
Phone: 330·893·2428
Fax: 330·893·2305

070208AM1
12239

Tears

of the

Rain

Canadian Family Resources
4473 Perth Line 72
Newton, ON N0K 1R0
Call Toll Free 1-877-595-7585
CFR Call for a free catalogue

Ruth Ann Stelfox

Table of Contents

1

A Change in Plans

September 10, 2001

It finally happened! For the last two years we have thought and prayed about the possibility of serving in a foreign country. Now the opportunity has come. My mind has been whirling since that phone call this morning. "Ruth Ann, this is Paul Weaver from Christian Aid Ministries in Ohio. We're just wondering if your family would consider going to Liberia, Africa, for a term of service. I know this is short notice, but could you possibly be ready by the end of next month?"

"Well," I answered when I could find my voice, "Wayne's in the hospital recuperating from appendicitis surgery, but I'll talk to him tonight. We'll let you know as soon as we can."

What a change in plans!

"This could drastically affect our lives for the next two years," I told the children, "but first we'll have to see what Dad says about it."

Wayne's first reaction when we visited him in the hospital this evening was a groggy, "Where's Liberia?"

"It's in Africa somewhere," I answered. "I'll have to look on the globe to tell you just where. But tell me now, *are we going?*"

"I really wanted to go somewhere cold, like Romania," Wayne reminded me, "but I guess if God wants us in a hot place near the equator, that's where we'll go."

Equator. I have always been intrigued by that word. Steamy jungles . . . tropical birds . . . fierce tribes. I've read about it. But to actually go there for two years is another story.

September 14

Wayne is feeling much better. It's getting hard to keep him from going back to his job as foreman for his carpentry crew.

"Well," he mused today, "if I have to sit here, I may as well decide what all I need to do in case we do go to Africa. It's impossible to be ready in a month though. I have to wind up all those jobs, sell the motor home, find a renter . . . We have to meet with the church to get their consent too. No, a month isn't nearly long enough."

"What about *our* consent, Dad?" the children wanted to know.

"I know *you* all want to go," he told them with a smile. "This is an opportunity of a lifetime, don't you think?"

They're not so sure. They know it's an opportunity, but they still need lots of reassurance—and so do I. Though I support Wayne fully, I still have to sort through all kinds of mixed emotions and free advice. We must make arrangements for our in-home daycare business, consider home-schooling, and make countless other decisions.

Our five children are bombarding us with lots of questions— questions for which we have no ready answers.

"Will we have e-mail?" nineteen-year-old Beverly and eighteen-year-old Julie wondered. "What about a telephone? And what about other young people?"

William, at fifteen, is more concerned about what they have to eat. "Do they have good food—or just rice?" he asked. "How long will we have to stay? I'm sure they don't play hockey."

"Who will teach us?" Charlotte wondered. At thirteen, she isn't too sure about being a missionary.

"Can I get a baby elephant, or a monkey, or maybe a parrot?" Larry had to know. I guess when you're ten years old, life is one big adventure.

I'm sure we'll have lots to talk about in the coming days as we struggle to answer these and many other questions.

September 21

Convincing some of our relatives has been difficult. "A person doesn't realize how earth-bound he is until that security is tested," I told our two dear aunts, Sarah and Anne, who stopped in to visit and to find out if we really were considering going to Africa.

"The very same God who is here is in Africa, don't forget," Aunt Sarah said comfortingly.

Auntie Anne, however, was not so encouraging. "I can't see it—I just can't see it," she lamented. "How anyone can uproot and go to some wild, far-off place where only God knows what will happen. You're needed right here. My, we will miss you!" She never did take kindly to the winds of change.

"We'll miss you too," I told them, smiling into their dear faces.

"How can you leave the church like this?" she continued.

"No one is indispensable," I answered. "People will manage just fine without us."

"Why can't someone else go from all those thousands of Mennonites back East? Why ask you?"

"We applied at Christian Aid almost two years ago," I reminded them. "They are graciously letting us have the opportunity. It's a *privilege*."

"What about your children?"

"We've been thinking it over for weeks," I replied patiently, "and we feel it will be a positive experience for them."

"The same God who's here is in Africa," repeated Aunt Sarah soothingly.

My mother seems to waver between the two—one minute giving us her full blessing, and the next minute wondering if it is the right thing to do.

"You have your answer already," she finally told me. "You do what Wayne wants you to."

September 27

Paul Weaver called again today. The Mark Yoder family will fill in until we can get to Liberia. He wondered if we could leave in January.

Wayne is enthusiastic. "Things are happening pretty fast now," he said. "We're scheduled to fly to Pittsburgh on November 1, drive down to see Mom and Dad in a rented car, and go to CAM's Open House all day Friday and Saturday. Then we'll drive to Berlin, Ohio, for a meeting with Paul Weaver, Kim Eichorn, and Mark Yoder. After a couple days there, we'll drive back to Pittsburgh. He said we'll stay at Mark Yoder's bed and breakfast close to the CAM headquarters. What do you think?"

"I think it sounds great—except I'm scared of meetings. What happens if we don't qualify?"

"We'll cross that bridge when we get to it," was his characteristic reply. "Meanwhile, I have lots to do."

November 1

This whole day was right on schedule. Our flight was wonderful.

We arrived at Dad Stelfox's in time for a big turkey supper and a large welcoming committee.

We visited and ate, then visited some more until we were exhausted. It was so good to see Wayne's family and many of our Pennsylvania friends again.

November 2

We pulled into the driveway at the huge CAM warehouse and noticed with consternation the rows and rows of vehicles.

"There must be hundreds of people here," I whispered nervously.

We were ushered up to the meeting area and shown to our seats, wearing nametags stating our new position. *Wayne Stelfox, Director, Liberia,* and *Ruth Ann Stelfox, Liberia.* It all seemed so final.

As we walked in, the former Liberia country director, Conrad Swartzentruber, leaned forward and studied us with a big smile on his face and eyes full of interest.

We found the speeches intensely interesting. They were packed with statistics, advice, and touching stories. I enjoyed the intertwined humor.

November 5

Berlin, Ohio, is just as beautiful as I remembered it. The gently rolling hills are swathed in their finest glory of autumn colors—from the scarlet maples to the golden oaks and every hue and shade in between. Little white breaths of mist hung in the valleys this morning, and now the sky is as blue as an Alberta mountain lake. Between the official meetings with the CAM staff, we drove around and reveled in the beauty of the countryside.

Mark and Betty Yoder's bed and breakfast matches the scenery perfectly. It is spotlessly clean and cozy. We feel like royalty under their excellent care.

The meetings with the CAM staff were formal, warm, and encouraging all at the same time. Between Paul and Mark and Kim, every avenue of mission life was covered thoroughly. "God will give you the grace to do whatever you have to do," we were told with certainty.

"I feel like Moses, who knew God was asking something impossible of him," Wayne confided. "I don't mind the other stuff, but all that bookwork scares me."

Yesterday's slide presentation of Liberia gave me a funny feeling. I kept trying to imagine actually being a part of those pictures, but I wasn't too successful. Everyone looked so poor, and their eyes all looked so sad.

We are leaving for home, however, with encouraged hearts and renewed determination. God *does* want us in Liberia, and we are willing to place our hands in His and let Him lead the way.

November 19

The countdown has begun—we're scheduled to arrive in Liberia on January 18. We plan to spend five days with Wayne's parents in Pennsylvania before we leave. We still have lots to do before then.

December 30

It is impossible to pack a week any fuller than this Christmas week has been. We have had no less than five farewells of one sort or another. It has given us a good opportunity to share what Christian Aid is all about.

It's been a bittersweet Christmas for all of us.

January 8, 2002

Tonight is our last night in Alberta, and we're all sleeping here at Mother's. Our beloved Western Plains Church held a farewell service for us Sunday morning. We've had many supper invitations, but some we simply couldn't accept. There just wasn't time.

January 9

Mother's house was full of visitors until it was time to go. It seemed like a dream, but suddenly it was late afternoon, and we had to say good-bye.

Saying good-bye is never easy—especially if you're facing the unknown and if you're scared inside. Especially if your mother and sisters and brother and all your friends are in tears. Especially if you're not quite sure you will ever see them again.

As we tearfully parted, thoughts of our wonderful God comforted us.

He sees our pain. He feels our fear. He is from everlasting to everlasting. Praise His name.

We drove three hours to stay with friends in Montana. Their home is only twenty miles from the Great Falls International Airport. They gave us a lovely supper of soup, dinner rolls, brownies, and fruit, but there was a sadness about the evening that could not be denied, though we all tried to be cheerful. We lingered long in the cozy living room and talked of many things. They gave Wayne and me the best bed in the house, but I have not been able to fall asleep.

2

Liberia—The Edge of the Earth

January 16

After five delightful days in Pennsylvania with all of Wayne's family, it was time to depart.

Everyone looked so precious as we waved goodbye. Though we had plenty of time before boarding, Wayne hurried us along "just in case we run into trouble."

"Are you sure you have our passports?" he wondered again.

"Absolutely sure."

Finally, it was time to board. My stomach felt queer, and I was literally shivering from excitement as we walked down the gangplank and into that huge DC-10 jet. It had nine seats across.

We found our aisle numbers, stowed our carry-on bags, and sank into those comfortable seats. Eventually we would try to sleep, but for now our excitement levels were way too high. I saw it in the faces of our children and in the brown eyes of my husband.

Larry was worried about takeoff. "Think we'll be okay?" he wondered for the third time as we taxied from the runway onto the takeoff strip. "Does the pilot steer down the runway like we do a car?"

"I'm wondering the same thing," I replied, "but don't worry—just enjoy it."

With a muffled roar, the great jet opened those tremendous engines and sent us hurtling down the runway and up into the darkening skies.

Larry's knuckles were white from gripping the edge of his seat. "Wow!" he exclaimed. "This thing has power!"

January 17

Dawn was sending pointed fingers of light over the pinking horizon when we landed in Amsterdam. It had taken seven hours to cross the ocean. We will never forget the experience of flying into the dawn at 600 miles per hour.

Several hours later, we were on another jet over the Great Sahara. It was like a sea of creamy white from five thousand feet. My eyes were glued to the window, straining to see an oasis or town or whatever else might be inhabited.

Our thoughts were interrupted by the loudspeaker. "Ladies and gentlemen, we will be landing in Mallam Ammin Kano International Airport in twenty minutes."

"Africa. We're landing in *Africa!*" Charlotte exclaimed, voicing all our thoughts. "Too bad it's getting dark."

"My heart is pounding!" said Larry.

"I sure hope so!" answered Wayne, trying to sound casual. "Dear, look down!"

"Aren't we going too fast?" I gasped as a patchwork of tin roofs rushed by below us. He didn't answer.

We hit the ground much too fast and the engines screamed and groaned with the sudden pressure put upon them to stop the plane. We were pushed forward in our seats and hung on until the plane finally slowed.

"That's the worst landing we've ever had!" Larry said when he found his voice.

"We're safe—that's what matters," Wayne told him with evident relief.

We taxied to a stop, and an old yellow tractor with smoke billowing around it came chugging up to the plane and began loading baggage. "It's their baggage cart!" laughed Larry, a bit shakily. "Oh, it's funny!"

"A bit different from Washington, eh?" Wayne asked.

We waited in the airport for about two hours. It didn't seem long with all the new sights and sounds. I hope we didn't stare too much.

Wayne found out we were in northern Nigeria.

After a short wait, we were up in the dark sky once again, in a much smaller jet.

After a few more hours of flying, we once again landed on African soil—this time in Abidjan, Ivory Coast. We had looked forward to the special time when we would step out into the tropical air. We had heard about it from several people and wondered what it would be like. Now the moment was upon us.

A wave of heat met us at the door of the jet. It was close and humid—heavy with unfamiliar scents. We looked at each other—and smiled.

All I ever imagined and more.

"You all look tired," Wayne commented as we staggered down the steps with our carry-on bags.

"We *are* tired!" everyone chorused.

"It's only nine-thirty, so we should still get a good night's sleep if it doesn't take too long here," Wayne assured us.

It was not to be. We waited in line, presented our Canadian passports, and promptly got turned away. "There is no stamp for the Ivory Coast, therefore we cannot allow you to enter our country," the officer told us politely but firmly. He refused to listen to any explanations. "I cannot enter your country without a passport, so neither can you enter here."

Thus began a two-hour nightmare—a crash course in the African way of life. Only after much praying, pleading, and even some bribing—a miracle, really—were we allowed to go to the motel for the night.

One more hop tomorrow evening and we'll be in Liberia!

January 18

It was almost dark by the time the jet arrived, and soon we were boarding for the short flight to Monrovia, Liberia. The flight attendants were efficient and served us a hot meal even though it was only a one-hour flight.

No one spoke as we disembarked to stand on Liberian soil. It was too wildly exciting. The night wind was sweet and warm and the airport looked strangely dark compared to American ones.

Almost immediately we were met by a short, pleasant-faced Lebanese gentleman who asked, "Selfoss?"

"That's almost us," we laughed.

"I am Tony Hage," he introduced himself. "You may come with me, please."

As we followed, Tony explained that he serves as a sort of mediator between CAM's personnel and Liberia's government officials. I watched the ease with which he moved us through the crowd and past the airline officials and wondered how we would have fared without him—and how much it would have cost us. He is obviously known and respected.

We entered the main building and were swallowed up in a milling, thronging crowd of people, all trying to go somewhere fast, all looking very harassed. Tony kept inching us ahead. He took our passports and health cards and said he would see that they got processed properly. We stood and waited around the conveyor belt and prayed that all our luggage had arrived.

We were overjoyed when Mark Yoder came through the doorway, smiling broadly. "They wouldn't allow me in, but I offered them five Liberian dollars, and here I am," he grinned. "It's so good to see you!"

"Same to you!" we agreed heartily. A familiar face at last!

At least an hour later we grabbed the very last piece on the belt—which happened to be ours—and followed Mark and Tony out to the luggage inspection room. More disorganized hassling and shouting and arguing followed. Tony edged up to the inspections officer and explained who we were and what we were doing. "Don't look through everything," he requested after suitcase number six had been raided.

"Okay, go on," the officer agreed.

We thanked Tony for his help. "You're welcome," he said,

smiling. "I'll be seeing more of you." With a wave of his hand he was gone.

We found a group of people waiting for us. It was good to see the rest of the Yoder family again—Mark's wife Betty and their five children. We were introduced to Curt and Evelyn Kauffman, who are part of the CAM staff here in Liberia, and to Amanda Troyer, Evelyn's sister. After extending happy greetings all around, we piled into Mark's white Land Cruiser for the hour-long trip to our new home.

Excitement was high as we slowed to a stop in front of the CAM compound where we are to live. The first thing I noticed was a high black and white stone wall, and over the wall a stately old two-story mansion with a large patio on the second floor. A security guard ceremoniously opened the gate—and we were home!

We walked into the kitchen and turned on the lights. Enormous scaly brown insects scurried to hide behind the fridge and stove.

"Horrors!" I exclaimed. "What *are* they?"

"Just cockroaches," Mark laughed. "You'll see a lot of them around here. But there are ways to keep them out."

After the Yoder family left, we walked around, trying to decide where everyone would sleep. We have three nice bedrooms, a large living room and dining room, and a dear little kitchen with white cupboards and a walk-in pantry. There's even a covered patio in front with a clothesline for rainy days. The laundry room is just outside the kitchen, and it's equipped with a nice wringer washer. I am so thrilled!

Someone had made a kettle of hamburger soup and set it on the stove. There was a batch of oatmeal cookies on the counter and granola in the freezer and peach cobbler in the refrigerator—but no one was hungry.

As Wayne pulled the light chain in our bedroom, a little yellowish-white creature scuttled up the wall.

"It's just a lizard," he said, knowing how I hate creepy-crawlies.

"I can't possibly sleep with one of them in the same room!" I shuddered, so he called Willie and the two of them chased the agile reptile all over the room. The lizard turned white in an effort to become invisible, then shed its tail when Willie grabbed it. He finally caught it and threw it out the window. "I wonder what that security fellow thinks of these crazy newcomers standing on the bed late at night swinging at something," Willie laughed.

"Yes, he peeked in to see what the fuss was about," Julie claimed. "He can easily see in since there are no curtains anywhere."

"Yes, and no screens either," Wayne said.

Sure enough, the windows were heavily barred and covered with long glass slats, but otherwise open. The slats closed somewhat with cranks, but closing them still left wide gaps. "Anything can crawl in here!" I cried.

"Don't worry, I'll have screens put on right away," Wayne assured me.

Maybe it is the super firm mattress and pillows, maybe the huge, barred, open windows, maybe the lizards and cockroaches that make me so uncomfortable, but I simply cannot sleep. Wayne is wide awake too. We both know those guards around the house are there to protect us from all kinds of thieves and criminals, and that isn't helping. Besides, it is our first night in Liberia—the edge of the earth. Who could sleep?

January 19

Wayne and I were awake at the crack of dawn. None of us have adjusted yet to the seven-hour time change. They say it takes a few days.

Bev is sick with a sore throat and fever, so I made her stay in bed.

"Those ambitious roosters crowed all night," she said hoarsely. "I thought roosters just crow at dawn."

There seems to be an awful lot of commotion for so early in the morning. People are yelling wildly all along the streets. They are carrying things to sell on their heads or in their wheelbarrows. Cars whiz by at alarming speeds, honking madly as they go. This is city life with a vengeance.

Dreaming about beautiful Alberta won't help at this point—except to make me cry.

At least we can see through the bars of both gates, and the walls aren't terribly high. I kind of feel like we're in a cage, but I guess we'll get used to it. I simply must get some curtains hung—but then, I can't imagine having the breezes stifled. Whew! I get hot just thinking about it.

The awesome Atlantic Ocean is just a block away. I stopped in sheer awe and amazement when my eyes first fell on that spectacular expanse of endless blue water. What a thrill to think of living so close! We can go upstairs and see it from the balcony anytime we want.

The boys made an exciting discovery as soon as they woke up. There's a big, sassy monkey living in the almond tree right outside the back porch. Charlie used to be Conrad Swartzentruber's pet and lived at the CAM base among his other pets.

"Mother, this is just what I dreamed about!" Larry said with shining eyes. "That monkey can do anything. He swings upside down by his tail or arm or leg or both legs—it's just unreal! He can jump through the air and climb a tree in two seconds. Now he's picking all the fleas out of Willie's hair—and eating them."

"Since when does William have fleas?" I answered. "And be careful—Mark said he bites."

"Don't worry," said Larry. "He won't bite unless you tease him or hurt him. He's such a nice old monkey."

We unpacked and sorted all day, filling drawers and dressers and closets and getting settled in. I could not figure out why I was so exhausted by evening—until I remembered it was about two in the morning back in Alberta. Our house is really hot unless the fans circulate the air. Most of the rooms have no electricity for several hours a day because the current runs on a breaker system. I am so thankful that the refrigerator always has electricity and we can have cold water anytime. Praise the Lord for cold water! Never before have I appreciated it so much.

The ceilings are all high, which allows the heat to escape a bit.

think we'll do some stenciling as soon as we can to put some touches of color in these white rooms. I really like the kitchen with its high windows and white cupboards. I never expected anything this nice. There's a set of couches in the living room and even a small end table. Our kitchen utensils and dishes are mostly borrowed at this point, but we can expect some supplies in about a month. In fact, CAM regularly sends shipping containers across the ocean from Pennsylvania, so if we desperately need something, there are ways to get it here.

We met some more of the CAM staff today when Iddo and Viola Yoder and their three children, Miriam, Maria, and Titus, came over to say "Hi." Iddo, we found out, is the director of CAM's agricultural projects and manages their sewing center.

"If you have any questions or need any help, we will be glad to come over," Iddo told us. He seems like such a gentle soul, and his eyes just twinkle. He has thick white hair and a matching beard.

"We have a French monkey," Viola told us. "Her name is Missie, and she's a lot smaller than Charlie."

"Sounds like there's a lot of monkey business going on around here!" I laughed.

Later, Curt and Evelyn Kauffman and Pastor Reuben Kaufman and his wife, Elva, stopped by.

I found it interesting that our compound is called "Residence," Pastor Reuben's is called "Chamber," and Curt's is "Charity." Iddo and Viola call their place "View," and there is another young family living at a place called "Mission."

Tonight the surf is pounding, and we can hear it clearly—a dull boom and crash, constant and low and powerful. Oh, I'm going to enjoy the night sounds of the waves!

Thank you, Jesus.

January 20

Words become weak when I try to describe this first Sunday in Liberia. Services were held at 9:30 in Iddo's carport up at View, which is a huge three-story building. (The Mark Yoder family lives on the second floor and the CAM sewing center is on the main floor.)

It felt different to wear flip-flops to church, but I cannot imagine doing otherwise. It was so warm and muggy.

Pastor Reuben and Elva were the first missionaries to start a Mennonite church here in Monrovia, and they have served here since CAM began work in Liberia in 2000. I sense a real bond between this elderly pastor and his flock.

Everyone filed in reverently and took their places on the hard, backless benches, then immediately bowed their heads for a few moments of prayer. It must be a tradition for the nationals, because it's the first thing they do when they sit down.

The church women wear cape dresses and white veils, and visitors wear traditional African dress.

The children really got my attention. What dear, eager little faces! What friendly smiles and shy glances! I loved them at once. They stared at us curiously, but we didn't mind. Some of the little girls were dressed in bright orange, yellow, white, or purple dresses, with frilly ankle socks to match and shiny black shoes. Others wore simple waist dresses and flip-flops. I'm sure they all wore their Sunday best.

I am fascinated by the way the native women braid their children. They start with teeny-tiny braids and create all kinds of patterns like zigzags, circles, diamonds, triangles, and squares all over their heads. It's just amazing.

I am also fascinated by the way they carry their small children. The native women almost all have a lapa . . . about two yards of straight-cut cloth that serves many purposes. A woman can wind it around her waist as a skirt, use it as a sack to carry things, or wrap a baby in it and tie the child to her back. The babies seem quite content to be carried in this manner and sleep through all kinds of jostling and commotion.

The people sing with great fervor, though a bit slowly. Wayne led several songs, but the congregation overpowered him. They led him right along, ignoring the rests or extra beats. I could hear one man above all the rest. They sang "Oh Lord My God" without any rests, and it was lovely.

Five men and a lady were baptized today. The lady was Dorcas, a woman known here for handing out Bible tracts.

After the sermon, there was time given for testimonies, and I saw that Pastor Reuben had to cut them short. How different from our congregations, where the minister has to wait in silence for someone to speak.

One tall, sad-looking fellow who just buried his wife got up and shared out of the sorrow of his heart. We found out he was the owner of Falcon Security, the company CAM hires to guard their compounds. His name is David Livingstone, but everyone calls him "Stone."

The people welcomed us warmly after services. "God bless you!" and "Praise the Lord!" we heard over and over. When they shake your hand, they snap your middle finger with theirs, or it isn't considered a proper handshake. I actually remember some of their names, like Moses Lamin (whom they call Doctor Lamin) and Moses Massawalla.

We also met Pastor Nathan Kauffman, his wife Kathy, and their two young children, Michelle and Christopher. Nathan will be in charge when Reuben leaves.

What a hunger these people have for God's Word! What tremendous potential in this little church!

3

Cold Fingers of Fear

January 21

With a cry of desperation, I fought the noose tightening around my neck. I struggled desperately for air, and my vision clouded. The cry in my throat strangled into a sobbing gasp.

Help! Someone please help me! Oh, God . . . !

With a sudden start, I awoke, my body trembling. Lying in the unfriendly darkness, I tried to remember where I was. Gradually, my senses became aware of my surroundings. Bars across the bare windows. Waves crashing somewhere close. A high wall outside. A flashlight beam working methodically across the roof. Ah, yes. *Liberia.*

Weak with relief, I realized that the awful strangling sensation had been a nightmare. Taking a deep breath, I tried to relax, the peaceful form of my sleeping husband helping to reassure me. Despite the intense heat of the tropical night, I was asleep again in minutes—but not for long.

Air! I need air! Someone's choking me! The vise-like grip of unseen hands felt like a band of steel around my neck, and I struggled with all my might. Gasping . . . slipping . . . *please, just let me breathe.*

Mercifully, I woke again, my heart pounding. Immediately, I

was drawing deep breaths, wide-awake now and trembling with the horror of the nightmare. What did it mean? I could still feel the sensation of fighting for air and the cold fingers of fear around my heart. Real fear—fear that clutched my whole being and wouldn't be dismissed.

All the warnings of well-meaning people were ringing in my ears—warnings of what we would face if we were foolhardy enough to come to this country.

Voodoo is still so prevalent in those countries, Ruth. These people are the devil's domain, and he's not about to let them go.

Witchcraft is practiced everywhere. It's frightening what they can actually do. Never underestimate the power of darkness.

To take a family out there is crazy. What will the children all do? Wayne, you must think of your family. Besides, your church needs you.

Many of the world's most poisonous snakes live in Africa, and what about all the diseases like AIDS and typhoid and malaria? What will you drink and eat?

The Saint Paul River runs right up against the city. I looked it up in the World Book *and the currents must be real dangerous, not to mention the ocean being a block away. Please don't let Willie or Larry or the girls swim, whatever you do. They wouldn't have a chance.*

Remember, the devil doesn't want you there. He'll do everything in his power to stop you. Aren't you scared?

That was it. The devil was trying to stop me from trusting in Jesus. My mind was drawn to the promise of 2 Timothy 1:7: "For God hath not given us the spirit of fear; but of power, and of love, and of a sound mind." *Oh Jesus, help!*

I sat up and begged God to deliver me from the clutches of fear—fear of the unknown and the devil and witchcraft and drowning and anything else that could ruin my peace with Him.

As the Lord brought precious promises to my mind, I was able to relax and actually fall asleep for the third time.

January 21, later

We are learning fast, although this is a whole new world. It is so different having security guards around at all times. They check the walls and all the dark corners periodically all night long with their flashlights to see if anyone is trying to creep into the compound. How do they expect us to sleep? During the day they keep a close eye on everyone coming or going, and they keep long lists of everything sitting around—every little thing. Even old plastic buckets or pieces of wood are listed, since they are responsible if anything gets stolen. When there is a basket of clothes or things to carry in from the Cruiser, they hardly let us lift a finger. I'm not sure I like it.

"Ah will take dat fo' you," they tell me firmly. Some call me "Missie" or "O'Ma," which means Old Ma. I don't like that. Others say "Muttah," which is "Mother," or "Mrs. Wayne." I love that.

So far we can only understand enough words to limp along in conversation. They chop off the last syllable of most of their words, and we really have to listen closely. I pity Wayne when they call him over the radio. He is forced to ask them to repeat several times. Our children are catching on more quickly.

We've been warned over and over to keep our passports in a safe place and our cash somewhere else—like around our neck. "You can't trust anyone," people tell us, but I wish they wouldn't say that. I already trust our guard, Elijah Beh—he looks honest out of his eyes. Nevertheless, I check every once in a while to see that all our important papers are still intact.

I have to admit it was a shock to see so many black people. I catch myself staring a bit—then I remember we are all of one blood. I'm sure they would have to get accustomed to an all-white nation, too, if they came to Canada. I'll get used to it.

Elijah is certainly Larry's favorite guard. He pays close attention to whatever Larry does and gives him good advice when he needs it. There's another very nice, tall young man on duty named William. He has some horrific scars around the back of his neck, above his eye, and on his mouth. I wonder what happened.

I can't believe how dirty everything gets. There's a fine, gritty dust in the air that coats everything and gets in everywhere. Today I asked Security William if he knew of an honest lady who could come once a week and help me clean this big house. His eyes lit up and he said, "Ah shore do. Ah shou' ask her to co' heah?"

"Would you please?" I answered.

"Oh, yes, praise God! Her name is Marie," he said, smiling happily. "An' she is ver', ver' hones', Missie."

January 22

Early this morning there was a gentle knock on the door and a slim, petite young woman stepped into the kitchen without waiting to be told. She looked about seventeen. She regarded me with big eyes, but only for a second, then she stared at the floor, nervously locking her fingers in and out.

"You must be Marie," I said. "I am happy to see you. Would you like a drink?" She glanced up at me again and shook her head slightly. She acted as if any sudden move on my part would make her run like a frightened deer.

I tried again, my words slower and more distinct. "You are Marie?"

"Yes-s . . . Marie," she said softly. "William say . . . you need so' help?"

"I sure do. Don't be scared," I responded, and proceeded to take her through the house to show her what I would like her to do. She nodded gravely when she understood, and shook her head when she didn't, so it worked out fine.

"Ah will do my bes'," she promised.

"Then we will see you on Tuesdays."

So we actually have a sweet little maid. Curt also asked Marie if she could help his wife two days a week. Now she has a real job. I found out she is the mother of a toddler and in her early twenties.

Marie helped me while she was here today. I was surprised how well she did.

"How is it that you know how to clean just the way I want

you to?" I asked. "I can see you get the corners and behind stuff—and you know how to make a bed better than I do."

"Ah cleaned for a whi' woman befo' the war," she explained softly, without looking at me. "Ah have naw been able to find work since. Ah praise God dat you need me."

At lunch time, we invited her to sit down and eat with us, but she looked genuinely scared at the suggestion.

"No, ah will jus' eat in the kitchen, Muttah."

I must tell her sometime that she shouldn't be afraid to look at me when she talks.

We were using a wringer washer, but since we've been out of water for several days, the girls wash all our clothes at the CAM base and bring them home, still wet and very heavy, to hang up. With the high humidity, nothing really dries unless there's a stiff breeze, and even then the heavy towels have a slight dampness to them.

We had been going to Pastor Reuben's house for showers and drinking water, and Wayne hauls what we need for daily use.

Toney George, the young CAM plumber, worked on the problem today. At one point, he paused at the door and laughed loudly and helplessly. I peeked outside to see Willie patiently sitting still while Charlie perched on his shoulders, parted his hair, and looked for edibles. Every once in a while he would pop something into his mouth—and it looked too real. Maybe . . . just maybe . . . but that was impossible.

"That's one monkey with a great imagination," I told Larry.

The CAM mechanic shed is right behind our house, and three vehicles are out there right now. It is a little shed with a roof, but no concrete to lie on to fix anything. Henry Cole is the head mechanic, and his helpers are Emmanuel Nyasiah and Peter Nimmo.

It's interesting to watch Emmanuel and Peter fall asleep when Henry is not around, then jerk awake at the first sound of a horn at the gate, leap out of their seats, and get busy fast.

29

Peter is a very sober, almost sullen type of fellow. He will barely say "hello," but maybe time will change that.

We have two personal hand radios for communicating with CAM staff. Wayne is "Sierra Fox," I am "Sierra Fox One," and so on down the line. It's really neat. We have to learn the handles of all the other staff.

January 23

Larry has a terrible time concentrating on his lessons, and I hardly know what to do. There's so much activity because of the mechanic shop, with really neat motor bikes coming in to be serviced and vehicles of all kinds roaring in and out. Then that funny little monkey always swings around doing the neatest tricks, and countless lizards just beg to be hunted. Plus, people come in and out of the gate all the time. It's just too interesting. Also, it's much warmer than we are used to, so we feel rather wilted by afternoon.

"I need a break at least every hour," Larry begged.

I wish I were a born teacher like some people seem to be. Maybe we'll be blessed with a real teacher by next year.

CAM has hired a lunch cook—a round, jolly little person called Sis Bea, who makes lunch for the staff every day except Sundays and holidays. I'm not used to that. She always sends rice with some kind of strange topping like oil of pumpkin soup, chopped cassava leaf, oil of cabbage soup, chopped sweet potato greens, dried fish soup complete with all the bones, or maybe oil of peanut soup. There's also a strong, orangish-brown butter made from palm nuts that most of the people seem to enjoy. This palm butter is hard to wash off the plastic dishes and leaves an ugly brown stain like tobacco juice.

I cannot force myself to taste all the various toppings yet. Maybe someday, but not just yet. There are plenty of bananas in this country for cowards like me. Fortunately, the rest of my family is not as queasy as I am. I'm glad.

Thankfully, CAM provides us with canned hamburger, sausage, chicken, and beef chunks, plus flour, sugar, oatmeal, canned vegetables, and all the basics we need. There's a small supermarket along the boulevard four blocks away. It is owned and run by Lebanese people, who own most of the stores and businesses in the city. It's surprising what all they have at the grocery. It's certainly not a Weis Market or a Sam's Club—or even an Amish country discount store—but it's pretty nice. We use powdered milk, which tastes not-too-bad when it's ice cold. Though I wish it wouldn't remind me so much of calf milk replacer.

Wayne shopped for vegetables and fruits today and came home with pineapples, some tiny limes, and a sad-looking assortment of discolored grapefruits. What a surprise to cut them open and find delicious, sweet, firm, pink fruit! The pineapples were sugar-sweet too.

4

Clouds on the Horizon

January 24

This morning, Mark Yoder and his two sons, Zack and Hans, along with Wayne, Willie, Julie, Larry, and me, all piled into the Jeep to go visit the displaced persons camp in Bellafoni. Tumba, a CAM driver, sat behind the steering wheel. I think Mark wanted to initiate my husband properly and show him what he will deal with in the future.

Tumba is a middle-aged, single fellow with a big voice, a hearty handshake, and a very pleasant face. We liked him at once. But how he drove!

"These people like speed!" Willie exclaimed to Zack as we flew over a hill and almost immediately turned a sharp curve. Tumba heard—and laughed. He sat slightly hunched in the driver's seat, glancing in the rear-view mirror every few minutes—and drove like mad. Mark gripped the handrail above the door, just in case, and Wayne enjoyed every minute. I did not.

The paved road was dotted with such deep potholes that we were forced to dodge them, resulting in some fantastic maneuvers. The speedometer hit 75 . . . 80 . . . 85. We were flying uphill when Tumba pulled out to pass a great, lumbering wreck of a truck, then quickly turned back to avoid hitting a taxi coming from the opposite direction.

I had been determined not to say anything about the hair-raising ride. After all, if no one else minded, why should I? But this was too much.

"That was close!" I blurted out.

"Better slow down, Tumba," Mark spoke up.

"Yes, sir," he replied cheerily. But not many minutes later we were back up around 85 miles per hour.

"What's the speed limit around here, Tumba?" Julie wondered.

"No speed limits," he drawled. "Ah jus' go."

Whenever we could force our eyes away from the road and the speedometer, we watched the countryside with great interest—rich green foliage and trees of all descriptions, including palm, coconut, and banana. We crossed dark, wide, winding rivers fringed thickly with overhanging trees and small creeks with women washing clothes or bathing.

Around ten o'clock we lunched on the canned Spam, street buns, and sodas from the cooler we had brought along. The drinks were cold and delicious.

Much later, we turned off onto a dirt road—a dusty, lurching, bouncing, brutal kind of road that made me think of riding a bucking bronco. No wonder the vehicles often need repair. Twenty miles of this treatment was enough to make us half sick, so it was a relief to finally reach the camp.

The steep hillside was literally covered with tiny mud shacks, all roofed with white tarps or palm leaves. Long lines of people waited in front of a dilapidated old block building, and CAM personnel were already handing out clothing and food parcels.

"They must have left really early," Wayne told Mark.

"Yes," said Mark, "they like to load up the day before so they can get an early start."

"Who are all these men?" Larry wondered.

"The fellow in the green shirt is our general relief director," Mark replied. "His name is Akin, and that other one is his assistant, George Wonlon, known as Pastor George. Both men are pastors at a church here in Liberia. That chubby driver is James Moore, or "Mo" for short, and the other one is Bundo Dakai. Don't worry, you'll get to know them all. I believe we've got a real good team. Let's go watch."

The people gazed at us openly as we stepped out of the vehicle. Hundreds of them, with hungry, bloodshot eyes and ragged clothing and worn-out flip-flops—a restless throng of desperate faces and protruding stomachs and skinny, scabby legs. They parted to let us through, and the heavy odor of many unwashed bodies enveloped us.

I realized this was the hidden side of Liberia. Their personal world of hunger and despair and hopelessness—a world of dehydrating children and elderly people—a world of waiting in long lines with no water.

The women stared at us. To look into all those dark eyes—one face after another—was truly a revelation to me. What did I read in their liquid depths? Hope? Despair? Pain? Hunger? They stood close to me, and yet I felt the great chasm between us. No words were spoken—they sized us up and we them. I felt a greater stirring of compassion in my heart than I ever felt before. I could see Julie felt the same way.

Every doubt I ever had about coming here was dimmed to near extinction. We are here to help pass on the incredible gifts of God's love. We are needed!

The lines moved slowly toward the CAM trucks. People craned their necks to see how far they had to go.

My heart nearly burst with the realization of it all. Generous people all over America had given of their bounties to places they scarcely knew existed. And now here it was, distributed right into the people's hands and hearts. It was just too wonderful.

We had much to think about as we drove home this afternoon. We actually made it without any major accidents, even though Tumba tried to get us there as quickly as possible.

January 27

Mark preached a powerful sermon this morning titled "The Devil, Our Adversary." The church was so full I didn't see one empty seat. We tried to rest in the afternoon, but it was just too warm to sleep, so we went visiting to Curt and Evelyn's and stopped by Nathan and Kathy's house. It's fun getting to know all the staff.

February 1

A dark cloud of worry hangs over our little group concerning Nathan Kauffman. He is suffering from terrible headaches—so bad that his vision is blurred.

"I can't even see that picture on the wall clearly," he told us anxiously. "I visited the clinic and they said I have malaria, but I think it's got to be more than that. Since when does malaria make your eyes blur?"

"Mark Yoder arranged for us to fly home next week and see a doctor," Kathy added, with tears shining in her blue eyes. "Nathan has so much pain most of the time that he can't do anything anyhow, so we'll try to take our most important belongings home in case we don't come back. It's hard to leave Liberia so soon. We have so many questions . . . but God knows best."

Words are weak at a time like this, but I recognize courage when I see it. Courage, and an unwavering faith in Almighty God.

Life is so uncertain.

Another thing that gives us little jabs of anxiety now and then is the unstable political environment of this country. Wayne recently saw the president along the boulevard. First came a police truck with its doors wide open, driving like crazy with lights flashing and horn honking. All traffic literally fled off the highway onto the side streets, sidewalks, or wherever they could squeeze off the road. Close behind whizzed some army trucks with camouflage and mounted guns, then a whole motorcade of fancy black cars with tinted windows, then more military vehicles and policemen. I'm looking forward to seeing the convoy myself. It doesn't sound like poor President Taylor trusts his fellow citizens at all.

We encounter checkpoints in every direction away from the city, and some right here in Monrovia. The soldiers usually recognize a CAM vehicle, so they don't give us much trouble. It's just that all those young, fierce-looking men with their huge guns look scary. They sidle up to our vehicle, glance around inside, look at us for a moment, then motion us through with a nod of the head or a short jerk of the hand.

After our family registered with the American Embassy, the consular officer said to us, "With the volatile situation that exists here, we need to know exactly who you are and where you will be staying. It is not my intent to frighten you, but you need to be aware that things can become unsafe very quickly."

We thanked him and left—and immediately dismissed any thoughts of danger. It may be present, but so is our God.

February 2

William, the scarred day security, told us what happened to him on "dat fateful Sunday, June 20, 1993." We sat on the porch and listened.

"Abou' four in da mornin', a group of armed ULIMO men entered our town an' ev'ry person was required to assemble, young an' old together. Dey carry each one and slaughtered him wi'ou' mercy. My own hands were tied in da presence of my muttah . . . she cried and yelled. Dey carried me behin' a house where dey slashed me in da back of my head wi' a cutlass. Ah yells 'Oh Lord, co' fo' me.' My head was bleedin' bad and den ah faint right down an' ah los' conscious. Den dey slash my tendons on my two feet an' cut me over heah," he ran his finger over the crooked scar across his eye, "an' heah," he pointed under his nose.

"Later, my muttah came wi' some friends an' dey carry me to a village where a nurse pu' on dressin'. He saved my life. Fo' a whole yeah he cared fo' me till the wounds healed."

"You poor fellow," I said softly.

"Ah mus' tell you, Missie, out of fifty-two people, only Zubah an' ah survived. Praise God ah am still alive. An' now ah lives wi' da scar, Missie."

Retelling his story had taken some effort for William. Pain shadowed his face and his jaw worked. "Thanks for telling us," Willie said feelingly. "It sounds like some kind of nightmare to me."

"Ah thank God da nightmare is over . . . *Praise God!*" he replied.

The ULIMO, or United Liberation Movement, consists of

soldiers known for their fierce, bloody ways. They torture and rape their victims and cut off their hands and feet. It is certainly a miracle that William is alive.

February 3

Paul Beachy, a visiting minister, preached this morning. Nathan couldn't come to church due to a raging headache, so the whole atmosphere was unusually sober.

"We were looking forward to this year *so* much," Kathy cried softly afterward. "I know someday we will understand, but right now it's pretty hard. The children were adjusting so well."

How do you comfort a person in so much pain? What can you say?

Wayne invited Moses Lamin and his family for lunch. Thankfully, we had beef barley soup cooking, and since it was way too thick anyway we could add some broth and more beef chunks. Brown rolls with strawberry jam and tapioca pudding finished it off.

I like the doctor. His sense of humor is alive and well, and he often makes a remark then chuckles at his own wit.

We walked outside with our guests and visited some more. A black and yellow lizard streaked toward us, and I shrieked. The awful thing did a fast sideways turn and nearly bowled over in its haste to get away. The security guards crumpled with mirth. I was so embarrassed.

"Ruth Ann, it was more scared of you than you were of it," Dr. Lamin laughed. He was still laughing when he drove out.

February 5

The Nathan Kauffman family flew home today. I'm sure it will be a relief to find out what's wrong, since he is in real pain. Kathy has been so brave through this whole ordeal.

Mr. Gurley, who works for CAM as an electrician, was here for a good part of the day trying to figure out what went wrong with our inverter system. There seems to be a problem with charging the battery bank, so Wayne called for him.

We all think dear old Mr. Gurley is one of the nicest gentlemen. He has twinkling black eyes in a weather-beaten face framed by a grizzled white beard and tight, graying hair. Since his knees are bad, he has to walk with a cane, but he is incredibly sharp and intelligent.

"Mrs. Wayne, ah praise God ah kin still walk," he said cheerfully. "Some days are much worse dan others, but today is a good day. Ah was able to catch a taxi wi'ou' much problem dis morning, so ah didn't have to walk to Redlight. It's a lo-o-ong walk fo' me, an' ah am not young."

February 6

This afternoon Wayne gave a short speech at the Baptist Seminary, where CAM is hosting a teachers' retreat for all the orphanage teachers.

There are some good, dedicated teachers among this group, and they show such interest in bettering themselves. After a couple days of lectures and sermons, combined with some good eating, I am sure they all feel refreshed and ready to continue their work. Their students are the future of Liberia.

"You'll be called on many times for impromptu speeches," Mark shared on the way home. "These people love speeches."

"I'm glad you're here to pave the way for me a bit," Wayne told him. "I wish you could stay a lot longer."

"Another thing I believe would be wise is to terminate work at five every evening, and take Saturdays off," Mark continued. "I have had little or no family time since we came, and I want it to be different for you."

"Sounds good to me," Wayne agreed.

February 7

Nathan Kauffman was admitted to the hospital today after some testing in the emergency room. His doctors found a brain tumor affecting his optical nerve. No wonder he had trouble seeing! It's amazing how fast the picture can change in one's life. We're wondering if they will ever be able to come back to Liberia.

February 8

So far I've made two major blunders since we arrived in Monrovia. A fellow I had never seen before came and knocked on our door about nine o'clock in the morning. "I came for your passports," he announced, without introducing himself. He was short and stocky, and wore glasses and a gaudy tailored suit. I could smell his cologne before I opened the door.

Instantly my warning lights went on. *There are master thieves in Liberia. Not everyone can be trusted.* Perhaps this man was aware we were new in the country, and thought he could convince the lady of the house to hand over her passports—then he would disappear.

"I'm sorry," I said icily. "I have been instructed not to give our passports to anyone without specific permission."

The man stood and stared at me in astonishment. He drew himself up to his full height and said indignantly, "I say, I am Mr. Seah, and I work for Christian Aid Ministries, and I need to take your family's passports with me to receive your legal documents to remain in this country."

"Do you mind if I radio my husband first?" I asked. I simply had to make sure he was authentic.

"I can do that for you," he returned coolly, and proceeded to pull out a CAM office badge and a CAM radio. "Sierra Fox. Sierra Fox. Papa Oscar, do you copy?" He held up his badge for me to see.

"Sierra Fox standing by," answered my husband.

"Do I have your permission to obtain the passports from your *Whiskey*?"

"Whiskey? . . . Ah, yes. Yes, you do."

"Thank you, sir," he said, turning back to me.

"Just a second. I'll go get them."

When I returned with the passports in hand, red-faced and apologetic, Mr. Seah just smiled and said, "Thank you very much."

"I think I will remember you from now on," I promised.

My second blunder was worse. The girls and I were exchanging a substantial amount of American money into Liberian. Since the exchange rate changes almost daily (one American dollar can be worth anywhere from fifty to seventy-five Liberian dollars), a person is at the mercy of the money changers, unless you want to stand there and count hundreds of five or ten dollar bills. As usual, several hopefuls came to the Jeep window.

I selected a clean-looking young man and proceeded to do business with him. I gave him some earnest admonition to digest on the side. "If you *ever* shortchange me—and I mean *ever*—I will have to go elsewhere," I said as he expertly counted out the stacks of limp, faded bills. "If I see you are trustworthy, we will continue to do business with you on a regular basis."

The startled man stopped counting. He looked at me with frank, horrified eyes. "I wou' *nevah* cheat you, Missie—or anyone else—*nevah!*" he stated emphatically, and continued counting.

Instantly, I felt cruel and mean and very, very foolish.

The culture is steeped in dishonesty, remember?

"Ah, I'm sure you wouldn't, Mr. . . . Mr. . . ."

"Reeves. Anthony Reeves," he said, not unkindly, with a hint of a smile. "Alright, I thank you very much." Before I could respond, he was gone.

"That's not fair, Mom," the girls chided me as we drove home. "There are lots of honest people in this place. We are sure of it."

"Don't worry. I've learned my lesson," I told them.

Imagine my consternation when I saw the very same Anthony Reeves consulting with Pastor Reuben a few minutes before the service started on Sunday—and found out later he is our pastor's trusted friend and adviser.

"I certainly hope I haven't offended that nice man," I confided forlornly to Wayne. "I will apologize to him the first time I see him. And do you know what? It's not up to me to decide if people are honest or not. I simply cannot go around suspecting everyone."

"Sounds good to me," was his reply. "I think CAM has some exceptional men working for them. It's interesting how they found some of these fellows. They're diligent and honest and I like working with them, so let's just trust people until we have a reason not to."

41

5

It Is Not Easy

February 9

This morning I decided to give Larry a haircut. I used an old, dull clipper set that made funny furrows all over his head. "Mom, it looks awful!" he exclaimed in genuine dismay.

"I don't know what to do—it just won't cut," I explained. "Maybe your hair is too damp. Anyway, I have to go pick up Dad now."

"I'll fix it up for you, Larry," Julie offered, examining his head critically from all angles. "Why not use the scissors?" Then, seeing the doubtful look on my face, she laughed and said, "Don't worry, Mom."

"Just be careful and take your time," I told her. "It's gonna be tricky."

We came back an hour later. "Mom, Dad, come here!" Larry called from his room. His head was under the sheet and his eyes peeked out—big and worried.

"Whatever is the matter?" I wondered. "Are you sick?"

"No-o-o, but my hair is," he said in a small voice.

"Let's see it," Wayne said, tugging at the sheet.

Larry's head looked like a shiny, pink egg. We stared for a few seconds, hardly believing our eyes.

43

"They really did you in this time, didn't they, Buddy?" Wayne said sympathetically, his eyes twinkling.

"Where's Julie?" I wondered, trying to keep a straight face.

"Still laughing somewhere—they *all* are. And now you are too," he complained. "I look like a scalped chicken. She tried to straighten it out, but it got worse and worse, so she just shaved it all off with a razor. I'm not going *anywhere* till my hair grows back."

"You'll fit right in with all your new friends this way," I reminded him. "It'll grow back in no time."

Just as we figured, he didn't stay in isolation long. "La-a-arry! Whazzup, man?" our security guards laughed, delighted at his new look. They wanted to feel his head and offered advice on the care and keeping of a bald palate. At first, Larry was mortified and embarrassed, but that soon wore off.

"Looks great!" was the general consensus, but I can guarantee our son will never be tempted to get such a short haircut again. I wonder if there's any place in town to sharpen clippers.

Larry wanted to go to the beach, so the girls went along to watch him while he romped in the water. Presently, they met a young woman with a small baby on her back. She was weeping and wandering aimlessly.

"Is something wrong?" they asked. "Can we help?"

The woman stopped, regarded them for a moment, then began to pour out her woes for their sympathetic ears. "Ah am Grace Allison," she began. "Ah don' have no one to help. My Shadrach's father won' pay me a thing, an' we are *hungry*. Ah wants to stop sellin' my body, bu' ah have no food, so ah canno' feed my chil'. It is naw easy. Ah want to go to church an' maybe school, but ah have nuthin' . . . *nuthin'!*" She wiped her bloodshot eyes with the corner of her lapa.

The baby's little arms were thin, and ugly scabs festered around the corners of his mouth. More scabs peppered his neck and arms.

"My Shadrach has a fevah," the woman continued. "He is hot."

"We are with Christian Aid Ministries," the girls explained. "I'm sure we can help you somehow, so just come to our place. We have some fever medicine at home, and your baby does look pretty sick."

"Praise God!" she exclaimed. "Ah have no money fo' medicine, an' it is naw easy."

"Come home with us," the girls invited.

Later, we sat around the table while Grace ate a big bowl of rice with cassava and told us about her life. Her boyfriend, an older man, wants to keep her as his mistress besides his wife, and though she was willing in the past, she is now desperate to change her lifestyle. He threatened to completely cut her off from any financial assistance if she dares disobey.

I feel so sorry for her. She's one of many unwanted young girls forced into the streets to obtain enough food to live. We arranged for her to eat lunch with us daily so she can nurse her baby until another solution can be found.

"Make sure you come to church," we reminded her before she left. "Don't forget to give the baby some medicine in four hours."

There is something wrong with our well again—we run out of water quite often. Wayne is not sure what he wants to do next. Pure water is so important in this country.

We are all faithfully taking our Mefloquine tablets for malaria prevention, but they make us feel half sick sometimes, especially Larry.

February 10

What a beautiful, breezy Lord's Day morning! Grace Allison met us on the steps before church services began. "Praise God, my Shadrach is much bettah," she said with relief in her voice. "You people are answers to prayer. Praise God! Now if ah could jus' have a business to help me—you know, maybe an ice business or a dry goods business—den ah wou' be happy. My room leaks in da rain, Muttah. We git co-o-old. Ah have no mattress, no blanket . . . it is naw easy."

45

"Let's go in," I said quietly, noticing all the curious onlookers. "We can talk later."

"Alright, Muttah."

The sweetest little girl sat down next to me and gave me such a smile. Then she proceeded to watch my every move and copy every word I wrote in my tablet. She dug in her little cloth satchel and produced a cherished candy—a cough drop actually—and gave it to me.

My name is Fatu. I am nine years old, she printed neatly. *I love you.*

After church, a well-dressed gentleman came up and introduced himself as Fatu's father. "I have never come to this church before," he said politely. "I will continue to come with my daughter since she does not desire to miss church."

"Please do that," I encouraged. "You are most welcome to come anytime."

I have a bad habit of looking around during church. I like to see the eager, interested looks on people's faces. I learned more about Dorcas today, the recently baptized lady who has inspired many by passing out thousands of tracts to her people. Her husband is living with another woman, and she supports some of their children. Such faith is rare indeed.

After church I saw her counseling with Grace Allison, who was crying quietly as she spoke. Dorcas reached over and wiped off the tears in the tenderest manner. "Don' cry, don' cry," she said softly. "God is able. He will help you."

Such love for a perfect stranger. It warmed my heart.

How do I greet visitors after church? Do I sneak by them and hope someone else will take the responsibility?

Tonight I was standing by the bathroom sink, only a few inches away from the window, when someone peeked in. It was so eerie. His head suddenly came into view about a foot away—and I was face to face with Charlie.

That old monkey looked half human the way he peered all around. I'm sure there was a smirk on his wrinkled face. I'm mad at him because I'm always giving him scraps and he still shrieks angrily at me for no reason. He has adopted Willie for his very own and gets absolutely violent if anyone else comes near when he is around. Of course, Willie loves it.

Our well is still giving us major problems, so Wayne scheduled some men to come drill a deeper one next week. We're all excited about having enough water so we don't have to bother Reuben and Elva anymore. They have been so gracious about letting us use their shower.

February 12

Nathan Kauffman had brain surgery, and they fear cancer. What a dreadful blow.

Wayne was called to an emergency NGO (Non-Governmental Organization) meeting this morning. There are serious reports of looting and killing somewhere north of Monrovia. Two more of CAM's orphanages have had to relocate to escape the soldiers. We haven't really seen any definite changes in the city, but there is a restlessness in the air. Our security guards hold their radios to their ears all day long to hear what is happening. I think they're scared.

Last night, two nice bed sheets were stolen off the wash line right under our bedroom window. Of course, Stone was here investigating the robbery and asking our security guards, Zaza and Robert, all kinds of questions.

"We canno' mess wi' armed men," Stone told us gravely when he was satisfied with the story. "It's naw worth my men's lives to try an' stop dem. Dey had guns."

"This all reminds me of a gathering storm, Mr. Stone," I said a bit anxiously. "Do you think there will ever be another war?"

"Ah don' think so, bu' ah don' know," he said. "Praise God, He will take care of us."

I felt admonished, just as I deserved.

The well drillers are at work. The machine they're using is beyond description—it's a combination of a roaring, hand-held auger and a pulley device. One man hangs onto it and the others sit and watch. No one hurries, no matter what.

February 15

We were delighted when Anthony Reeves offered to go with Wayne, Larry, and me on a shopping trip to Paynesville this morning. Wayne, especially, was glad to have him along, as he knows the area so much better than we do. Driving is a real art in this country, with no traffic lights, no speed limits, and no stop signs.

Shortly after reaching Paynesville, Wayne pulled out into an intersection, and a traffic control cop held up his hand. Wayne stopped sharply, but just over the line.

"May ah have yo' license, sah?" the officer asked haughtily.

"Of course."

"Hold onto it," cautioned Anthony, so Wayne held it up with a firm grip.

"You have vi'lated da law. Ah need to have dis license righ' now," said the officer sternly.

"He will keep it!" warned Anthony.

"Come on, my man, what did I do wrong?" asked Wayne.

"You di' naw stop in time," the man insisted, grabbing for the license. This time he got it.

"He's getting mad," I whispered, as the cop motioned two more of his fellow policemen over. They stood a few feet away and inspected Wayne's license. They talked in agitated tones, gesturing and muttering and casting angry glances in our direction.

"What should I do?" Wayne wondered.

"Please, dear Lord, help us," I prayed aloud.

"If dey come back now, it will naw be easy," said Anthony.

Suddenly, from out of nowhere, Mr. Seah appeared with Mr. Gurley, hurrying as fast as his crippled knees allowed, behind him.

"I'll take over," Mr. Seah announced, quickly approaching the policemen.

"And ah will help," Mr. Gurley added breathlessly.

"Praise God!" Anthony exclaimed.

In the fierce argument that ensued, Mr. Seah stood his ground a few inches from the first officer's furious face, and dear old Mr. Gurley waved his cane as he tried to convince the other two. Curious onlookers crowded the sidewalk beside us.

About ten minutes later, smiling triumphantly, Mr. Gurley and Mr. Seah emerged from the fray, waving Wayne's license. "Go now—go quickly," Mr. Seah said, and my husband needed no coaxing.

"The police don' like to talk to Mr. Seah—he's too good," was Mr. Gurley's parting remark.

"What a fuss over crossing the line!" Wayne exclaimed. "Now we won't have much time to shop."

"Would they have put us in jail?" Larry wondered, laughing a little with relief.

"Naw, dey need food," Anthony explained. "Da gover'men' don' pay dem, so dey has to beg or cheat."

"I want you to get an African dress for a souvenir," Wayne decided suddenly as we passed the tailor shops full of gaudily embroidered clothing.

"It's not my style," I countered.

"Just try one on," he persisted.

We entered a dark little shop called "Sew Corner" where several men were sewing. The walls were covered with embroidered dresses, blouses, and shirts.

Some of the ancient machines were tied together with strings, rubber, or twine—but they still worked. What incredible workmanship! What fabulous embroidery!

We picked a rich green, wildly bright gown, and I dutifully wrestled it on over my dress. It was heavy and stiff and much too tight.

"I love it!" said Wayne.

"Yo' muttah look like a butte'fly." Anthony told Larry. That's just how I felt, very bright and broad-shouldered.

"It will surely rip the first time I wear it," I told Wayne.

"Okay then—we'll keep looking."

I'll never again go shopping without wearing shoes and socks—*something* was biting my feet—something invisible and

49

very hungry. My feet started to itch fiercely, and when I scratched, it became worse.

"Dus' mites," said Anthony.

This evening, all the CAM staff met at Mamba Point for supper. It is an old Lebanese restaurant in a lovely spot above the ocean. They had a long table prepared for us on the outside upper patio. The menu was printed very stylishly and the wording was perfect, but the prices were exorbitant.

The surf rolled gently below the magnificent clouds. We sat and ate and watched the sun play peek-a-boo in the mist above the water. The stiff breeze was warm and salty and my heart thrilled again and again to think of the God who spoke this all into existence.

It was a wonderful evening of delicious food and warm fellowship, yet there was an unspoken sadness in the air—the Mark Yoder family and Pastor Reuben and Elva will soon leave us for good.

Life is just too full of changes.

February 21

Nathan Kauffman *does* have cancer. He is at home recuperating from brain surgery. We've all seen what that dreaded disease can do, and I always wonder how people handle it without having God as their ever-present help.

Mark Yoder preached for the last time here this past Sunday. After lunch, his family and Wayne and I were already in the church van to leave for the airport when Wayne decided to call Tony Hage and ask if Ghana Air would be on time—only to learn that the flight had been canceled. So they had to unpack what they needed to stay another night in Monrovia. Living in Liberia teaches great patience.

Fifteen beautiful cabbages were stolen last night from the CAM garden next to the office. "We planned to cut them the next day," Iddo said ruefully. "They were really nice this time. I wonder who could have taken them, anyway?"

Wayne decided he would like to host each of the native CAM staff for supper at least once while we're here, so this evening we enjoyed having General Relief Director Akin, his wife Evee, and their baby son Emmanuel, and Varnee, the warehouse manager, and his wife Anna.

We served Coke and Indian fry bread with all the toppings. The bread is a simple flour dough rolled into tortilla-like rounds and deep fried. After finding out how to pile all the toppings on the crispy shell to eat this strange new food, Akin and Varnee both had seconds.

Evee and Anna hardly spoke unless addressed. They sat and smiled at us and murmured thanks for every little thing. I liked them both.

"When will you start terminating work at five and on Saturdays?" Akin wanted to know.

"It's almost impossible," Wayne answered. "I hardly finish what I need to this way—you know what I mean."

February 22

We woke up in the wee hours to the sound of pouring rain—*bucketing* rain, I should say. The wash still on the line was flapping madly about as it was re-washed. I dozed off for a while only to be awakened by the sound of a deluge like Noah must have heard in the ark. It was accompanied by sudden, brilliant lightning and heavy thunder like the sound of crashing cymbals. Crash after rolling crash roared right above us, with lightning that would convert a sinner. It was fierce—but awesome.

I love mornings after a storm—that delicious "don't have to get up yet" feeling, with the windows wide open and the air so fresh it hurts. I was still in bed when I heard an unearthly commotion in the bathroom. I jumped out of bed to find the bathroom door shut and Wayne inside.

"What's going on?" I yelled.

"I'm chasing a mouse," he replied in muffled tones. "Don't open the door!"

Evidently they were having a fierce battle, because I could

hear things flying everywhere.

I laughed to myself. I just knew security thought the Missus had lost it. When Wayne finally emerged, he was holding the remains of our only broom in one hand.

"You fought with a *mouse?*" the grocer asked him when we went looking for a new broom. "What kind of mouse would that be?"

At least *I* wasn't the laughingstock this time!

In the grocery store, a young fellow followed us up and down the aisles, then asked, "Where do you an' Mr. Wayne live?"

"Over there a ways," I said cautiously.

"Well, could I come visit?"

"Do we know you?"

"No, but could I come to church?"

"Of course! Everyone is welcome at church."

"Could I see her at church then?" he asked, eyeing one of our daughters.

"Her? No. Church is for meeting God."

"Well, could I come see God first, then her?"

"No." I felt sorry for the young man. Many Liberians dream of reaching America one way or another. This young man hoped to do so by marrying an American.

6

African Wedding

February 23

This afternoon, Wayne rounded up our family to go to Emmanuel and Linda's wedding. Emmanuel is an official at the Ghanaian Embassy just across the street from the CAM office, and he insisted Wayne bring his family.

"I think this will be interesting," I said. "I've never seen an African wedding before. Let's make sure we're not late."

It took us a while to find the wedding compound, a tumbledown, walled enclosure down Jamaica Street. A lone man ushered us in under a large blue umbrella tarp and gave us seats.

We were basically left to ourselves after the initial welcome. We waited, and waited some more. The merciless sun and that heavy tarp created an oven-like atmosphere.

A scabby dog with its ears half eaten off wandered through, stopping often to scratch desperately. Lizards ran along the crumbling cement blocks, stopping to stare at us, their tongues flicking in and out.

"Maybe the wedding has been canceled," Larry said. "Let's go swimming instead."

It must have been an hour later when more people, including the young pastor, arrived and took their seats. The women swept in wearing bright, elaborate cotton gowns with exaggerated flowing sleeves, matching head ties, and pointed cuffs. A few wore dark, silky dresses. All were heavily embroidered with gold, silver, navy, or green. Their spiked sandals and shoes were high and pointed and glittering. They wore all kinds of colored jewelry on their necks, wrists, ears, and ankles. Their nails were a brilliant variety of colors with stars, diamonds, snakes, and all kinds of tiny designs painted in contrast. Even their toenails were wildly colored. Some of them wore bold hues of green, blue, or black paint on their dark eyes, and bright tones of lipstick. They looked like Egyptian royalty.

A Muslim gentleman arrived. He was wrapped in multiple folds of russet cotton fabric, which he soon let slide down so he could cool off.

Suddenly, the music started with a tremendous bash. The first song was a strange wail with a chorus that ran like this: "Satan, I hate you-u-u. I don't like you-u-u. Some people ask me, and ah say . . . my Jesus makes me fine." It must have been repeated fifteen times, and it was a relief to hear it end.

Right on its heels, Johnny Cash belted out a country hit, then there was another African spiritual, and so it went. Unfortunately, the loudspeakers were in perfect working condition, and the whole neighborhood could hear.

Presently, the groom and his attendants came in amid much laughter and jesting from the crowd. Emmanuel wore a long, heavily-embroidered white dress with a matching round cotton cap, the top of which lay over to one side and down over his ear. The groomsmen wore duplicate gowns in baby blue and yellow. Whenever they sat down they would hoist up their skirts, revealing matching trousers.

"Da bride has arrived!" someone shouted into the microphone. The music changed. All eyes turned toward the curtain at the front of the tent. Slowly, ever so slowly, the first bridesmaid waltzed in, taking small steps in time with the music, bowing and swaying left and right. She wore a long, simple blue dress and carried a bouquet of green rice. Her false hair was piled high on her head in loose curls and studded with blue orchids. The people clapped and hooted and nodded with obvious approval.

Soon Linda appeared in the doorway on the arm of her father. The crowd erupted, smiling and clapping and yelling, "Yes! Yes!"

They slowly waltzed in. Linda's long, lavish white gown glittered with shiny embroidery; her hair was done in jet black ringlets and she wore great gold bangles on her wrists. Her nails were painted snow white. She carried a similar bouquet, tied with white ribbon.

"Beautiful!" a man shouted over the strains of the music.

"A-men!" shouted another, and the chorus was on. Everyone was impressed.

The pastor eagerly shot to his feet. "My theme for the sermon is "Be Loyal to Each Other!" he hollered.

"It's going to be a long day," Julie said soberly, "but he's got good English."

The pastor kept up his stentorian yelling for a whole hour, often repeating phrases and never drifting far from his admonitions about marital loyalty. "Are you listening, Emmanuel?" he would holler periodically. "Are *you* listening, Linda?"

"They must be deaf if they aren't," Bev smiled.

He went into great detail about the sin of homosexuality. "It is blasphemy against the Almighty God, and those who do it will burn in hell. They are in hell right now!"

We thought the sermon would never end. People were fanning like mad in an attempt to cool off, and the attendants faithfully mopped the face and neck of the bridal couple.

Finally, the vows were exchanged, and the pastor had one final yell: "What God hath joined together let no man, no woman, no boy, no girl, and no *busybody* put asunder!" Everyone snickered.

A young man pulled his chair up to his keyboard, which was sitting atop two cases of wine, and proceeded to play and sing "Jesus Is the Answer" in a cultivated, rich baritone. He sang so reverently and quietly that a hush fell over the whole congregation.

"Now that was beautiful," Wayne commented when he was done.

We were served paper plates full of macaroni and potato salad, some kind of meat, and a piece of cake. The food was warm and salty.

The air smelled of sweating bodies, cheap perfume, fried food, and fish. "I've got to get out of this heat," Wayne declared. "Let's go."

People were starting to stand up and foxtrot. "Looks like the celebration is just beginning," I told him.

We thanked our hosts and made our way out. People of all ages were clustered around the compound, having their own private little dances to the free music.

February 24

I love Sundays in Liberia. Pastor Reuben has such a gentle way of expressing things, yet you know he is very serious about them. The only drawback of going to church is the volley of letters we receive every Sunday—desperate letters. Most of them greet us in the name of "our Lord and Saviour, Jesus Christ," and no amount of pleading or sternness can make the people stop begging on Sunday. Some of them come a long way to church and see it as an opportunity to appeal to CAM's country director.

The letters express terrible needs and plead for "whatever assistance the Lord Jesus may lay on your heart." They have no food, no clothes, no job; the children are starving and sick; they need money for schooling and tin and shoes and rice. They have no hope of life unless we help immediately. Could we please give them just a small job so they could eat? Or help them start a small, small business so they could feed their seven children? Could we just help them rent a room so they could sleep "in the dry"? Any small thing would help.

I always feel depressed when I read their letters. It is a tremendous job for the CAM staff to decide which are the neediest, because it is impossible to help them all. It is tremendously satisfying, however, to see a new business prosper.

CAM's Self-Help and Special Needs programs are truly put to good use.

After lunch today, Wayne, Larry, and I filled the Cruiser with literature and followed Curt and Evelyn Kauffman to the football stadium near Elwa Junction, where a "Pray For Liberia" crusade is in progress. Thousands of people walked along the highway and in the ditches beside the road. Thousands more filled the huge lot outside the stadium, and people said there was not an empty seat in the whole stadium.

Sam Kargbo, the orphanage administrator for CAM, and Akin were there ahead of us and eager to help. "There are at least sixty thousand people here today," Sam told us. To me it looked like a million.

We drove slowly up to the gate, parked the vehicles, and began happily handing out literature. Before long we realized this could get dangerous. The crowds began pushing and milling about, trying to grab the literature from our hands. I'll never forget that sea of faces, those reaching hands, and all those determined eyes.

"Dad!" Larry yelled urgently. "*Da-ad!*" I looked around and barely saw the top of his head and his hands clutching *Nature Friend* magazines above the crowd.

Wayne saw him too. Quick as a wink, he made his way to Larry's side, grabbed him up, and carried him to the Cruiser.

Larry's face was pale. He rolled up all the windows and locked the doors.

The literature was gone in a very short time, so we drove back to the office for more. We loaded twenty-two boxes of Bibles, *Seed of Truth, Reaching Out, Nature Friend, Sword and Trumpet, Beside the Still Waters, Companions,* quarterlies, and more.

We began passing them out as fast as we could, but not fast enough for the people. They actually started to mob the vehicles to get inside and help themselves, so Wayne and Curt had to drive away and come back again when things settled down.

Meanwhile, I found myself all alone in the crowd of people, and my boxes were empty. I felt a stab of fear, realizing I wouldn't have a chance if the crowd got ugly.

Sam Kargbo suddenly emerged from the crowd. "Come with me!" he said loudly, and I needed no urging. He grabbed my hand and pulled me from that jostling mass out to the safety of the sidelines. He explained that my crew had gone to turn around and had told him to look after me.

When the others came back, the soldiers on duty made the people form lines inside the gates so they could come out a few at a time in an orderly fashion. Then they stood right next to us to see that we would be safe, and before long they were requesting literature to pass out. Those long AK-47 rifles slung around their shoulders contrasted sharply with the Bibles in their arms.

Wayne made sure they each got a Bible of their own. It is thrilling to know the Word of God has reached so many more souls.

So shall my Word . . . not return unto me void.

February 26

Reuben and Elva received word today of the death of Elva's only sister. What a shock for poor Elva, who was greatly looking forward to seeing her. We all got together for a short service at church—a sad one, because these people hate to see Reuben and Elva go. Then they had to pack quickly because they have to leave tomorrow morning. Reuben plans to come back to tie up all the loose ends before the new pastor arrives.

Larry came home with a tiny baby monkey hanging around his neck. He bought it for 300 Liberian dollars, and he is so tickled. It cried and screeched when he put it down, literally begging to be held.

"Her name is Jillie," Larry announced proudly.

Bev walked by and the monkey threw itself into her arms and clung like a terrified baby. "Oh!" she gasped, then, "It's really cute!"

"I knew you'd like it," Larry grinned. "Julie will too. Do *you* like her, Mom?"

I looked at the ugly little creature, and then at Larry's shining eyes. "It is kinda cute," I finally admitted.

The Sam Kargbo family came for supper tonight. When they arrived I heard Wayne say, "They're here—and Sam is wearing a black and white striped gown."

I don't think I'll ever get used to men in long dresses, no matter how prettily embroidered, but here in Liberia this is an accepted standard for special occasions. We had pizza, Jell-O, potato salad, and cake for supper, then we sang hymns and visited some more. It was wonderful.

March 4

I sat up in bed and glanced at the clock—2 a.m. What had awakened me? I looked out the window and caught my breath—a shadowy form was slowly sneaking toward the sleeping night security. Willie! Without a sound he glided through the tiny office, picked up a stick, and tickled Zayzay's nose, then quickly stepped back.

Zayzay jerked awake with a little start. He stretched and yawned leisurely, stood up, and walked a couple steps before he turned and saw a gleaming white man spread-eagled against the wall. His breath left him in one huge gasp, and he started babbling into his radio—his eyes bulging out in terror. It took a few seconds before he realized it was only our laughing son.

"Ah was only restin', naw sleepin'," he declared. "Ah wou' nevah sleep."

A sleeping security guard can't expect to keep his job, and they both know it. We had a good laugh at the breakfast table.

All the responsibilities of school weighed heavily on my mind this morning. Are Willie, Charlotte, and Larry getting all the concepts? Are we being thorough enough? Since that monkey came, Larry's interest in school has waned even further. I have to admit she's awfully tiny and cute, and it's incredible what an acrobat she is. But I'm still scared of her.

Larry was halfway through memorizing the different layers of the atmosphere in his social studies book when the screen door banged in the kitchen. We all turned to see who was stopping by when in walked the baby monkey on all fours. By the disdainful expression on her tiny face, she may as well have told us how unfair it is that she's tied up on a little rope and we are all free to move about as we please. Without warning, she took a flying leap and clutched me tightly around the neck.

Laughing hysterically, Larry loosened Jillie, who shrieked in protest, and went to tie her up while I scrubbed with medicated soap. Grandpa Stelfox had warned us about the rare diseases monkeys carry.

"Mom, you looked so funny!" Larry giggled.

"Get busy!" I told him sternly. "No wonder you have such a hard time concentrating."

The door banged again. Jillie was around my neck before I could stand up to ward her off. Her scratchy little hands hung on as if I were mama monkey herself.

Larry flew to my rescue, prying her hands off my dress. She screamed with indignation and looked at me pleadingly.

"Larry?"

"Yes, Mom, I'm going. I'll see why she gets loose, so give me some time, will you?"

"Sierra Fox One, Sierra Fox," crackled my radio.

"Go ahead, I'm standing by."

"Want to go along to the port with Mr. Seah? Bring Larry too."

"Oh, sure!" I replied. I needed a break from hugging monkeys.

When we got to the port, one massive steel ship was being loaded with raw rubber from the huge Firestone plantation in Harbel. Another was unloading rice with a crane, right over the heads of all the people milling about. I thought about all the rigid safety rules in Canada and shuddered to think of one of those cables breaking.

We walked farther down the wharf and gazed down into the water at a ship that had sunk. It was listing badly in the murky water, and two shipping containers sat at a crazy angle on top.

"Those are Christian Aid's containers," Mr. Seah informed us. "Many men have died trying to get the goods. They dive down and try to get in, and they either suffocate or drown."

We stood and stared silently at the watery grave. I looked up over the glittering expanse of water beyond the ship and tried not to think about the desperation the doomed men must have felt. Maybe their children were waiting at home, crying for food, or maybe the rent was due and there was no way out.

March 9

Early this morning, Wayne, Bev, Larry, a CAM orphanage administrator named Borbor Zolue, and I delivered some supplies to Our Lady Fatima Rehabilitation Center. It was teeming with hundreds of handicapped children—some in leg braces and crutches, some with badly twisted limbs, some with sightless eyes. The sight of so many disfigured and crippled children was heart wrenching. Sister Fatima, confined to a wheelchair herself, takes care of them all. I marvel at the courage and determination of that small, powerful lady who knows each child personally and loves them as her own.

"These children could never survive without her," Borbor informed us.

A small shed serves as a woodworking shop where children were busy fashioning limb braces and crutches for their own use. There were boys on ladders white-washing the walls; others were up to their elbows in laundry tubs, tackling the piles of laundry; still others were ironing, mending, and doing other small jobs.

I think wise Lady Fatima dreams up work to keep them all busy. She sent one of the men along to show us their garden projects about a quarter mile away.

This is impossible, I thought as we lurched and skidded down to the valley where they grow corn and watermelons. It is beautiful along the hillsides, but the washouts in the road tested Wayne's driving skills.

Eager gardeners showed us around the little mounds and craters of soil where tiny corn and watermelon plants were being carefully tended. Every inch of claimed space had to be cleared of thick foliage and heavy grasses.

"Do you ever see any snakes around here?" I asked on impulse.

"Oh yes, yes," they assured me.

"Wh-what kinds?" I asked faintly.

"Oh, dey be cobra . . . big, big, like dat," and the smiling fellow proceeded to show us a piece of plastic tubing fully five inches thick.

Immediately, I noticed all the cracks and holes under the crumbling concrete walkway.

"Dey come along da rocks righ' heah, where you be standin'," but to their astonishment, I was speeding for the safety of the Defender.

"Oh, Mom, this is nothing compared to Haiti," my brave Bev informed me, but she was scurrying along right behind me. The obvious mirth of the gardeners didn't bother me one bit. I wasn't going to chance meeting a cobra.

This evening we had the privilege of being invited to Dr. Lamin's country home for supper. Dr. Lamin pulled frosty bottles of pop out of his ice-filled cooler and wiped off the moisture before opening them, then he gravely handed each of us one. We were all sitting on his small front porch. The air was heavy with the scent of rain, and welcome little breezes fanned our cheeks.

"Now come and eat," he told us, passing around a tray piled high with sandwiches. How nice of him to invite us all over to get acquainted and have a bit to eat.

Dr. Lamin's wife, Gertrude, his daughter Florence, and his two sons, Moses and Paul, helped serve the sandwiches and pour the drinks. His sweet little granddaughter, Acie, made friends with the girls.

Wayne coughed suddenly as his face turned red and the tears stood in his eyes.

"You okay?" I whispered.

"I'll be all right," he smiled. "Just a bit of a kick in these sandwiches."

"A bit of a kick" was mildly stated. The first bite felt like fire in our mouths. We coughed and sputtered, took drinks, and smiled through our tears at each other.

"I like it," said Julie. "What's in here anyway, red pepper?"

Dr. Lamin chuckled and offered us some more. He was in a

jolly mood. While eating, we discussed his new clinic and the pros and cons of opening another one somewhere.

"It is a dream come true for me to open a clinic in Redlight," he smiled. "To God be all the glory. It was not easy, but by God's grace it became a reality."

His heart's concern is for his people. You can see it in the way he relates to them and takes time to listen to their troubles.

March 10

Six men were baptized this morning, and Dr. Lamin was among them. Our hearts rejoiced with them as they took their vows and became members of the church.

It's especially touching to see these people reaching out to God. They have such a terrible, sad history—a history almost unbearable to reflect upon.

Pastor Reuben's whole face shone with the love and concern he has for this little flock. He has carefully nurtured and guided them from the beginning. He has spent sleepless nights and anxious days trying to sift them out and determine who is sincere and who is not. In turn, the people love him fiercely. They marvel that Pastor and his wife were willing to sacrifice for them, spending years in a strange, forbidding country.

A peaceful reverence permeated the group, while the devil gnashed his teeth at the new little group of saints in Liberia.

7

Stay Away from the Beaches at Night

March 12

Even before full light this morning, a boy was out selling his frozen Kool-Aid. I saw him from the porch where I was hanging out laundry, hoping to beat the rain.

"Koo-ay! Koo-ay! Koo-ay!" he hollered, pushing his loaded wheelbarrow expertly. He walked with the peculiar, lilting gait of the typical Liberian, ending each step on his toes. He came to the gate, motioned to me with his hand, and flashed a big friendly grin. "Koo-ay?"

"No thanks. Not today," I answered—*or ever*, I thought. That Kool-Aid is stirred together in huge, dirty buckets, with flies swarming everywhere. It's a sticky mess by the time they're done filling all those little plastic bags, and there's no place to wash all those dirty hands with soap and water. No Kool-Aid for me.

"Mornin' calamah! Mornin' calamah!" rang the next breakfast offer.

Morning calamah is a watery white liquid made from rice soaked overnight, then stirred vigorously and drained. It is pretty bland, but I've been told a dash of dry milk powder greatly improves the taste. The remaining rice is not wasted, but is pounded to a pulp and pressed through a wire sieve, creating small knots to cook for the next meal. Only the rich can afford a teaspoon or two of "sugar to taste."

Last evening, Larry suddenly appeared at the door and announced, "There's a lady at the gate with a gift for us, Dad."

"A gift?" I wondered. "Tell her to come on in." Imagine our surprise to find a lady outside with a plastic tub balanced expertly on her head. In it was our gift—a fish. The red gripper fish was so huge that the head and tail curved out over the tub.

"How can such a thin neck hold so much weight?" I wondered.

"Thank you," Wayne told her. "We sure appreciate this."

He stood looking down at the scaly monster, dreading the next job. "Elijah, do you know how to clean a fish?"

"Yes, sir," Elijah assured him, grinning from ear to ear.

We watched, fascinated, as the scales flew. The memory will remain with me forever—the man working amid the tubs of water, his coal black skin glistening in the porch light, and a young white boy leaning close, his questions flying as fast as the scales.

"Do you eat the head?" I wondered.

"Sure," he said with evident relish. "Dat's da bes' part."

"What about the eyeballs?"

"Oh, yes, ah eat dem too," Elijah answered, rolling his eyes with pleasure at the thought.

Silence.

"Maybe your mom will want to cook dem?" he wondered, tentatively looking at Larry, then at me.

"I'll let you have them," I answered generously.

"Ahhh, it will make good soup," he grinned. "Thank you *very* much."

Dear, faithful Elijah took not only the eyeballs, but the head and some of the entrails as well. He has a family of five and a young wife to feed—and tonight they will celebrate.

Marie, our cleaning lady, was just as grateful when I gave her a portion of the fish to take home. "Thank you *very* much," she said, regarding me gravely with big, dark eyes. "My little Freddie will love it so much."

March 16

"Let's go visit Barbara Christie today," Bev suggested this morning as she breezed into the kitchen. "She's that lady we talked to at church with a little baby named Elva. I heard she has malaria. C'mon, Mom; it's Saturday. Come along."

"I'm coming too," Charlotte said. "I'd like to see that sweet little baby again."

"Okay," I agreed. "Let's take some formula along for her."

The delicious ocean breeze danced along the cracked sidewalk with us, lifting some of the endless pieces of garbage and letting them settle lazily back to the pile. There is rubble wherever you look; it half covers the road and is scattered all over people's yards. There are millions of small plastic bags—most of them blue—lying along the crumbling block walls. Hideous old cars and army vehicles have been left to rot where they crashed.

"Why couldn't an army of jobless men launch a great clean-up campaign in this messy city?" I asked, but got no answer.

The same friendly breeze that brought us the tang of the ocean caused us to groan with the stench of the rotting debris. Everywhere, the tangled creeping vines and wildflowers were attempting to cover the filth with their exotic blossoms and green foliage. Energetic hens clucked to their bright-eyed babies when we passed. They love the garbage dumps.

"This is Barbara's place," Charlotte announced as she ducked into the tiny, two-room dwelling where the sick woman lay. The ceiling was low and covered neatly with rows of newspapers. There was a tiny bedside stand and a small table with a few dishes.

On the floor lay baby Elva.

"She's still nursing, but she can't while I'm sick," Barbara whispered.

I stood and looked at the neat little room, the dear, sleeping child, and the sick mother, and I marveled at how little it actually takes to live. We sat and talked and gave her the milk and pudding. How grateful she was! All too soon it was time to leave.

When we walked past the CAM base on the way home, Mr.

Gurley and Pastor Reuben were talking to a mother whose daughter had been badly burned when marauding soldiers set fire to their hut. The two had traveled for days through the bush, and they looked exhausted.

"Come, look," Pastor Reuben beckoned us.

The girl's back was a mass of blackened skin with angry, swollen ridges as if she had been whipped. Streaks of dried blood added to the gruesome sight. Her upper arms were swollen and blistered, her hair matted and singed, and her eyes bloodshot.

"She needs Silvadene!" Bev exclaimed.

"I have suffered a lot in the war, but not as she has," kind old Mr. Gurley said, shaking his head.

Dr. Lamin was waiting at the Good Samaritan Clinic, looking like an angel of light to all of us. He helped her into a clean white bed and with loving hands applied a softening cream to her blistered back.

"Now we will use Silvadene cream," the good doctor said, "and she will be all right."

Their nightmare was just about over.

March 17

A gentle rain was falling outside the old church garage this morning, but Pastor Reuben held everyone's attention once again. There was a sad note to the singing today, as if we were already missing him.

All during church, the busy black and orange lizards darted back and forth along the garden wall, or lay still, watching us with beady, unblinking eyes.

"I'll miss those little fellows when we move to the new church," Wayne told me later.

After church, Larry, Wayne, and I drove Iddo and Viola Yoder to Robert's Field Airport. They are leaving us for a while.

On the way back we followed an ancient Toyota transport truck. Heavily loaded with coal, bamboo sticks, and bananas, it leaned precariously to the side. The tires were worn and squatting under the weight.

"Please don't get too close," I told my husband. "Just look at those men clinging to the back—and a woman too."

As we slowly approached the crest of a steep hill, we suddenly noticed that the vehicle ahead of the Toyota had lost its load right in our lane—and another car was just coming over the hill.

The Toyota slowed quickly, the driver cranking the wheels hard to the right to avoid hitting the oncoming car. Swaying precariously, it finally shuddered to a stop—and then started drifting back toward us.

"Back up, quick!" I cried, but Wayne was already backing out of harm's way.

We watched helplessly as the Toyota drifted slowly backward toward the steep embankment. Suddenly, one of the riders hopped out of the cab and with lightning speed thrust a large block of wood behind the back tire. The tire hopped over the wood as if it wasn't there, and the last thing we saw was the terrified girl clinging to the back before the truck plunged over the side with a sickening crash.

Seconds later, the girl came scrambling up out of the ravine, unhurt except for a gash in her leg. Her eyes were wide with terror.

"She must have jumped just in time!" Wayne exclaimed.

We hurried to the next checkpoint and reported the accident. It is hard knowing just what to do in such a situation, but one thing we do know. God protected us mightily.

Tonight, the wind is cool and refreshing and the giant fruit bats are darting around in the pale moonlight. It is so wonderful to know God is totally in control.

March 18

Larry is sick again. I felt his forehead; it was hot to the touch. His head ached and his eyes hurt. I can tell he is miserable.

"You must stop eating off the streets," I admonished. "Just sleep—it's the best thing for you. I'm slipping down to the office to see how they're getting along."

I drove the six blocks down to the CAM office and parked the

Cruiser outside the gate. I was humming a little tune when I stepped out—right into a pile of big red ants. Instantly, they swarmed on my feet and legs, biting with searing, painful little stings. I stomped and swatted, trying to be dignified at the same time so the passersby wouldn't stare.

"Ants," Tumba told Wayne as they watched me from a second-floor window. "You all right?" Tumba asked when I came upstairs.

"You aren't supposed to laugh," I told him sternly.

"That's true, Muttah. That's true," he said. "Ha, ha, ha."

My legs ached with about twenty bites. Calamine lotion would be just the thing.

The base was like a hive of busy bees this morning, though it seemed sometimes that things weren't working as efficiently as a beehive does. Excitement hung in the air.

Most of the staff were busy scraping off old paint or painting walls, scrubbing black ceiling fans and light fixtures, sorting out old junk, or doing small repairs. Many of the men wore ill-fitting clothing from the clothing bags at the warehouse, and they looked hilarious. Usually they dress immaculately for work, and this was such a change.

Wayne hurried about, looking a bit harassed as he gathered supplies, wiped up paint, and helped with countless other jobs.

March 20

Mervin Lantz, the new pastor from Lott, Texas, along with his wife Mary and their two daughters, Staci and Angela, arrived at two o'clock this afternoon. I'm really looking forward to meeting them.

Larry feels much better, but these quick fevers worry me.

March 22

A shipping container with supplies and other goodies from the folks back home was scheduled to arrive today, which caused no little excitement for a certain schoolboy. But first the science book had to be studied.

"What does the liver help the blood resist?" I quizzed.

"Temptation," came the ready reply. "Do you know it's my birthday next month?"

"Larry," I reprimanded with a mixture of amusement and exasperation, "you *must* keep your mind on your work. Of course I know it's your birthday. Now let's try that question again . . ."

It took some perseverance, but we waded through the whole science book before the container arrived. With a note of triumph Larry finally shouted, "Daddy's here!"

We drove through some extremely busy traffic to the CAM warehouse, where Varnee welcomed us with an ice-cold drink.

The tireless workers were already carrying bags of heavy clothing back to the storage area. Hundreds of bags of clothing, all collected and sorted and bagged by willing volunteers in the clothing centers back in the States. I imagined them visiting and talking as they worked. I wish I could thank each of them personally.

I couldn't believe all the donated shoes. Thousands of them— all bagged and ready to wear. I watched in fascination.

"By the way," Willie announced suddenly, "I saw Dave Waines, and he said they are coming for supper."

"Bev, you'll have to go home and start something!" I exclaimed. "There are nine of them. Just add some cans to the soup, put out the buns, and make some brownies. We'll be home as soon as we can."

"His brother is coming too," Willie added.

With the wonderful canned meat and mixed vegetables we had in the pantry, I wasn't one bit worried. Having a Canadian family over for supper sounded like fun.

When the container was empty and all the personal boxes for the CAM staff were loaded onto the Cruiser, we drove home. Our guests were already in the kitchen.

"I'm Dave," he began. "Please meet my wife Audrey, and this is Janelle, Daniel, Joshua, Rebecca, and Matthew—and these two are Naomi and Manwo," he finished, affectionately indicating a small black girl and an older black boy who was obviously handicapped. "This is my brother Brent; he's here for six weeks."

"A family from Canada, and a *large* one at that!" was Audrey's comment when she saw all of us. She was small and slim with a thick reddish braid. She looked tired and worn.

"Hello," said Manwo, grinning from ear to ear and extending his hand. "We brough' you somethin'."

Dave dug in their black plastic bag and produced Pringles chips, smoked almonds, flat pita bread, juice, and golden delicious apples, then he fetched two pineapples from the car. "We didn't want you to supply everything," he smiled.

The Waines have been missionaries in Liberia for about thirteen years, fleeing to Guatemala for two years during the war.

"We live right in the leprosy compound there in Ghanta," Audrey said. "I teach classes for the young girls, but our own children sure aren't getting their education. It's just too hard to do."

"Have you seen many snakes around your place?" interrupted Larry.

"Oh, yes," Dave replied. "Let's see, we've had green mambas, which are long, slender, and very fast. Their bite is deadly. We also drove over a cobra at least nine feet long, and last week we chopped the head off a night viper and out popped two toads— *and hopped away.*"

"Gross!"

"Horrors!"

"The worst one is the night adder with the white tip on its tail," Dave continued. "It lives around buildings, and many people are bitten because they walk around at night with no shoes and no flashlights. It's especially dangerous to reach for wood without checking first. That's why we do not allow our children outside after dark."

"I think the worst was when Matthew came running with that dead cobra around his neck," grimaced Audrey. "Its head was chopped off and he was a bloody mess." She shook her head at the memory.

"Change the subject, please!" Bev exclaimed.

"We're really concerned about the ritualistic killing going on all the time in the villages," Audrey confessed. "The devil they worship demands human blood. You really wouldn't believe what they do. Someone has to be the sacrifice."

My mind struggled to comprehend what she was saying. I thought of Baal, Ashera, Molech—way back in Bible times when the heathen raged—but now, in 2002? It was unthinkable.

Stay away from the beaches at night, whatever you do. That's where they perform their sacrifices.

"Well, I know God is on the throne, and if you fear Him you have nothing else to fear," I answered, to the agreement of all.

March 23

Wayne and I took off early today to do some grocery shopping. I love to get up and sneak off with him sometimes, and he needs the break too.

People already jammed the streets, and none of them were in a hurry. They called and waved to each other and slowly went about their business.

On Benson Street I wisely stayed in the Jeep and let Wayne do the fresh vegetable bargaining. Immediately, he was surrounded by a determined crowd of merchants trying to outdo each other for his attention. He peered into the ring of blue plastic bags and occasionally his arms waved in the air. I laughed helplessly.

"Missie, Missie!" a toothless old woman begged. She made sharp little gestures from her mouth to me, over and over. Her head hung sideways in the most dejected pose she could muster.

I dug into my black plastic bag and pulled a twenty-dollar bill from the thick wad at the bottom.

The old eyes lit up. "God bless you, Missie, God *bless* you."

A few minutes later, Wayne emerged from the fray. "Sometimes I win, sometimes I lose," he commented dryly. "It's like a war zone in there."

As Wayne parked in front of the hardware store, I settled down to read while I waited—but not for long. There was too much going on. I watched as a taxi screeched to a stop just ahead of me.

The back door flew open and all eyes turned toward a tremendously fat lady ambling toward them. Little by little she worked her way into that car, while the other passengers gamely sucked in their breath to make more room. Somehow they got the door slammed shut and the car roared off, its back right bumper dangerously close to the road.

Seconds later, a battered old van swerved into the same space, loaded to the shocks with greasy oil drums, coal bundles, hangers of green bananas, and sticks of every size. Heads stuck out of every broken window and many more heads filled the spaces between.

A man hopped out, followed by the lady in command.

"Take dem bananas off!" she ordered, so he jumped up and grabbed a large hanger, dropping two or three in the process. They rolled off the other side of the van. He either didn't see them or didn't want to see them.

"Git dem other ones!" she barked.

"Wha-where . . ." he began, but Ms. Sharp-eyes stopped him cold.

"Git dem."

Instantly, they were face to face, shouting and screeching, giving little hops of rage. I could almost see the spit flying. The man was backing up, inch by inch, and suddenly he turned and went around the side of the van, growling angrily as he went. She stood glowering after him.

"How much?" Wayne asked her, indicating the bunch.

She smiled a dazzling, white-toothed smile. The bangles on her plump wrists danced as she parked her fists on her hips and rolled her eyes heavenward in deep thought.

"Two-fifty," she stated. "Ah really needs two se'nty five, bu' fo' you ah will let dem go for two-fifty."

"No thanks," he replied, starting for the truck. "I can get them in Buchanan for a hundred and fifty."

"Yes, but we have to bring dem heah an' it is naw easy," she countered.

"It's a deal," Wayne agreed, and it was, at four U.S. dollars.

March 24

Today we had our first service in the "new" church. How exciting! It's nice and big compared to the carport, and there is room to spare.

Pastor Reuben delivered his sermon with zeal and ended it with a plea for the congregation to remain faithful to the end. He handed all his responsibilities over to Pastor Mervin and prayed for him. Many of the people wept.

Later this evening, some of the staff met at Iddo and Viola's house for a small private farewell. It was a perfect opportunity to become better acquainted with Mervin and Mary Lantz and their family. I'm sure we will get along just fine.

Changes are inevitable. Even though they tug at your heart, they're also good, because God is in control. His angels hover over us day and night.

March 25

Last night we grouped in the open kitchen doorway to watch the fury of a thunderstorm unleashing its power into the African night.

"I've never, ever seen such lightning," I murmured in sheer awe.

It would start with a sheet of blinding white, then a tremendous earth-to-sky bolt that flashed so often it seemed to stand in the heavens. Right on its heels, another one danced in the sky—then another. The thunder followed in a series of ear-splitting crashes and rolls and jolts of sound, and the rain slashed the leaves off the trees and overflowed the eaves with a rushing sound.

It was so beautiful it defies description. The rain lingered through the night, swelling and subsiding, and finally, when the first rays of dawn streaked the sky, it turned to gentle tears.

8

Hungry Beggars

March 26

Larry felt so miserable this morning that we decided to go see Dr. Lamin.

The Good Samaritan Clinic was packed by the time we arrived. "It's only 8:45," I marveled, "and look at all these people."

They were squished on the benches in the hallway, with arms full of babies or toddlers. Others stood in the small entry or spilled out on the steps. Many more waited in the gazebo. Old and young alike waited eagerly but patiently for help.

"I've never seen so many infants in one place before," I told Dr. Lamin. The newborn ones looked like perfect dolls with incredibly cute faces and hands. Their curls felt as soft as corn tassels and as curly as wedding ribbon. Some were wrapped in colorful, carefully made patchwork blankets that came straight from American sewing circles.

Dr. Lamin chuckled. "Well, we have a good staff here, Ruth Ann, an' this is what happens here every day. Jus' come this way," he added, leading the way through the hall. He opened a small wooden door and motioned us inside. "Sit right here an' fill out this form while I get Joseph, the lab technician."

I looked around the room curiously. The small table and two

chairs felt sticky—as if the varnish never had a chance to dry. There was an open shelf for the patients' records, and assorted boxes of medical supplies were stacked on the concrete floor against the wall. A bucket of water stood in the corner sink.

I thought of the Raymond Clinic in Alberta, with new oak cabinets, spotless floors, private waiting rooms, and sterile, wrapped instruments, and my heart went out to Dr. Lamin. He was doing the absolute best with his situation.

The lab slip was four by six inches and named all kinds of disgusting parasites and exotic diseases to be tested for—hookworms, roundworms, pinworms, tapeworms, E-coli, cholera, malaria, and typhoid.

"I am sorry you must wait, but Joseph is not here yet," Dr. Lamin apologized, sticking his head in the door. He looked agitated.

"Daddy, it's so hot in here," Larry complained, his face flushed. "Let's go home."

"We have to find out what's wrong with you," Wayne answered firmly.

An administrator came in and turned on the fan to circulate some of the hot air. Still we waited. A half hour passed, then forty minutes . . .

Dr. Lamin came in, paced around the room, and apologized again for the delay. He looked down the hall and finally planted himself in front of the luckless administrator.

"I purposely did not let you know ahead of time that the director was bringing his son. This is an embarrassment to us. These people make it possible for us to have this clinic in the first place, and here they sit and wait and wait some more."

"Yes, sir," the man replied meekly, fiddling with his pen.

"If Joseph is sick," Dr. Lamin continued, "he should send a message that he cannot come. If he has business to take care of, let him do it after he looks after the people. If he cannot do the job and is not here by eight o'clock, we will have to find someone to replace him. And if you, as the administrator, cannot see that Joseph is here on time, we will have to replace you as well."

The administrator clasped and unclasped his hands—the doctor's message was clear.

"Let's go," Dr. Lamin told us. We climbed into the Jeep and drove in silence toward the main road.

A man in a white lab coat was walking leisurely toward us. Joseph?

"Stop the car, please," Dr. Lamin requested, then, "Get in, Joseph." Joseph obeyed.

Larry's eyes were big and round and expectant. I felt like holding my breath.

"Joseph," Dr. Lamin began in a quiet, controlled voice. "Why are you an hour and a half late? These people have been waiting on you." His whole demeanor suggested an effort at self-control, and Joseph knew it.

All the bumpy way back to the clinic, Joseph received a kind but stern lecture that none of us will soon forget. I couldn't help but admire the doctor. He had every right to lash out in anger, yet he displayed a truly controlled spirit. "Now let's take care of our patients properly," he finished.

I felt a tiny bit sorry for Joseph, as he seems like an enterprising young man. The carefree, unhurried manner in which he was strolling to the clinic was gone. We were through in ten minutes.

March 27

I was both relieved and worried when Dr. Lamin told us he found malaria and a stomach parasite in Larry. I know malaria can cause brain damage and death if not treated properly. And a stomach parasite? How would we ever survive two years or more?

"It's not a bad case, but it has to be looked after, or it will become bad. You must understand, Larry can get parasites from walking barefoot or swallowing any kind of soil," Dr. Lamin told me. "The worms may also enter through the skin when he wades in the water or bathes on the beach. They are everywhere, Ruth Ann. Just make sure he takes his pills like I told you."

This morning, Dr. Lamin joined Wayne and me to look for a

farewell gift for Pastor Reuben. After three weeks of being back in Liberia, the pastor is leaving for home this afternoon—for good this time.

Almost immediately, we found the gift—a detailed little African village with little huts all around and an elephant outside. It was perfect.

It was almost two o'clock when we finally headed for the airport in the Liberia Mennonite van with Pastor Reuben and all the church members who could possibly fit in, packed as tight as sardines. Reuben, Wayne, and Larry sat in the front and ten more church friends and I filled the back. More would have gladly come—gladly sat on the front hood or hung onto the side doors, or better yet, opened the back hood and sat there.

On the way down, Alfred Gibson told a hair-raising story about a seventeen-foot snake that killed five of his chickens one night before he and his neighbors killed it with their machetes. Gibson lives right in the city close to Fiama Market—only about ten blocks from home!

Seeing Pastor Reuben leave was a sad occasion. "If we don't meet here again, we will meet in heaven," Reuben comforted us as he said good-bye. The women cried into their handkerchiefs, and the men swallowed hard.

Dorcas summed up everyone's thoughts. "We will miss 'im so-o-o much."

March 30

"Happy birthday to you, Happy birthday to you . . ." we sang as the Cruiser ate up the miles.

"How old am I anyway?" Wayne teased us.

"It sure is hard to tell looking at you," I said. "This pace of living could age you fast, though," I added, thinking of all the long, strenuous days spent at the office. "At least we can relax today at Tony's farm. We have to meet the rest by eight."

Two hours later we pulled up the steep, rocky lane leading to Tony Hage's farmhouse. It is a quaint, round, two-story rock building with large windows all around the second floor and a wide stairway leading up.

A large, circular cement pad faces the house, encompassed by metal rails that rise high above the sloping ground behind it. Tremendous old shade trees lean out over the concrete. The undergrowth and jungle foliage stretch for miles in every direction, affording a spectacular view. Birds warble in the trees and brilliant butterflies sail everywhere. No wonder William Tubman, the former president of Liberia, loved to relax here.

"I want to take you to see the lions at President Tubman's home place," Tony informed us. "My men will cook the dinner."

The presidential grounds were once magnificent. The stately old mansion boasts crafty stonework and big garages. The house is surrounded by beautiful, spreading grounds with huge old trees of every kind. A long, paved lane curves up to it, lined with flowering trees and fruit trees. Animal cages of all sizes are rusting away in the damp shade. The president enjoyed keeping elephants, giraffes, goats, lions, and even rats for his entertainment. Only the lion pair remains. Gaunt and mangy, they are fierce-looking beasts with brooding yellow eyes. When we approached, they both began to roar at once—a wild, primeval, haunting sound that belongs in the jungles and plains of their old hunting grounds. It was only natural to feel a shiver of fear, but I felt sorry for them.

Back at the farm, a feast was being prepared. Beef kabobs and chicken franks were dripping juices and smelling like the American Golden Corral. French fries crisped in the frying pan and chicken sizzled on the grill. On the worktable lay a heap of chopped greens, sliced onions, minced garlic, and squeezed-out lime shells. The men had arranged round white plastic tables and matching chairs on the big patio for us. Tony ripped open bags of cheese balls, mixed nuts, and Pringles, poured them into small bowls, and set them on the tables. Two coolers were loaded with soft drinks and fruit juices submerged in crushed ice.

"Would you please say grace for us, Mr. Yoder?" asked Tony.

There was laughter and visiting as we gnawed the chicken and ribs from the bones, dipped the Lebanese flat bread into the humus and the French fries into the ketchup, swigged our drinks, and licked our fingers.

"Mom, look at those little boys!" Larry exclaimed, drawing our attention to the small, ragged beggars creeping along the wall behind us. They were grabbing every bone and scrap we tossed away, tucking them into their pockets. They moved silently and swiftly, their watchful eyes darting here and there. Not a morsel did they miss. Their eyes looked hollow and too big for their faces, and their bellies protruded above their shabby trousers.

Suddenly they all disappeared like frightened deer as one of the cooks came toward us with more trays of food. The cook didn't notice—or didn't want to—and minutes later the little beggars glided around the corner once more.

"I'm gonna leave some meat on these bones from now on," Larry declared, voicing my intentions. "But just imagine chewing someone's leftover bones and picking up those dry crusts. It's like eating from the slop bucket!"

"It's a good reminder of how richly God has blessed us," I reminded him. "I'm sure He hates it when we grumble."

Our eyes were drawn to a tall, smiling young man with ragged clothes walking jauntily up the lane carrying a bamboo basket.

"My name is John," he introduced himself. "See what ah have in dis basket? Four baby crocodiles! Is dere any watah aroun'?" he asked. "Dey need to git wet."

Someone brought a plastic tub half full of water. John carefully grabbed each foot-long baby behind the jaws and one by one let them slide into the water. One of them jerked around and cut a slice in his finger.

"Ah've had dem since dey was as big as my thumb," John grimaced, shaking his finger. "In five more months, dey will be as big as my thigh. When da muttah wen' lookin' fo' food, ah stole the babies. Ah have two men and two women, an' ah wan' fifty dollahs fo' all four of dem."

"Fifty U.S.?" Willie wondered. "Are they really that valuable?"

"Ah yes, dey make purses an' shoes. Dey git big. Like dis," and he showed us a length of about twelve feet. "Make lots of purses an' shoes. If ah can sell dem, ah will buy some tin fo' my roof."

We stood around and stared at the sassy reptiles. They made funny little grunting noises and bit fiercely at each other and at the stick William was poking them with. "Be careful," John laughed. "Dey can bite yo' finger off."

"Where is your family?" Bev asked.

"My muttah lef' us an' ah have no idea where my father is, so ah takes care of my sistah," he answered, smiling broadly. "Do you want to buy dem?"

"No . . . no thank you," she told him hastily.

When the enjoyable day was over, Tony filled the back of the Jeep with pineapples, wild honey, bananas, limes, and plantains before letting us go. Crocodile John promised to visit us in Monrovia. "Ah will bring dem along," he smiled, nodding at his reptile investment.

9

The Blind, the Maimed, the Fatherless

April 1

What a memorable day! This morning we set out to visit several nursing homes and orphanages in the Buchanan area to evaluate them for possible CAM funding. Wayne, Julie, and I went with Pastor George and Esther Akoi, a wonderful young lady from our church in charge of CAM's Self-Help program. She had some loans to collect in that area.

The most unforgettable stop of the day was the blind center. The center is in a small room on the second story of a horrible old building with a hideous washroom that consists of a couple of filthy buckets and a broken commode.

"Some of these folks lost their eyes during the war when ammunition exploded and the extreme flash of light caused burns," George explained quietly. "Some have diseases, but no cure, so here they sit, waiting for someone to come help them."

I can only imagine the horror of opening your eyes after such a shock and realizing you can't see.

The blind people sat in a circle on chairs, awaiting the visitors. They felt around and brought us a few chairs. I chose to stand.

"*Everyone's* blind," Julie whispered in an agonized tone.

It was horrible. Some of their eyes were only slits in their faces. Some were open and blank, others nothing more than gaping sockets. Some were a strange whitish color, and others had a running discharge.

A young blind man started talking in a high monotone that lacked feeling or expression. It was clear he had memorized the whole speech carefully, he talked so fast.

I pitied him desperately. So young, yet so destitute. Such deplorable living conditions. If they at least had one good meal a day to look forward to, or even a decent washroom so they could take care of their personal needs. If they had just a little comfort to make their endless days a bit easier . . .

All the sightless eyes were getting to me. I knew I needed some fresh air, so I slipped outside.

Seconds later Julie joined me, tears running down her face. "I just couldn't handle that speech," she explained.

We walked down to the Jeep and stood there, grieving for what we had just seen. Suddenly, someone lightly touched my arm. I turned and looked straight into the eyes of a blind young girl. White cataracts covered the area where the irises should have been. It gave her an unreal, alien look.

"Oh, no . . ." I groaned.

Her mother stood beside her and spoke the only two words of English she knew. "Mommie, pleeease!

I held up my hands in mute appeal. A desperation welled up inside. What could *we* do? I didn't know whether to scream or cry—it was just too awful. Maybe we could write back to the States and beg for money. Maybe we could ask people not to go out for supper or buy that new dress or fix up the house. But then what?

"We'll talk about it," Julie answered. "There's got to be something we can do."

Oh God, have mercy!

We drove away from that place with a deep, unsettling horror clouding our thoughts and memories.

"Now we come to Group 77," our driver announced.

Group 77 is a center for maimed war amputees.

"We're staying in the car, if you don't mind," we told the men. They understood. Enough was enough for one day.

Wayne just shook his head when he came back outside. "They are in dire straits. It was just horrible in there."

After tracking down Esther's clients, we started the long trip home—sadder and wiser, and a whole lot more thankful for what we had.

April 3

Wayne's face was grave when he came home for lunch. "Two of Tony Hage's cousins have been shot to death in Kakata. Some young soldiers demanded money, which they got, but they killed the men anyway. We'll have to go over to Tony's tonight for a bit."

I could tell there was unusual tension in the air. The mechanics stood around and talked with our security guards in low tones. People are actually serious about a coming war.

Wednesday evening prayer meetings are such warm, close times of fellowship. Sometimes the group is rather small, as people cannot afford the taxi fare twice a week.

Alfred Gibson had devotions about David and his incredible bravery in fighting off an angry bear. "Ah wou' have run so-o-o fas'," he stated. "Yes, ah wou' have run away fas'."

You killed a seventeen-foot boa in the pitch dark—and you would run from a bear? I don't think so.

After church, several men lined up to speak with Wayne, as usual.

"Jus' gi' me a chance. Pleease! No work, no money. My children are starvin' . . . no school funds, nothing. Please gi' me a job. Ah will do anything. Ah will sweep, ah will clean up da yard. Ah will do my bes'."

And then the next one came. "Sir, I must beg you. Since the war we have had almost no food. I lost my job and my six children need to eat. Is there anything I could do in your organization? Please?" The man was obviously educated. He hated to beg.

Soon another came, and yet another. Able-bodied, desperate

men with no future in sight. It is sad to hear them plead, especially when every available CAM job has been taken, plus many extra jobs that really don't have to be done.

They turn away with the hope crushed out of their eyes—disappointed again. Many of them quit coming to church when they realize the church is not an unemployment center.

"This is really getting hard on you, isn't it?" I asked Wayne sympathetically. "And you haven't opened nearly all the letters yet."

"I have to brace myself every time I go to church, or anywhere for that matter," he answered. "It's just never-ending."

April 6

"Anthony Reeves said he'd love to come shopping with us again," Wayne informed me when I said we needed groceries. Anthony knew all the little shops in the back of Waterside—an unbelievable labyrinth of stores and shops and stands of every description. We followed him through the maze, trying to stick together, but the paths were unbelievably narrow and so crowded with goods and people that we had to duck to miss them all. We wove through clothing shops, hanging shoe shops, curtain shops, and cosmetic shops.

Children in school uniforms slouched around their family shops. Mothers arranged small beds right on the floors or among the clothing piles for their tiny infants. Other babies stared at us from their mothers' back lapas. Some slept, their tiny heads lolling around and sweating in the sun.

"Somehow they make it," Wayne said for the umpteenth time. He always remembers how carefully we supported our babies' heads when they were too small to support their own. "Just maybe that's why they have such strong necks—and they never fuss, either."

Wherever we looked, women were having their hair done. They lounged on the floor with their heads leaning forward or backward or sideways. Hair was everywhere. Fake, real, crimped, curled, straightened, braided, knit, crocheted, twisted, spiraled, spiked, black, brown, reddish, or glittering gold is plaited into the existing hair on the ladies' heads.

"Who *thinks* of all these styles?" I marveled. "Isn't it hot?" But Anthony didn't know. His hair is cut so short it's almost nonexistent.

Other shops had all kinds of cheap perfumes, purses, knick-knacks, and millions of other things.

"Two seventy-five," a man said to Wayne when he indicated interest in a bottle of shaving lotion.

Anthony's head ducked under the canopy. "Two seventy-five for Identity lotion? Oh no!" And he proceeded to tell the man what the right price was. "Da minute dey see a whi' man, da price goes way up!" he explained. "Identity don' cost dat much."

"We paid fifty Liberian dollars for tomatoes last week, and today they're a hundred," I told him. "Since you're along, you can bargain for me."

And he did. We got things at their normal prices, without haggling.

"We're definitely interested in paying what it's worth," Wayne explained to Anthony. "We don't want to cheat the people in any way—but three times more is just too much."

April 10

"Now *this* sounds like fun!" Larry exclaimed when Wayne told us what was being planned.

"We want to take two full days to tour all the orphanages," Wayne warned him. "You may get tired of it before we finish."

"Not me!" Larry insisted. "It's a perfect social studies project."

"I think he's right on that," I laughed. "Where else could a boy get such excellent hands-on experience?"

We left around nine-thirty with CAM's Orphanage Sponsorship Program administrator, Sam Kargbo, at the wheel and Wayne, Julie, Larry, and me riding along. Sam is a good, safe driver, and we could watch the sights along the way without worrying.

The Caring for Tomorrow orphanage in Buchanan welcomed

us happily. "I am so blessed. My soul has found rest . . . O Lord, we give thanks for all you've done. I am so blessed," the children sang.

The schoolrooms were constructed of new bamboo sticks overlaid with long grass. The sun glinted through and made dancing patterns everywhere. "This reminds me so much of when we were children," I told Larry. "We used to build tents and Indian forts all the time." It even smelled the same.

Sam led the roll call and each child answered. The smallest ones had to be prompted; they were too busy staring at the white people to hear their names.

"They're not just a number," Wayne observed. "See how they interact with Sam—he seems to know them all. Look how they hug him and hang on to him."

"Children know when they're loved," I returned.

"Where is Kabah today?" Sam asked the caretakers in charge. "She should be here. I don't like it when the caretakers are not all here with the children. You must tell her."

The dorms we toured were neat and clean. Well-worn CAM quilts splashed across the narrow, wooden beds. An old man followed us, blessing us as we walked.

We came away thinking, *It's real.* Here are happy children, kind caretakers, schoolbooks, and teachers. No distended bellies and filthy clothing. The pantry is well stocked with rice, chicken, oil, flour, sugar, cornmeal, salt, beans, soap, and more. It was thrilling!

"God will make a way," they were singing as we left. "He will make a way when it seems there is no way."

Next we visited the Lighthouse Ministry Children's Village. It boasted sixty-four orphans, and they, too, loved to sing. A lad with an old shampoo bottle and a stick was beating his "drum." The littlest ones were so fascinated with us they forgot to sing. They stared with big, solemn eyes.

I felt a wave of gratitude for the sponsors of these innocent souls. "I wish every Christian in the world could see this," I said.

"Can you imagine how many new sponsors would respond?"

After the speeches and introductions, the children thawed out. They slipped their sweaty little hands into ours and smiled up at us with shining eyes. We marveled at all the dusty little feet in flip-flops and the joy on the children's faces—and felt our hearts melt.

"It's so different here than at the blind center!" Julie exclaimed. "Here there is hope, and the children are happy. They're actually getting enough food. Mom, we have to be sponsors when we get home."

"After seeing all this I feel like sending a letter across America," I agreed. "Just think—if a person or a family would not go out for supper just *once*, they could feed a child for a month. It's almost unbelievable. Julie, look how nice that Amish dress looks on that old lady. I wonder which lovely sewing room it was sewn in?"

"Oh, Father," a small boy prayed at Preparing Our Future Orphanage. "Bless Christian Aid."

"Amen!" the rest agreed, peeking through their fingers at us.

"Oh, Father, God. Send us some mo' rice."

"Amen."

"Father God, send some mo' shoes, mo' mattress, an' mo' zinc fo' da roof."

"Amen."

The Hannah B. Williams Home had clothing drying on the ground all over the yard. Some children were being treated for scalp fungus and had white cream smeared all over their heads. A large pile of mud lay where some bricks had been destroyed by the recent rains.

The dorms needed a good cleaning and smelled like many unwashed bodies, but at least the children were being fed. The condition of these children's homes, we are finding out, depends on the personal commitment of the caretakers and, as always, some are in it just for the money.

That's why CAM is so persistently sending out administrators, so they can keep a close eye on things.

Flowers bloomed in profusion along the porch at the Catherine Home. The singing was excellent—"God, you are wonderful . . ."

"I'd rate this one a B+," I told Julie. "Look how clean it is."

The children at the Good Samaritan Home screamed out "Glory Be to God in the Highest." A little old man stood there and watched, his hands planted firmly on his hips, just taking it all in. A pleased smile played on his lips.

Ninety-seven children crowded into the Hawa Massaquoi Home, but Mrs. Hawa is building larger quarters.

"All wha' you see is from Christian Aid," she told us. "Praise God. Dey give us all da building materials—all da' zinc an' cement an' everything. Praise be to God."

The children's small, clean faces glistened with sweat as they sang, but the heat didn't wilt their happy smiles. They slept in homemade bamboo beds, with CAM quilts everywhere. How those quilts brightened those rooms!

The Children's Rehabilitation Home had sixty-three children, a little black billy goat, and two very skinny pigs.

"Evidently there aren't many scraps around here," Julie observed. "See how the rain washed away the kitchen wall. They really need help in this place, don't you think?"

"I sure do," I agreed, looking at the ramshackle old dorms, the rundown kitchen, and the leaking roofs.

"Soldiers threw too many dead bodies into this well," Sam told us as we peered down a deep, black hole. "The other well is dry, so we need a pump or some way to get water. They must carry all the water they use."

Sixty-three children? Carry all the water?

The church was made of bamboo, with a thick palm frond roof covered with tarps. The benches all around were constructed of hard, round bamboo stalks. "Ouch! I couldn't sit here for too long!" Larry declared.

"Many, many other orphanages want to come under CAM's roof," Sam informed us as we drove away. "CAM has such an excellent food basket and consistent monthly deliveries. Other NGOs may bring food for a few months and then not show up the next few months. They only have bulgur wheat to offer and maybe oil sometimes."

"What's an NGO?" asked Larry.

"It stands for Non-Governmental Organization," Sam answered. "That means people who come to countries like Liberia to give the suffering aid. Like Christian Aid Ministries," he smiled.

"Are any of these children ever adopted?" I wondered. "It seems like there's a child of every description in these homes."

"Once in a while a relative comes searching for a child and finds one," he answered. "It certainly is rare though; most of these children's parents are dead."

"This is our next stop," Sam continued as we pulled into the Elwa Home. "This place has one hundred and ten children." It was old and dark, surrounded by walls, but the children literally swarmed around us, shouting wildly, "Christian Aid! Christian Aid is here!" Obviously, they knew the truck on sight.

I noticed an unusual number of little ones around one or two years old. "This is a lot of children for one place," I told Sam.

He chuckled. "Currently, we sponsor two thousand two hundred and ninety-five children," he said, eager to let us know the figures, "in forty-one places."

All those motherless children.

In the kitchen, rows and rows of supper plates were being filled—generous, heaping portions of rice with pepper soup on top. The cooks smiled broadly and thanked us for coming.

Our attention was drawn to a small boy with a grotesquely swollen leg. "What happened to him?" we all wondered sympathetically.

"A snake bit him," we were told. "Out in da dark las' night, when he was playin' outside. We don' know wha' kin' of snake it was—maybe a cobra or yard snake."

Two dark fang marks showed just below the boy's ankle. A tight piece of grass was tied around the ankle itself, but the swelling was already up to his knee.

"Shouldn't Dr. Lamin see him right away?" I asked in consternation. "It looks like the circulation is cut off."

"Yes, the doctor will see him," Sam assured us. "This is not the first snake bite and won't be the last."

"Mister Wayne, the roof is leakin' bad," the caretaker complained. "We git all wet durin' da' night."

"We will be sending your zinc this week yet," Wayne told her.

"Thank you! Praise God! Oh, praise God!" came the replies.

"Why such excitement over some old tin?" Larry wondered.

"Just imagine living in a cold, dark building like this," I answered. "The rains would come and pour into the place, and all your stuff would get wet. If someone would fix the roof, you could sleep in comfort and not have to worry that the walls will dissolve and crumble during the night."

The girls' dorm was badly damaged, with no screens on the windows. "Check that out," Julie said, indicating all the quilts. "The shoes are all in order too. Look at all these mosquitoes though. I'm getting out of here."

"The director here is one remarkable woman," Sam declared as we jerked and bumped into the Gloria C. Home. "She had to flee from Cape Mount with all these children because of the recent fighting, so this is just temporary."

A large clothesline hung full, and more clothing lay all over the yard, draped over the bushes and on the old surrounding wall. "Think of washing clothes for sixty children," I groaned. "The girls all have to have their hair washed and braided too. I can't imagine!"

"I'm sure they don't get braided too often," Julie mused. "They probably take turns, and the bigger ones can braid too. They sure look nice and clean though."

A small boy had fallen asleep right on the floor, but he was quickly awakened to help sing. "Come we dat love da Lor'!" they yelled with tremendous volume. The director watched them fondly, with pride in her eyes. Judging by the orderliness and cleanliness, her heart was definitely in the program.

One little lad wore a pair of cowboy boots with missing soles, but he didn't seem to mind.

One caretaker brought out a chubby, adorable baby with satin, ebony skin. "May we please hold him?" I asked. His cheeks felt smooth and soft, like the petals of a rose. His damp little curls were loose and thick and smelled of scented oils. He gazed at us quietly, his eyes full of wonder.

"What a perfect doll," Julie said admiringly. "It's my turn now."

"This is really impressive!" we praised the cooks as they gave us a mini-tour of the orderly kitchen. The dishes were covered with a cloth to keep out the flies, and everything was as clean as possible. The pantry was in perfect order.

"She *is* remarkable!" Wayne declared on our way out. "It's not hard to tell which caretakers really care about the children."

"Our next stop," Sam told us, "is my own orphanage." The note of excitement in his voice was unmistakable.

Children were already pouring out of the buildings when we slowly pulled in at the Zion Praise School and Children's Relief Home. They were clapping and dancing with excitement.

Some of the younger ones were busily weaving beautiful mats on a wooden frame studded with nails. They carefully threaded the yarn over and under, making wild, colorful African patterns. Shy smiles lit their eyes.

An older man sat before a treadle Singer sewing machine, his gnarled feet rocking the pedal grate back and forth with swift, perfect rhythm. "He is training the younger boys to sew, and they are doing very well. Christian Aid sent the machine," Sam informed. "Children! Let's sing for the visitors."

Instantly, the children obeyed, setting up their usual formation with the bigger ones in the back and the toddlers in front. "Let all da people praise you, oh Lor'," they sang lustily. "Let us praise da Lor'!"

I leaned toward Wayne. "The caretakers look weary to the bone," I whispered. "And see the eye infections some children have? They can't even open their eyes all the way."

The tired orphanage building had once been a grand mansion. Rich black marble floors lined the spacious room, but now they were scuffed and chipped and beaten. I could only imagine all the wild parties once held in the huge, open-air courtyard, and all the unrestrained drinking at the circular bar above the sunken living room.

The bedrooms had boasted private baths and modern facilities, but they were modern no longer. They were broken, cracked, and shattered, just like the dreams of the owners.

Perhaps there had been babies born here . . . weddings and funerals held . . . perhaps the people had laughed and cried and finally fled in the face of great danger.

The war has destroyed the beauty of Liberia. It is a shell of its former self. It was hard not to feel the utter sadness of the place.

Suddenly, a dark, dignified woman approached us. "Wan' to hol' da chil?" she asked as she carefully handed me a baby girl and stood back respectfully.

For a minute we were speechless—stunned by the child's astonishing beauty. "Who is this?" we asked wonderingly. "She looks half white."

The baby had a diminutive, oval face. Her eyes were large and framed with soot black lashes that contrasted with the paleness of her nut-brown skin. She had full, drooping lips, a perfect little nose, and deep dimples in both cheeks. Her oiled hair was arranged in tiny braids all over her head.

"She's gorgeous!" I breathed.

"Let's keep her!" Julie exclaimed, her mind aflame with eager plans.

"She sure has plenty of hair," Larry chirped. "How can they braid such a little kid?"

"Wow! She's *really* cute!" Wayne agreed, as he and Sam approached. "Where did she come from?"

"This child was found in a hut after the village had been raided," Sam explained simply. "There was no one around; the parents were either dead or gone, and the child almost starved to death. This is what happens, Boss. It is a terrible thing. Many times after a raid bush people will search the houses to see what is left. They found this baby—and brought her to us."

In my mind, I could see the child lying helplessly on a filthy, bloody, dirt floor crawling with ants and roaches, her cries becoming weaker and weaker.

"Thank God she was found!" I breathed, stroking her cheek as my heart broke for her. God was using this child to open my eyes. The dilapidated condition of the building became totally unimportant. There was love in action here. Hope for the hopeless, the starving, and the abandoned children of Liberia.

"Oh, thank God!" I breathed again, hugging the child tightly. Tears welled up in my eyes, dimming my vision. "If only the mother could see her now."

We left Sam's orphanage with a renewed sense of purpose. *Truly we have so much to be thankful for. Lord, help us use our blessings to serve others.*

"One more place today, and this one is bad," Sam said quietly. "They had to flee their original home, so we combined two homes in one. They have over a hundred children."

We soon saw what he meant.

How is this possible? We were all horrified at the broken-down, crumbling walls, the splintered door, the patchwork roof with jagged tin hanging everywhere. *This place looks dangerous!*

The beds were built of blocks and cement—but they were swathed in warm blankets. *At least they keep warm at night,* I consoled myself. I tried not to think of all those bony frames sleeping on the unyielding concrete.

The windows were all broken out and open to the hungry mosquitoes. Even the warehouse had an open window. Gaping holes decorated the walls, and the ceilings were patched and sagging.

No one spoke. We were trying to comprehend the enormity of the need in this place.

Ragged, dirty children were everywhere—along the walls, on the crumbling porch, and in the yard outside. I knew their swollen stomachs crawled with parasites.

"What do they do when it rains?" Larry wondered.

"They get soaked," was the reply.

There in the middle of all the need was a little sewing circle in progress. We watched as several young girls worked on dresses and shirts while the matron kept the shiny sewing machine whirring.

"What a bright spot!" Julie said with little satisfaction. "The one bright spot in the whole place."

Later tonight, when supper was over and Larry was in his clean bed, he called me over. "Mom, I'm so glad I'm not an orphan," he said. "I feel so sorry for them."

"I'm glad too," I told him fondly. "We have much to be thankful for."

April 11

Once again, we were on the road early this morning to visit more of Liberia's orphanages. "One orphanage we want to visit today is near an immigration point where the soldiers can get very nasty," Sam confided.

"Just give them some Bibles—that usually works," Wayne said confidently.

"I'm sure glad I could come today," Charlotte said with satisfaction. "I want to see some of those children you're all talking about."

A van sped past us, piled high with goods. Two or three men stood on the back bumper and hung onto the sides or the window frames. On the very top, swaying madly back and forth and tied on by ropes, was a long couch. Lounging on the couch were three men.

"They must have absolutely no fear," Wayne chuckled. "The

way they hang from the back of vehicles or sit on the open end gate—I just don't know."

"Stop here a minute, please," Wayne said suddenly, sitting up straight and reaching for his wallet. "I want to give this fellow something."

It was a young schoolboy, terribly crippled, dragging his feet along the dusty road to school. His crutches kicked up little puffs of dust as he went. His uniform was all disheveled and wrinkled and little lines of dust were visible around his mouth and nose.

We stopped and waited until he was alongside, then Wayne said, "Here, Sonny," and handed the surprised boy some money.

The child's eyes shone like two black stars. "Thank you, sir!" he said in perfect English, with a little salute of his hand. "God bless you, sir."

Soon we came upon a stretch of road "under construction," which meant one or two men leaning on a shovel using clumps of grass as road dividers. The job looked absolutely hopeless.

"If all the unemployed men in this country did just one small stretch, it could be fixed in no time," I mused.

"Yes, but they must be paid," Sam answered.

As we traveled on, the road became so dusty we had to roll up the windows.

"Uh-oh, there's the immigration point," Sam said, slowing down the car.

"An immigration point *here?*" I wondered out loud. "Who would be immigrating, and where to?" It seemed ridiculous.

"Let me see your passport," the stocky, uniformed officer demanded. Sam kept a firm grip on his passport as he held it out the window.

"What you doin' heah?"

"We have an orphanage near here," Sam responded patiently.

"You lie!" the man snarled. "I wan' your proof of citizenship an' your proof of ownership of da' car."

There was a long pause. "We don't have the documents you are asking for, but we do have a Bible for you," Sam responded politely, holding out a new Bible.

The officer's eyes softened for a moment, then he scowled and waved us on.

"He just wanted money, like all the rest," Sam explained. "Since the Taylor government doesn't pay them, they rob the people just to eat."

Hours later, as we drove home, I was thinking about the incredible events of the past few days—the bright-eyed children, the hundreds of plates of rice, and the evidence of hope we witnessed everywhere. I could still feel the gentle pressure of those little sweaty palms in my own and see the shine of those dark eyes.

Without warning, Sam slammed on the brakes, coming to a quick stop. A man on the road ahead was slashing wildly at a long, very slender green snake. Finally he looked up, sweaty and triumphant.

"It is dead," he said simply.

"Don't get too close!" I urged frantically as they all jumped out for a closer look. "It's a green mamba!"

"Six feet long, at least," Wayne marveled. "Make sure you get a good picture."

"This is one dangerous snake," Sam confirmed.

The man dug a hole, carefully severed the wicked-looking head, and buried it. Killing a deadly snake was all in a day's work for him.

10

A Spiritual Battle

April 12

Gibson and his crew arrived early in the morning to begin a new shed for the mechanics, since it was impossible for them to work when it rained. They began by digging large, deep postholes by hand—slow, back-breaking work. Next they poured rocks, cement powder, sand, and water onto a heap on the ground and proceeded to mix it like a huge batch of cookie dough.

The blistering sun caked the mingled cement dust and sweat on their clothing and their faces, and their eyes took on a peculiar, hollow appearance as the dust formed ridges around them.

"Are these your building tools?" Wayne wondered, looking at the odd little assortment they had brought along. He opened his mouth to say something, but decided against it.

"They don't even own a level," he confided later.

"Not every one is so particular about things being straight," I reminded him.

April 14

"Let's walk to church this morning," Bev said gaily. "It's just too gorgeous to drive."

"Go ahead and walk with the girls," Wayne suggested. "I have to haul the speakers."

The gentle, rhythmic cooing of the doves accented the booming surf as we made our way to church. Chicken families scratched around in the dirt and trash. The tiny balls of fluff did exactly as the old hen commanded.

"There are diamonds in this country. We're probably walking over fields of them," I told the girls. "I think Liberians could be rich if they would forget all the demon worship and witch doctors."

"They grew up with it," Bev reasoned. "They don't know anything different. Do you really believe all this weird stuff happens—this sacrificing and casting spells?"

"I'm sure most of it is real. I just hope we never meet up with any of it," I answered, remembering the noose around my neck.

"Look at all those nests in that tree," Charlotte urged. "Looks like about two hundred."

"They're weaverbirds of some kind, and it looks like they're killing the tree," I answered. "I wish we had a good bird book; the people around here have no idea what kinds of birds or flowers they have. I've asked them often enough."

Pastor Mervin preached on the inerrant Word of God—a powerful, moving sermon that made us realize what a priceless gift the Bible is. Woe to the person who counts the Bible as nonsense. The church was so full I was sure not one more could fit in. Several latecomers had to squeeze themselves in like sardines.

The singing was so tremendous it seemed to shake the ceiling boards. No one noticed that Wayne was four words ahead of everybody else in an effort to gain a bit of speed. They seldom glanced up from their books.

Tonight, we hosted the youth meeting. It is so inspiring to listen to their fervent singing. They all sat in a large circle in the living room—all forty-two of them. Among them were older men, some of them above forty years—but as long as you are single, you are a youth.

Only Moses Massawalla seemed listless. He had recently been

baptized and was a sincere young man.

"Excuse me, Ma, but I think I will have to go home," he said, approaching me. "I am not well."

"I'm sorry," I sympathized. "I hope it's not malaria."

It wasn't. At 8:15 Wayne answered the phone to find Pastor Mervin calling.

"Wayne, could you please come down to the church right away? Moses Massawalla is in great pain. He's writhing on the floor and crying and I don't know what to do."

"I wonder if it's his appendix," Wayne said as we hurried to the church, where Moses lived as a caretaker. We made our way up the steps in the pitch darkness, feeling along the walls to keep our balance. The dim light of the candle flickered as we entered the little chamber where Pastor Mervin and Curt stood beside the inert form lying face-down on the floor, still as death.

Wayne knelt down beside the sick man. "Moses. Moses. Can you hear me? Talk to me, Moses!"

No response.

"Are you in pain? Can we help you somehow?" he continued urgently.

Moses gave a sudden jerk of his arm and lay still once more.

The candle dimmed. Shadows danced across the faces of the little group.

"He's been face down on the floor since he came from your place," Pastor Mervin told us. "That's almost two hours now."

"I wonder if this isn't a spiritual battle of some kind," Wayne said quietly.

"I agree," Curt added. "This isn't normal."

"Dr. Lamin," Pastor Mervin said into his cell phone. "What shall we do? He's not responding at all anymore." He listened for a moment.

"Lamin says to get him to the hospital right away. He thinks it may be serious."

"Bible! Bible!" gasped Moses suddenly. Someone placed his Bible in his arm, and he clutched it desperately.

"Pray, please PRAY!" he cried beseechingly.

The men formed a close circle around him and called upon the name of the Lord. They commanded the demons to flee in the name of Jesus, claiming the shed blood of the Lamb.

"Water?" Moses said faintly. "Put it on my head, please. Did you pray?"

"We sure did!" Wayne assured him.

"Where is my grandfather?" Moses asked suddenly, lifting his head and looking at us in a puzzled manner. "Where is he? I was fighting with him jus' now. What happened? Was I sick?"

He looked at Mervin. "Pastor?"

"Hello, Moses," Mervin said softly. "Let me help you sit up. Here, drink some water."

Moses' hand shook as he took the cup. His dark face glistened with beads of sweat.

"He's still weak as a kitten," William observed.

"He's talking, though," Curt said.

"I sensed it was witchcraft of some kind," Wayne added. "We are in Africa, you know."

Haltingly at first, then like a flowing stream, the story came forth—all in his own language. We had to wait until he was finished before someone could translate.

"His grandfather paid him a visit and tried to force him to take some medicine, which he refused, so the grandfather gave him a blow in the area of the heart," he explained. Hence the excruciating pain. "In the battle that ensued, he killed three spirits."

Moses felt his side gingerly. "No more pain. I will be alright now, I am sure. Thank you!" He sank down on his mattress, asleep before we could leave the room.

Asleep in total peace. Weak, but victorious. It was a miracle. One minute in mortal unconscious agony . . . a prayer sent to the throne . . . the next minute sitting up and talking.

How chilling to realize the awful power of the devil and his agents. How comforting to claim anew the all-powerful, almighty power of the blood of the Lamb. "*For we wrestle not against flesh and blood, but against principalities, against powers, against the rulers of darkness of this world, against spiritual wickedness in high places.*"

As we stepped outside into the black night, the innumerable stars seemed brighter, and I felt a great sense of peace.

"God is in His heaven, and all is right with the world," I quoted softly.

11

Goodies from Home

There is a sandstorm in the Great Sahara. I can tell by the gray, early morning haze that has spread out over the ocean and blanketed the city, and by the new layer of dust that has settled on everything.

It's Larry's birthday, so I had to scramble to get everything done.

"I'm eleven today, Mom!" shouted Larry, appearing at the laundry room door. "Did you remember? Can I invite everyone I want? What's for breakfast?" and he disappeared as quickly as he had come.

After breakfast, the girls scattered to the office with Wayne, and the rest of us tried to concentrate on school.

"There's a shipping container coming tomorrow, *finally*," Willie said.

"Our boxes are on it," Charlotte added. "That shipping thing lists all kinds of stuff—like candy and cookies and cheese."

"Maybe even a birthday gift!" Larry said, his eyes shining with anticipation. "Why can't I just have today off, since it's my birthday?"

"Either today or the day the shipping container comes," I

107

reminded him. "You can't have both—so let's get busy."

Evening finally came, and with it Larry's birthday guests—Stone and his daughter Gloria, Zaza, Anthony, Harris, Tony, and others. "I'm not going to have enough hot dogs," I worried as more guests filed through the gate. "There's plenty of cake, but just give one scoop of ice cream to begin with."

"Don't worry, they're not big eaters," Bev said comfortingly. "How many friends does Larry have, anyway?"

"Okay, guys, listen while I tell you how this treasure hunt works," Wayne announced. "We hid small notes all over the yard, and you have to look for them. The one who finds the note reads it out loud so everyone can hear. We have a treasure hidden at the end that I know you'll enjoy—although I'm not sure what it is. So when you find it, wait for everyone to come around before you open it, okay?"

The hunt was on.

What a hootin' and hollerin' when someone found a note! What pounding of feet and frantic searching! I caught sight of Larry's flying white feet in the midst of them when they passed.

"Just like a bunch of kids with a new game," Wayne laughed. "Looks like Stone is the leader."

"Yahoo! We found it!" someone yelled, pulling the brown treasure bag out of the discarded washing machine in the back yard.

"That was a good time," they agreed, happily munching on the homemade caramel corn, complete with roasted "ground peas."

We served ice cream and cake, finger Jell-O, and cups of slushy Kool-Aid. They all ate heartily and took generous second helpings.

"Stone's plate is *heaping*," I whispered.

"You always worry we won't have enough, Mother," Bev smiled. "That game must have made them all hungry by the looks of things."

"If there is no rice, then I have not eaten," Stone said gravely, scraping his plate and licking off his spoon. He leaned back and patted his belly. "Naw, I have not eaten."

April 17

The tardy container caused much excitement.

"Hurry, Dad," Larry begged as we stopped at the bank on the way to CAM's warehouse. His mood was contagious, and I found myself nearly as excited as he was.

The first container was from Indiana, and full of clothing bundles, shoes, and comforters. It was fascinating to watch the unloading process. The men would stand right next to the truck, receive the heavy bundles on their heads, and carry them to the back room of the warehouse. It was hard work, and they were soon drenched with sweat.

Curt supervised the counting and helped stack the bundles.

The duty officers sat in a row along the side, alternately jotting on their slates and peering through crooked glasses in their most official-looking manner. Frequently, the stress of the job called for an ice-cold soft drink from Varnee's dwindling supply.

Hours later the container was empty. "Four hundred and forty-eight bags of shoes!" I exclaimed in wonder as the final tally was drawn. "Twelve hundred bundles of clothing. Hundreds of quilts. This is unreal!"

The old truck pulled out, slowly and laboriously, with much creaking and groaning amid the shouts of the directors.

During the ensuing lull, Akin arrived with his crew, loaded a shipment for distribution, picked up Willie, and rushed out—in a hurry as usual.

Meanwhile, a smaller truck arrived with a load of flour and had to be quickly unloaded. The men hoisted the hundred-pound bags on each others' heads and carried them effortlessly to the assigned place. Flour dust sifted through the bags and turned their hair white.

By the time the flour was unloaded, a truck had arrived with canned chicken, beans, cornmeal, schoolbooks, and medical supplies. Wayne ran the forklift, and it was unloaded in record time.

Just as the truck pulled out, Akin arrived for another load. I knew they were distributing at the displaced camps near

Monrovia. Julie, Maria, Evelyn, and Willie were among the helpers for the day.

"When can we come along?" I asked.

"Presently, Ma, you and my Boss may come," Akin answered with a smile. "Good day, and God bless you," and he was gone. Akin is a man of action.

"Wonder where that other container is," Wayne said, as time slipped away. "Here comes a truck now."

It was a truck full of rice from Tony Hage. "C'mon boys, let's get this done before the next truck," Wayne urged the tired men.

Once again, they carried those one-hundred-ten-pound bags of rice on their heads. "Wonder if I could do that," Wayne mused.

"Of course you could," I told him. "You'll damage your neck though, because you aren't used to it like they are."

The burning sun was slipping into the dark Atlantic when the last container had been unloaded and we finally left the warehouse. Clutched in our arms were the eagerly anticipated packages from back home.

"Not just one box, but three!" Larry said with delight. "Big ones too. I can hardly wait to open them."

Eagerly, we gathered around the tempting array of boxes.

"You'll have to divide this evenly," I cautioned as we lifted out the bags of goodies. "Just make a pile for each person, and if you want to eat it all or give some away, you can. Or if you want to save it, you can."

"You always save yours till it's not good anymore," they laughed.

"Oh-h-h, pure milk chocolate," Bev sighed. "Caramels and licorice . . . and more chocolate."

"Wow! They must think we're starving," Willie decided. "I haven't seen so much good stuff all at once since last Christmas."

There was pie filling and poppy seed, cookies, flax seed, Velveeta cheese, tea, a sheet set, birthday stuff for Larry, tea towels, and all kinds of lotions and soaps.

"Missionary barrels sure aren't what they used to be," I mused. "In those 'Uncle Arthur' stories, it was just used clothing or old dolls that were sent. Children, we are *spoiled.* Look at this!"

"This won't happen very often, I'm sure," Julie decided. "Now, I will divide the spoils," she added dramatically.

"I will write the thank-you notes," Charlotte offered.

"Well," said Wayne, chewing on a piece of dried beef jerky from Grandpa, "now that the 'spoils' are all unwrapped, maybe we should get some sleep. Akin is leaving for a widow food parcel distribution tomorrow, and he would appreciate our help."

12

Poverty—A Way of Life

I set the alarm earlier this morning to make sure we wouldn't be late to go along with Akin. "You know how he hates to be late," I warned.

"For sure," Wayne agreed. "He's always going at high speed."

True to form, Akin, Pastor George, and the drivers, Bundo and Mo, were ready and waiting at the warehouse when we arrived.

"Sierra Fox for Golf Five Zero," Akin barked into his handset.

"Standing right next to you," Sierra Fox replied.

"We canno' linger," Akin smiled. "Sir, you, Ma, an' Larry come wi' me and Bundo, an' the rest go with Mo in CAM 23—there is no time to waste."

We passed a car-washing business in full operation. Three yellow taxis and an old, beat-up pick-up truck were backed into the lake. Several men busily scrubbed and rinsed them while the owners waited.

"They just back their cars into the water and get a scrub!" Larry marveled. "I wonder if they expect them to be clean after being washed in that muddy water."

Soon CAM 23 turned off the main road and crawled along ahead of us. The tires were squatting and the side tarps bulged with widow parcels and comforters.

"That thing is loaded!" Larry remarked.

The road turned to red silt and wound around deep gullies and washouts, but our overloaded Defender trucks struggled gamely through them all. "This sure tests their mettle," Wayne said admiringly as we eased out of a deep rut. "These Defenders are tough as nails. I really appreciate how careful you are, Bundo."

Bundo smiled in his easy way. "Thank you, Boss," he said.

Thick, tangled brush grew in green profusion along the roadside, occasionally breaking to let us view a pathetic group of huts. "Just see how these poor people live," I told Larry. In some places the brush was so thick we could just see the tops of the hut roofs over it.

The huts looked desperately poor, especially the roofs. Everything imaginable—pieces of jagged rusty tin, torn burlap, plastic sheeting, pieces of wood—had been tacked on in an attempt to provide shelter from the relentless rain.

Women and children stood in the doorways as we passed— often a nursing mother with two or three naked little ones around her.

Still meditating on the lives these people lead, I suddenly noticed what appeared to be several fallen logs across a gully on the road ahead. "This *can't* be a bridge!" I gasped.

"This is a very *good* bridge," Akin assured us as we slowly crossed. "Ma, on one of the worst roads we travel, we must cross at least twenty *dangerous* bridges—very, very dangerous ones."

"Well, I'll never go along on that run," I told him.

As we neared the village of Johnsonville, an old lady saw us, dropped everything she was holding, and came running after us in the dust. "Can she run!" Larry cried. "See how fast that old woman is peddling! Dad, look!"

She ran all the way to the nice little country church where all the old folks of the county were already assembled, dropped into a vacant seat, and brushed at her clothes. Her face was streaked with dust, and the rags she wore did little to hide her skinny frame, but her eyes shone with anticipation. *A Christian Aid distribution was no small event.*

"She's *tough!*" concluded Larry.

Within minutes the small clearing was filled with children and curious onlookers.

Drums boomed in celebration as we were graciously directed into the church. The sound reverberated in my ears and tickled my feet. "You may sit right here," the usher said loudly, indicating an extra-low double-seater bench covered with a clean, threadbare cloth.

As Wayne and I sat down on the bench, the elderly people rose to their feet and began swaying to the music and clapping their hands. *Some must be over a hundred years old*, I thought, fascinated.

Some of them had shiny black eyes; others' eyes looked dull and dim; some had bent, twisted bodies; others stood straight. Still others had shriveled, parched skin, while their neighbor's skin was almost wrinkle free. But they could all dance. They stamped their skinny, slippered legs to the music and chanted the same phrase over and over. I caught the words "Christian Aid" and something about "Almighty God." Their smiles were wide and toothless in their leathery faces.

When the bundles and boxes were brought into the church, the music reached a crescendo. It became insistent, demanding, compelling.

"This is truly Africa!" I yelled to Wayne. "It's hard to sit still, isn't it? Look at Larry."

Larry was leaning against the wall, staring open-mouthed at the people, eyes wide with interest.

"He'll never forget this," Wayne chuckled, wiping his brow with his ever-ready hand towel.

"Neither will I," I returned. "I won't forget the heat either— you look so-o-o hot."

The music stopped with a sudden crash of all the different

instruments at once. The silence was deafening.

Akin and Pastor George went about their business with a truly professional air. George immediately set up a table of widow parcels so he could register each candidate.

Then Akin stood and preached a sermon on repentance. He commanded our attention—and every eye fastened on him as he spoke about the coming of death to the body and the need to be right with Almighty God.

"Moses knew his name could be blotted out of the book of life at any time, and just because you were once saved doesn't mean you *stay* saved!" he warned with great emphasis. "Is your name in that book? If you canno' forgive someone, your name will be blotted out. If you don't repent from your sins, you will go to HELL!"

Glittering dark eyes stared at him. Slight bodies swayed back and forth, back and forth, in their seats. The stout bamboo walls fairly quivered.

Pastor George then rose to his feet. In his calm, quiet voice he offered a prayer with the people repeating after him. "Lord, ah have fallen away. Ah changed my mind an' turned my back on you." There was a murmur of agreement. "Now ah ask you, Jesus, to forgi' my sins. It is so *serious* fo' us to repent. Now let us clap for Jesus!" he finished, and the mini revival meeting was over.

We nearly melted. The people outside the church were cutting off the last hope of any circulating air. They cupped their hands and peered through the cracks, chattering excitedly. Wayne twirled his face cloth in a vain attempt to cool off. Little rivulets of sweat ran down the side of his face. Larry was so hot he ran outside to cool off.

"You may NOT use the money we give you fo' tobacco!" Akin admonished them sternly, shaking his finger. He stood strong and tall in front of the ancient group, leaning forward so they could understand every word.

They gave him their undivided attention. They stared up at him intently—eagerly—not wanting to miss a word he said. "You may use the ten dollars to buy charcoal an' make some food fo' yourself. We have rice fo' you, an' we have beans, an' we have chicken. We have tablets because we want you to be strong. We have shampoo for you," he said, pausing dramatically, "because we want you to be shiny, shiny, shiny old ladies. Now we will proceed."

There were grins and nods and a feeble clap or two. One by one they shuffled up to George's makeshift desk, where they sat down and answered his questions.

"Ol' lady, what's yo' name?" George asked.

Sometimes recipients answered the questions, but often there was a son or daughter present who spoke for them.

"How many chil'ren do you have? Where are yo' living chil'ren? Where's yo' man? What happened to him? How are you eatin' now? Do you live by yo'self?"

"What a thorough investigation!" I remarked to Wayne. "Most of their husbands died in the war the way it sounds, and many of their children as well. Good thing CAM has such a program here."

"Ol' man, how many children do you have?"

"Ah has twelve, an' dey has all died—an' den my wife left me too," he replied slowly, his dark old eyes full of pain. "Ah live on da sympathy of others."

"We will help you, ol' man," George answered softly. "Jus' sit down here."

"Ah have plenty of land, but no one to take care of it fo' me," one old lady explained in a reedy voice.

Akin led a very weak, trembling man up to George. He was so old his skin hung in folds under his neck and half covered his cloudy eyes. He couldn't lift his badly swollen feet to walk, so he just dragged them along. His clothes were so filthy they looked stiff.

Akin gently helped him sit down. "Jus' give him what he needs," he instructed. "He is most vulnerable."

A very young girl came in with the cutest baby on her hip. The child's bright little face was a beam of sunshine in the room. George noticed her immediately, and something seemed to click in his brain. "I think too many people's chil'ren have all died!" he exclaimed. From then on, he questioned them more closely.

"You don' need to lie to get a parcel," he told them sternly. "Some of these people think they will receive no parcel if they have living chil'ren," he explained, turning to us.

"Yo' chil'ren are standin' outsi' dis church!" he informed the next old woman. "You tell me dey are dead. If dey heah you, dey will say, 'Ma, we are still alive! Do naw kill us jus' to git a parcel!' "

Everyone who heard him had to chuckle. "We are passing out the comforters now," Akin explained, "Would you care to help?"

"Look at these quilts!" I exclaimed in genuine astonishment. They were lovely pieces of work, with small, neat, colorful patches that would brighten any room. The old folks hugged them rapturously, their eyes shining. They ran their gnarled hands back and forth over the fabric, savoring the softness and smiling to themselves. One actually laughed aloud, burying her face among the patches. She looked at the quilt, then at the others, with unbelieving eyes. *Her very own quilt! What joy!*

Then it was time to dole out the rice—ten heaping cups for each person, with a can of chicken for good measure. "I never worry about containers," Akin laughed when I wondered what they would put it in. "They *always* have something handy, just in case they get a handout."

The rice was poured into old shawls, rags, lapas, and even the quilts if there was nothing else.

When it was time to leave, the place suddenly crowded with people again. "I see some people's chil'ren have resurrected!" George shouted.

On the way home, George talked about the forces of evil in Liberia.

"Our country is *full* of demonic powers," George insisted. "There is a place on Benson Street where human sacrifices are offered daily. There are secret societies everywhere, an' if you do naw belong to one, you canno' git a job. It is true that people were, an' still are, cannibals. Even a monkey will refuse to eat one of its own kind, but people do it all the time. No wonder Almighty God allowed what He did in Liberia."

After making plans to meet George at the Doe Community the following day, we turned our faces homeward. I feel overwhelmed with thankfulness for the home we have—soft beds, ceiling fans, plenty of food and clothing—every need fully supplied.

God is so good.

April 25

Wayne, Julie, Larry, and I went along for another orphanage tour today. Sam wants to make sure CAM gets all the reports about them. I have much work to do, but Wayne wanted me to go, so I went. I am so glad I did.

"They have fifty-six children here," Sam informed us as we pulled up beside the Calvary Orphanage. "See the gardens?" Close by was a swampy area where several banana trees, a lone almond tree, and a few straggly cassava plants swayed in the breeze. A very thin old pig stretched out in a small pen, soaking up the sunlight. His hooves stuck out under the bamboo fence, and occasionally he would shake off the flies tormenting his ears.

"There are no scraps around here," muttered Wayne.

We walked back to the outdoor cook shack where rice bubbled merrily in huge aluminum kettles. "Look at that funny monkey!" Larry giggled as the agile creature flipped upside-down, landed expertly on his feet, and stared at us curiously from the safety of the bamboo rafters. "Jillie is way cuter, isn't she, Mom?"

"Shoo!" yelled the buxom cook to her motley crew of animals when she saw us coming. Not one moved.

The family of ducks meandered here and there, under the tables and the lone bamboo chair, looking for stray kernels of rice and big crunchy ants. "Watch your step!" I warned. "They can bite."

"De ants be bad heah," the cook said gravely. "Dey eat people. Shoo!" and she pretended to be annoyed at all her pets.

Her mangy, malnourished puppy opened one eye and looked around. He flicked his tattered, bloody ears in a half-hearted attempt to ease the dreadful itch of the merciless fleas. Every rib showed as he gave a long, shuddering sigh and put his head back down.

My stomach felt sick. "Does the dog ever eat?" I asked pointedly.

"Oh yes, he can eat plenty-o. Shoo!"

The monkey dangled by his tail above the table and chattered excitedly. Several thin black hairs floated erratically earthward.

A small cloud of dust rose and resettled over a hen as she wriggled farther into her deep dust bowl alongside the cook shack. "Why does the cook even try to chase them? They *live* here," said Larry, with his customary candor.

"Yes, they're stationed here all right," Julie laughed. "Just so we're not invited for dinner."

"A wolf could blow these over!" was Larry's next observation, as we toured the children's dorms.

"I have these on my list," Sam was telling Wayne. "See the blocks drying in the sun? They're for a new dorm. I have already put in a request for more bedding, as well."

"I sure hope it happens soon," Wayne answered. "This is terrible."

Just before we left, we opened a five-gallon plastic bucket of Life Savers and passed them around. "Thank you!" the children chorused, thrilled with the unexpected treat.

"She's eating it all at once," Larry noticed as a small child unrolled her candy and daintily licked it lengthwise. "She must not know they come apart."

The blazing sun was quickly melting the candy—and the visitors. "We will be back!" Sam cried as we pulled out.

The Mary Himmie Home was next on Sam's long list.

"Oh, you are welcome. Oh, welcome. Oh, welcome. CAM, you are welcome today!" sang the orphans happily. They offered us chairs which were actually discarded seats from demolished vehicles, but we declined and went on with the tour. Walking into the dorms was like entering a low, dark mud tunnel with broken doors and ragged ceilings. The beds were hard and close together, and the window open to malaria-infested mosquitoes.

"I can't believe this. I just can't," I groaned.

"Oh, the poor little things!" Julie agreed. "Can't we do something for them? Look how good we have it—and these innocent children sleep like this."

Dinner was being cooked in a small, smoke-filled brick room that served as a kitchen. I was sure the cooks were being smoked right along with the rice. They were sweating profusely and smiling at us. Their oven was crafted from welded tire rims, and the kettles on top were boiling madly over the charcoal. They stood and patiently stirred the rice with long sticks. One hundred plastic bowls stood waiting to be filled—*and still the cooks were smiling!*

"That kitchen is one big oven itself," Wayne marveled, shaking his head. "How would you like to cook like that, dear?" he teased.

Day after day . . . month after weary month . . . cooking inside an oven.

"I'll never complain again," I said with finality.

The laundry room consisted of two huge tubs and a bucket of CAM soap. "How would you like to wash for a hundred and three children by hand?" I asked Julie.

"My imagination stops," she answered.

We waded through all the speeches and introductions while not a breeze stirred. A small boy with infected eyes blinked incessantly against the sun. Time hung suspended on the heat waves. Flies crawled all over the face, neck, and arms of a handsome toddler asleep on the floor. He didn't even feel them. Another child pulled himself along in the fine dust, dragging his dirty, crippled feet behind him.

But there were smiles all around when the candy was passed out. "I don't get it, Mom—they are so happy over a bit of candy—when they have *nothing!*" Larry confided.

Take a lesson, Son.

The Great Commission Home boasted eighty-two happy orphans and several large shade trees. We gathered gratefully in their welcome shade as the children came running. "God will make a way," they yelled, "when it seems there is no way."

One of the caretakers slapped a tardy child sharply. "Beating?" Sam queried, his eyes flashing. "Such is *not* necessary."

Fourteen mentally handicapped people reside in the Antoinette Tubman Cheshire Home, and it was refreshingly clean and airy and well kept. "The former first lady used to support us, but not anymore," the director told us. "CAM has been an angel of mercy."

"Do you still wash the floors twice a day?" asked Sam teasingly.

"I sure do!" she answered proudly.

"You must have a heart the size of Texas!" Wayne exclaimed as we toured and saw all the handicapped inmates. They were very crippled and helpless. Many were blind or twisted out of proportion, yet they were well cared for and clean as could be.

"I make it my business to see that they do all they can to care for themselves, and learn everything they can," she explained, fondly ruffling a big boy's hair.

"What is that girl doing?" I asked. A teenaged girl was sitting in a corner, chewing on the edges of a large hole in the front of her blouse.

"During the war we had to flee, so we took as many children as possible the first trip, thinking we could come back fo' the rest. But the soldiers would no' let us back in, so the children stayed two weeks withou' food or care. They got so terrified that they piled up in a corner, an' by the time we reached them, the ones on the bottom of the pile were dead." She paused and looked at us sadly. "Ever since, she has eaten her clothing. No matter what we put on her, she eats it. Then we jus' turns it aroun' an' she eats the back too. Nothing can make her quit."

"I'm growing weary," I complained on the way down the steps. "It's just too much to see all this in one day. Maybe the next orphanage will cheer us up a bit."

"I don't think so," Sam ventured. "The lady in charge is on probation with CAM."

Old Hannah B. Williams greeted us warmly and led us all into a dark hole of a room. A pair of tiny twin boys and three other small babies lay asleep on the bed.

"How old . . . what age?" Julie asked in a whisper.

" 'Tween three an' five months."

"Where did you find them?"

"Da twins' muttah died an' da others co' from da Social Services."

"I smell pigs!" Larry whispered, too loudly.

Hannah heard. "Yes," she said, "Those beasties once lived in heah."

The sandy courtyard spilled over with children—seventy-six of them. They were a pitiful-looking bunch. We walked into the dorms and felt the gritty sand beneath our feet. The mattresses were filthy and all the bedding full of holes.

I was speechless.

"This place reeks!" Larry insisted as we entered the kitchen. A swarm of flies lifted off the table and settled back down, feasting on the greasy top. His eyes got wide. "Oh, a pig pen?" Sure enough, three pigs lounged lazily in a pen not far from the kitchen, accompanied by several fat ducks. "No wonder."

As Sam went through all the necessary paperwork, we stood and observed the children.

"They look sick and hungry, and they need clothes," Julie said.

"Look at those infected eyes, and that scalp fungus," I pointed out.

"We have lots of stuff ready to distribute," said Sam, "but if she's on probation she gets nothing, right?"

"If that's the case," I countered, "look who's suffering."

"Yes, I know."

Hannah shuffled up and escorted us to a bamboo building where assorted chairs and old benches were set up. "You sit heah," she directed us. She walked out and returned minutes later with a fragile little girl in her arms. As she set the child down in the sand, Julie gasped in dismay.

"She was foun' in da' garbage where her muttah lef' her—she is blind from da measles," Hannah explained.

The child turned. One eye was the light blue of the blind; the other was severely ruptured and protruded like a marble from the small face. Her mouth was small and sweet beneath her perfect little nose. She held her head erect, straining to hear and trying to decide what was going on. I noticed the severe scalp fungus and the running sores at the corners of her mouth. She was painfully thin, with a swollen stomach that revealed a serious worm infestation. Her scrawny legs were scratched raw in places from the merciless itch of scabies.

We all sat and stared.

The child reached her arms ahead of her and tottered unsteadily toward Julie. She put her little hands on Julie's knees and lay her head on Julie's lap. Tears pushed my eyelids.

She has found the right person, I thought as Julie scooped her up, scabies and all, and held her close. She didn't put the child down until she absolutely had to.

"I want that child," she told Sam as soon as the vehicle door was shut. "How can I get her? I want to clean her up and take care of that eye. What do I do first, Uncle Sam?"

"Wait a minute—not so fast!" Wayne answered. "We can't be taking all the needy children into the house."

"Daddy, she will surely die if I don't! That's what we're here for, isn't it? Here in Liberia, I mean. Please?"

"You will have to contact Dr. Lamin, as she obviously needs medical attention," Sam put in. "Otherwise, I see no reason why you couldn't take her, at least till she improves."

"Dad?"

"Well, okay, I guess," Wayne conceded at last, "but be careful about those scabies—I don't want to get them."

We were still thinking about the little girl when Sam pulled in at the next orphanage. "This is My Brother's Keeper, the last one for the day," Sam announced. Director Ralph greeted us as if we were royalty, his voice filled with obvious pleasure.

"Don't leave me, Jesus," sang the children. "I don't believe He brought me this far to leave me. No, don't leave me, Jesus." Their English was pretty good.

Ralph delivered a mini-sermon on how to be prayerful and take nothing for granted. "We are so fortunate—so privileged!" he stressed.

"The kitchen is a breezeway!" I exclaimed with delight.

"Compared to some of the others, they *are* fortunate," Julie stated. "Do *you* care if I take Princess?"

"Who's Princess?" I wondered.

"Oh, Mom, you know. That little blind girl. I named her Princess."

"I'm sure she already has a name, Julie."

All the way home Julie could talk of nothing else. I really don't know what to think, but the memory of that blind, suffering little waif is just too much.

13

Generous Hearts

April 28

What a treat to have Bishop Andy Mullet from Lott, Texas, here for a visit! He is so interesting to listen to. The church was filled to overflowing, but no one complained or whispered. A visiting speaker is quite rare, and no one wanted to miss a word he said.

His face sober, Andy appealed to the congregation to maintain high moral standards, reading verse after verse to make his meaning clear.

Eight baptismal applicants sat in a semi-circle in front of the church. I mentally calculated that these would make a total of twenty new members since we arrived in January.

Listening to their vows and seeing the joy on their faces, I could only imagine how the angels of God were rejoicing. It was a warm and special service, with plenty of food for thought.

"Let me help you out, Steve," Larry said to the blind man after the service, taking his arm and guiding him outside. He fished in his pocket and pressed five dollars into Steve's hand. "Five dollars to buy some water," he whispered.

"Thank you, Larry." Steven smiled.

It did my heart good. It was just what I had hoped to see . . .

Larry's heart was softening toward the unfortunate.

"Daddy," asked Larry this afternoon, "is it true that there's fighting close to here?"

"It's at least two hours away," Wayne comforted him. "I hardly know what to think of all the rumors, but you never know what will happen in this country. I don't think it's anything serious yet."

We hear ominous rumors of sporadic fighting close to Totota. How true are Jesus' warnings about the last days—there shall be wars and rumors of war!

April 29

Iddo stopped in today with a stack of eggs from the egg farm and a twinkle in his eye. "Wait, I have more stuff for you," he said, disappearing out the door.

"Two huge bags of broken pretzels!" Willie exclaimed. "You'd better hide those before the girls get here."

"I'm not worried about the *girls*," I informed him. "Grandpa must know you love these things."

I asked Iddo about the rebel fighting close by. "Aw," he said, shrugging it off. "I'm not a bit worried. God is in control."

May God give me the faith this man has.

We have been giving Grace Allison and her little boy, Shadrach, a bowl of rice for dinner every day until she can find a job. I affectionately call her Garlic Grace, because you can tell from far away that she loves garlic. Today, as usual, the strong odor of garlic reached me before the woman herself.

"Hello-o-o?" she called in her high trademark greeting.

We sat and ate rice topped with pumpkin oil soup while I listened once again to the woes of her existence—her stomach problems, her lack of a job, her need for assistance. "Muttah, ah nevah, evah wants to go back to dat man to make my livin'. Ah jus' hate livin' like dat. Da man has a wife . . . an' ah knows it's wrong. But ah can't find a room an' feed my Shadrach if ah don' have a job. My room leaks in da' rain and da' cold gi' me a har' time. It is naw easy."

"Wayne is looking for a freezer for you," I reminded her.

"Meanwhile, you have food to eat and clothes to wear—just be patient."

"Ah eats dis garlic fo' my bad breath," she reminded me. "My stomach can gi' me a har' time, Muttah."

"Maybe you have ulcers from worrying too much," I suggested. "In that case, I don't think chewing pure garlic is the answer."

"I have two mo' children besides Shadrach," she announced suddenly, looking at me warily.

"Two more . . . what . . . where?" I asked, staring at her in disbelief. "Just little ones?"

"Oh, dey are fine wheah dey are," she said casually. "Dere gran'muttah takes care of dem . . . an' dey are small-small." She expertly deposited a large spoonful of rice into her mouth without closing her lips against the spoon.

"When did you last see them?" I asked sharply.

"Naw fo' a long time," she returned, smiling at my surprise. "It is far, Muttah."

"How can you have children and never see them?" I wondered in dismay. "What if someone steals them, or worse?"

"Oh, Muttah!" she laughed helplessly, emitting another fresh wave of garlic. "Oh, Muttah, dis is Liberia! No one steals children. No one! Children are plenty-o."

"That's just the problem—no one really cares if they live or die," I answered a trifle bitterly. "How can poor Grandmother feed them if you can't?"

Long after she left, I thought of those two small children, unwanted and unloved, no doubt regarded a nuisance to feed and clothe.

Suddenly Elijah stuck his head in the door.

"Dere's a fish lady at da gate," he said hopefully.

"Yes, Wayne said she was coming," I told him. "He's counting on you to clean them, though—if you don't mind."

"Ah will clean dem," and he shut the door, only to pop it open again. "Ah will bring my wife to church again on Sunday."

"Sounds good!" I answered, thinking of last Sunday when he

first brought Ellen to church and proudly introduced her to us. She is slim and of medium height, with a frank, open gaze and a certain gracious air. I think she is beautiful. "How did you get such a young wife?" I asked without really thinking.

His eyes lit up. "My Ellen an' ah are da' same age. We have five chil'ren together."

As we headed outside, we met Larry. "Wow, those are huge fish!" Larry exclaimed.

"Red gripper—very good fish," Elijah said.

"That man's got a heart of gold," I thought, watching him industriously sharpen the kitchen knife. I couldn't resist asking, "Elijah, what *do* you do with the fins and eyeballs? Tell me truly."

"Eat 'em."

"How can you eat an eyeball? Doesn't it kinda roll around in your mouth?" Larry wondered.

"Some folk jus' don' know wha' da best part of da' fish is," he returned, grinning wickedly.

In no time, Elijah had those huge fish cleaned and the entrails, eyes, and head in a bag to take home.

"These will be perfect for supper on Thursday night," Wayne declared, admiring the long, white fillets I was preparing to freeze. "By the way," he continued. "Sam wants us to go shopping tomorrow morning for supplies for the orphanage teachers' seminar at the Baptist Compound. Want to come along? I'm taking Anthony Reeves too."

"Sure, but you look so tired again," I observed, noticing the weariness in his eyes and the slump of his shoulders. "I wish you could sleep in for a change."

"I know. I'm trying my best to make it home earlier, but it's hard . . . it's hard. This office work is harder on me than shoveling concrete all day long."

April 29

After picking up Sam's long list of needed items, Wayne, Anthony, and I headed for Waterside Market. Larry didn't mind staying at home, as shopping is not his favorite pastime.

"I think it's fun," Wayne grinned. "It's working out great. Anthony seems to know all these little shops back in here."

"How many more things do we need?" I asked wearily.

Why hadn't I worn shoes? I know the dust mites are bad in public places.

"Just let me check these prices yet—so far the UN market is about the best," said Wayne, and he and Anthony disappeared into a crowded shop.

I stood and watched the street vendors—and tried to avoid eye contact with any eager salesmen. The slightest glance of interest is a signal for them to rush to my side with their wares. They could have ten pairs of shoes or eighteen pairs of sunglasses dangling in front of my eyes in a matter of seconds.

Please, don't bug me today.

A lady was vigorously rearranging her tiny partition, hauling the bags of charcoal from one side to the other, lifting heavy buckets of rice and meal, and stooping to pick things up. She worked as if she were alone, but a small baby slept on her back, the dear little head lolling around with every energetic movement. Once in a while she would give a short hop to bounce the baby higher onto her back, but the child slept on. She bent over double and started sweeping the dirt floor. She reached way up on tiptoes and fumbled around near the ceiling—and still the child slept. The throng swept by noisily, merchants hollered, sales boys shouted, and countless women chattered incessantly. Vehicles droned by, honking loudly and often—but the baby slept.

I used to sneak around the house when Bev was a baby so she would sleep longer—and sister Carolyn tried valiantly to keep the house quiet so her children would sleep for more than ten minutes. Why didn't we just put them on our backs?

The dinner bun boy passed with a cheerful grin and a slick maneuvering of his wheelbarrow. The well-used plastic which covered the buns was cloudy with condensation from the heat.

A lady stopped him with a gesture. He set the wheelbarrow on its haunches and carefully unrolled the end of the plastic, spreading a clean rag to make a bit of table space. He reached back under the plastic and fished out a jar. Then he opened the bun, and using a long knife, slathered it thickly with the warm mayonnaise. The customer eyed the big white blobs approvingly. She handed him ten Liberian dollars and took a big bite before merging into the crowd. Little flecks of mayonnaise stood at the corners of her mouth.

I approached a small cubicle where a beautiful mulatto woman held her black-eyed baby boy. "How much are your ground peas?" I asked.

"Twenty-fi' dollah," she smiled, settling the child on her hip.

"Give me three cups, please."

She dipped three heaping tin cans of small brown peanuts into a pink plastic container and added another half can for good measure.

"Thank you very much. What's your fine baby's name?'

"Yontyn," she answered proudly.

Clutching my bag of peanuts, I thought of the extra half cup the lady had given me. I thought of the generous helpings of mayonnaise, and of Anthony's flat refusal to be reimbursed for the drinks he had purchased—and my heart was humbled.

Generous hearts. In the abject poverty of their existence, unselfish, generous hearts . . .

14

Little Blind Princess

May 2

Julie's dream came true—Princess has arrived! After getting all the necessary permission, she finally has the right to bring her to our house from the Hannah B. Williams Home to try to nurse her back to health.

I was straining the various insect parts out of the wild honey from Tony Hage's farm when Bundo arrived with Julie, Charlotte, and little blind Princess. I have a few misgivings. Am I really willing to take a blind, filthy, diseased child into my heart and home? I feel guilty and ashamed, but not quite sure what to think or feel, especially when Julie is so excited about the whole adventure.

They came slowly to the front door, with the child taking small, halting steps, one thin arm clinging to Julie and the other stretched out in front of her. Bundo followed, his kind, mellow face beaming. Now and then he would pat the child's curly head with a tender hand.

"Mom, here she is! Isn't she adorable?" Julie asked as they entered. Princess's protruding eye blinked painfully; the other shone with an unnatural blue color. She promptly sat down on the floor, pulled up one knee, and cradled her head in her arms. She looked small and sick and vulnerable. The dress she wore was ripped and faded and very dirty.

I felt a strange stirring of pity and revulsion. I noticed immediately the ugly scabs all over her ankles where she had scratched until they bled. I saw the crusted sores on her nose and mouth and the matted curls. *Suffer the little children . . . suffer the little children . . .* kept going in circles through my mind.

"She's wondering where on earth she is now. Come, Sweetie," Julie said. She picked Princess up as if she were a feather and hugged her close. "*Finally* I can take care of this poor thing. She needs eye drops immediately. See how she has to strain to blink over that bulging eye? Dr. Lamin said we have to take her to an eye specialist right away—to a Dr. Guizzie. He thinks they might have to take out that eye. And look at these awful sores by her mouth. What can we put on?"

The child's strong, unpleasant odor began to permeate the room. "I think you should bathe her immediately. Put in lots of bubble bath and make the water really warm. Let her soak for a long time and then we'll see to all those sores. Make sure she has her own comb—that white fungus looks worse than ever. Try not to touch her too much because scabies is very contagious, okay? Put all the towels and washcloths in the laundry immediately. I'll put Detol in the water. And please don't kiss her—not till she's healed. Do you think she has rickets?"

Understanding dawned in Julie's brown eyes. "Don't worry, Mom," she said consolingly. "I had to get used to her too. Now, let's make a list of what we need—de-worming medicine, fungus cream . . . I plan to look for some of her relatives one of these days and find out what really happened."

"We had to get her out of there," Charlotte said seriously. "No matter how much trouble she may be, we *couldn't* leave her at Hannah B's."

"I'll shampoo her hair and leave the soap on the whole time she's in the tub," Julie decided. "Dr. Lamin is coming over this evening. Come help me, Charlotte," and they whisked Princess away.

I joined the girls just as they were coaxing Princess into a deep, sudsy tub. She gasped and hung on, no doubt wondering wildly what this was all about. The girls talked in soothing tones. "You're okay, Princess. This is fun. See? Water. Smell the soap. Um-m-m."

Princess held her head high and made funny, hysterical little noises as she felt the water's warm embrace. One little brown hand slapped the water. Then she laughed—a low, musical chuckle that became louder and higher and turned into a treble of pure delight. She laughed and laughed, and we laughed with her. She dipped her hands down into the water and up again, over her head, feeling the water on her hair and letting it trickle down her face. Julie handed her a washcloth, and quick as a wink she brought it up and sucked out some water. Then she put it on her head and squeezed it so the water ran.

"Give her that cup," Charlotte suggested, and Princess immediately dipped it full and drank of its soapy contents.

"No, no, Princess, don't drink it," said Julie, quickly pulling the cup away from her mouth. "Pour it over yourself, like this." Princess giggled as she felt the water running over her body. Again and again she filled that cup and poured it on her head, letting it run all over her hair and face.

"She's smart," Charlotte said happily. "Let's not get soap in that one eye. I'm sure it would hurt like crazy."

"She *loves* this water," Julie said. "We'll have to take her swimming sometime. No, no, Princess, don't bite the soap."

"If she needs surgery, you will have to get her tested for AIDS," I reminded Julie. "I don't think she has it, though."

"I certainly hope not!" Julie exclaimed. "But you're right, we need to know.

Princess took another drink. "Let me get her some cold water," I offered. She drained the whole cup.

"I believe she didn't get enough water till now," Charlotte said. "With all those children running around, how could anyone have time for a blind one?"

"Well, she's mine now, aren't you, Princess?" Julie said with satisfaction. "I'll get Marie to plait her hair tomorrow. I think it's long enough."

They lotioned and powdered and fussed until Princess looked like a different child. All the while, she was exploring their faces and the countertop and everything within reach with her busy little hands.

The dresses Julie picked out for her were all too big around the waist and hung down around the ankles, but they couldn't hide the bony little frame. Julie picked out a dress with a pale blue background and small white daisies. She tied the belt loosely, but Princess's waist still looked much too tiny. "Give her a snack before she goes to sleep," I suggested. "Something like milk and toast with lots of peanut butter. She needs frequent healthy snacks for a while at least."

"I know she loves peanuts," Charlotte said. "She ate a whole bag on the way home."

True to his word, Dr. Lamin came over with vitamins, fungus lotion, scabies cream, and de-worming pills for Princess. He checked her hair. "Put this stuff on three times a day," he instructed. "If the fungus isn't better in a few days, you will have to shave her head. This is for the scabies, an' this for the worms. She has a bad case of them. These are vitamins an' minerals for her to take twice a day."

"I think she can see light," we told the good doctor. "She goes through open, lighted doors without crashing. And it seems she follows with her eyes when someone walks against the light." We demonstrated to show him what we meant.

"Praise the Lord!" he exclaimed.

Princess turned her face toward him. "Aw-w-MEN!" she shouted suddenly, and then laughed with us.

"I will tell Dr. Guizzie about it, an' he will check it out," Dr. Lamin assured us.

"I'm going to raise the money to get her to America if it takes me a whole year," Julie told him. "Wouldn't that be a miracle if they could operate on her one eye and restore her sight? I *have* to try—I just have to!"

Dr. Lamin regarded her gravely through smudged spectacles. The whole idea seemed impossible. "Well . . . I guess you can try," he said finally.

I had a few more questions on my mind. "Is it true that the rebel soldiers are closer than ever?" I asked. "We've been hearing about war and rumors of war. Tell me truly, Dr. Lamin, is there danger?"

Dr. Lamin paused before he answered. "It is true," he said simply. "We must pray, Ruth Ann. They are not far away an' coming for the city. I don't want to scare you, or the boss-man will be upset—but it is true."

"How close?"

"Maybe twenty miles."

"Are you scared?" I asked the kind doctor.

"I am a Christian now," he replied fervently. "Praise the Lord!"

"Aw-w-MEN!" yelled Princess.

Later, when the rest of the family came home, they were awed and amazed at the sight of the poor little orphan. "That eye must hurt!" Larry exclaimed.

"They didn't feed her," Willie commented, "but I like her hair—it's nice. How old is she anyway?"

"We're not sure, but probably about three," answered Julie.

Wayne sighed. "I hope she sleeps all night," he said. "I need my rest these days. We heard today that the rebels are advancing toward the Poe River bridge. It doesn't sound good."

Later on, Julie dressed her little charge in a long cotton nightie and applied more lotion. "I can't seem to get rid of this smell. It's engrained in her skin," she said.

"I think it will just take time to cleanse her from inside out," I replied. "She smells ninety percent better already."

During family devotions, Princess fell asleep. Afterward, Julie carried her into the bedroom and laid her on the soft mattress. "Did you see what they slept on at the orphanage? This child won't know what happened to her!" she said happily. "Good night, my little angel."

May 3

Marie came to clean as usual this morning. When she saw Princess, she stopped short, her big eyes full of questions and her brow puckered with surprise. I knew she would never ask, because she so faithfully minds her own business.

"This is Princess, Marie," I said, drawing the child closer. She stood with her head tilted to one side, listening. Her lips parted and her poor blind eyes wandered from side to side. She reminded me of a wary deer sniffing the breeze for some sign of danger. When Marie leaned down, she reached toward her and gently touched her face, running her fingers along her cheeks and over her nose. "Say Marie," I prompted.

"Maree."

"We're all taking care of her till she's healthier. I'm not sure what will happen then. Julie was wondering if you would plait her hair when you have time. She had to work today, but I said I would ask you."

"Ah surely will, Muttah," Marie agreed, trying not to stare. "Is she . . . blind?"

"Yes, she had such a high fever with the measles that it literally burned her eyes. I don't think she will ever see, but we think she can see some light. How else could she walk through all the doors without crashing?"

Marie had barely started combing Princess's hair when she gave a startled outcry. "Muttah! She has *lice!* Big ones! Co' see on da' comb."

I instantly recognized the horrible, squirming vermin on the white comb. "Oh no, Marie! Now what? She slept in the girls' bed last night!"

I felt sick. Some of the daycare children we had in Alberta had been infested with lice, and what a nightmare to get rid of it! "We must strip all the sheets and wash them in boiling water. We must sweep the floors, beat out all the couch cushions, spray the rooms really good, and shake out the clothes in the closets."

"Ah will help," Marie agreed. "Firs' ah' will comb all da lice out of her head."

I called Dr. Lamin and told him about our emergency. "Please bring the stuff right away," I pleaded.

Dr. Lamin laughed. "It's just head lice," he said, surprised at the urgency in my voice. "Nothing serious, Ruth Ann."

I tried again. "They're huge, Dr. Lamin! They'll get in everybody's hair . . . please?"

"I will come right after work," he promised, which meant several hours.

I called Julie. "She slept with me part of the night, so I'm sure I have them," she said sadly. "In fact, my head is starting to itch."

"Mine too. What do you mean, part of the night? Where else did she sleep?"

"She was on the floor when I woke up, so I put her back in bed. But this morning she was sound asleep on the bare floor again."

I tied a tight cloth around Princess's head, and then Marie and I cleaned and disinfected the whole house. When Julie came home we treated poor little Princess with some horrid-smelling lice shampoo. We did it twice to make sure, then combed her hair all over again.

Princess took it all quite calmly, scrunching her eyes shut just as we told her. She hung on to Julie's wrist the whole time we scrubbed, but she didn't cry out once.

Marie checked her hair again, slowly and carefully drawing the comb through the curls. "Da fungus is bad," she said. "Maybe you shou' cut it off?"

"Let's do it," we agreed.

Marie gave Julie directions to the closest barber shop and Julie lost no time getting there. So now our little charge is running around with a closely-shaved head and a handkerchief for a head tie. She really *is* beautiful.

Tonight, just before we fell asleep, something drew me into Princess's room to check if she was asleep. I nearly tripped over her slight form. She was lying on her stomach with her head pressed against the floor, sound asleep.

"You poor little lamb. Can't sleep in a soft bed, eh? Well, let's try again—cockroaches run around here at night."

I felt that stirring of pity once again, but this time there was no revulsion with it. I hugged her a few seconds before tucking her in.

May 6

There simply hasn't been time to write like I want to. Julie is sick with malaria, so I need to keep an eye on Princess between the laundry, cooking, and schooling. Charlotte is busy with her books, and it's really making her exercise some self-discipline.

Julie did a huge pile of laundry on Monday, but the humidity hung like a close, wet blanket over the city, so we had to let it hang overnight. This morning it was still damp. Later this afternoon, I noticed a sudden darkening of the kitchen, and at the same time Henry, the security guard, appeared at the door. "Da rain comin' fas', Missie!"

I lifted Princess off the cupboard where she had been "helping" me shape cookies and dashed outside. Elijah was already gathering the clothes.

"Hurry! Hurry!" he called, fumbling with a stubborn clothespin. We both hurried, but not enough. The rain swept in like a miniature flood. There was nothing to do but dash for cover. The rain lashed down in great gray sheets and whipped streams of water across the yard, shredding leaves off the mango trees and pouring off the roofs in rivers. It beat a loud staccato on the tin of the old security shed, where the men were only vague shadows through the veil of water.

"Whew!" I exclaimed, and instantly Princess echoed, "Wee-yew!" It was fast becoming a habit with her.

"It's pouring, Princess! Just look . . . I mean . . . *listen* to the rain!" I led her outside on the porch and we stood with the rain bucketing down a mere two feet away. She stood perfectly still, listening, her face turned toward the little clouds of mist that reached us. Then she reached out a slim brown hand and smiled.

"Watah!" she said.

I gazed in delight at the awesome fall of the rain, at the limp clothes dancing on the line, the beaten trees, the large puddles collecting in the yard, and I thought of the blank darkness behind those sightless eyes. Suddenly I felt like weeping.

"Jesus, thank you for my two eyes!" I exclaimed aloud.

"Two eye," she echoed happily.

Go for it, Julie. Do everything in your power to see if she can be helped—and may God in heaven bless your efforts.

The storm lasted a full hour, with the thunder trying to compete with the noise of the raindrops. Finally, it tapered off to a gentle shower. The thunder growled a few more times, and it was over.

"Awesome, just *awesome!*" I commented over and over, and that spunky little scrap of a child repeated my words.

"Aw-w-SUM. Jus' aw-w-SUM!"

I'm learning to love her.

15

"We Have Not Eaten for Four Days!"

May 7

I'm not sure how I was roped into it again, but before I knew it, I had consented to go with the distribution team. "Mom, you're gonna *love* this!" Bev said excitedly as she filled the jug with ice water and packed the peanut butter cookies in the cooler. "There's really nothing to be scared of with Pastor George and Joseph Pawah and Mo along. They always look after us. And if it gets ugly, we leave."

"What do you mean, gets ugly?" I wanted to know.

"We-e-ell . . . the people are desperate, so any little delay makes them angry," she answered. "I kinda wish Akin were along, but he's over at another camp today. They're honking at the gate—hurry!"

We stopped at the CAM warehouse, which was buzzing like a hive of bees. Two distribution trucks were loading ahead of us. Henry Cole was servicing the forklift, with his tools spread all around him, and way back in the medical room Cleo Hardy, one of the church ladies, was packing medicines to go. Varnee scurried around in his spotless white shirt, giving orders and checking delivery notes for accuracy. The guards kept eagle eyes on all the developments, and Pastor George didn't seem in much of a hurry to get anywhere.

Finally, however, everything was ready, and we were on our way to Blamasey Displaced Camp near Hotel Africa.

The displaced persons camp was a vast expanse of small bamboo huts built close together and only high enough so a man could comfortably stand up inside. Thousands of them were stretched out across the dusty soil.

A slender young woman marched past us balancing an extremely long bundle of sticks on her head. She held a bucket of water in one hand and carried a baby on her back. I stared in amazement. "Where do you think her husband is?" I wondered aloud.

"Maybe he ran from the soldiers and they shot him . . . or maybe they forced him to fight," came the sober reply. "Some of these displaced go back to their homes; some stay here; some die here," George continued. "*All* are hungry."

The Defender lurched over a skinny plank bridge and plowed through a stretch of deep sand. An open shed stood close to the road, and people came running as Mo backed up to it. A tremendous crowd assembled within minutes. Two heavy ladies were already sitting on strained chairs in the small, tarp-covered building, looking through their log books, ready for action. Their fingers wore sparkling jewels and their bright dresses boasted many yards of frilly ruffles.

I felt a tinge of trepidation as I scanned the faces before me. They looked weary and sullen—even threatening. Their black eyes glittered, and sweat ran from their faces as they looked us over, chattering incessantly all the while. They shifted their feet restlessly and showed no inclination to smile.

I remembered the words of warning from Akin. "We must be very careful when dealing with displaced people," he had warned. "They are traumatized; they have seen tragedies in their own families, and they can vent their feelings on you. You must serve them with a spirit of sympathy, because if they think you are hiding food or cheating them in any way, they will become ugly. Hunger is a terrible foe!"

"What . . . what's wrong with them?" I whispered to George.

"These people are *very hungry*," he said grimly. "We will need to act fast."

Only a thin rope separated us from the throng.

George quickly conferred with the two ladies and decided on a system of distribution, then began calling out names. It soon became apparent that many of the people had been here yesterday, and a royal mix-up ensued.

"I wish Akin were here," Bev confided, which didn't help my worries. "He's never lost a distribution yet—to chaos, I mean," she added, seeing my puzzled expression. "I don't really like what's going on here. The tickets are all mixed up. I'm going to help Joe hand out the parcels."

George would bellow out a name through the microphone and wait a few seconds. If no one answered, he tried another name.

People began to thrust their tickets toward us impatiently, deaf to George's entreaties for order. "This is stamped already—now go!" George shouted. "You jus' got rice yesterday."

The camp director began haggling with the people, describing the tickets we were serving. "Those who have a *blue* ticket—only a *BLUE* one—come here!" he yelled. "Rules are rules—you mus' obey."

The list looked endless. Faces became anxious. An old man with a thick, woolen toque took his time to fish a ticket out of his worn Bible.

The ladies in charge waxed hotter and hotter. "Dey think you are a new people, an' dey are comin' fo' seconds," one of them told me, fanning her poor face with a towel.

I'm sure you would too.

Suddenly she spied someone in the crowd. "Why are *you* heah?" she yelled angrily, rising half-way to her feet. She fixed him with a fierce gaze and shook her finger briskly. "You are a Red Cross man. Why are you heah—tell me! Now *git!*" The man "got."

George was having problems of his own. "Dixie Swain. C'mon Dixie. Where are you from? Wha' part of Bupalo? How many chil'ren?"

"NO, NO!" he roared. "Not five. Only two. One bag of rice fo' you." Evidently the original number of children had suddenly increased, and the information didn't match the ticket. Poor George.

A persistent old woman kept plucking at his sleeve. Pick . . . pick . . . pick. "Help me now, *ri' now,*" she insisted for the tenth time.

"I beg you, Ma. I beg you—jus' wait!" he said, trying hard to remain respectful.

"Help me now! Ah los' ma ticket in da swamp. Can you help me *now?*" Pick . . . pick . . . pick.

George put both his hands on her stooped shoulders and explained the situation. It was touching to see. "We have to stay organized or we lose all—understand?"

A young woman came to claim rice for her husband.

"What's his age?" George countered, checking her ticket.

She hesitated. "Thirty-nine," she said.

"Sorry. Your ticket says *sixty-nine.* Next?"

Another thwarted effort at dishonesty.

Slowly, the line moved along. I could see how necessary it was to stick to a rigid program in such a sensitive situation to prevent utter chaos. The two ladies paged slower and slower while George patiently kept calling out names. The pile of rice in the back of the Defender dwindled noticeably.

"It is time to begin with the influx now," George informed us all. We waited another half hour while the ladies tried to make sense of their logbooks and George lined the people up according to their ticket dates. Suddenly everyone was claiming to be among the new influx. George shook his head in despair.

"If you can't act properly we will leave this camp!" he hollered indignantly.

The people must have known he was near the end of his endurance. They relaxed a bit, the tension eased, and the distribution continued. A smiling Bev still handed out bag after bag of rice from the Defender, and sprawled out against the remaining bags was Joe Pawah, sound asleep.

George noticed too. "Joseph? What's this?" he yelled, and the startled Joe leaped from his seat in confusion, much to the amusement of the people. He sheepishly started helping again.

George was shouting again. "Please open this place! Open this place! You must not behave like gorillas. We will not serve you if you are not in line!"

From the crowd, a woman's wild screams sent chills through my blood. "My baby!" she shrieked, bursting through the throng with desperate strength. "Dey squish my baby . . . Oh God! My baby!"

The pressing crowd had very nearly suffocated the tiny boy she had on her back. "You shoul' carry da' chil' in yo' arms in such a place!" she was told sternly, as many willing hands helped her untie the little mite. She was trembling all over. I met the gaze of her dark eyes and saw an incredible mother-love shining from their depths.

The rice was almost gone, and there wasn't a sign of the next truck.

Four days without food. Running from your home in terror, with all your goods upon your back—and the rice is running out.

We felt a sudden surge of dismay among the remaining people. The merciless African sun beat down upon their heads and bare backs, and they had to squint against the glare. They pushed against the ropes menacingly.

George noticed at once. "Listen! Let us understand one another," he pleaded, raising his voice above the din. "We came to serve you, but we can only give to those who hold a ticket. They were here first—they are the hungriest. We will come back tomorrow with more rice. I beg you!"

"My son, I am h-u-n-g-r-y," an old man answered, spelling out the word. "We will all be dead befo' you co' again. Please, we have not eaten in four days!"

"Oh God! Liberia is going!" George exclaimed, pulling out his handset. "Golf Five Zero. Golf Five Zero."

"Golf Five Zero standing by," came the welcome reply.

"What do we do if relief does not come? We are almost out of rice."

"Pull out! Pull out!" Akin ordered.

"Be ready to get to the truck—fast," George warned us. "We'll come back tomorrow."

I glanced up over the crowd in time to see a woman who had just been served offer a few words—and her ticket—to another female, who instantly got in line.

"Hunger drives a man to dishonesty," Akin had said.

Before the last bag of rice was handed out, Bev and I hurried to the truck and woke a napping Mo. Shortly after, the men joined us, and we took off, but not quickly enough to keep several hopefuls from clinging to the back. "Stop the truck," George ordered. Then, "Please, get off!"

"What a day!" sighed Bev. "I can't imagine keeping up this pace for too long."

On the way home we stopped in at the Center for Malnourished Children, "Jus' to check it out as a possibility," said George. "These are the chil'ren of the warfront—chil'ren who have been abandoned or displaced."

Words failed me as I gazed upon the smallest sufferers of Liberia. Such thin little scraps of humanity. They were all eyes and bones. Their little legs dangled like sticks, without an ounce of strength. We all stood silently for several minutes, trying to absorb this new, pathetic scene.

"Ah have twins—den triplets—an' ma' husband was taken by da army. Ah have no idea where he is," a woman said quietly.

"Oh, these poor children!" Bev breathed. "Does CAM help them?"

"That's why I'm checking today," George answered. "Even if we do not have sponsors for them, we can give them aid. That is the beauty of the General Relief program."

Larry came running to the gate as we arrived at home. "Mom! They're fighting two hours away—really bad fighting, they said. Will there be a war here, Mom?"

"That close?" I asked. "What does Dad say?"

"He said we don't have to worry till it gets closer, but two hours is only from home to Waterton Park. That's close!"

"Too close," I agreed. "But Dad's right, worrying won't help. Praying will."

"I'm going to *dream* about displaced camps," Bev said wearily as we entered the house.

May 8

It's a whole new experience living with a blind child. We have to remind ourselves that she can't see when she knocks over cups or trips over something. Her hair is growing again, slowly but surely. She flinches a bit when she takes her vitamins, but we think she's incredibly brave. She can eat rice like a full-sighted person or better, and she doesn't need a spoon. We're trying to teach her, though. Her mind is as sharp as a whip.

I look forward to the day when she can sleep all night. I think her life has been far too traumatic for her to relax for too long at a time.

Julie has to constantly take care of that ruptured eye; it gets dry, and when the eyelid is closed it doesn't cover the hemorrhage. That must really feel awful.

Hannah B. visited Sam Kargbo at the CAM office and wanted to know what had become of "her chil'," but Julie is positive she is no relation. She *told* us the child was found somewhere.

May 10

Bev had arranged for the two of us to go with Akin's distribution team this morning. Right after breakfast they drove through the gate.

The team's smiles widened as they eyed the brown paper bag Bev carried. "You brought some relief with you!" Akin remarked. "Praise God!"

"Ah kin smell the cookies," Joe commented, grinning from ear to ear.

I couldn't help but notice the incredible azure blue of the sky as we dodged and bounced along the road toward the warehouse. The dim gray of the misty rain was replaced by warm golden sunlight. Tremendous piles of snow-white cumulus clouds stood along the horizon way to the north.

We stopped at the warehouse to load rice. Varnee greeted us warmly. "Wou' you like a drink?" he asked courteously, extending his hand and bowing toward the small fridge that cooled his soft drinks. Varnee was always giving short, slight bows, and his friendly smile was quick and frequent.

"You're dressed for church today, Varnee," I told him, noticing the highly polished black shoes, the clean, wrinkle-free blue shirt, and the matching navy dress pants.

"Ah like to look good fo' my job," he grinned.

The men were loading black plastic bags of rice into the Defender. They worked fast, but not fast enough for Akin. He kept hurrying them on. Bev and I made sure we were on board as soon as the truck was loaded. It wouldn't do to keep Akin waiting.

At the very first checkpoint, a young soldier sauntered up to the door and looked us over. Another one approached the other side door. "Christian Ay-yed," one read aloud. It was strange, the way they stood there and stared, as if they were trying to decide what to do.

I noticed there seemed to be an unusual number of soldiers standing by, but I didn't suspect a thing. Some of the guns they held were old and taped together, but that didn't make them look any less menacing.

"What you carryin'?" the soldier asked in a heavy, slurred accent. His shifty eyes peered through the plastic windows of the Defender, where the bags of rice were bulging.

"Rice for Rick's Institute," Akin replied coolly. "You *know* us, my man. You know what we do."

The man paused again, trying to feel his way. "We are hungry! No food . . . no-o-o food fo' three days. Kin you gi' me one bag—jus' one?"

Akin didn't waver. "No," he said. "This is not for soldiers. It is for the starving influx at Rick's Camp. Now let us go."

The man hesitated. His dark eyes smoldered. He looked at Akin's impassive face—and waved us on. The other soldier's face was sullen, even angry.

Hunger. Hunger showed in their eyes—in the grim, gaunt lines of their faces and the weary stoop of their shoulders.

"It is not our fault they have no rice!" Akin exclaimed when we were out of hearing distance. "They destroy; they kill; they steal. They are part of Satan's ministry. Sometimes we are forced to give them rice or they will not let us through." He paused for a moment, clearly agitated. "And now I will give you all your job descriptions. First, we must confirm that this is indeed Rick's Camp. Second, we will serve the outstanding ones first, meaning the ones who have been here the longest. Third, we will separate the old, vulnerable ones from the rest. You, Bev, will serve them. I want every baby ma and the pregnant women in another line; the only trouble is there will suddenly be many, many pregnant women. You, Mrs. Stelfox, will serve them."

"Are you sure I can?" I quavered.

"Absolutely!" he said. "There is no need to fear. Joseph, you get the bags out of the Defender."

I felt a thrill of excitement that we could actually be a part of CAM's hands-on distribution team. It was a major job to pass out thousands of plastic bags of rice, beans, and chicken to all the displaced camps. It took planning, bookwork, and plain old-fashioned stamina.

"The people will bring many babies, either their own or someone else's," Akin was saying. "The child will cry as if it is hungry, but it really just wants its mother. Do not let them fool you. Just tell them, *"Give that child back to its mother!"*"

"They must think you can read their minds!" I piped up.

"It is worse than you think, Mrs. Stelfox—just watch and see. These people have come from far."

Rick's Institute was once a beautiful, sprawling campus with long dorms and a huge university building. We backed up slowly to the battered step of the biggest building and parked right against the concrete so we could be higher than the enormous crowd that milled around in front of us. Akin leaped up the steps and faced the crowd with his Bible in one hand.

"He'll probably preach a bit before starting," Bev explained. "He can't pass up such a great chance."

Akin immediately picked four likely-looking young men to help with general law and order. In a loud voice, he explained their specific duties. "I need only you four men. I will call you my SOS, meaning Security On Security." The men beamed and jostled each other.

"Listen. I do not want you calling anyone else to help. Do not refer me to your family at any time—and do not pass rice under the table or I will fire you. Do not say, 'Here is my friend; help him.' And do not put your own friends first. I will give you NOTHING for helping me this day; you are here to work—now WORK."

To the people he shouted, "Are there any fighters here? Please, if you cannot listen to me, go away NOW. I do not want you to stand in the hot sun all day. See this old man here . . ." and he effortlessly set an old man on the step in front of him. "If you are as old as he, but not as old as his hat, you may get in line over here."

The people stared wonderingly at Akin's team. I, in turn, was amazed and a bit awed by the size of the crowd. I was impressed by the weariness in their posture and the wretched hunger in their eyes. They couldn't go rest. They needed to stand in line for food to keep them alive, no matter how tired they were.

And we *get impatient waiting at the checkouts in an air-conditioned supermarket.*

"Akin, the microphone is ou' of battery," one of the helpers stated.

"Now I cannot preach," he answered disappointedly and put away his Bible. "Let us show them where to form the lines."

Half an hour later, three long lines were being served quickly and efficiently. Akin showed us how he wanted us to sign each ticket—*5-10-CAM.* "Make sure you watch closely," he warned. "Ask me if you have any questions."

Joseph Pawah handed out bags as fast as Bev could sign the tickets. There was no sign of Mo, who must have been overcome with exhaustion and stayed in the truck. Akin helped all three lines at once.

It wasn't long until I could recognize the signs of a forgery. People would erase the previous CAM signature or simply tear it off, or they would alter numbers and dates and names. I must admit I was tempted to give the cheating women another bag of rice. I knew they needed it, but rules are rules.

The baby mas would usually turn slightly so I could see their babies. I couldn't resist. I had to touch them. Some slept soundly, with great beads of sweat standing on their faces and necks, their heads lolling about with every move the mother made. Others were tied securely—so tightly that it looked like their mother's lapas would strangle them. Some were awake and stared at me with wide, unblinking eyes. The smallest ones had cloths draped over their faces to shield them from the blazing sun. All were precious little souls in the sight of Almighty God.

Desperate people tried to sneak in ahead of others when Akin wasn't looking. "If you continue to allow others before you, I will not serve them!" he exclaimed.

He leaned down to face a frail senior. "Hello, O'Ma—you alright? We have served you already—remember?"

Her hopeless old eyes stared at him uncomprehendingly. Her white, kinky hair was a gnarled mess, with little bits of dry grass clinging to it. An unmistakable odor permeated her whole being. She held out her ticket again, making signs and gestures.

"Someone has taken her rice!" Akin fumed, putting another bag of rice in her arms. "They lie in wait and steal the rice, and she can do nothing about it. Come here, Membah," he ordered, motioning to one of the four men enlisted to keep order. "See that this old lady gets home this time."

Turning to us, he said quietly, "Firmness with compassion is the key."

A beautiful young baby ma with tiny, diamond-shaped braiding all over her head and bright yellow fingernails handed Akin her ticket. He glanced at her skimpy embroidered halter-top and tight shorts, then at her ticket. "Is this your husband's or boyfriend's ticket?" he asked suspiciously.

"My husban's."

"Three children? You have three children?"

"Yes."

"Did he pay a dowry for you?"

"No . . ."

"Then he is not your husband. How old is he?"

"Forty-nine."

"How can a forty-nine-year-old man be married to such a

child?" Akin fairly spat out the words. "Get home and put on some more clothing—you are not fit to be in a public place."

The startled girl melted into the crowd with the bag of rice on her head. Next time, she would come fully dressed.

"That's just the trouble," Akin said despairingly. "Just look how the old men treat the young girls. When they tire of them, they find a mistress—and have more children. May God have mercy on Liberia."

I showed Akin a ticket with a smudged date in the corner. "What is your age?" he asked the girl who had been holding the ticket.

"Ah don' know," she said softly. "Ah think maybe fifteen."

"Is this ticket for you? Are you sure? Not for a friend or relative? Varnee is a man's name, and you are a girl, so I am not convinced that it is yours. Move on now."

The girl stayed. "It is fo' my fathah," she wailed suddenly. "Ple-e-ase gi' me some rice!"

"Where is your father?"

"He has gone t' pray . . ."

I was wishing I had not asked him about this particular ticket when he looked my way and smiled faintly. "I must do this to relieve the tension sometimes, Mrs. Stelfox," he smiled. "Give her the rice."

An ancient, toothless granny went through the process and received two bags of rice. She quickly hoisted them over her shoulders and scurried away as fast as she could, literally bending under the load. "Ma! Can I help you?" Akin called after her, but she never slowed a step. She didn't even look back.

The morning wore on and on, with the merciless African sun frying the skin on our faces and arms. I was so glad for the height of those concrete steps. I simply could not have stood down there among that anxious crowd without getting claustrophobic. The young men who were helping did a wonderful job of keeping the people at arm's length. I was glad they took their job so seriously.

Finally, the rice was all gone, and we all jumped into the Defender to go get another load, trying to answer all the anxious questions about our return. They didn't seem to believe we would come back.

Bev and I dug out the cookies and ice water and passed them around. Never had water tasted so good.

"I turned a lady away because she had been served, so she went over to your line," Bev told Akin on the way to the warehouse. "I knew you would catch on to her trick, so I didn't worry about it— but the next thing I knew she was leaving with *two* bags of rice."

For once, Akin was speechless. When he found his tongue, he fairly sputtered with indignation. "Each bag of rice is worth $125 in Liberian money, and I am responsible to screen them carefully."

When we were all loaded and heading back, Akin had more to say. "This time I will be very strict!" he declared. "More so than before."

How is that possible? I thought.

As luck would have it, the first person in line was a very young girl with a baby of her own. "Babies borning babies!" Akin stormed. "No school, no education, no nothing. Where is the future of this country? And *why* are there so many more people here?"

A well-meaning man had gathered all the people he could find and brought them around. Poor Akin hardly knew what to do. "Why do you get these people's hopes up when you are aware that we can only serve those who have tickets?" he shouted above the clamor. He threw a ticket on the ground, saying, "You have fooled with the signature. We are here to serve you—why do you make it so difficult for us?"

I picked up the ticket and looked at it. Sure enough, someone had nearly succeeded in erasing the small "CAM" in the top corner.

A fierce verbal bickering broke out among the older people, so Akin had to settle the matter. They were all hard of hearing, so he picked up the bullhorn and shouted to them. "As you know by now, Akin will never compromise!" he bellowed. "I am doing this in your interest, and the Almighty God will judge me if I am not. Look at all the human beings standing in the sun. Now, let's get busy."

"No ticket?" Akin asked a poor old widow. "Here, hang on to this so no one takes it. Understand?" She looked up into his face with utter gratitude shining in her eyes.

"God beff you!" she told him with a toothless smile.

As the rice supply dwindled, Akin suddenly turned to us. "Mrs. Stelfox, Bev—you must enter the truck immediately," he told us in a low voice. "We are almost finished." Bev and I hurried to the Defender, where Mo was just rousing from his second nap of the day.

When the people realized that the last of the rice was being handed out, they broke out of line and rushed toward the Defender, begging and pleading for rice. "We canno' wait till Monday!" they cried. "Please, I beg!"

I felt like weeping. I will never forget the faces of those people pressed against the windows—holding up their babies and showing us all their boils and whatever else ailed them. It was desperately sad, but twilight was not far away, and we needed to get home quickly to avoid any problems at the checkpoints.

We slowly, carefully pulled out, with their cries ringing in our ears. "You will co' back? You will co' back?"

The ride home was quiet. We were all thinking of those poor people who will go to bed hungry. What a hopeless feeling it must be.

"We thank you very much for coming along," Akin said respectfully as the gates to Residence swung open. "You may come again at any time. God bless you."

All the CAM staff had arrived for our biweekly unit meeting by the time Bev and I cleaned up and ate some leftover rice. As it has been for the last several meetings, the main topic was the threat of war and the necessary precautions in case it actually happens.

When the meeting adjourned, everyone really began talking, as usual.

"I can't see it coming for a while yet," Iddo remarked. "There have been so many threats and scares that I just don't get excited too fast anymore." He shrugged his shoulders in his customary way as he spoke.

"All the signs point to a real fight somewhere, though," Curt said with conviction.

16

War Draws Near

May 11

Today, Tony Hage asked Wayne and me to come with him and his cousin to Kakata to visit the warehouse of his slain cousins. They died on the third of April, but all the legalities had to be taken care of before Tony could open their warehouse to CAM. He wanted to know if CAM could use any of the goods at a reduced price.

We reached the town of Kakata around ten-thirty and drove right to the warehouse. The blue and white building was marred with jagged bullet scars.

Going through the warehouse was a sobering experience. Unfinished projects littered the countertops and half-empty boxes of goods stood in the aisles waiting to be shelved. It was all so real, so chilling—the owners had been gunned down without mercy.

Tony and his cousin looked grim as they showed Wayne all the garden tools, the groceries neatly stacked on the shelves, and all the other items for sale. The whole atmosphere was unutterably sad.

It was intensely disturbing to see the victims' home, with the locks shot off the doors and the blood on the bedroom floors, where the desperate men had tried to barricade themselves in. I simply couldn't finish touring the place—it was too awful. How barbaric and senseless could human beings actually be? Two souls hurtled into eternity.

I didn't enjoy today at all. Not even the changing landscape or the lovely thundershower on the way home. The rain seemed to be tears, the heavens weeping for the two lives so senselessly snuffed out.

May 12

Sundays have become such a balm for the weary. Sometimes the pressures of living in Africa threaten to suffocate us—then Sunday rolls around, and we can sit under the sound of the Gospel and feel our tension drain away. We feel rejuvenated and full of determination to make every day in this needy country really count.

Early this morning, a rain shower hurried over and only managed to heat things up. The ocean looked like a giant Jacuzzi.

When we walked the five blocks to church, steam was rising from the roads and garbage heaps. Great red blossoms of exotic bushes along the road shone like flames against their dark green foliage. The long, droopy banana leaves dripped with moisture. Little trails of mist wound upward among the creeping vines and undergrowth.

We made our way inside the church building and found our seats. When Wayne got up to lead singing, he looked as if he had dunked his head in a bucket of water. He tried speeding up the songs, but there was no response.

Pastor Mervin Lantz has a reputation for being very prompt. He gave the announcements, preached a wonderful sermon on mothers, and because of the heat, skipped the usual testimony time.

Fellowship dinner was at Iddo and Viola's house today. And what a lovely meal awaited us! We dined on chicken and beef enchiladas, rice, refried beans, lettuce salad, iced tea, and peanut butter pie. No restaurant in all of Monrovia could have done better. We didn't even have to help with the dishes.

"Those refried beans were better than store-bought," I gushed.

"But we did buy them this time," they told me.

"Well, they're as good as homemade ones," I allowed, laughing along.

"Miriam really enjoys cooking," Viola told us. "It gives me a lot more time for the sewing center.

"I can't imagine how you keep all that straight," I sighed, thinking of all the projects they had going. They have women sewing there almost every day. Several sewing centers from Monrovia and beyond do regular sewing for them. The clothes have to be counted and distributed among the orphanages. Ladies piece quilts and baby blankets, sew diapers, and do a host of other things. Huge donated shipments of cloth, zippers, thread, and all kinds of sewing notions have to be distributed where needed.

"Do you want to come help us sometime?" Viola wondered.

"I think you're doing a wonderful job," I told her. "It takes all I've got to homeschool right now."

Iddo is also in charge of the agriculture projects, teaching the people how to grow rice and vegetables. He loves it, but he's a busy man.

Later this evening, we drove out to the beach to watch the sun sink into the gray-blue mist of the mighty Atlantic. Of course Princess was along. She has added such a dimension to our lives. Tonight she was in a laughing mood.

"Who let the dogs out?" Larry asked her.

She puckered up her sweet baby mouth and yelled, "WHOO! WHOO!"

"Remember that older man who had lunch with us on Thursday—the one who stared at Princess all during lunch?" asked Wayne.

"Yes, he didn't eat his rice."

"Well, he told me later he could hardly eat because of Princess's eye. He wondered why on earth we didn't pick a pretty child if we were going to take care of one."

"What did you tell him, Dad?" one of the girls wondered

indignantly. "Princess is *beautiful*."

"I just told him to be glad *he's* not blind."

"The more dependent a person is on you, the more you learn to love them," I commented. "It took me a day or two to get used to her, but now she's sunshine to my days."

"Shunshine," agreed Princess.

May 13

We were just finishing up school around three o'clock when Wayne and the girls burst into the house. They were all talking at once. "We're stuck! The war front is only thirty minutes away. They heard the gunfire at Pastor Mervin's house so we have to get our suitcases totally ready *now*. We can't get through on any of the phones; Curt thinks the lines have already been cut."

"Oh, *Dad!*" Larry cried, his face blanching. "I was scared this would happen!"

"What can we do?" I asked more calmly than I felt.

"Nothing but wait and see what happens," Wayne said soberly. "Let's pray right now—this could be serious."

In the next few hours we made sure all the suitcases were packed with necessary supplies. "Just take what you need," we were told. It was all so new and unreal. War? Killing?

Lord God of heaven . . . take care of us, please.

"I can't imagine leaving Liberia!" Bev exclaimed. "What will happen to all our friends?"

"I feel like a traitor—running away," Julie said. "We can leave, and they all have to stay and face the music. It's just not fair."

"That's true," said Wayne, "but we must realize that staying is a lot safer for them than for us. We are prime targets, whereas they know just where to hide and what to do."

"I can't believe we're really in danger," Willie decided. "There have been so many false alarms. I agree with Iddo. When it actually happens, we'll have plenty of time to be scared."

"Rather be safe than sorry, Son," I told him. "Look how frightened Elijah is. *That* is what concerns me the most."

Princess, too, sensed there was something wrong. She sought

out Julie's lap and curled up for a nice long stay. Every once in a while she would whisper "Juwee?"

"She knows there's something going on," Charlotte said. "She won't leave you for a minute."

Wayne became increasingly restless. Finally, he got through to Paul Weaver from CAM Ohio. Paul, always a source of encouragement, promised they would all pray.

"Make sure you declare Code Red if it gets any worse," he told Wayne.

Code Red stands for an explosive situation in which CAM Ohio asks all their American staff to leave the country. If any of the staff would refuse to leave, they would remain at their own risk and without CAM support. Wayne was encouraged to call CAM Ohio every two hours on the even hour, from 10 a.m. until midnight if needed.

Around five o'clock, President Taylor gave a long, drawn-out speech on the radio. *I'm sure he is scared. Elijah will know everything he said.*

"Let's sit down and review the security codes again," Wayne suggested, pulling them from the drawer. "We're in Code Orange right now. *(1) Director should coordinate all staff movement and know their approximate locations at all times,*" he read aloud. "That's not hard with all our radios, but what if they are stolen? *(2) Be packed and prepared to evacuate at a moment's notice. (3) Make sure passports, evacuation money, and airline tickets are ready for evacuation. (4) Any person wanting to leave the country is given the opportunity to go to the destination CAM Ohio specifies and remain there. (5) Be in contact with the CAM Ohio office at specific times throughout the day.* Looks like we're right on track so far."

"You look tired, Dad," Julie commented. "Maybe we should all go to bed early—like Princess here. Did you know I have to have her in the hospital by nine o'clock this Friday to have that eye removed? War *can't* be coming!"

Is this really happening? Will the ruthless rebel soldiers storm our gate tonight and pounce on us, killing us all? What will happen to Princess? My imagination has been spinning, yet I am not as scared as I think I should be. The rest of the family is even more unconcerned—but then, none of us has ever been close to a war.

Security Sam is patrolling round and round the yard, never stopping for a minute. He looks like he is on full alert for any possible signs of danger.

Elijah, too, is constantly listening to his radio, pacing about like a caged animal, checking out the gates. He couldn't even eat the sandwich we made for him, but wrapped it up to take along home.

"Those men know what war is all about," Wayne observed, watching through the open door. "They're really scared."

It was late when we finally quit visiting and decided to go to bed. I went out onto the porch and gazed up at the starry night sky. *And He made the stars also*, I quoted to myself, remembering that favorite verse fragment. It is comforting to realize God is in control.

May 15

The war scare subsided as fast as it came. People are going about their business as if it never happened, but we were instructed to keep our suitcases packed, just in case. I hate this threat of what might be hanging over us. I refuse to worry until it actually happens.

Curt seems to think war is inevitable. Iddo thinks there's no danger yet. Wayne doesn't know what to think, but he sure isn't worried about it. The native staff—especially Dr. Lamin, Akin, and George—are confident God will never allow war in Liberia again. They seem to have a real, solid faith, and I just praise the Lord!

May 16

Things happen so fast around here I hardly know how to cope. Now the American CAM staff leaders want us to go to Sierra Leone to do an assessment to see if there is a need for help from

CAM, so it sounds like our family, Akin's family, and Dr. Lamin and his son Moses will be leaving on Tuesday.

If we go to Sierra Leone, Merci Evans will keep Princess until we get back. She is a single Nigerian lady in the church whom we have come to appreciate highly. We've had many excellent discussions with her about all sorts of things. She has such a sense of stability about her—such a merry laugh and such sparkling eyes. Princess took to her instantly.

"Sis Mercee, I love you," she says. "Come eat some rice wi' me."

And Merci laughs and says, "Oh-h-h, *Princess!*" and they head for the table to eat rice. Merci has the patience Princess needs right now.

Just this morning, again, Princess was up much too early, roaming all around the house and singing "Jesus loves me, dis ah know." As long as she sings I'm not too worried, but as soon as she gets quiet I start to wonder and drag myself out of bed to see what she's up to. Usually it's still dark outside, but how would *she* know? Sometimes she's "looking" in the fridge, feeling all the cold containers and holding some to her cheek. Or else she's out on the front porch, balancing on the round concrete fence with her toes gripping the edge. She lets me lead her back to bed and on rare occasions she even stays there until we all wake up.

Julie faithfully cleans the pus out of that ruptured eye and keeps it moist with eye drops. Princess sits quite patiently through it all.

Last time she came to clean, Marie brought her little Freddie to meet Princess. He stood and stared at Princess's poor protruding eye and her cropped hair. She, sensing his presence, approached him and ran her eager little fingers over his face. He tried to back off, but she pursued him and insisted on becoming acquainted.

"This is Freddie," we informed her. "You may play with him today."

"Dis is Fweddie," she repeated. "Fweddie, Fweddie," and gave him a sudden shove.

The startled child let out a wail for his mother, but Marie was so overcome with laughter she wasn't much help.

"Princess! That was not nice," Charlotte said reproachfully.

"Naw nice."

"Now say, 'I'm sorry.'"

"Ah sorry," she giggled.

Charlotte had a great time with the two little ones and the garden hose. The temperature hung around ninety degrees, so it was a wonderful way to cool them off. They splashed wildly on the back porch in a clothes tub and didn't want to quit. I could hear Princess's shrieks of delight and Freddie's high laughter. Charlie, the monkey, scolded loudly from the branches. I'm sure he was aching to get in on the fun.

After dinner, the new little friends napped on the floor, so there was peace once more. I can't imagine how dull it was around here before Princess came. I am rather confused about how to discipline her, but I'm trying my best to teach her not to be quite so aggressive. I think she had to fight for what she got in the orphanage.

Wayne went over to meet with Iddo, Curt, and Mervin about this war scare again. They must have all broken curfew tonight, because he came back really late.

I will be so glad when tomorrow is over. Our sweet Princess is scheduled for surgery to remove that diseased eye.

17

Eye Surgery

May 17

When Princess woke this morning, Bev and Julie bathed her and lotioned her fuzzy little head. "Ah wanna eat rice!" she begged, and although we had received no pre-surgery instructions, we knew better than to let her eat anything.

"Julie will feed you as soon as we get home, okay, Princess?"

"Me eat rice!"

"Give her a little water, Julie. You never know how long this could take," I cautioned.

"Dr. Guizzie is really nice, and I'm sure he will take good care of her," she said as they were leaving.

Bev drove them to the hospital, and I got busy with school and laundry and tried to keep my mind occupied. The house was quiet—much too quiet. No little brown hands explored the countertops and smelled the cucumbers as I peeled them. No one grabbed hold of my skirt and propelled along with me wherever I went. No one called me "Muttah," and no one sang "*Halle-e-yew-w-yah!*"

"Sure is quiet around here," Willie commented. "I can actually concentrate on my books."

"I hope they know what they're doing," Charlotte worried.

"Imagine taking out an eye! Won't there be a big hole there?"

Four hours later, Wayne drove into the yard, honking as he came. "We have to go pick up Julie. She doesn't have a phone with her. There was some mix-up and she couldn't get hold of us. Hurry!"

I hurried. We dodged through the heavy traffic, over the bridge, did a U-turn—and there was Julie, walking along the road with Princess in her arms. She looked weary and upset.

"Where were you so long?" she asked, carefully crawling into the front seat. "I've been waiting a long time."

"We didn't know you were ready. When Bev mentioned that you didn't have a phone, I flew over here as fast as I could," Wayne explained. "I'm sorry."

Princess lay like a rag doll—her eye socket covered with a bloody bandage. There were traces of dried blood on her cheeks and her skinny little neck. Her forehead was burning hot.

"It was *horrible!*" Julie exclaimed feelingly. "They did the surgery around noon, and it didn't take long at all. I waited and waited and *waited* for Princess to wake up, but she never did. I tried putting a cold cloth on her head and everything I could think of, but she still hasn't moved. Is she going to be all right, Mom? It's like she's dead!" She paused to wipe the beads of sweat from Princess's forehead. "There's really no one around to take care of the patients, and there was no one around when I left the hospital except the receptionist—and all he wondered was if someone was going to pick us up. I didn't need any permission to get up and walk out with a child who's still heavily sedated and just had major eye surgery!"

It was heart-wrenching. That pathetic little bundle with the bloody bandage where her eye had been—and no one in the world who really cared except us.

There is One who loves Princess much more than we ever could. Who knows what wonderful plan the loving Heavenly Father has for her?

At home once again, we ate supper and put away the dishes—and still Princess slept. I called Dr. Lamin. "Ruth Ann, you jus' have to wait till she gets up," he said calmly. "She will be alright."

Merci came over and rocked Princess for a long time while we discussed our pending trip to Sierra Leone. "I will take excellent care of her. It will not be necessary to worry at all!" She smiled at us reassuringly.

"Dr. Lamin thought it was a great idea to have you come stay here," I told her, "so I am comfortable with the situation. We really hate to leave her right now, but it can't be helped. Just make sure you boil all the water you give her and keep that eye socket clean. Julie will have to show you how tomorrow when we put a new bandage on. Are you *sure* you can handle it?"

"I am sure," she smiled.

"Don't forget to give her lots of apple juice and children's Tylenol till her fever goes down. If you need anything else, just go to Mary Lantz. She'll help you."

"I am looking forward to it," Merci said seriously, "but when will she wake up?"

"We have no idea," Julie said. "How much anesthesia did they give her, anyway? Doesn't anyone measure it—or do they just estimate the amount? It's been nine hours already. Merci, do you think there's any way of finding her relatives so we can discover what really happened to her—why she was abandoned and all that?"

"I am sure there is," was the reply.

"Well I'm sure going to try. I'd love to know the real story."

May 18

All night long Princess moaned and groaned in a restless, trance-like sleep. Every time we put her on the bed she became more agitated than ever, so we let her sleep on a light sheet on the floor. It must have been cooler. I wanted to give her something for her fever, but there was no way we could force any liquid through her clenched teeth.

"This child is in agony!" I told Julie. "You need to take her to the Good Samaritan Clinic as soon as they open. Imagine how that eye socket throbs, and how dehydrated she is with no fluids since that water yesterday morning." I felt almost desperate.

About six in the morning Princess sat up, whimpering like a lost puppy. Julie was there like a flash. "Mom, get me some water!" she called.

We held the cool water to her parched little mouth and she eagerly tried to drink—and promptly vomited it up. "Watah, watah," she begged, so we tried again. Same result.

"Maybe she isn't keeping it down, but she's getting a tiny bit," I said. "At least she's wetting her mouth and tongue."

There was no more sleep for us anyway, so we gave her a bath and got her ready to go to the clinic.

Dr. Lamin was waiting when Julie and Princess arrived. After several tries, the nurse managed to find her tiny vein and start the IV. Princess still wasn't fully awake, and when they came home she was fast asleep once again.

"They put another sedative and some fever reducer into the IV so she wouldn't have so much pain," Julie explained. "That's good—at least she's not crying. She was able to keep some water down before she fell asleep again. I forgot to tell you yesterday— Dr. Guizzie took pictures of her eye, and he thinks there's an excellent chance of a cornea graft! But it would cost at least $2,500 U.S., so I guess there's no chance . . . is there? Do you think I could raise the money?" she asked hopefully.

"Well, I certainly think you could try," I encouraged her.

"I'm so desperate for her to see again, Mom. I'll beg all over the world if I have to, just to give her a chance. Maybe . . . just maybe God will see fit to heal her."

We stood and looked at Princess's slight form on the floor. Her cheek was pressed against the concrete and her little hands were outstretched, palms down, as if trying to cool them off. "It's the only way she'll lie still, so let her sleep, I guess," Julie whispered quietly.

"Poor little thing!" I answered.

A sudden dazzle of lightning made us run to shut the doors and windows, because that meant another sudden storm. It moved in with amazing speed, slicing the leaves off the thrashing trees and sending sheets of water over the edges of the roof.

Marvelous are thy works . . . and that my soul knoweth right well . . . kept running through my mind over and over. *Marvelous power and marvelous works!*

Inside our big block house it was cozy and dry, but the thought of some poor locals trying to keep dry in their mud huts took away a lot of the enjoyment for me. I know poor Elijah fights a losing battle during every rainy season—the water literally runs through his house. I know, too, that the huge amounts of water cause the sewer systems to overflow, increasing the chance of disease.

Yet I love these storms!

Princess woke up again around ten o'clock and asked for more water. This time she wanted to hold the cup herself, but her dear little hands are still too weak. Julie patiently helped her take little sips until the whole cupful was gone, and then we gave her a good dose of Tylenol. I think the sedative has worn off because the poor little girl whimpered in the most pathetic way until the pain reliever kicked in. She fell asleep again around midnight.

May 20

Today we packed for Sierra Leone between the many visitors who came just to talk. They usually ended up staying a while, but we didn't mind. Princess could tell there was something stirring, and she cried whenever we left her alone in a room. Finally, Merci arrived and took charge in her capable manner. "She is feeling *much* better!" she smiled. "You jus' do your work—I will take care of her."

"She's probably hungry. See if she'll eat, will you please?" I asked.

I feel really good about Merci coming over until we get home. God is so faithful! He knows our needs before we ask.

18

A Trip Blessed of the Father

May 21

"Everyone looks so sad," I said as we were pulling out of CAM's base for our trip to Sierra Leone early this morning.

Dr. Lamin chuckled as he waved a final farewell out the side front window. "They all want to go along," he explained.

"I was afraid of that," Wayne commented dryly, "so I made sure there would be no hitch-hikers, except for the pastor here. Even he's lucky to be along."

Pastor Amos Gaby, Larry, and I were sitting in the sturdy, uncomfortable back seat of the new CAM Defender. Pastor Amos had come to Monrovia to plant a new church, but his home was in Freetown, Sierra Leone, so this trip was an answer to his prayers. He was immaculately dressed in a dark green African shirt with gold spiral embroidery all around the neck and flowing sleeves, and a matching set of trousers with more embroidery around the ankles. His brown dress shoes were polished to a shine.

"The blessing of the Lord is on this journey—I can feel it!" he said jubilantly, rubbing his hands together. "The Lord did soften your heart, Mr. Wayne, and you let me come along. Praise the Lord for His goodness!" His English was just about perfect.

Behind us, in his small blue car, came Akin, his wife Evee, and

171

their baby Emmanuel. Then the rest of our children and Moses Lamin Jr. brought up the rear of the small convoy in the CAM Cruiser. We each had a radio hand-set so we could easily communicate.

I tried to think of anything we had missed and might need. "Do you have the passports?" Wayne asked, as if reading my thoughts.

"Yes, Dear, and the re-entry booklets, and the permanent resident ones, and the health ones."

I had over a thousand dollars stashed away in three clever hiding places, but I didn't offer that information. If we were robbed or threatened along the way, our passengers could truthfully declare that they knew of no more money.

"We go through Bomi and Grand Cape Mount before we reach Sierra Leone," Pastor Amos offered. "It's a long way, but my heart is so full of joy that the miles will seem to disappear." He grinned broadly, his white teeth shining. "Are you not happy, Mrs. Wayne?"

"Well . . . I guess I am," I said lamely. "It's a bit scary to think of meeting soldiers along the way . . . and I hope Bev can handle all the driving she has to do."

"There is no need to worry. God has control, and the Bible tells us to be anxious for nothing. Let us praise the Lord!"

"What have you heard about Pastor Kauffman?" Dr. Lamin asked. He always shows a real interest in Nathan's treatment and recovery.

"They're trying to find a treatment that will work for him," I answered. "Kathy wrote that he has some good days, but he's still really weak and has a lot of pain."

"War takes some and disease takes some," Dr. Lamin mused. "He is but a young man."

The miles flew under our wheels. We opened all the windows since the new Defender doesn't have air-conditioning and let the warm, dusty air circulate around us. I never tire of the real-life moving pictures of the African roadside, so it seemed only a short while later that we came to the Klay checkpoint inside Bomi County. A few uniformed men stood alongside the metal gate.

"Let me talk," Dr. Lamin said.

I glanced at Pastor Amos and saw his huge smile disappear. He kept his eyes downcast while the soldiers peered inside. They asked Dr. Lamin a few questions, and he explained our mission and told them that all three vehicles were together. Without another word, they waved us on through.

"It is a *miracle!*" exclaimed the pastor. "God has extended His blessing upon us this day."

Several hours later it became disturbingly evident that there was an unusual amount of activity along the road. People were moving. At first there was only a thin stream of travelers, then more, and finally it seemed there was always someone walking. They had enormous bundles on their heads and carried all they could in their arms. Some pulled small carts or pushed a wheelbarrow.

"Refugees," Dr. Lamin muttered.

"They look terrible!" I said anxiously. "Where do they all come from—and where are they going?"

"I do not know for certain," Dr. Lamin answered, "but I believe they want to enter Monrovia." He sat up suddenly and peered ahead. "I see the Tiene border checkpoint just ahead, Boss."

As we approached the sagging rope strung across the road, a soldier broke away from his group of buddies, sauntered over, and untied the end. "You mus' all go inside an' register," he informed us.

I noticed all of them carried big rifles. Around their chests or waists were belts of ammunition. I didn't like the way they handled their guns—as if they were always ready for something.

As we were getting out of the Defender, I noticed the pastor hanging a piece of cloth in his window. Then he slouched way down in the corner. "Why aren't you coming?" Larry asked. "Why are you hiding?"

"I stay *here!*" he answered somewhat urgently. "I will not leave this place. Go on."

Larry shrugged and hopped out.

We entered the dim office, signed our names, and answered all the questions they asked. The officers in charge were not satisfied. They began asking all kinds of questions about the new Defender. Dr. Lamin looked worried. "You wait for me outside," he said in a low voice, so we went out and waited around the vehicles. At least they offered a bit of shade.

Dr. Lamin conferred long and hard with the officials, hurrying from building to building. We could hear his loud arguments from time to time.

"There is nothing an African official likes more than to argue!" Akin declared. "All they want is money, money, MONEY! If they have a position of any kind, they take full advantage of it."

It was over an hour later when Dr. Lamin finally reappeared, mopping his face. "They wanted money, an' lots of it," he explained as we lurched out of the yard. "I told them we were an NGO an' they dare not harass us or the government will step in. *That* made them think!" and he chuckled in a relieved manner.

Pastor Amos uncurled and stretched his legs. "They didn't even know I was along!" he smiled triumphantly. "Truly God blessed me, and truly He will bless the whole journey."

It was good to get back out on the road, dusty though it was. "Is there still war in Sierra Leone?" Larry asked Pastor Amos. "I mean, are there rebels and soldiers all over the place, like in Monrovia?"

"No, Sierra Leone is at peace," he answered. "Yet it was not always so. It is not a nice story, but I can tell you of the days before the foreign peacekeepers entered my country."

"Yes, please do," we told him.

Pleased at the attention and interest, Pastor Amos drew a long breath. "The rebel soldiers who roamed about the bush were absolutely merciless. They captured anyone who happened to be around and made them stand in long lines. They would say, 'Do you want your hand cut off at the wrist, or do you want it cut off above the elbow? Do you want short sleeve or long sleeve? Or do you want your foot cut off? It is your choice.' The soldiers laughed and joked. The people begged, they cried and screamed, but it did no good. They had to stand and watch all before them get cut, then it was their own turn. Sometimes they cut a hand and a foot, or both hands and feet. Whatever the soldier wanted, he did. Even the baby ma and her baby."

Pastor Amos paused, his dark eyes full of pain. Larry's eyes were like two saucers. I was filled with horror.

"Yes, any fool whim of the soldier, that's what he did," he continued softly. "And no one stopped them. No one could! The people were innocent. They did nothing wrong. They just happened to be in the bush when the soldiers came. Most of them went away bleeding to death. Some hollered and got help in time. But most died some hours later from shock and loss of blood. The soldiers' bare arms and chests were all spattered with the people's blood, but they made jokes and laughed. All through the war the rebel soldiers did this. Now the people who survived are in camps. We will show you."

I found myself wishing we hadn't asked about the times before peace. What kind of man—or beast—could grasp the tiny, fragile hand of a baby in his own, then, while looking into the terrified little face, lay the hand on a wooden block and chop it off . . . toss it into the bloody grass . . . hear the agonized screams of pain . . . see the spurting life-blood . . . *and then do the same to its mother?*

Almost two hours later, Pastor Amos glanced ahead and slowly settled himself deeper into the seat. Soon we were stopped by a very young soldier who manned a twisted wire gate across the road. He looked like a child in a uniform much too big. As he hurried over, he passed his rifle from one hand to the other in the most unprofessional manner. "Ah need jus' a bit' of bread . . . jus' a little bit," he begged.

"We are three—THREE!" Dr. Lamin said, holding up three fingers and pointing back to the other cars. The boy nodded. Dr. Lamin handed him a sandwich and a warm, bruised apple. He snatched it like a starving man and kicked at the end of the wire in passing. It settled down on the road in a small cloud of red dust. The boy leaned his rifle against a tree and unwrapped the sandwich without once looking up.

"If it were only that easy all the time!" the good doctor chuckled.

"It is unbelievable how the Almighty God has blessed this journey!" sang out Pastor Amos, sitting up straighter than ever.

The road became worse and worse as we drove along. Finally, we were creeping, dodging deep potholes the size and depth of an industrial kitchen sink and crossing deep pools of water. Larry would look back to see how Akin was making it through the puddles in his little car. "C'mon, Akin, floor it! Wow, that's deep! He made it, Dad!"

"Another checkpoint ahead!" Wayne called out, and slowly, almost imperceptibly, Pastor Amos shrank to half his size. Larry motioned for me to look and frowned a question with his eyes. I smiled and winked at him.

This time the soldiers were not so docile—and not so hungry. "Your passports!" one of them barked, hoisting his rifle up on his shoulder and holding out his grubby hand. Several more stood closely around, and some approached Akin and Bev behind us.

"This is a matter of principle," Dr. Lamin told him gently but firmly. "We are NGOs in this country an' you mus' let us go! We are here to serve da people—jus' like you. Now let us go. We are three—three together."

The man glared, but Dr. Lamin didn't flinch. "Let us go," he repeated more gently. "We will soon stop at immigration, an' we need time."

Still the man stared. Goosebumps broke out on my skin. I was getting awfully nervous about all those rifles hanging just a few feet away. Pastor Amos was as still as death. The tension mounted.

The soldier looked past Dr. Lamin at Larry, and quick as a wink, Larry saluted. A smile started to erase the anger on the soldier's face. I could see the others relaxing around him. They, too, began to grin.

"Huh, huh, ha!" the man laughed. "A small whi' man soldier, eh? Huh, ha, ha!" He waved us on by, still grinning.

"Sierra Fox Two, just drive on through," Wayne said into his radio.

Pastor Amos let out his breath in a long, quavering sigh. It took a while for him to straighten up this time, but finally, "Oh, God, I *knew* this journey was blessed by you!"

"You're funny!" Larry giggled.

"I believe they jus' wanted money," said Dr. Lamin.

Finally, we reached the border of Sierra Leone. At the guard's instructions, Dr. Lamin went inside to show all the legal vehicle registrations and passports. He came out much later, his face sober. "The registration on this Defender has a problem, Wayne, an' they want forty dollars. There is no dealing with these men!"

"Hey, this is the border—just give it to them," Wayne decided instantly. "You've saved us that much many times over!"

Sierra Leone was different. I could see it in the huge tracts of cleared land that grew heavily with bananas, pineapples, cassava, and sweet potatoes. The people were industriously burning brush and clearing more farms all along the way. Wherever you looked there was a garden of some sort. It was lovely to behold.

"This is sure different from Liberia," I observed. "These people know how to work."

"Yes, Ruth Ann," said Dr. Lamin sadly. "The people of Liberia have no courage—an' less energy. Jus' look what they could be doing!" he exclaimed, waving his arms about.

A couple hours deeper into Sierra Leone, the traffic got heavier. We encountered many UN trucks, and they all had one thing in common—they drove like crazy.

"The Zimmie checkpoint is just ahead," Pastor Amos finally announced. Larry and I both looked at him, but he was grinning with delight and not one bit afraid. "This is an army camp, an' we will be fine," he assured us.

The UN camp was huge. The officers at the checkpoint were professional and abrupt, but Dr. Lamin was just as good. In forty-five minutes we were on our way. The taxis on the road all passed our convoy as if we were standing still. Their wheels bumped madly over the holes and hills in that awful road. They swerved and dodged and careened wildly along—and the passengers just sat there impassively watching the countryside fly by.

"Sierra Fox Two . . . Gulf Five Zero, watch the oncoming

traffic!" Wayne would warn over and over when a wild army truck or taxi would come barreling toward us.

"How do they stay together?" Larry marveled.

"They don't!" Dr. Lamin almost shouted, laughing heartily and pointing at a car alongside the road. Its hood was up and the engine was smoking like a fire pit just quenched with water. "They don't stay together. Ha, ha, ha!"

Right after twilight, a strange white mist rolled up from the road, making it very hard to see, especially when a car came our way. I was chewing my fingernails in the back seat. "We are approaching Bo soon," Pastor Amos stated.

"How soon?" we wanted to know.

"About two hours—maybe three."

"Pastor Amos, 'approaching' means coming near to, like maybe ten minutes away from," I explained. "Three hours is a long time!"

Suddenly, without warning, a white wall of sand bags appeared in the headlights. Wayne braked hard and we swerved wildly around the first pile—then a second one and yet a third. They were staggered so the traffic could drive around them, but what a death trap if you were unaware of them!

"Sierra Fox Two . . . Gulf Five . . . slow down!" Wayne yelled into the radio, and just in time.

"Thanks, Dad!" Bev's voice trembled. "There was no warning of any kind!"

I cried a bit in the darkness, I was so shaken. Why hadn't there been any signs?

The mercies of God are new every morning! Great is thy faithfulness!

Finally, the town of Bo. We drove around and found a seedy motel called Madam Wokie. We unpacked everything since the Defender is not thief proof, carried it up three flights of stairs, and made ready for bed. But not before Dr. Lamin had enjoyed his bowl of rice. "I can eat American food, but it is jus' not like rice," he chuckled.

There were no washcloths and only one towel per room, but we were all too tired to notice the small discomforts. About 2 a.m., some other small discomforts made themselves known. Cockroaches began to invade the room and rustle among the empty food containers in the trash.

"They must be as big as mice," I told Wayne wearily—but he never heard. No cockroach would rob him of his sleep!

To make matters more interesting, a violent rainstorm blew in and made the curtains flap . . . flap . . . flap against the edges of the lumpy bed. Wild blue shadows danced on the opposite wall and tiny drops of rain found their way through the slated window glass.

Sleep? I laughed softly—helplessly.

Oh, Africa—never a dull moment!

May 22

It was still dark this morning when I awoke. Something with sharp, prickly legs scurried along my arm toward my neck. I gave the covers a jerk and bumped my knee hard on the edge of the wooden mattress frame as I climbed out of the cavernous bed. Limping to the door, I ran my hand along the wall to find the light switch—and felt something crawling over my bare feet.

Suppressing a shriek, I found the switch and flipped it on—and watched the cockroaches fleeing in all directions. They hid under our flip-flops and under the bed, beneath the dresser and in the sleeves of the clothes hanging on the edge of the chair. Some of the braver ones sat near the back of the small table, waving their long brittle feelers.

It didn't take us long to clear out of there. We shook everything out carefully before wearing or packing it.

After everyone had assembled in the open-air dining room and eaten a free breakfast of eggs scrambled with green peppers, we were on the road again. It was barely passable. Now the biggest potholes measured two feet across at least. We were forced to crawl along over miles of heavily damaged highway.

A very large cloud of dust moving up behind us disgorged an ancient twelve-passenger van carrying about twenty people. The wheels danced wildly in the potholes while the whole thing swayed like a crazy giraffe. The men on top yelled and waved, grinning widely. I read their dusty logo aloud—"In God We Trust."

Dr. Lamin laughed. "They better trust in God!" he said.

Closer to Freetown, the road became wider and smoother. Helicopters hovered overhead and army vehicles were numerous.

"This place is *crawling* with soldiers," Larry observed.

"About seventeen hundred," Pastor Amos agreed. "Almighty God saw the people had suffered enough. He sent the peacekeepers for relief. Praise Jesus. This *whole trip* has been blessed of my Father."

Freetown is built right along the ocean, and the hills bank sharply up from the beach. Houses are perched all the way to the tops of the hills, but we saw no roads going up.

"They *climb* home," Pastor Amos grinned, his white teeth flashing. "Ah-h-h, it is good to be back. I will never leave again." He rubbed his hands together.

"You have to show us where to go," Wayne told him as we approached the checkpoint near the city.

Pastor Amos leaned forward in his seat, smiling and nodding at the soldiers when they looked his way. After a few general questions, we were waved on.

"You sure aren't scared anymore," Larry stated.

"Me? Scared? I never was!" Pastor Amos countered. "Praise God!"

The streets of Freetown were miserably narrow and high, with crumbling edges and drainage ditches on either side. They sloped steeply down into alleys where children abounded and many families lived. People would look up as we passed and squint against the sun.

"I would say the streets need fixing bad," chuckled Dr. Lamin. "Monrovia is not this bad—not even close."

I agreed. "When I heard how modern Freetown was, I was imagining something more like our cities in Canada," I admitted ruefully. "It's Monrovia all over again, except it's older, busier, and happier. I get the feeling that everyone is celebrating."

"Yes, people speak in terms of before the war or after the war," Pastor Amos said. "Now they are full of happiness."

The marketplace was a seething mass of humanity that made Waterside Market in Monrovia look like a park. We were forced off the road whenever we met another car. Horns honked incessantly and children chattered and laughed and frolicked everywhere, pausing only to stare at us with wide, curious eyes.

After forty-five minutes of maneuvers that would make a jet pilot proud, we came to Amos's fellow pastor's house, where all the necessary introductions and some future plans were made. Our new friend gave some detailed instructions as to where overnight lodging could be found.

"I thank you, my friends," Pastor Amos told us warmly. "It has been a memorable trip—one without incident, and surely blessed by God. This is where I will take leave of you until tomorrow. Praise be to God!"

A bit later we ventured back into the streets to find a place to sleep. Presently, Akin spotted a lone room for rent and radioed us of his intentions to stop for the night. We circled back and the men made plans for the morning. "We will see you tomorrow," he smiled as he helped his little family toward the door. "God bless you."

The next motel was so crowded there was no place to park, so we kept bravely on. Half an hour later we found a darling little guesthouse on the outskirts of town with a bright "VACANCY" sign hanging on the black iron lattice.

"I think this is the place!" Dr. Lamin crowed. "Ruth Ann will have no problem sleeping here."

And I won't. The large rooms are spotlessly clean and cozy with king size beds and hot running water.

"I am so grateful!" I told Wayne happily. "God knew I couldn't handle another night with cockroaches."

May 23

"I have never tasted anything better than these mangos!" Bev exclaimed over breakfast this morning. I had to agree. They were arranged in thick orange slices on our plates—cool, sweet, and utterly tantalizing.

"The coffee is excellent as well," Wayne commented. "But we need to go."

The fresh morning air was alive with the sounds of a million birds warbling. The sky was a clear azure, the trees a brilliant green.

After meeting up with Akin and Pastor Amos, we drove to the main amputee camp in Freetown. The devout Muslims were already at prayer, bowing with faces to the earth over and over.

"They rise before dawn and begin to pray," Pastor Amos said. "They fast often. But they know not the true God."

We parked on a hillside and walked down into the camp. I had dreaded this visit, but nothing could have prepared me for what we saw. People of all ages sat around the doorways or went about their daily duties as best they could. It would have looked like any typical African community—except for the awful fact that they all had missing limbs.

A young man with dark, hopeless eyes welcomed us. "I am Rupert Beh. I will show you the place," he said simply, gesturing with his two stumps that dangled where his arms should have been. Somewhere he had been to school, because his English was flawless.

"There are at least one hundred fifty souls here," he said despairingly as we walked along. "We all need help. Some of the families have children, so they need to go beg in the streets every day. I myself cannot dress without assistance. I cannot eat. I cannot tie my shoes. I cannot even pick something up from the ground." His voice faltered. "I am young—and yet I am useless."

Akin groaned aloud. "It is a serious thing!" he lamented. His strong face was working, trying to hold back the tears.

Dr. Lamin exclaimed and muttered under his breath, his dark face highlighted with sweat. For once he had no words.

Julie stood with ashen face, trying to absorb what she was witnessing.

"The soldiers herded us like goats and made us stand in line," the young man went on. "We begged and screamed and the women cried aloud, but it made no difference. My little brother tried to hold onto my neck, but they grabbed him from me and cut off his foot. He died in much blood, and there was nothing I could do."

Stop! Stop! I wanted to scream. *Let's get out of here!*

Horror settled about me like a stifling blanket. I found myself automatically, unwillingly checking everyone's hands and feet.

A woman lay in the dust in front of a building, both feet missing. A young girl smiled at us shyly, holding up her mutilated stump to shield her eyes from the sun.

The voice of our guide went on. "This happened in 1998. You can see how small that boy must have been when he was cut."

We turned to look where he had indicated. A lad of about six years was leaning against the side of a mud block building, watching us. He had a thick mop of loose curls and a beautiful, sensitive face. When we looked at him, his whole face lit up with a broad smile. He held his arms behind his back.

"He was one of the luckier ones—though they took both hands, he did not bleed to death."

The child giggled and held one stump in front of his mouth to stifle the laughter. "White man. White man," he said clearly.

I felt sick. Julie's eyes swam with sympathy.

Haltingly, the stories came out. The people wanted us to know what had happened to them, even though their eyes clouded with pain at the memories. Again we heard the awful facts that Pastor Amos had told us, except this time we were actually looking at the victims.

"I believe our tormentors actually started to enjoy this mutilation," our guide told us. "Some of the people would go into immediate shock, and literally thousands bled to death. In some cases it took a day or two. If medical help was unavailable, there was no choice. Now we 'fortunate' ones are at the mercy of others once again." He paused and turned to look at us. "I wish I had died," he said softly.

"The government has plans for us," he continued without enthusiasm. "They plan to disperse all the amputee camps and build us our own homes. I am unsure when this will take place, but it really makes no difference to me. There is one thing, though, that I must tell you."

For the first time since we came there was a glimmer of happiness on Rupert's face. "I am a Christian," he said. "If Jesus came today, He could heal us all."

"Praise God!" Akin exclaimed.

"I know, too," continued Rupert, "that someday I will be strong again. I will be whole and have my two hands."

We were all fighting tears. It was hard to turn away from him and from them all. We all felt that maddeningly helpless feeling when you know there is not a thing you can do.

Rupert had reminded us all of that glorious day when the sky will split to reveal the Son of God in all His glory.

The dreadfulness of that amputee camp stayed with me the whole day.

The next place scheduled for assessment was a large displaced persons camp that looked like it had been there for a very long time.

We were given a tour of the whole place and saw that it was an established community. We soon learned that this particular camp administration was annoyed with the NGOs that were currently assisting. They only received twelve kilograms of bulgur wheat per person every month, plus oil, peas, and salt. They wanted rice, sugar, and maybe cornmeal.

Mr. Sengah, the camp administrator, took us to his hut and loudly proclaimed how needy the camp was and how seldom they received used clothing. He was wearing a Tommy Hilfiger hat and designer jeans, and his ample stomach belied his claim of being undernourished.

I looked at the children, who gathered like curious little black woolly sheep, staring at us unashamedly with bright eyes. They looked well fed and decently clothed.

"The government wants us to disperse, an' rainy season is upon us," the man whined.

"Looks like you do well, my man," Dr. Lamin countered. "You have a fresh water spring and your own market an' even a sewing center. You are doing *well*."

Wayne agreed. "Look at the children," he observed. "They look just fine to me."

May 24

We toured more today. Akin wasn't along since it was decided we could cover more territory if he spied out the land by himself, but Pastor Amos had his usual seat in the Cruiser.

One of our stops was at the office of the Freetown health director. Mr. Teah was an eager-faced gentleman with graying hair, a booming voice, and a perpetual smile. He led us up the stairs to his office. It was large and musty, all overlaid with dark wood and furnished with matching chairs. The floor creaked in complaint as we filed in and sat down.

Two more officials quietly entered and took their places opposite us.

Mr. Teah sat and smiled at us for several seconds. We smiled back.

"I am so happy you are here," he began. "So happy that I will overlook the fact that it is a holiday today."

"We are wondering about bringing subsidized medicines into Freetown," Dr. Lamin informed him. "I need all the information you can give us, an' we will go from there. Christian Aid has its own program, an' we will stick to it closely. Jus' so you know."

Mr. Teah leaned forward. "Take us on board," he begged. "We wou' be so happy to join you. We have jus' come out of the war, so there are many needs . We like to have our needs met at once," and he smiled broadly.

We listened politely for several more minutes, then got to our feet to leave. "There's so much more to inform you of," Mr. Teah smiled. "Remember, we like it when things happen fast."

As we pulled out of the lot, Dr. Lamin voiced everyone's thoughts as he commented dryly, "I am sure there is no great need here."

"Tomorrow we leave for Monrovia," Pastor Amos suddenly stated.

"Are you coming along back?" Larry asked in genuine surprise. "I thought you couldn't wait to get back to your home here."

"Yes, if you will permit me," Pastor Amos smiled. "Freetown is nice, but Monrovia has become home. I am certain God will bless the trip."

I looked at Wayne in the rearview mirror. He winked. "You're welcome to come back with us, Amos," he said.

"Thank you, Mr. Wayne," Amos replied. "May God bless you."

19

The Tall White Commander

May 27

We left the next day, as Amos had suggested. Akin decided to stay in Freetown for a few more days to do a more thorough assessment. He wanted to stay and look things over, and perhaps even move to the area.

It was so good to be going home, though "home" was a war-torn town in Liberia. Excitement ran high as we packed and started our journey.

We traversed the same awful roads until we finally came to the town of Bo. There we found a rather nice motel and unpacked everything. Since it was still early in the day, the men decided to look the town over in case we ever had to flee Monrovia.

Meanwhile, black rain clouds began building up in the west with surprising speed. Before we could get back to the motel, the storm broke in all its awesome fury. We were able to pull off the road, but found no shelter. I sat with my face pressed to the window and enjoyed every second of the display.

"I don't think I've ever seen a storm move in so fast," Wayne commented.

It was still pouring when we ran for the shelter of the motel. Long into the black African night, the lightning illuminated our whole room with brilliant, blue-white light—and long after everyone else was asleep I thrilled to the distant thunder. I know I will someday think back with great longing to see such a storm again.

The next morning was fiercely hot. No one felt like talking. There was a subtle threat in the air—a sense of wondering and waiting as we pondered the uncertainties ahead. Would we get through the checkpoints all right? Was war any closer to home?

It was a long, tiring day. Wayne let me drive for several miles so he could rest, but I didn't go fast enough for Dr. Lamin. "You are too slow, Ruth Ann," he chided me. "We will get there too late."

It was four o'clock when we finally reached Kenema. No one wanted to risk the imminent checkpoints in the dark, so we decided to stay for the night. The guesthouse we found had no running water and no screens in the windows, so we had to carry water from the well outside and rely on two small fans to circulate the air.

Dr. Lamin went in search of rice while we took our baths out of a five-gallon bucket.

We ate the delicious rice and drank warm, bottled Fanta out on the verandah as the humid tropical night closed in. Mosquitoes droned around the bare light bulb on the porch. Far away, a night bird cried a lonely *keeakeeakee.*

We awoke around three in the morning to unwelcome silence— the generator had shut off, leaving the room stifling. I breathed deeply to get more oxygen into my lungs.

"I'm burning up," Wayne said. "It's not going to help opening the windows, either." He dressed and hurried out.

Groggily I became aware of something abnormal in the bed. It was like a slow prickling sensation starting at my feet and working its way up. I got out so fast I was dizzy, then turned on the dim light and closely examined the mattress. Meanwhile, my feet and legs began to itch unbearably.

What on earth?

I heard the girls laughing, then Willie and Moses and more voices.

They were all on the porch, fully dressed and looking as if they were ready to leave that very minute. Dr. Lamin, Pastor Amos, Larry, and all the rest were leaning against the porch railing or sitting on the chairs as if it were the most natural thing in the world to be doing at three-thirty in the morning.

"What's going on?" I asked, reaching down to scratch those merciless, stinging bites.

"They must be in your bed too, Mom," Bev said. "I have never been so bit up in all my life."

"We can't see a thing," said Charlotte, "but my legs are all red."

"It's in *our* beds too," said Willie. "What is it, Dr. Lamin? Did you get bit too?"

"Just bed lice," said Dr. Lamin nonchalantly. "This is Africa, you must remember."

The bites were swelling up noticeably and forming little blisters wherever a person scratched. We tried every cream and lotion and salve we had along, but nothing helped.

"It will go away in time," was Dr. Lamin's only comfort. "Kerosene may stop the itch."

The rest of the long, hot night inched by. We were so desperately sleepy that we tried lying on our towels to ward off the lice. Finally, the light quickened and daylight appeared. No one had to be urged out of bed, and in short order we were on the last stretch home.

"There's something different around here," Wayne observed as we drove south. "It looks deserted or something."

"You're right," Pastor Amos agreed nervously. "There is a lack of people in the area. Oh, that God would bless our return as He did our exodus."

The next village we reached was empty. Not even a few chickens scratched around. "Not good, not good," muttered Dr. Lamin, unbuckling his radio. "I will try to reach base. Kilo Alpha. Kilo Alpha. Mike 47," he called into the handset.

We waited anxiously.

"Mike 47. Mike 47," came Curt Kauffman's welcome reply. "Come in, come in."

"We are reaching the first checkpoint. First checkpoint . . . do you copy?"

"Copy loud and clear. News is not good. Soldier activity in your area and near Klay crossing . . . do you copy?"

Dr. Lamin's hand shook. "Copy loud an' clear. We will keep in touch."

"Sierra Fox Two, stay close behind," Wayne told Bev.

"I will. We heard what he said."

Pastor Amos was praying silently. His lips moved, but his eyes remained on the road ahead.

I felt apprehension, but I wasn't really afraid. I tried to envision the host of Syria surrounding the city in Elisha's time and how insignificant it was compared to God's chariots of fire. The mental picture helped. I knew that no matter what happened to us, God was able to deliver. He just might choose not to.

"Checkpoint, Boss," Dr. Lamin said quietly.

"I remember this one," Wayne said. "Sierra Fox Two, drive right on through behind us," he spoke quietly into his radio.

There was a long, rough board across the road with many wicked looking nails protruding from it. Several equally wicked-looking soldiers stood around, and sitting on the ground right close to them was a little girl.

"I will speak," Dr. Lamin said.

We pulled up to the men, and they leaned down and looked into the vehicle. One of them gazed right at Pastor Amos, whose eyes fairly bugged out with terror and whose Adam's apple danced madly.

The man slowly stood up and began firing questions at Dr. Lamin, who answered them all politely and decisively.

I looked at the child, and she met my gaze with dark, vacant eyes. She was dirty and scratched and wore a red bandana, rebel-style, over her hair.

"We wan' you to take da girl," the soldier commanded. "Da muttah is lost, an' she needs a ride to Monrovia. We haven' seen her muttah for a week now."

My heart leaped. What if the mother would come looking for her and she would be gone? Dr. Lamin explained that Christian Aid allowed no passengers, and the man nodded in understanding. He waved us on. I looked back at the forlorn little figure hugging her knees—alone and motherless. "God have mercy," I whispered. I refused to let myself think of that poor young girl at the mercy of those godless men.

Bev drove right on through without looking left or right.

Before long we encountered another checkpoint. "This one wasn't here when we came," said Wayne as we pulled up to the makeshift barrier on the road. A crooked stick was driven into the ground and something round was positioned at a weird angle on top of it.

"Is . . . is that a *skull?*" Larry wondered.

It was. With dark eyeholes and a grotesque, gaping mouth.

"I bet these guys are cannibals," Larry continued fearfully.

"Quiet, Son," Wayne told him.

Dr. Lamin opened the window a crack. "We need a ride. To Monrovia," one of the soldier boys told him. He made short, jerky little movements the whole time he talked. His eyes darted here and there, back to the Cruiser and to us again. "Gimme a ride." Then he said something violently in another language.

Again Dr. Lamin explained the rules. "We would have no room fo' ourselves if we took all of you," he explained. "Let us go, my man," and he pressed a small token into the boy's hand.

"Thank you!" the fellow fairly hollered. "Let 'em go."

The rope was lowered to the ground, and we both pulled through as one vehicle. Bev wasn't taking any chances.

Dr. Lamin lost no time calling base and letting Curt know we were fine. "There are no people aroun' . . . *no people . . .*" he emphasized.

"They're all pouring into Monrovia," Curt answered.

My nerves were getting jumpy. I had never seen a human skull before. "I wonder what horrible fate befell the poor man," I said.

Pastor Amos didn't want to discuss it. His eyes had a strange look that I didn't like.

"Are you going to be okay?" I asked. "Don't you know that nothing can happen to us unless God allows it? Try to enjoy . . ." but he wasn't listening. His eyes stared ahead.

"Klay Junction," Dr. Lamin announced.

We rounded a bend in the road and came upon a huge group of soldiers milling about, holding their tremendous rifles and rocket launchers in their arms.

"Shut your windows!" Wayne yelled to Bev, while we cranked ours up as fast as we could. We drove slowly toward the gate, the tension increasing with every yard.

"Wayne, jus' keep going, jus' drive slow, and do not point anywhere," directed Dr. Lamin unsteadily. He was frightened.

I was totally unprepared for poor Amos's reaction, however. He slid halfway down the seat so he could barely see out and began praying aloud in the most desperate tones I have ever heard.

"Oh, Je-e-sus!" he cried. "Deliver us, I beg you! Bind the power of da' devil, I beg you! Oh, Je-e-esus, save us!" He peeped out the window, and his eyes bulged with fresh terror.

I couldn't help but notice how he resorted to a Liberian accent.

Larry sat like a statue, staring wonderingly at Amos, then at the scene before us.

The soldiers *did* look menacing. We were right in among them. Their eyes were bloodshot and glassy and stared openly as they milled about the Defender. We could see they looked desperately tired—even ill. The sweat glistened on their faces, and their expressions were sullen and fierce.

Their rifles were varied and plentiful. Some of them had two barrels; some had a brass-colored, spear-shaped attachment; some were cut off abruptly with a scope mounted on top. Most of them had large, black bullet clips hanging underneath. Several men carried rocket launchers.

We inched ahead. I felt the beating of my heart in my ears. Dr. Lamin was powerless with fear. All he could do was mop sweat from his neck and face.

We passed the mangled carcass of a burned-out car. Little spirals of smoke rose here and there from the blackened metal. "That car wasn't here before," Wayne said quietly.

I looked around fearfully—and suddenly noticed a very tall white man in army fatigues standing to the left side, waving our vehicles through with short, sharp movements of his arm. Just as suddenly, the tall man turned and disappeared down the embankment. Instantly the soldiers opened the gate.

"Did you see that tall white commander?" I asked breathlessly when we were all safe. No one had.

"Wha' a miracle!" Dr. Lamin exclaimed, smiling faintly. "God is good!" he yelled into his radio to Curt. "We are now approaching Monrovia. We will inform you of conditions when we arrive . . . when we arrive. Over and out."

I'm sure everyone at the CAM base was wondering greatly about Dr. Lamin's fervent, periodic praises over the radio.

Pastor Amos didn't speak. He lifted his arms heavenward and his lips moved in mute thanksgiving. I wondered if he was still thinking that the trip was so "blessed of the Lord." He looked wilted and worn out.

We passed through a small village that was totally deserted. It looked strange and empty—like a ghost town. Not a single person was to be seen anywhere.

"I sure hope that's the last of the soldiers, Dad," Larry said fervently. The words were barely out of his mouth when we came upon a scene that made our blood run cold.

Eight wild and fierce-looking men were standing side by side across the road, their feet planted firmly apart. It was such a shock we hardly knew what to do.

Amos gave a strangled yelp and almost slid under the front seat. "Bandits. Dissidents. Robbers. They kill at random . . ."

"Sierra Fox Two. Don't stop *no matter what*. Keep coming," Wayne told her urgently. "I'm going on through."

We held our breath as we neared that formidable barrier. "Go, go, Wayne," Dr. Lamin hissed through clenched teeth, and Wayne went. Slowly but surely he kept on driving—and at the last second the bandits parted and let us through.

Bev was so close I thought I felt the bumper of her vehicle nudging ours.

Pastor Amos became almost hysterical in his prayers. "Oh, Father God, *Father God*," he moaned.

"Do not point!" instructed Dr. Lamin, as if any of us would dare.

The bandits made a frightening picture with their various tattered T-shirts, their multi-colored shorts, bandanas, and flip-flops. One wore a heavy toque on his head, a gray lined parka, and white jeans. I wondered what hapless victim had yielded such a set of clothing.

I didn't dare look directly at them, but it was hard not to notice the heavy artillery they carried. The young man standing closest to us carried a long, slim weapon that tapered down to a wicked-looking knife. His gaze was lethal.

"Dad! That was close—did you see all their guns?" Larry exclaimed.

"Sure did. I wouldn't want to tangle with those guys."

"We're past them now—you can sit up," Larry told Pastor Amos matter-of-factly.

The pastor's face worked. "This was a se-e-erious thing," he marveled after composing himself. "If those men want something and you refuse to give it . . ."

"Sierra Fox, Sierra Fox," the radio barked.

"Go ahead, Sierra Fox Two."

Relief dripped from Wayne's voice as he talked. "We made it through the bandits!" he shouted jubilantly, without the formalities of names. "Praise God we made it! Over and out." He whipped out his towel and wiped his face.

An hour and two checkpoints later, we pulled into Monrovia. How sweet the sight of the CAM base! How warm the welcomes from our friends!

Pastor Amos slipped away so hurriedly that we hardly noticed his departure. I wonder if we will ever see him again.

We didn't even bother to unpack. Weariness drove us to bed. Tomorrow will be another day, but meanwhile, the angels of God have been very close.

May 31

This afternoon, Wayne asked me to come with him and Pastor George Wonlon to look at the new Sawegbeh displaced camp.

When we got there, we could hardly drive up to the building. Great masses of dirty, hungry people sat around, looking as if it didn't matter whether they lived or died. Many, many children lay on the ground, sleeping soundly, and it was only mid-afternoon. Most of the people there were from the Klay area. No wonder the villages were deserted.

I have never seen such quiet despair. These people had been driven from their homes with nothing but what they could carry on their heads. They were scared and hungry and exhausted. They stood or sat quietly, their faces mirroring their pain. It was haunting.

"I'm afraid, dear, that the war just may come," Wayne said soberly as we drove away. "These men said the soldiers have no mercy, especially on white men."

"What did you decide to do?" I asked.

"We'll be there first thing in the morning," Wayne replied. "They're in bad shape—and there are lots of little children."

My heart swelled with thankfulness at the thought of the CAM trucks pulling into the camp in the early morning and unloading precious bags of food. I could see the people dusting off their dented little kettles and building small fires to cook the rice. I felt like singing.

June 2

Crocodile John arrived here yesterday just before church. He reported that thousands of starving people were pouring into Totata.

"Where are your crocodiles?" Willie wondered.

John looked at the floor. "Dead," he said simply. "Ah lef' dem in da cage, an' da fierce red mission ants attacked. In da mornin' dey was half eaten—an' still alive."

"Horrors!" said Willie. "There goes all your profit for your zinc."

"God will make a way," John told him softly.

Pastor Mervin's sermon was on forgiveness. The stress of carrying a grudge in one's heart passes on to all those nearest and dearest to you. We sang "By a Crowd of Worshippers," as usual.

The people love the message and the hope offered in those lyrics.

We were invited to Pastor Amos's house for a snack this afternoon. It was around four o'clock when we found Amos's house near Barnersville—just beating an approaching storm. After meeting Amos's wife and little girl, we went outside to watch a bit. The community people were hustling to fill containers and the children were having their baths under the drainpipes. The whole world was gray with the driving downpour.

Mrs. Amos had fixed jalapeno pepper chicken, fried plantains, and french fried potatoes. "This is just a snack," Pastor Amos told us after we were seated in their small living room. "When a person serves rice, then it is considered a meal."

The food was so hot that our fingers burned from holding the chicken. At the first bite, our mouths and throats burned like fire and our eyes watered. Even Princess didn't finish her chicken.

Amos sat across from us and urged us to eat. Thankfully, the darkness of the storm and the dim lantern kept our hosts from seeing our discomfort.

When they were sure we actually didn't want any more food, Pastor Amos and his wife helped gather our plates.

"I must tell you people something," he began. "I have asked around and it has been confirmed that those men across the road were indeed the feared dissidents. They stop people at gunpoint, rob them, and harm the women. Let us praise God that He brought us safely through."

"There is awesome power in prayer," Wayne answered, "and you did your share of it for us. Thank you, Pastor."

Pastor Amos brought out his keyboard, and we sang lovely old hymns for an hour or so. It was so cozy in that little room, with the wind and rain buffeting the house and the flickering lantern casting little shadows on the walls. The beautiful words of the songs filled us with joy.

"We have a curfew, Amos—we must go," Wayne announced finally. "We sure enjoyed your hospitality."

"Ah, God is good!" Pastor Amos responded. "Let us praise the Lord!"

20

Twins in the Family

June 7

While walking home from the office today, I passed a very tall, skinny white man with a great bush of brown hair and sad brown eyes. There was something vaguely familiar about the way he walked. He nodded his head in a friendly "hello" and passed by on the other side of the street.

He must be new in these parts. He certainly isn't Liberian.

This afternoon, just before the CAM office closed, a very distraught family brought a set of twin boys to the gate. The mother, a woman named Eva, had hemorrhaged to death soon after they were born, and their father and a sister-in-law had brought them in all the way from River Cess, a city along the coast about a hundred miles southeast of Monrovia. The babies had had nothing but water from a spoon in the four days since they were born.

Something about the tiny babies tugged at Wayne's heart. "Has Julie seen them yet?" he asked Willie.

"I don't think so."

"Well, tell her to come quickly."

Just as Julie approached, one baby fainted and started turning an awful grayish-blue. Julie grabbed the baby and put it over her shoulder, patting its tiny back. Slowly, faintly, the child began breathing again.

"We have to get to the hospital right now!" Julie cried.

Meanwhile, Willie had made a fast exit, saying, "I don't want to see this." He was sure the baby was dying.

Julie and Evelyn got all excited over the situation. They unwrapped the two baby layettes that happened to be in the office and put them to good use. Soon those two little babies were in St. Joseph's Hospital. Since the nursery had no extra bottles, the ones in the layettes became life-savers.

I wonder which sewing circle in America made those particular layette bundles. I wish they could see the drama unfolding across the ocean in West Africa and realize what precious things those bundles are.

When Wayne got home from work and told us the story, it didn't take Charlotte and me long to decide that we wanted to go to St. Joseph's Hospital immediately. We just *had* to find out how Julie and Evelyn were making out with the newest little people in our lives. We found the hospital old and ill-equipped, but cleaner than I expected. There was no electricity, so the halls and rooms were getting dark.

"How can they run any machines with no current?" Charlotte wondered.

"They probably have it for a few hours at a certain time," Wayne guessed.

We were fascinated with the twins—perfect little boys. They weighed about four pounds each, with dear little wrinkly faces, perfect hands, and lots of black hair.

"Oh-h-h, they're cute!" Charlotte and I said in unison.

"Their names are Oliver and Alosious Dixon," Julie told us. "This is their father, Isaac Dixon, and their Aunt Musu, and their cousin Susanna."

Dr. Lamin had supplied a soy formula, so they had been fed and were sleeping soundly. I had a good chance to look around the intensive care unit.

It was bare, unsanitary, and full of suffering children. The little boy next to Oliver's crib had a stomach as big as a football, arms like a man's thumb, and legs like a measuring ruler. I had to look twice to see if I was seeing right.

"His name is Amos and his mom is Agutta," Julie said. "He needs spleen surgery and there's no blood available. He's been here for three weeks, Mom. Imagine! The poor little guy."

The mother looked desperate. She motioned with her hands toward her suffering boy and begged pitifully. "Amos needs blood. No blood. Amos will die soon."

"Where should I get blood from?" I asked her.

"Ah don' know. Please! He's dying!"

"I'll see what I can do," I promised, wracking my brain for a solution.

I stood by the crib and looked down at the child. His eyes met mine unwaveringly and followed my every move. They were like huge black pools of misery in his wasted little face.

"Muttah, ah *beg* you," the mother pleaded again, with eyes as miserable as those of her son.

"Where is his father?" I asked.

"Away," and she gestured with her hand.

Across the room, another beautiful, chubby baby girl fought for her life. She choked dreadfully and wheezed and sputtered until I was half out of breath watching her. The veins bulged on her temples and along her neck, and her eyes looked frantic.

"She has fluid in her lungs," Evelyn said.

A nurse wheeled in a large tank that looked just like a propane tank—tall, gray, and chipped all over. Liquid oxygen bubbled merrily into the scarred plastic dome on top. The nurse wiped off the end of the plastic tube with a cotton ball and stuck it right down the baby girl's nose.

"She got it the first time," Evelyn observed. "I sure hope these guys don't ever need oxygen, though. How much do you think we should feed them, Ruth Ann?"

"I would give them as much as they'll drink for now," I answered. "It will probably only be a few tablespoons at a time."

I can see those babies have her wrapped right around their

little fingers—and she's not the only one.

"Think we could take care of one of those babies?" I asked Wayne on the way home. "I'm sure Evelyn will want one."

"We could easily handle it," Charlotte added hopefully. "They're just too cute, Dad."

"We'll see what happens," he said.

June 8

Bev, Julie, and Charlotte visited the hospital this morning to see how the little twins were doing.

They found the babies doing well. Their Aunt Musu is taking good care of them, and their father hangs around the hospital all the time. He wonders who will care for them when they leave the hospital, and I know some girls who would love to.

After seeing Agutta quietly weeping again this morning for her poor little Amos, and seeing the distraught father as well, Bev and Julie decided then and there to have their blood types checked out in case they would match. The happy father went down to the lab with them. Everyone was very excited to find out that Julie has the blood type anyone can use, and Bev has the same type as Amos.

In no time, with no further testing or questions, the lab technicians began drawing blood. They had Julie sit down and did a good job of finding a vein and collecting the blood. Then Bev sat down for her turn. She almost immediately felt light-headed, but the feeling passed.

Julie, however, took one look at Bev's ashen face and fainted right on the spot. Instantly, the lab turned chaotic. The staff was in a frenzy and ran for the wheelchair. Amos's bewildered father asked Charlotte, "Wha' happen? Wha' happen?"

After several minutes, Julie opened her eyes and, finding herself on the floor, began to laugh. Then everybody relaxed, and they all laughed together.

The life-giving blood is safely stored. That's all that really matters. Agutta is so happy she is singing aloud.

Tonight, we all had to go peek at those darling twins again. Oliver seems to have a constant wheeze; I hope it's not too serious. They have to be some of the dearest babies I've ever seen.

When we arrived home, a lady and her teenage daughter who knew Conrad and Katy Swartzentruber were waiting at the gate . She had a sack of fruit under one arm and a big gray rooster under the other. She said her name was Ellen.

"I jus' want to co' meet you, Missie," she told me softly after we had invited them in to sit down. "Ah knew Conra' an Katy very well. They helped me wi' a laundry business when my husban' died. Christian Aid has kept me an' my ten children alive. Now ah kin sen' dem to school an' feed dem all. Dis is my daughter. Dis rooster is fo' you."

"Thank you! This will make good soup," Wayne said to Ellen. "I'll just let it go outside for now."

June 9

That rooster began crowing hours before dawn and didn't stop until we were all awake. Princess had heard lots of roosters in her life, so she didn't mind it at all, but I'm determined he has to go. I see he roosted on the new motorbike seat all night.

Little Oliver has pneumonia, so they put him on intravenous antibiotics. I had to force myself to stop thinking about those two little boys in the hospital, or I wouldn't have heard a word of Pastor Mervin's sermon. He spoke on the hope of the Christian. It was perfect for the poor man who recently approached one of the CAM staff in tears and poured out his frustrations in utter despair and told how he planned to kill himself.

Today, he was sitting under the sound of the Gospel, drinking in every word.

June 10

Today was the grand opening of Dr. Lamin's clinic in Paynesville. The program was to begin at ten o'clock, but we all knew that meant at least noon, so we didn't hurry too much.

It was so exciting to tour that old, rundown building which had been transformed with some cement, paint, and tile—and lots of elbow grease. Dr. Lamin had chairs set up in the waiting room, which was actually a lean-to off the main building.

Mr. Seah was the emcee, Wayne was scheduled for remarks, and Iddo came just in time to cut the ribbon of tissue paper across the doorway.

There is a nice-sized delivery room and an adjoining room for observation of new mothers, two examination rooms, a small office, and a well-stocked pharmacy. Prescriptions will be handed through the window. The separate bathrooms are outside and not far away.

"It is really the nicest little clinic in the whole country!" I told a beaming Dr. Lamin.

The sky was showing dark signs of a heavy rain by the time the program ended. Some of us offered to help with the meal, but it was evident the cooks had everything under control. The whole kitchen was a whirlwind of activity, and from that melee came heaping plates of rice with potato greens, potato salad, Sis Bea's cake, and Fanta to drink. Everyone ate quickly, with one eye on the approaching storm. Varnee ran for his bike and left in a great hurry.

Outside the back door, several ladies were on their knees in the dirt, washing the plastic bowls as fast as they could. Scrawny little neighbor urchins hung around just out of reach, their eyes begging for a bite to eat. Bev and I saw to it that some of the skinniest got the leftovers from the feast. One little girl sank down along the wall and ate quickly, enjoying every morsel.

Meanwhile, a great storm was rolling in. When the driving wind announced the rain, we all scrambled for the vehicles—just in time. It came in torrents that defied the windshield wipers and created instant rivers along the footpaths and a layer of water on the highway. We had to slow down to a crawl until the worst was over.

As soon as we got home, we went to the hospital to pick up little Alosious, who was well enough to be released.

Oliver seems to be holding his own, and Curt said he is much better than yesterday. He is getting oxygen and they feed him through his nose. I just hope the little guy pulls through.

When we got home, we all had to take turns holding Alosious. He has straight black hair that waves when it's wet, and he makes the funniest little screwed up faces.

I bathed him in the kitchen sink and shampooed his dear little head. He was so tiny in my hands, I hardly knew how to handle him. Everyone hovered around and offered little bits of advice.

"He looks so funny!" Larry laughed. "Look how he hangs on to you."

"His arms are like my finger," Wayne said, coming in on the scene. "What's that tied around his waist?"

"It keeps evil spirits away," Toney George said darkly. "Better leave it on."

Bev gave me a pair of scissors from the drawer. "Cut and pray! Cut and pray!" Toney George cried suddenly. I ignored his fears and cut the thing off.

I nearly lost him in the soft towel when I wrapped him up. Only his tiny annoyed face peeked out. I dried him gently and put lotion all over his bony little frame.

"What a doll!" the girls said when he was all dressed and wrapped and had his curls combed. "What a perfect doll!"

We are thankful for CAM's Special Needs program that makes it possible to give these little ones a chance at life.

Julie is praising God for the "Sight for Princess" funds coming in. A youth group in Ohio is donating $1,000 for the surgery. Jessie Hein, a little neighbor girl back in Alberta, made lots of homemade suckers to sell and raised over $300! She was thrilled, and so are we. Just maybe Princess will be able to see again.

June 12

At three o'clock this morning we were awakened by the most unearthly yowls right below our window. Sam, the night security, was screaming, "Rogue! Rogue!" in an eerie, high-pitched voice of anger and fear. He dashed to the back where a man crouched in the generator shed. He chased him up the wall, grabbed his pants, and tried to bite him as he scrambled over. Sam told us the man went for a knife, so he let him go. We think he was grabbing for his jeans!

Anyway, Sam became an instant hero. The would-be thief had cut all the barbed wires along the top of the back wall, and when Sam's patrol had taken him to the front, he had sneaked inside.

"If any more rogues come over, call them in and I'll cook them some rice," I told Harris, the other security guard.

"Oh-h-h, no-o-o, Ma'am," he said, laughing. "Ah couldn'!"

Alosious has been here for two days, and we're all in love with him. Princess feels all over his tiny face so gently, and he opens his mouth and follows her fingers, thinking she wants to feed him. He doesn't have the lusty cry that Oliver has, though. He seems weaker.

This morning, Wayne radioed for me to come along to the new Sawegbeh displaced camp to give Akin a microphone. He simply can't yell anymore. I jump at the chance to go anywhere with my husband; it happens too infrequently for my liking. I knew the baby would be fine in Bev's care, so we were soon lurching along the picturesque cow path leading to the camp. It was raining, and the potholes were full of water. It was like driving along a rock-hard riverbed that has been washed and eroded away for years.

As we crested the little rise before the camp, we could see all the thousands of stick frames that had sprung up overnight.

We spied the distribution truck backed up to a sea of umbrellas. Akin and his helpers were busy distributing. People stood huddled in groups of four and five, trying to keep dry. Hundreds of faces peered out from under the umbrellas—hungry, expectant faces. The water poured off the edges of the umbrellas and seeped down the backs of their necks—and still they were smiling at Akin's antics. He was pretending he was an immigration officer in charge of would-be passengers of a huge jet.

"Final flight for June the fourth!" he roared through the microphone, startling everyone, including himself. "If you hear your name, come forward! You cannot board without a ticket!"

He grinned happily. "This works just fine."

We climbed up into the back of the truck to watch a bit. A young man handed in an old ticket. "This plane left a long time ago," Akin told him. "It is probably in Jerusalem by now."

Turning to us he asked, "Would you help sign tickets? Then we can all go home earlier." We were happy to oblige.

There were 1,920 bags of food to deliver, and they dwindled very slowly. Only one or two of the people said, "Thank you," but we didn't mind—their eyes said it all.

"Next flight!" shouted Akin, and read a whole list of names at once. Then he leaned back against the side of the truck, very unlike himself.

"What have you eaten today?" Wayne asked on impulse.

"Nothing," he replied, and we discovered that his whole crew had missed lunch. They were very hungry and thirsty.

"Something has to be done about this," Wayne decided immediately.

Finally, the last bags were handed out. "I thank you once again," Akin told us gallantly. "I have to have a little humor on the job. You do not mind?"

"Not at all," we assured him. "You do well."

"I cannot blame the people for getting anxious," he continued. "They have children to feed. But order is a must."

Little Oliver is home from the hospital and has moved in at Curt and Evelyn's house, along with his Aunt Susanna. I have to marvel when I see how things are working out.

21

Place of Suffering

What an exhausting day! We went grocery shopping this morning on Benson Street—Wayne, Charlotte, Larry, and I. I have learned to enjoy picking out the produce and leaving Wayne to haggle about the price.

When we were finished, Wayne discovered his keys were missing. I was sure someone had pulled them out of his pocket, as they have a long leather strap attached.

Wayne has a second set on his key ring, so we just got in and drove away. We drove around a little, praying that we could find those keys somehow, because all of Monrovia knows CAM's vehicles and we would be forced to replace the locks.

We stopped to park a little farther up on Benson Street, and a man came hurrying up. He was dirty, ragged, and barefoot, with a meager set of teeth and long, wild dreadlocks.

"I'll give you something if you bring those keys," Wayne said without pretense.

The man feigned surprise. "I haven' seen no keys, bu' ah kin look," he offered, and left in a hurry.

Another man hurried up. "You lookin' fo' somethin'?" he asked. "Ah saw some boys wi' a set of keys, jus' playin' aroun'."

"Yeah, sure," Wayne answered. "Now get me those keys!"

"You gi' me twenty dollah?" he asked.

"What should we do?" Wayne wondered. "It will cost a whole lot more than that to replace these locks. Okay, it's a deal. Hurry!"

In two minutes the first man was back with the keys. Then the second one arrived, breathless, and the fight was on.

"No money till I have the keys!" Wayne shouted. They both reached in the window, trying to grab the twenty-dollar bill.

I was getting scared. Wayne grabbed the keys, thrust the money into the second man's hand, and drove away.

"That was one expensive shopping trip," Wayne muttered. "That guy's a con-man—he has kids steal for him. I'm sure of it!"

As soon as we entered the house, I saw that something was *very* wrong with Alosious. He lay limp as a rag in Beverly's arms. His dear little eyes looked like burned holes in a blanket, all sunken and bluish and hollow. The soft spot on his head had caved way in.

We packed a little suitcase with some formula and the layette we had gotten from the office. There were two bottles, two receiving blankets, two dear little garments, booties, socks, diapers and pins, powder, washcloths, and a small bottle of baby lotion.

"Mom, I am so scared," Bev said tearfully, as she and Julie and I drove back to St. Joseph's Hospital. "If he would die now, I just couldn't handle it."

It had started to rain. Things suddenly looked gray and dreary— our baby was in danger!

As I stood by that hospital bed in the emergency unit, my feelings were as turbulent as the storm outside. I wracked my brain. Was there something we could have done differently?

I thought he had been eating a bit more, but he had been fussy during the night. Even the re-hydration salts hadn't stopped the milk from going right through him. Guilt washed over me like a wave.

Now his cry was faint and weak—not unlike a lost kitten's pitiful meow.

No one seemed a bit concerned. The doctor wrote and wrote and wrote some more, firing questions at Julie all the while.

I couldn't go near while they started the IV. His cry was so pitiful I had to stop my ears. Finally, we were transferred to the infant ward upstairs. It was very crowded, and all but two small cribs were full.

"At least we're in the corner of the room," Bev said thankfully. "Here comes the doctor again."

"Someone mus' stay for the night," the doctor told us. "We have no staff to care for him, and he mus' eat every two hours. I am changing his formula immediately. Did you boil all the water for at least four minutes?"

"No, we didn't," I said miserably, trying to swallow the awful lump in my throat. "I thought our water was pure."

"Not pure enough!" he said, studying me for a minute. Then . . . "Do you want to see a child who is *really* bad off? Come!"

We didn't want to, but he was already leading the way. We didn't like to leave Alosious for even a minute.

"His name is Mumadee," said the doctor as we approached the bedside of a small boy about three years old. He lay on a blood-stained sheet, his poor little arms thrown up above his head. His skin was coming off in pieces, like the skin of a burn victim. Bloody patches alternated everywhere on his torn little body where infection had set in. One eye had fallen out and the socket was covered with a plastic patch.

We gazed in horror. "This is a result of malnutrition," the doctor explained softly. "He doesn't have a chance."

Oh God, have mercy.

Julie offered to stay overnight, but I hated to see her stay alone, with no place to sleep. "You need to rest, Mom," she said comfortingly. "Don't worry about me. I'll be fine. Look at all these mothers in here. I'm going to make some new friends!"

June 17

Weeping may endure for a night, but joy cometh in the morning!

Wayne drove me to the hospital this morning. We left early because we knew Julie would be really tired. The sun was bright and the day beautiful. I hated to miss church, but I knew God understood.

Two women sat by Mumadee's bedside. One cried softly. Maybe today the angels will come for him.

Alosious is better. The precious liquids have rounded out his dear little face once again, and the soft spot in his head is no longer caved in.

"Maybe they'll let him come home tonight," Wayne said hopefully. "He looks much better."

Julie was exhausted. "I couldn't sleep," she said. "The floor is too hard, and Agutta and I just visited most of the night. And I had to feed this little fritz every two hours. There are some really nice ladies here, but just don't be too upset by what you see—this is *Africa,* Mom. The nurses on duty today are Patience and Mema, and they're really nice. See you tonight!"

There was a chorus of "G'bye, Julie!" from every direction. "You will co' back?"

"I'll be back tonight if the baby doesn't come home," she promised.

I arranged my bags at the foot of the tiny crib and put my box of assorted *Seed of Truth* and *Pathway* papers underneath it.

I was aware of many pairs of eyes watching every move I made. Almost every bed in the room was occupied except for the corner one next to me and one more a few beds down. Some of the children lay as still as death with tubes coming out of their noses. Others sat in their cribs or on their mothers' laps. All the women grew quiet for a time, but when I smiled at them they thawed out and began visiting again. I was glad.

"You Julie's ma?" they asked.

"I sure am!"

Agutta still sat by Amos's bed, a diligent picture of devoted motherhood. She held a raggedy old Bible, which she had been reading to Amos. She gave me a tired smile. "Julie is a fine girl—a *fine one!*" she repeated.

I smiled down at Amos. "How are *you?*" I asked, taking his hand. It was burning hot.

"Amos needs one more pint of blood—just one more fo' the surgery," his mother told me when I wondered what was happening.

"Agutta, try and get some sleep, or you'll be in here *with* Amos," I told her. I noticed how gaunt and thin she was. Her cheekbones protruded sharply, and I could see the outline of her jaw. Her clothes hung like a loose sack over her sparse frame.

What a patient, caring mother she was! Day after weary day, for over a month, she had scarcely left her child's bedside.

"I brought Amos some juice," I whispered to her so no one else would hear. "Give me your bag, and I'll put it in."

The orange juice was still cold, so she turned her back and poured a little bit into her cup. She held it to the child's lips. His eyes widened with wonder and delight as he sipped the cool liquid.

"More, Mam," he squeaked hoarsely. She gave him a tiny bit more.

"Take some yourself," I urged. She hesitated, weighing in her mind whether she should drink some of his juice. Then she poured out about a tablespoon and drank it, smacking her lips.

"It is *good!*" she said happily. "Amos has a cough, so they're waiting to do the surgery," she added.

I couldn't imagine his cough getting better with all that pressure on his lungs. His belly was huge! Every breath he took was labored. His cheeks burned with fever.

A nurse came over to me. "I will need $40 Liberian for the drip," she said.

"No problem. Are you Patience?"

"Yes."

"This IV tape is too tight," I told her as I fished the money out of my handbag. "Look how blue his hand is."

"I will fix it righ' now," she said, and went to get the supplies.

Minutes later, Doctor Saah himself brought me the change. "The child is doing well," he said. "Any questions?"

"Can he come home?"

He laughed. "Not so fas' . . . not so fas'. We mus' make sure."

I changed Alosious and prepared some formula with the water the nurse gave me. He was awake and alert, and those dear dark eyes of his looked at me as if he knew exactly who I was.

A lady came in to visit with a child in tow. Patience was

incensed. "I am surprised that security let you in here," she said sharply. "Take the child out! Shoo! There is disease in here!"

The lady glanced around fearfully and almost ran out the door.

Out in the hall, a woman started chanting a low, undulating song. More voices joined in, then Patience started clapping and swaying and singing "What a Mighty God We Serve!" in a very strong voice.

Hadn't they read the "Quiet!" sign above the ICU door?

Soon it seemed everyone was having a devotional period, singing and clapping and praising the Lord. One of the lady preachers had a short sermon right there in the hall. Some of the singing was actually pretty! If these poor ladies couldn't go to church, let them sing. I sure didn't mind.

Cleanup was a snap for the janitor. He swept that whole room in half a minute, not bothering to sweep under the beds or chairs. He squirted some fluid all over the floor with great sweeping motions and spread it all over with a waxing brush. Done!

I was coming back in with another bottle when I saw him push the pile of trash all the way down the hall in front of the broom in one long sweep, smash the end on the floor several times to dislodge the dirt, and step on all the hair and string it had collected along the way.

As Alosious slept, I hovered close so the mosquitoes couldn't get to him. They were everywhere. They hung under the beds, up on the ceiling, and on the damp walls. They whined around my face and legs—small, deadly, and hard to swat. I was half sick with fear that one would bite Alosious and give him malaria. He wouldn't have a chance.

Cobwebs hung in the corners of the room. Occasionally, I spotted a certain evil-looking species of spider, big and jumpy and black—horrid creatures. I nearly panicked when one came right into Alosious's crib.

"Please get that spider!" I begged Agutta. She laughed and complied.

The women looked at me with amusement and pity in their glances. *What a strange woman!*

Baby cockroaches ran along the edges of the floor all day. I knew without asking that the big ones came out at night.

All day the sky wept, but my heart rejoiced at the improvement in Alosious. Once in a while he gave a small jerk, but I decided it was nothing to worry about. My mind traveled back to the circumstances surrounding the twins' birth. Oliver had been born first, and for eleven hours the poor child had lain naked on the bare ground until Alosious was born. No wonder he had gotten pneumonia.

The wicked plan had been to let both babies die, since they were twins and held an evil curse. These people actually believe that one twin is conceived by an evil spirit and the other by a human father. Since you can't possibly know which is which, you just let both babies die a slow death by starvation, or get eaten by the ants, which would have been the case with Oliver and Alosious.

I couldn't bear to think about it. I lifted the sleeping baby out of the crib and held him as tightly as I dared. He smiled in his sleep.

It was a pleasure to care for him. Meanwhile, I had plenty of time to look around.

I noticed the dark tattered rags the other mothers used for diapers. A thin cotton lapa served for a blanket, even if the child was shivering with malaria. Instead of private stainless steel nightstands, everyone had his belongings in a little plastic bag beside the bed. There was no hot water to wash out the bottles unless the kitchen happened to be boiling water for tea.

Several times today, Patience came to take Alosious's vital signs. She would fish a thermometer out of her pocket and stick it under his arm, singing "Oh, Beulah Land" or "Glory, Glory Hallelujah!" the whole time she counted his pulse. How accurate was *that*?

There is a terrible smell of urine—and worse—permeating the nurses' station and hallway just outside the ICU. The washrooms are pathetic. Neither commode has a seat or a lid on the tank, and nothing to flush with except a wire sticking up from the tank. There is only water at certain times in the day, as well as electricity, so the washroom is semi-dark. Water stands on the floor from the showers, which are nothing more than a cold trickle. Wet diapers

213

are draped over all the doors and everywhere else, creating a powerful ammonia stench. There are no privacy curtains anywhere.

I realize much of this can't be helped. Who should fix all this stuff? Who can buy cleaners and disinfectants and baby bottles and a washing machine to wash the diapers and bedding? Who can afford to do *anything?*

Around ten o'clock, a breakfast of cooked cornmeal and shortcake was served. Agutta pulled out a tiny bag of powdered milk and stirred it into hers before she ate it.

Hawa, the beautiful, fair-skinned young woman next to us, fed her chubby little baby girl most of hers.

"Is your baby better?" I asked her, trying to start a conversation. The baby certainly looked fine to me, adorable, dimpled, and black-eyed.

"She is much better. She had malaria, but she kin go home fo' a long time already."

"Then why are you still here?"

"No money to go," she admitted softly. "Ah can't go . . . "

"You mean you have to stay until the bill is paid?"

"Yes, Muttah."

"Ah kin read," she said shyly when she saw my stack of *Pathway* papers.

"Why, of course!" I answered eagerly, "I have a lot more, if anyone else is interested."

How satisfying it is now to see all those heads bent intently over those wonderful magazines!

Right after breakfast, the visitors started coming. I am convinced they have nothing else to do, so they just come to wile away their time at the local hospital. They walked around the room from crib to crib, sometimes draping their arms over the crib and staring intently for several minutes. Worse yet, they reach over and touch the sick children's faces and ask all kinds of questions about each child.

"A baby like this has no resistance," Patience reminded me. I decided immediately that we would hold Alosious during visiting hours, and no one would touch him.

About mid-afternoon, the air was rent with a blood-curdling scream, followed by more shrieks and wails and moans. I felt the chills go up and down my spine. The sounds were primeval in their intensity.

"A child has died," someone whispered loudly.

It was Mumadee, the little sufferer with the flaking skin.

Praise Jesus! I rejoiced quietly. Imagine the shock of joy he received when the angels came for him.

Meanwhile, the wailing went on and on until I thought I couldn't handle another shriek. The mother and another woman lay on the floor in the hall banging their feet against the concrete. People walked by as if they weren't there, and only a few showed sympathy. The nurses were obviously used to such scenes.

Everyone except me calmly went about their business. I was mesmerized.

Patience came to start a new IV for Alosious. For some reason the other one had quit working. I can't stand to hear him cry, so I left for a minute. The wailing in the hallway reached a tremendous crescendo, then stopped just as fast as it had begun. The women got up, straightened their dresses, and went on their way. I was actually trembling when they brought Alosious back.

Blessed quietness, I told myself. I gathered him into my arms and rewrapped him carefully. He was still whimpering. I fed him some formula and rocked him to sleep.

Dinner was served—a small bowl of rice with peanut soup—but I could not eat. I went out to the hall and gave mine to Hawa, who enjoyed every morsel.

Another commotion began in the next room. Mumadee's father had arrived. Immediately he began screaming and yelling at the top of his lungs. "Ah want to carry the chil' home, an' you say *no!* Ah will naw pay! Ah will jus' go righ' now!"

While he screamed, I was thinking, *Thank you, Jesus, that the child is safe*. It was all so horrible. I was relieved when the distraught man finally quit bellowing. Hadn't he read the sign?

Things had barely quieted down when more wild screams reached our ears—from the street this time. All the women hurried to the window. Through the dirty windowpane, I could make out a woman thrashing and wailing on the wet sidewalk. *Another death.*

Amid the confusion, Nurse Mema calmly appeared to take Alosious's vital signs. She scribbled them onto a piece of cardboard ripped from the edge of a box. She then changed Amos's catheter and kicked the bag back under his bed.

Throughout the day I listened to some of the women's stories about their children. One dear little fellow from Lofa County has a shattered shoulder where a bullet struck him, but they have no funds for surgery. This means he will lose the use of his right arm.

Special Needs Fund, I thought.

A baby named Hunee is losing her sight due to measles. She cries all the time unless she's nursing, but she is just skin and bones. Her mother asked for some baby clothes. We have lots of those. I'll bring some tomorrow.

Little Calle is so thin she can't sit up. Her mother is just as thin. I think they're both starving. I see the nurses give them food a bit oftener than the rest. The father came in and looked at Calle, then sat there for a long time. He never spoke or even glanced at the mother, who sat in the chair and gazed straight ahead, as if he weren't there. Dr. Saah mentioned something about her not being competent, so there's something wrong. Maybe she's dumb or deaf.

One father came in twice today. He sat and held his little Blessing and visited with the mother and laughed with them both. It was wonderful to see.

One more father showed up just before visiting hours ended. He was young, about sixteen, the perfect age for Chaka, who is only fifteen. They acted like two children, which they are, but at least he comes to visit. Their little boy has a skin infection caused by dog or cat hookworms, which are picked up by walking barefoot through moist sand.

This evening, my whole family and Esther came in to pick me up. Esther was being tested to see if her blood was a match for Amos.

"I offered to give blood too," Willie told me, "but they said I had to be twenty years old. The girls aren't that old!"

They all fussed over Alosious while Julie stashed her bulging bags under the bed. I knew someone would benefit tonight.

"He hardly cried at all today . . . I wish he would," I told Julie, and reminded her to feed him often.

"Oliver is sure doing well," she said. "He's got a funny wheeze, but he's gaining weight like everything. Evelyn just loves him."

On the way out we met the lab technician. He staggered a bit, then steadied himself against the wall, hiccoughing drunkenly.

"That man took blood from you?" I asked Esther in amazement.

"Oh, yes," she said nonchalantly. "He's drunk, though."

I've earned my rest tonight, I thought wearily as we pulled into Residence.

June 17

After helping Charlotte sort the laundry and firmly telling Larry to stick to his studies, I left for the hospital again this morning. I hated to leave, but there was no alternative. I arrived at the hospital at 7:30, just in time for Dr. Saah's visit.

Julie left amid the hugs and sighs of the women. "She brings joy," Hawa told me. "Ah wish she'd bring funds for me too."

Poor Hawa has been forced to move out in the hallway to make room for newcomers, so the cribs on either side of Alosious are empty.

Agutta wanted me to go down to the lab with her to see if all was in order with the donated blood for Amos. Rows and rows of people sat on the benches, waiting for some form of blood work. The old lab technician we had met the night before was working at the counter, whistling as he dug through supplies and records.

I tried not to stare at the piles of blood samples lying askew all over the stained counters, the dirty plastic bucket of assorted needles and syringes, and the odd assortment of papers everywhere. The unmistakable smell of blood made my stomach churn.

The floor was discolored and greatly in need of a broom. The nurse on duty was shaking a vial of blood vigorously. She tossed it on the counter and sauntered over to the technician. "You say it's Bodo? Mr. *Arthur* Bodo? You sure?"

He nodded, and then glanced at us. "Come back later," he said. "Too busy."

Alosious still has a runny stomach, and he hasn't gained any weight. I feel like calling Dr. Lamin to come in and take a look. He looks awfully thin.

There's an intelligent, capable nurse on duty today. Her name is Alice, and I can see she takes her job seriously. She brought me a small pail of warm water so I could give Alosious a good bath. I had to use great care because of the IV, but it was fun. I used the Johnson's baby soap from the layette, and then rubbed lotion all over him. Some of the women gathered around the crib and stood there with their hands on their hips watching every move I made. Alosious looked so worried through it all that I just had to kiss him. I love the little guy!

As I looked around the hospital room this morning, I nearly got a lump in my throat—Julie and that bulging bag of hers *had* made a difference! Hunee now wore a lovely little blue dress which I recognized from the box of baby clothes Aunt Lucinda sent, and the smallest babies each had a new patchwork baby quilt. Calle's starving mother was eating roasted peanuts. She ate with pleasure, dropping all the skins on the floor—then she threw the empty bags on top and left it all there for the janitor to sweep up.

But that wasn't all—Julie had given all the women a copy of *101 Bible Stories*, and many of them were paging through it.

Agutta was thrilled. "I've wanted a *101 Stories* book fo' a long time!" she told me. "Now I kin read to Amos."

She spent almost the whole day reading. She would lean on Amos's bed and in a low murmur tell him stories. She acted out the parts a little, and he gazed at her with big, solemn eyes, and every now and then he would nod slowly in agreement.

It was a touching scene I won't soon forget. The old raggedy Bible was not forgotten, and she read from that, too, pointing to the words with her finger, and reading slowly and distinctly.

While Agutta read, Nurse Mema came in to give Amos a shot for the fever. "Oh, man!" he cried pitifully. "Oh, *man!*"

She changed his catheter, accidentally dropped the full bag, and left it lying there while she continued her rounds. It leaked slowly, forming a dark puddle on the floor, until she came back and picked it up.

Agutta found a rag from somewhere and wiped it up.

Right after lunch, a boy was brought in. He was too long for the crib, so his feet stuck out at the bottom end. I nicknamed him "Little Longfellow." Nurse Alice barely had him situated when he vomited and thrashed about dreadfully until his head hit the sides of the crib. Malaria had gone to his brain. Because the disease had been left untreated, it was literally taking away his sanity.

He was deathly ill, with high fever and chills, yet sweating profusely. His eyes were wild and staring, and it was all his mother could do to keep him from tearing out his IV. He fought almost constantly.

Where was his father?

Little Longfellow vomited again and again. My stomach, not being the world's strongest, did flip-flops. The nurses changed the sheet and wiped it all up with soapy water while the child looked around deliriously and cried out in pain.

"Wha' you lookin' fo'?" his mother asked him gently.

Meanwhile, another party arrived—a very young girl holding a lovely baby, followed by her mother and a scowling old woman. I had to squeeze closer to the empty bed so Alice and Mema could situate the newcomer in the corner crib and make room for the oxygen tank. They bumped Amos's bed constantly as they put the baby girl down. Alice deftly threaded the tube into the baby's nose, scolding the whole time.

"You tried *country medicine* first!" she spat. "Look at the chil'! Did it help? Huh? Did it help? This chil' is sick—*very* sick! Shame on you!"

She taped on the tube, arranged the IV closer to the wall, and left, muttering all the while. Mema followed, and the old lady glared after them.

The child gasped for every breath. It was a terrible sound. I found myself holding my own breath until she would finally exhale and then gasp horribly again. Her tiny chest heaved in short, jerky spasms as she fought for air. The timid baby ma sat by the bed and sniffled constantly, while her mother stood stone-faced and the old lady growled around.

"Do naw cry!" hissed the old woman again and again, as the young mother blinked away the tears. She looked terrified.

Where was the father?

When visiting hours were over, the fierce old woman gave a parting admonition. "Don' you cry!" she snapped. "You heah? *Don' cry!*"

When the two miserable comforters finally left, I asked the young woman her name. "Abby," she said shyly.

"And your age . . . ?"

"Sixteen," she told me.

No wonder she was crying.

Back in the other corner, Little Longfellow had calmed down a bit. Every once in a while his whole body would jerk convulsively and his mother would leap up and grab the IV. She looked tired and nervous.

It was dark outside when another beautiful, sturdy little boy was admitted with malaria. I heard him screaming when they started the IV. They put him in the only empty bed, two feet away.

His eyes were wide with terror because he, too, had difficulty breathing. He must have wondered what was happening to him with all the needles and all the strangers milling about.

His mother, dressed in a stylish blouse and blue jeans, wore gold bracelets and rings on her hands. It was plain to see she was wealthy.

I reached through the bars and took the child's dear little hand in mine. He didn't resist, but held onto my hand and regarded me with fascination.

The mother smiled. "His name is Bobby," she offered. "He's sick wi' malaria."

"Would you like a book for him?" I asked gently.

She eagerly accepted the *101 Bible Stories* book and the *Seed of Truth* magazine.

When Wayne appeared at the door with Julie, I was ready to go.

"Just watch the mosquitoes," I begged her. "We *can't* let him get malaria. I'm hoping the doctor lets him go home tomorrow."

June 18

I arrived at the hospital to find my anxious daughter watching Dr. Saah add malaria treatment to the IV for Alosious. "He whimpered a lot last night," she said. "He wouldn't drink a thing."

"How do you know he has malaria?" I agonized.

"Although the tests showed negative, I am sure he does," Dr. Saah responded. "I have seen a baby three hours old with malaria, and this one surely has it too. There are resistant strains that the tests do not reveal, and since the child has fever, it backs up my diagnosis."

"Abby's baby died during the night," Julie whispered before she left. "Everyone gave her a hard time for trying country medicine before she came here. She's just a baby herself."

"That child is in heaven," I answered.

Now Abby was sitting alone, dry-eyed and emotionless. The crib was empty.

Agutta was in high spirits. "Amos will have surgery tomorrow," she told me with shining eyes. "The paper is signed."

"I brought some apple juice and cookies for him," I told her. "Make sure you eat one too."

Amos knew I had something in that bag just for him. His face broke into a sunny smile as he watched me pull out the goodies.

Bobby was sleeping on his mother's lap, his breathing slow and even. "He is better," his mother said happily. "No more tube in his nose. He will be fine."

"Praise the Lord!" I rejoiced with her.

She had tied a bright red bandanna around his curly head and he looked absolutely adorable.

Little Longfellow lay in a coma, his eyes open and staring vacantly, his breathing slow and shallow. His mother flitted in and out of the room like a frightened bird. She would glide in, look at him closely to see that he was still breathing, then hurry out again. She looked terrified.

A newcomer across the room got my attention. Her pretty five-year-old daughter lay unconscious. I asked Agutta about her.

"That is Diris," she told me. "They came late las' night. The chil' has malaria."

The woman wept quietly. She stroked the child's hand and softly called her name. "Sophie. Sophie chil', talk to me! Sophie . . . "

The child began jerking so hard that her whole body lifted off the bed. Diris stood up, hesitated, then sat down again. She buried her face in her hands and began to pray.

"Oh-h-h, Father God . . . have mercy. Have mercy!"

A man joined her by the bedside and laid a comforting hand on her shoulder. She lifted her grief-stricken face and looked at him with tear-filled eyes.

He knelt slowly by the bed, and there, in front of everyone, they prayed for their dying child. I will never forget that scene—the old, dilapidated hospital room, the sick children, the nurses hovering in the background, and those two dear people beseeching God for their precious Sophie.

Where two or three are gathered together . . .

Longfellow's father came in today. He stood by his son and scolded gently, shaking his head and acting very unhappy. Although he never touched the child, I think it was his gruff way of showing concern.

"He had it befo', but nevah this bad . . . *nevah* this bad," he muttered. He looked bewildered and helpless, trying to comprehend the awfulness of this invisible foe that was destroying his son.

I kept a wary eye on the mosquitoes. So small—yet so deadly. I couldn't find one bite on Alosious.

Suddenly Abby let out a shriek. Her tribe burst into the room, shattering the stillness with the most unearthly screeches and cries I've ever heard. At least seven relatives joined Abby, and the din was so great I had to protect Alosious's ears.

The sullen old woman of yesterday did her own little dance while she wailed, head down on her chest, feet shuffling with short, jerky steps. The steady crying went up and down, up and down, reaching a certain high peak, then trailing off to a low, long moan.

It was creepy.

As if by signal, they all trotted out of the room, single file.

Thank you, Lord, that it's over.

My nerves felt raw. I looked at the clock. It was only 10:15. I cradled Alosious and refused to let myself worry that he had malaria. He *had* to get better.

Little Longfellow started bleeding from his mouth. His mother's cries brought two nurses, Patience and Korpo, who yelled for a suction machine.

A male assistant came hurrying in with something that looked like an oversized vacuum cleaner from the sixties. Patience stuck the thick plastic tube down into the boy's lungs without sterile precautions of any kind. She turned on the suction. Instantly it filled with fresh red blood. It swirled into the glass bottle—dark red and sinister. Both nurses looked grim.

Curious onlookers filed into the room and stood gawking. One man's mouth stood open in disbelief. They slowly surrounded the bed, only moving aside for the nurses. I had to resist the urge to send them all out in a hurry. This was supposed to be the ICU.

Meanwhile, the distraught mother vacillated between his bedside and the hallway, wringing her hands and crying openly. She came into the room repeatedly and stopped about five feet from the bed, stood staring at him, then rushed out again, her face contorted with pain.

The curious people slowly straggled out again in search of more excitement. Korpo thrust a wooden stick with a piece of gauze on the end into Longfellow's mouth so he couldn't swallow his tongue. Soon it was bright red.

Bloody froth began to bubble slowly out of his mouth. I could almost feel the angels hovering over that bed, waiting for the final command from the giver and sustainer of all life.

Patience, Korpo, and another nurse worked on a sick baby, trying to start an IV. The child screamed pitifully. After what seemed like hours, Patience brought her in, still struggling, and put her in the corner crib. Their efforts to find a vein had been unsuccessful.

"We will try again later," Patience told the two women who had brought the child. She methodically administered oxygen from an awfully old tank, inserting the tube and turning the dial this way and that. She leaned down and studied the gauge intently. Then she turned it up some more.

The mother was also young and scared, but she had a dear old grannie with her who was just as concerned as she was. They never strayed from that crib. They dipped a white rag in a cup of cool water and sponged the infant's face, neck, and her bare little stomach and the bruises on her arms from the needles. They held her hands and crooned African lullabies in a slow, soothing chant. It was wonderful to see the love in their eyes.

I gave them a copy of *101 Bible Stories* and asked them about the baby. She was four months old and her name was Famutta. The mother's name was Awena.

I suddenly felt claustrophobic in my small cubbyhole, with sick children on all sides, mosquitoes everywhere, and no place to hide. I wanted to run down to the ocean and feel the salt air and leave this awful place behind.

By now, Longfellow's father was gone, and the little boy was dying. There was nothing more the nurses could do. His poor mother came in from wailing in the hall and threw herself on the floor in front of the crib. She crossed her arms and bent over double and swayed to and fro, crying and calling out, "Why me? Why me?"

She lifted herself up on her elbows, then her hands, and made another beseeching appeal to all of us in general. She tossed her head from side to side like a spirited horse. She beat on her chest and thumped her heels on the floor—then she stood up, brushed off her dress, and walked out.

No one was by his bedside when little Longfellow died—no one to hold his dear little hand and whisper words of love or tell him good-bye. He simply drew one last, shuddering breath and lay still.

I cried into the comforting folds of Alosious's soft blanket. I couldn't help it.

Minutes later, Longfellow's mother came back in. She looked at him with wide, horrified eyes and let out a wild shriek. I can imagine the cries of the lost sounding like she did. The commotion in the hallway was unearthly.

Nurse Korpo came into the room, her face void of expression. She removed all the tubes and removed the tape from the little corpse, then covered his face. Patience brought a stretcher alongside the bed and together they wrapped him in a cloth, lifted him, and wheeled him out.

His forlorn little heap of belongings lay beside his bed, and on top of the pile, his new *101 Bible Stories*. He no longer needed a *101 Bible Stories* book. Mighty angels had already borne their precious burden to the realms of heaven—to Jesus Himself.

Bev, Marie, and Charlotte brought me some rice with pumpkin soup topping, but I could not eat, even though the noise in the hallway had finally subsided.

Agutta gathered a small group of ladies around her and was telling them all the story of King Solomon and the two new mothers. She held up the book so all could see the picture. Her quiet, trusting attitude had a calming effect on the whole room.

Diris, the praying mother, sat transfixed, drinking in every word. "Ah, yes. Yes!" she breathed. "God is able to do *anything*."

The girls had barely gone when baby Famutta started jerking. Her eyes grew wide with fright—she tried to cry, and her breath came out in sobbing gasps.

Grannie held the child's hands and talked to her soothingly, while her mother, Awena, began crying—quiet, controlled, heart-broken sobs that seemed worse in their intensity than the wailing we had heard earlier.

Right in the middle of it all, the hospital secretary arrived, pulled out her tablet, and demanded they show all their receipts to prove they had paid. The weeping mother searched through her bag, her eyes blinded with tears, trying to find the elusive papers, while her baby convulsed and the secretary waited. Finally the papers were found and the secretary was satisfied.

Famutta had just started breathing more easily when Patience came in and announced that they would try again to start an IV.

By the time they finished, I felt like screaming myself. Famutta's little hand was bloody where they had tried for so long to find the vein. I hoped desperately I wouldn't have to see her die.

Wayne, Willie, Larry, Georgie, and Harris brought Julie in tonight. They all wanted to see Alosious. Julie was full of energy and actually looking forward to staying overnight again. I told her Alosious had a runny stomach and needed to be changed often.

"I can't wait to take him home," I told her tearfully. "Longfellow died and now this darling baby Famutta is so sick . . . and Diris over there has a *very* sick child. It's just too much."

"You go right to sleep," she returned. "You'll feel better tomorrow."

I've been trying to sleep, but I keep wondering why God allowed me to witness such suffering. The screams of the children keep ringing in my mind and with them the verse, *Weeping may endure for a night, but joy cometh in the morning.*

June 19

"He still has a *really* runny stomach," Julie told Wayne and me when we arrived this morning. "I held him most of the night because the mosquitoes were bad."

Alosious's eyes were bright and alert. He smiled at me, trusting me completely. I felt fiercely protective and a bit desperate.

"I'll talk to the doctor. There's something wrong here," I said to Wayne and Julie as I picked up Alosious. "See you tonight."

Dr. Saah was late in coming, but when he did, I pestered him and the nurses, Alice and Sando, and asked all kinds of questions. They finally admitted that the water they had been giving me to mix the dehydration salts came straight from the tap.

"You gave me strict orders not to use any water I hadn't boiled for four minutes," I told Dr. Saah in astonishment, "and now your nurses have been giving it to me all along. He'll *never* get better at this rate!"

Thoroughly vexed, I called home on the radio for some boiled water. "Bring it right away," I told Bev. "I think that's the whole problem."

Famutta was sleeping without oxygen. Grannie and Awena beamed.

I saw that Diris's little girl was conscious and nibbling on a biscuit. "She's much better!" I exclaimed.

"God is in control," she said simply, with great joy in her eyes. The *101 Bible Stories* lay on her lap.

Joy truly cometh in the morning.

Hawa was still camping in the hall. She took charge of the morning devotions to help pass the time. I marveled at her patience. What if no one ever paid that bill?

Amos left for surgery at 11:15. By 12:30 he was back. The nurses lifted him, limp and unconscious, onto the bed. They tied his feet fast to the foot of the bed, checked his vital signs, and left.

"That surgery took only an hour and fifteen minutes," I told Agutta. "That must be quite an efficient team."

Amos looked thin and shrunken with that huge, offending spleen removed.

"Come down an' look at the spleen," Agutta urged me, smiling, but I simply could not.

Amos regained consciousness in a surprisingly short time. "Where did you go?" Agutta asked him.

"I had operation," he whispered weakly.

"Wha' did they do to you?" she asked.

"I don' know."

Before long he was sobbing in pain, wanting to sit up, but the rags held him fast. "If you sit up, you will come apart," Agutta told him over and over.

He didn't give up. "Let me si' up . . . let me si' up," he begged.

"He probably has a bad headache. Or maybe he feels like throwing up," I ventured. "Go call Alice, Agutta."

She ran for the nurse and came back with a bucket. Amos tried to sit up.

"If you sit up I will beat you!" his mother cried out fearfully, afraid that his stitches would tear. He settled back down, whimpering.

Bev and Julie arrived with two thermos bottles of water, one hot and one ice cold. I washed out Alosious's bottle and mixed a batch of fresh, warm formula. He sighed contentedly as he drank. We watched with real satisfaction.

"We scraped our money together and came up with $780 Liberian for Hawa," Julie said in undertones. "Now she's out on the streets begging for the rest. She needs $1000 in all. We can't just let her stay here; her baby will get sick again. I'll come in around seven."

After the girls left, I tried to help Agutta make Amos comfortable. We fanned him with the *Family Life* magazine and wiped him off with a wet rag. He was miserable with fever and pain, but finally he slept.

Evening devotions were different tonight. The women started prancing around the room, singing lustily, clapping, and swaying. There was an air of celebration that has been sadly lacking since we came. Children are improving.

We all recited the Lord's Prayer, then Diris led a personal prayer of praise. We ended by reciting some verses in Psalms. I was so blessed.

When I left, Amos was still in pain. I'm not sure why they refuse to give him water.

June 20

Dr. Saah took one good look at Alosious and ordered the IV unhooked. "Take him home," he said. "He will be fine now."

We told our new friends and the staff good-bye and walked downstairs. The old lab technician was just leaving.

"Praise God," he said clearly and distinctly, and this time I could smile back.

We were going home.

22

The Forces of Evil

June 21

Merci arrived at our door tonight, her face drawn. "I am out of a home!" she cried. "The soldiers came and knocked at the door with their rifles and told me to get out now. The president says all his secrets leak out from the airfield where I live. Now the whole area is sealed off."

She will be staying at Iddo and Viola's house until another place can be found. Poor Merci—suddenly homeless with no place to go.

June 22

Charlotte is actually fourteen today. She informed me gravely that she could drive if she were back in Canada, but I don't think it would be wise to buy her a license in this country.

It was extremely easy to obtain our Liberian driver's licenses. All we had to do was get a photo taken, answer a few questions, and pay $20 U.S. Never mind a driver's test.

There are no traffic rules or lights, and no speed limits or stop signs. Most people drive fast and furiously, honking as they go, dodging around other cars and people. I like to say a little prayer when our men and women and boys go out into that wild melee.

It always amazes me how traffic stops to let people cross the busy boulevard. Maybe that is an unspoken law of Liberia, because if you step out onto the street, they will come to a grinding halt and let you walk across.

We were surprised when Agutta appeared at our door this morning. Amos had sent her, she said. He was begging for "some juice from Muttah." I was delighted to give her some cold apple juice.

"I thank God for you people!" she said. "If not for you, my Amos would be dead. My two-year-old son has the same thing. I will carry him to the office to show him to Dr. Lamin.

"A chil' came when you left," Agutta continued. "She was a two-year-old. Someone threw scalding water at her and her belly was cooked. It was all white an' red, and the skin was coming off. She died while they tried to connect the IV."

"Oh my," I shuddered. "That hospital is not equipped for a burn patient. I'm glad I wasn't there, Agutta. Too much is too much."

Larry plays soccer with the neighbor boys after school right in the next lot. Charlie Boy and Darling Boy are around his age. He really enjoys them, but I keep a close eye on their activities. Elijah knows this culture, and he assures me Larry will be fine.

"Ah will watch him close, Muttah," he told me. "Ah know where Larry is at all times."

June 27

William is sixteen today. He was at the warehouse part of the day with his friend, Georgie, helping unload containers.

Tonight we celebrated Willie's birthday by inviting some of his friends for sausage pizza and homemade ice cream. The ice cream turned out really nice and creamy, even though we used powdered and evaporated milk.

Georgie, Harris, Toney, Patience, and Pastor Amos and his wife joined us for the birthday supper. The lights didn't work, so we ate by candlelight.

"Dad, who is that really tall white man walking around the

streets?" Willie wondered while we ate.

"I saw him once too," I added. "He looked familiar."

"That's Neil Dimocopoulos," Wayne answered. "He was in my office today asking for rice. And guess what? He's the commander you saw at Klay when the soldiers were all milling around. He's the one who got us through. I invited him to church."

Pastor Amos sat very still. "Neil Dimocopolous is a very bad man," he said finally. "I know him."

July 4

American Independence Day. Wayne and I were invited to a banquet with the American Ambassador, Bismark Myrick from Virginia.

After listening to various speeches and dining on finger food, we were glad to get home to our dear block house on Payne Avenue, where the young people were playing games and eating popcorn. Princess was "helping," and Georgie was rocking Alosious in the living room.

"What's the matter, Georgie?" Willie asked when Georgie said he didn't feel like playing games.

It took some coaxing, but finally Georgie admitted it made him sad to think of his childhood during the war.

"Tell us your story," the young people begged.

"I will write it down," he promised. "It is too hard to tell."

July 7

Georgie handed me a piece of paper after church. "My story," he said simply. I couldn't wait until lunch was over. Finally, the little ones were sleeping and I could curl up in a chair to read it. It went like this:

The war of 1990 was a terrible one. My father left me with a young uncle and went to look for my brother and sister, who were on vacation with my grandmother. They all got caught up in the war when the rebels overtook the area and never came back. My uncle was very afraid. Sometimes we never ate for days. Our house was a short distance from the army camp and there were such evil things going on there that we went to live at a friend's house.

After the rebels captured President Doe on September 9, 1990, the AFL (Armed Forces of Liberia) became ruthless. They began killing civilians. They killed hundreds of innocent people seeking refuge in a church. The street smelled of dead bodies for weeks.

My uncle and I decided to cross the bridge where the rebels were in control. There were dead bodies all along the way. Only ten years old, I was very afraid. The dogs were all over the city, eating dead body parts. My uncle settled with another friend across the bridge, and when they went to look for food I was left alone. My uncle and his friend never returned.

I had nowhere to go, so I began running with other kids like myself. We ate anything to keep us alive. One day my friend and I were taken to the rebel base where they had set up an orphanage. Life started getting better. I could eat once a day. I started getting healthy again.

On October 15, 1993, we were attacked by another rebel group. All the children in the orphanage got caught up in the fighting. Under the heavy shooting and launching of rockets, God helped us, and Prince Johnson and his guys managed to cross us over the river with canoes to the other side. I was then taken to the SOS children's village.

One time there was a whole night of shooting. We all thought it was a rebel attack, but it was not. It was a group of loyalists of the late President Doe. They were shooting and killing civilians who were redoing a church. These people were killed because they were all from the Gio tribe, who were said to be loyal to the rebels.

The next morning the streets were quiet except for the cries of the babies and wounded people. There was blood rolling from under the church door. A friend of mine lost his legs that night. They even killed the babies. The dead bodies were left there for weeks, and it smelled terrible.

I was just a child when I went through all these nightmares. Now that I am a man I don't want my children to go through the same. I grew up in an orphanage, but it gave me a good life. Thank God He brought me through, and I am still alive.

See ya,
Georgie

July 13

Princess is getting over a bout of malaria. Dr. Lamin wasted no time in putting her on Mefloquine, and she is much better today.

Julie recently took her to Dr. Guizzie, and they tried to fit her with a glass eye.

"Are you sure she's ready for it?" Julie wondered. "Her eye cavity is still red and sore."

"Oh yes, she will be fine," the nurse assured her as she attempted to insert the offending object.

Princess was not impressed. "Ah will beat you!" she cried.

She didn't get the glass eye. Maybe some day a competent eye specialist can help, but not today.

Dr. Guizzie gave Julie his official diagnosis. "The left eye needs a cornea graft," he explained. "Just imagine if I would drop hot wax on my watch lens. The engine inside would still be running, but you could not see the time. All you have to do is change that glass and you will be able to see the time once again. I am confident that the child will be able to see. I have a friend connected with Operation Eyesight in Calgary, Alberta. I will give you the number."

Julie is thrilled over the response to her "Sight for Princess" request. The donated funds are above and beyond what she ever dared to hope.

"I wish all those dear people could see Princess," she said wistfully. "Just think what Princess will say when she *sees* us. It's better than any storybook. Dr. Guizzie said we should request a free eye surgery, so I'm going to get Aunt June involved."

July 21

After Pastor Mervin's wonderful sermon on the fruits of the Spirit, Moses Massawalla requested prayer because he is approaching his birthday with dread. It is the day his family wants to initiate him as sole heir to all their demonic powers.

"Ah am the oldes' in the family," he explained. "My two younger brothers have been sacrificed fo' me so that ah could inherit even more power from the devil. My grandfather is in America, but that does not deter his curses. Dey will try to take my life if ah do not agree. Firs' dey will torture me to make me change my mind. Then dey will kill me. Please, ah need prayer. Ah do not *want* Satan's powers."

Moses' face was lined with deep distress and fear. I had to adjust my thinking to absorb this new piece of information. There are still witches and many satanic customs, even if it is 2002.

This horrific realization was reaffirmed when Borbor's wife, Felicia, asked to come speak with me after church. They are administrators at one of CAM's orphanages.

Felicia brought two of their four children along, and she is pregnant with the fifth one.

"Sis Ruth," she began in quiet, even tones. "I was put out of my home when I was jus' ten years old, like my daughter here. My family tried to convince me to go join the Devil Bush, a satanic cult that requires the drinking of blood and eating of human flesh to become one of them. After that a person supposedly has powers straight from the devil."

I felt a chill go up my spine. Felicia's big, dark eyes never left my face. "I would run like crazy when the scouts came looking for young girls. They want girls jus' beginning to develop—like my daughter here. They would circumcise them in the most awful ways, Sis Ruth. The girls would sometimes die from infection and loss of blood. The ones who lived were pushed out of their homes and encouraged to give themselves to some man, *any* man, who would take them."

She paused, her eyes filled with pain. "It can make my mind weak to think back. I was so afraid that I could not sleep at night, in case they would come for me. I hid deep in the bush and didn't come out until I was sure they were gone. My mother told me, 'Get out of my home and find yourself a man.' "

"You are a Christian now, Felicia," I said gently. "No one and nothing can harm you unless God wills. Try to forget the horrible things—think about Jesus and how He loves you. I beg you, watch your children closely, especially this little girl."

"I can never forget, Sis Ruth," she said. "Even now the devil and all his hordes are looking for a way into my home. They can appear as people and come in, watching all I do—waiting for a chance to enter. If anyone in the family does not have a right heart, the devils can enter through them."

I encouraged her to become acquainted with the Bible and claim verses for her own, such as "Resist the devil and he will flee from you." She left soon after, promising to come again.

Felicia was barely out of the gate when the twins' father, Isaac Dixon, and Aunt Musu stopped to talk. Isaac was carrying a little girl.

"I must go back to River Cess, so I say good-bye to you," Musu said, offering her hand. "I am grateful to God for you people."

"Who do you have here?" I asked, smiling at the beautiful child. She had a great abundance of thick, curly hair done up in many colorful ribbons and barrettes. Her nose was slightly upturned and her eyes were big and fringed with heavy lashes.

"This is my daughter, Susan," Isaac answered.

"Susan? But I thought . . . "

"She is Bonita's child," Musu offered. "Isaac lived with Bonita five years."

"Who's Bonita?"

"She was Isaac's girlfriend before Eva."

"Oh."

I liked Musu immediately. She is soft-spoken and gentle, and the more we visited, the more I saw that she is a Christian. She cradled Alosious in her arms.

"He is a fine baby!" she exalted. "He is getting fat."

Isaac showed no interest in Alosious. "What do you plan to do with the twins?" I asked, almost fearfully. He shrugged.

"I have no one to care fo' them. My Eva die, an' I am alone."

"Why don't you go back to Bonita?" I blurted. "You lived with her for five years."

"She wa' unfaithful . . . she does not understand me," he said miserably. "If I would consent to take Bonita back, she would do the same thing again."

"Musu, what happened anyway?" I asked, changing the subject. "How did you get the babies?"

She smiled and began. "When I came to the village, they told me about Isaac's twins. So I went to the house and said, 'Unlock the door.' 'No!' they told me. 'There are two, and they are cursed. See how they killed mother Eva?' The babies cried dreadfully, so I broke the window and picked up the babies and came to Salvation Army in Monrovia. 'We cannot help,' they said, 'Go down to Christian Aid.' An' you helped us."

"God will reward you, Musu," I told her happily. "Think of how happy Eva would be if she knew you saved her baby boys."

"To God be the glory," she said modestly.

When Wayne appeared from his room, Isaac repeated the whole sad story. Before long the two were discussing the plan of salvation. A spark of hope kindled in Isaac's eyes.

"How can I get my life back together?" he wondered sadly. "It's jus' too mixed up."

"I believe that man has a good heart," Wayne told me later. "We need to keep after him until he can see the light."

23

More Pets

July 24

Larry was excited when someone appeared at the gate today with a mongoose for sale. He brought it into the house. "For just a few bucks, Mom," he begged, his eyes shining. "It takes everything shiny and digs a hole to put it in, then it stands guard so no one can get it."

The agile little creature pushed a sharp nose into Larry's pocket, then explored along his neck and under his shirt.

"You mean he'll take all our keys and paper clips and nail clippers and hide them?" I asked, my voice filled with doubt.

Larry changed his approach. "He can kill a full-grown cobra, Mom!"

"Okay, I guess so. But make sure you keep him out of the house."

During the night I started feeling sick. Chills like the north wind swept over me. Wayne got more blankets and piled them on top of me. I broke out in a sweat.

"It's malaria," I told him. "Quickly get me the Meladox tablets—three of them." Now I know how a malaria patient feels.

Although we all take preventative medicine to ward off

malaria, it is not very effective against certain strains of the disease—and avoiding mosquitoes is impossible.

July 26

Wayne and I have been married for twenty-two years today. So tonight we stole away to Mamba Point for supper. It was raining, so we couldn't sit outside on the terrace, but we could still see the mighty ocean breaking all along the shore. He ordered cassava fish, and I had shrimp with garlic butter. We reminisced and marveled at the changes in our lives since our wedding day.

Now we are here in Africa, so different from the wide, endless plains near the foot of the Rockies, where minus 35 degrees is normal in winter and the wild Chinook wind howls across the drifts. We are here, and we are happy.

July 31

We have two wee little men living with us now. Curt and Evelyn are going to Togo, Ghana, to try to sell the old Suburban and the Explorer, so they brought Oliver over here last night. We think it's a good idea to have the twins together anyway.

"He still wheezes with every breath," Evelyn said. "Maybe he'll grow out of it; I sure hope so."

"The baby . . . he is so *harish!*" Marie said when she saw Oliver.

"What does that mean?" I asked.

"He is harish; he has plenty of hair."

Actually, both babies have a lot of hair. Oliver has thick tight curls like new lamb's wool, and Alosious has loose, feathery curls like a duckling's down. Oliver's skin tone is much blacker than Alosious's, and he is at least a pound heavier. They have their own personalities too.

We try not to worry about Oliver's breathing problem. It sounds like he is very, very congested all the time. Wayne has taken a real shine to the little guy.

The only cloud on the horizon is the thought of someday giving them up.

Princess has a new little musical guitar that plays all kinds of tunes and makes animal sounds. She carries it wherever she goes, held close to her ear. For the first time in her life, she has something all her own. Julie and Charlotte are making an effort to teach her how to eat properly, sit on the chairs instead of squatting on the floor, and remain in her bed at night. My heart just melts when tears run out of those sightless eyes, so I have a hard time being strict enough. Julie took her to the clinic this morning because she was burning hot during the night and refused any breakfast.

Rikki-tikki-tavi, as Larry calls his pet mongoose, is the friendliest little creature. He loves to explore every dark hole he can find—under the steps, behind the oven, behind the fridge—anywhere. Nothing escapes his scrutiny, not even the smallest piece of food or fabric on the floor. He sleeps a lot during the day, and his favorite place is in the crook of someone's arm.

Larry and Charlie Boy hunt lizards for Rikki every day, and they have to be alive or he just turns up his nose. The workers gather round to watch the fights between Rikki and the hapless lizards. They're usually over in a second or two, because Rikki is lightning fast.

A young lad appeared at the gate today with the sorriest looking puppy I have ever seen. It has a crooked gait and tattered ears, but something about its eyes speaks of intelligence and character.

"Oh, he's cute!" cried Larry, scooping him up in his arms. "Mom? You *know* how long I've wanted a dog."

The puppy wriggled in his arms and licked his cheeks and ears and neck, whimpering and wagging its tail frantically. It was definitely puppy love at first sight.

"It's fine with me," I agreed, "but you have to ask Dad."

"I'll go right now. Just come along with me," he said to the owner.

"Wait a minute. How much?" I asked.

"Five dollah'."

"I've got the money," Larry told him. "Remember, Mom . . . from Uncle Ben?"

"Next we'll have a *parrot* around here," I said with resignation.

Surprisingly, Wayne gave his consent to buy the little mongrel, and as an added bonus, Willie promised to help Larry build a shelter under the steps leading upstairs.

"My dreams are coming true," Larry sighed with satisfaction. "I think I'll name him Ranger."

Julie came home after supper carrying Princess, and I could see it had been a hard day. "She has malaria," she wailed. "They put her on drip immediately, but it was so awful, Mom. They couldn't find a vein for the longest time, and she just started yelling, 'Save me! Save me, Juee!' When I didn't respond how she thought I should, she yelled, 'Muttah! Muttah!' I felt so helpless when she clung to me and begged me to rescue her. She couldn't figure out why I would let them poke her arms."

"Put her in bed, Julie. Someday you can explain to her if you need to."

August 1

Julie woke me before the sun was up. "Mom, Princess is really sick. She threw up three times and she's shaking all over."

"Why didn't you wake me sooner?" I chided.

"Maybe I should have," she answered. "I've been holding her since three o'clock, when Bev and I were up to feed the twins."

As soon as it was feasible, Julie left for the Providence Clinic in Redlight. An hour later she radioed home. "I'll be here a while," she told me. "The doctor said she's badly dehydrated. Tell Bev I won't be at the office. Over and out."

Julie came home alone around six o'clock. "Dr. Lamin didn't want to take her off the IV till he was sure she was better," she said wearily. "I bought some coconuts so she can drink as much as she wants. She threw up again, and her fever was up to 103. When I left, she was sleeping because they sedated her a bit. Wake me up *early*."

August 2

Somewhere between midnight and morning, a terrific clap of thunder roused the whole family and made the twins scream with fright. We raced around the house to shut the windows, but already puddles of rain stood here and there. The wind hit with such force that the curtains flapped horizontally and the rain was driven under the overhang into the house.

"Be careful! The glass might break!" I gasped. "I've never seen such a storm."

"The lightning hit somewhere close," Wayne declared as he cuddled Oliver. "This is sure a cute little fellow. I wonder if peppermint oil would cure that rattle in his throat."

Everyone's eyes seemed too big in the brilliant flashes of lightning. "Maybe it's a typhoon," Willie suggested. "You should see the branches in the yard. Do you know that rogues love it when it rains? That way Security can't hear them come and go."

As the storm subsided to an angry growl, I tried not to think of the poor natives who live in low, poorly drained swamps, with big holes in their shacks where the rats and snakes have easy access. What would it be like to live as they do?

Julie left right after breakfast. She brought Princess home shortly after lunch and tucked her right in bed. I had to look twice when I saw her. Her head was shaved on both sides, Shawnee style.

"They couldn't find a vein, so they tried on her head, but they couldn't get it in there either," Julie said in disgust. "Finally they got it in near her wrist. They shaved her hair for nothing, just when it was getting really nice."

"We'll cut that strip off and start all over," I said as comfortingly as I could.

Dr. Lamin came by after work. "Princess was *very* sick, Ruth Ann. I was afraid it was too late. God be praised!"

It made me realize just how precious Princess has become to all of us.

When she woke up, she asked for juice, and later for rice, so she's on the mend.

I can almost feel the desperation of all the mothers who cannot afford malaria treatment. No wonder malaria is a leading cause of death among the children of Liberia.

August 4

Agutta was in church today with her little Amos. She had to help him along, but he smiled bravely and said, "Thank you fo' everything," and hoisted up his shirt so we could see his bandage. His little hand was hot in mine.

"Muttah, should I come visit?" Agutta asked me hopefully.

"Of course," I told her. "I have some homemade salve for Amos's scar."

We had a houseful of friends for dinner guests. The native people are always so grateful for a plate of food. It is so easy to think of myself and what I want, but what about the "thousand million sobbing souls" in need?

We are troubled more and more by the incredible poverty of the Liberian people. They live among the rats and dogs and chickens with leaky roofs for protection and hideous old cots to sleep on. They battle scalp fungus, pinkeye, scabies, ringworm, and crab lice. Typhoid lurks in the wells, and all manner of dangerous parasites lurk in the sand and the food and the streets. Mosquitoes take their deadly toll, since there is no way of controlling them. People lose their teeth and their eyesight and their toenails to disease and decay. Some die of snakebites and some of a witch doctor's curses.

What a tiny dent all the missionaries in the world are making! I am comforted by an illustration we heard not long ago.

A man was out on the beach throwing stranded starfish back into the ocean. "Do you really think you're making a difference?" someone asked him. "There are thousands of starfish dying on the beach."

He tossed yet another starfish to safety. "I made a difference for that one," he replied.

Just before supper, Dave and Audrey Waines and their family arrived, bringing with them Tim and Titus Wengerd from Oregon. Tim is involved in foreign adoptions and has adopted two black children of his own.

The Waines work under a Baptist group called *EQUIP*, and recently had to evacuate from Ghanta and resettle in Ivory Coast until things settle down. Now they are visiting Monrovia.

Dr. Lamin and several of his family came just in time to help us eat. I asked him to check on Princess, and he said she was just fine. "But I am somewhat worried about Oliver. He seems to have aspiration pneumonia," he told us. "He has no fever, but his breathing is not right."

Elijah poked his head around the corner. "Agutta is here. Shou' I call her?"

Now? I groaned inwardly. The house was full, it was getting late, and we were getting tired. But she had walked all the way from her deplorable room behind Fiama Market.

"Yes, tell her to come in."

Agutta came in, limping badly. Behind her were Amos and two more boys. "This is Jallah an' this is Francis," she said proudly. "My sons."

I immediately noticed a huge, all-too-familiar bulge under the littlest boy's shirt. "He has the same big stomach," she said as she saw me looking.

"What's wrong with your foot?" Bev asked.

"I stepped on an open lunch meat can," she answered. "My heel is almo' gone."

"When?" I cried.

"Today. That's why I am so late. I wa' at the hospital."

"Agutta! You shouldn't have walked all the way over here . . . and with Amos besides. You'll get a horrible infection."

"But you said I can come!"

Bev gave Alosious to Audrey, fixed some sandwiches, and poured some juice. The little family ate hungrily.

Agutta lingered after all the other guests had gone home.

"Is there something I can do for you?" I finally asked.

"Muttah, you need to know about me," she said. "My first boyfrien' an' I were separated for ten years durin' the war. I bore Jullah from him. Then my parents forced me to go out to find someone to take care of me. I found an older man, and then Amos was born. I hated staying with him, Muttah. I ran away when Amos was a new baby, an' looked for my first man. I found him in the bush, a highly educated man, scraping a small-small living out of the land. Now he is here, an' as soon as he can find a place, he will send for me."

"I surely hope so, Agutta."

"I'll give you a ride home," Wayne told her. She gratefully accepted.

They had barely walked out when the screen door banged, and in walked Moses Massawalla. "There's one sausage sandwich left for you," Willie told him.

The dishes waited as Moses briefly described his recent adventures. He had been captured by the militia because he was passing out free tracts and they thought he was a spy. They gave him a subu haircut (cut off totally with a razor), but otherwise he was unharmed.

"Moses, you *must* write it all down," I told him.

"I will write it down, but I canno' give it to you until it would be safe to do so," he answered. "I also have some photos fo' you to see, Sis Ruth. I will bring them."

August 10

Bev, Julie, and Esther decided to go look for Princess's family after work. Julie has been asking around and found a few definite leads. She needs valid information to get a passport for Princess.

Princess has an incredible sixth sense that tells her who enters the room. Today Georgie brought her some bananas. She stood still for a few seconds after the door banged, listening, holding her beloved guitar in one hand.

"Gorgee!" she exclaimed, walking swiftly toward him with one arm stretched out in front of her. "See? See?"

"Wha' do you have, Princess?" he asked.

He squatted down to her level, and they visited heartily in Liberian slang. She showed him her guitar and played the songs for him, and even jigged to the tunes.

When Georgie finally left, she walked around the house consoling herself over and over, "Gorgee going to come back."

Princess has also made friends with Elijah. She often goes out onto the porch, and he will come and swing her over the rail and hold her. They jabber like only two Africans can. Today I gave her a piece of pound cake to give to him, and she held it out gingerly, took a quick bite, and gave him the rest. She just couldn't resist.

Tumba is another one of her favorites. He has driven her to the clinic once or twice, so she knows him well. "My Princess," he says whenever he comes, caressing her bald little crown.

The girls came home from their fact-finding mission brimming with news. They talked to the lady who found Princess under the table in Leprosy Market.

"Princess had been in the market for a day and a night in pouring rain, so the dear lady took her home and mothered her until she was forced to give her up," Julie said. "She is very poor herself, so she had to call the police to get Princess, especially since Princess was sickly and weak. The police took her to the Hannah B. Orphanage. The lady has no idea who any of Princess's relatives are, though, so we'll try at Fiama Market next time. Maybe someone will recognize her."

"One other time a girl in Fiama claimed to know Princess," Bev added. "She said Princess's name is Whyayeh Karnque, or something like that."

"Don't give up," I encouraged. "She didn't just appear out of nowhere."

August 16

What a reward to see Oliver and Alosious grow! Now they can roll over and wiggle themselves into all sorts of funny positions. When they bump heads they start crying lustily. They look like two dolls when they're asleep, and when one starts crying, the other soon puckers up too.

During lunch break today, Dr. Lamin breezed in here in his usual brisk way. He listened to the twins' breathing, then bent over Oliver and made some startling sucking noises. Then he almost ran outside.

"What did Dr. Lamin just do?" Wayne queried, with a strange look on his face.

"Just gave Oliver a kiss . . . I *think*," I replied.

"What did you just do?" he asked Dr. Lamin, who had come back inside.

"I suctioned out his nose," he replied, chuckling heartily at our faces.

There was such an outcry of protest that the good doctor was astonished. "That's what we need to do in Africa when a child is unable to breathe," he told us seriously. "We have no modern suction machines."

"Would you like some cookies?" I asked faintly.

"Thank you, I might have one or two. You need to come to the clinic with Oliver tomorrow, Ruth Ann. I believe he needs extra attention."

August 17

Esther Akoi and Cleo Hardy dropped in this evening to see Julie to discuss their upcoming girls' classes. They decided to include all girls from ages nine to nineteen and try to teach them some basic principles of purity.

"I was taught nothing!" Esther exclaimed. "I knew *nothing*. So many girls are pushed out by their parents. 'Go! Find someone to take you'—and they are ruined."

Julie ordered all kinds of free literature from the States, and it finally arrived, so they can go ahead.

For some reason I had a wave of homesickness this evening. It is almost September, and at home in Alberta the nights will be getting much cooler, the wild Canada geese will be winging their way south again, and peaches and pears will need canning.

I love autumn in Alberta. I miss the tang of the crisp air, the blazing sunsets, the endless blue of the open skies, the enormous harvest moon at night, and the piles of fresh fruits and vegetables waiting to be stored in the root cellar.

Yet, I am glad to be here. Africa has enriched our lives. The trials have strengthened us. Best of all, the very same God of heaven who dwells in Alberta dwells here too.

August 18

I feel like a zombie today. For some reason, the babies were restless and didn't want to drink much at a time, so they woke oftener than usual last night. By three o'clock I hadn't slept more than an hour. The rooster crowed faithfully, and I decided to give him to the next needy person I meet.

After church today, a woman came up to me, silently handed me an envelope, and melted into the crowd. I had never seen her before.

We had so much company this afternoon—people just dropping in to talk—that I didn't get a chance to read the letter until later.

> Dear Mrs. Wayne,
>
> I do greet you with pleasures of gladness in Christ's name and do wish all of your endeavors come true. I am a mother of six children and they are starving for food. I have no money to put them in schooling. I am kindly begging and appealing to you for assistance since I am suffering greatly. I have been on my own since the war, with no mother and no father because they died in the war. There is no rice and the children cry in our poverty. I shall greatly appreciate any help your organization can give me, especially food, clothing, and medicines. For Jesus' sake, help me, Mrs. Wayne.
>
> Respectfully yours,
> Aleece Bonyer

My heart bleeds for the poor lady. I feel the awful despair and mingled hope in her words. I will see to it that the letter gets into the right hands. I feel suddenly inspired to send several e-mails asking for used baby clothing, bottles, formula, and layettes. We need them!

August 21

"Look at my license!" Willie cheered as he stepped in the door this morning. He is naturally a good driver, but it will test his skill to drive in Africa. CAM has already scheduled him to make a delivery to the C.O. Smythe Orphanage here in Monrovia.

Curt and Evelyn flew home from Togo today, so Wayne and I went to the airport to pick them up. They will not have much time in Liberia because they are scheduled to fly to the U.S. on furlough tomorrow evening. I guess we have little Oliver for keeps.

The first girls' class was held from 3:30 to 5:30. One by one the girls filed into the kitchen, where our committee of three awaited them. Cleo began with prayer, then Julie tried to explain the purpose of the meetings, but no one understood. She gave up.

"Esther . . . help!" she said, and that worthy lady took over. Talking Liberian English, she explained in minute detail what the girls could expect from now on, and wondered if they were still interested. She talked so fast that I was hard put to understand.

The girls understood, however. When Esther would pause after a stream of sentences and ask "Yah?" they slowly nodded their heads.

Each one received a questionnaire to fill out, a cup of ice water to drink, and a cookie to munch on. I feel very optimistic about the whole project.

Afterward, Julie and Esther took Princess down to Fiama to continue searching for her family. They came back several hours later with great news.

"Sit down and tell us!" we chorused.

Julie began, "We just walked along and asked everyone, 'Do you know this little girl?' Almost immediately, the same child who had approached us before came and asked us if she should call the mother. She came back with an older woman—about sixty-five, I would guess, by the name of Matta."

"Yes, at least that old," agreed Esther.

"I looked her straight in the eye, and she looked back at me," Julie continued. "I asked her if she knew this child. 'Yes, I do,' she said. Then I asked her what the child's name was and she replied, 'Whyayeh Karnque'—exactly the same name Bev mentioned. We made an appointment with her tomorrow. We also talked to a man named Dennis Johnson, who says he actually lived in the same apartment as Princess, even though he is no relation. He will also be at the meeting tomorrow."

"I will listen too," Esther promised. "I will tell you if they lie."

August 22

Julie is convinced she is finally on the right track concerning Princess, who is really Whyayeh Karnque. Never once did Matta contradict herself. This is the story she told.

> *"I am an aunt to Whyayeh. When she was very small, she lived with her mother, Naomi. At the age of two-and-one-half years, the child became sick with measles. Naomi, a wild and uncontrolled teenager, did not want the responsibility of raising a child, so she brought the little girl to me. She got sicker and sicker, so I carried her to the Catholic hospital. It was too late. Her eyes were already destroyed. I was at my wits' end, and as a last resort, I visited a female witch doctor, a relative of the Karnques. This doctor agreed to help and took Whyayeh into the bush. I didn't hear from her for a long time, so I made inquiry. The doctor vowed that Naomi had come and demanded Whyayeh, so she had no choice but to give her up. Naomi had taken Whyayeh home but her lover didn't want the baby around. 'She's sick and she's ugly and I don't want her near the other children,' he said. 'I want her gone.'*
>
> *"That is how I lost track of Naomi and Whyayeh. I first saw her again with you. I do not know who her father is. I have never seen him."*

"This is so exciting!" Julie said. "If we can only find her mother now."

Later today, a lady with enormous black eyes and high, sharp cheekbones came to the gate, begging for some rice. She was tall and thin, and on her back she carried a baby girl, so small and fragile, with the very same eyes. One little black hand rested on her mother's bony back. I could see they had never had enough to eat.

"Elijah! Catch the rooster, please," I said, as sudden inspiration hit.

There was a great squawking and flying of feathers as the mechanics joined the chase, and behind them galloped Ranger, wild with excitement. The rooster ran with his head outstretched, his wings flapping madly, and his feet churning up the dust. Elijah made a quick lunge and caught the rooster. He didn't resist as Elijah tied his feet and brought him to the gate.

"Here, take him home for supper," I said happily. "If you need more help, just go to the CAM office."

She acted as if she wanted to kneel before me. Instead, she did a small dance of thankfulness right there. The little girl tied to her back grinned with delight.

They will have a feast.

24

From Darkness to Light

August 25

"Look who's here," Wayne said quietly, nudging me. "I can't believe it."

I followed his gaze to the doorway of the church and caught my breath. There stood the tall white man we had heard so many rumors about—Neil Dimacopoulos. With him were a beautiful black woman, a small, fair-skinned lad, and another black man. When Neil spied Wayne beckoning, he strode into the church with the others following. He shook hands with us and took a seat on the front bench to the left of us. He looked gaunt and haggard and ill.

A hush fell over the congregation. Many pairs of fearful eyes fastened on Neil. He seemed oblivious to the stares and focused on Pastor Mervin, who rose to welcome everyone.

The morning sermon was on a lying tongue, and Pastor elaborated on all the different forms of lies. A person can even lie by keeping quiet.

Neil sat transfixed, drinking in every word. I stole a glance at the child sitting between him and the woman. He had huge brown eyes and an abundance of loose, rust-colored curls.

After the sermon, three people were baptized. It was a

beautiful service.

When church was dismissed, the people hurried outside without delivering their usual letters of request. Neil introduced the woman as Abigail Grey, the mother of his son, Georgie, and the other man as Solomon, a close friend. Wayne invited them all for lunch.

I was so glad we had prepared a rice casserole with cornmeal biscuit topping, fruit salad, fresh brown rolls, canned green beans, and coconut cream pie. Abigail wanted to help set the table and pour the ice water.

Neil stood by the twins' crib for a few minutes looking down at them. He reached down and let Oliver grab one of his fingers. "Cute little fellows," he remarked.

He sat down in the living room, his eyes darting all over. "You have a nice place here, Mr. Wayne," he said. "I like these curtains—and all the books around here. Kind of brings back memories."

When dinner was ready, Wayne asked the blessing on the food and on our new friends. Neil's eyes glistened as he surveyed the table. "Solomon, look at this. This is unreal!" he exclaimed unashamedly, addressing his friend. "This is absolutely unbelievable. Real food. Meat and salad and vegetables—and pure water. My dad was a great cook; in fact, he cooked gourmet most of the time."

He took a mouthful of casserole. "Delicious! The beans are wonderful. And the bread . . .

"Did you folks know you were in a very dangerous position when you came through Klay? I saw your two vehicles approaching the checkpoint in our controlled area, and I saw clearly the logo of a cross and a dove, and the words 'Christian Aid.' Something just told me to intervene and control the soldiers. (This fruit mix is excellent . . . excellent!) They were very undisciplined and extremely intimidating and molesting. I ordered that the checkpoint gate be opened and that you be allowed to pass safely through and continue on to Monrovia. (My father made some sort of rice like this, only spicier. He used all kinds of spices in his cooking.)"

"Did you actually see who we were?" Wayne asked quickly.

"I saw every one of you. I never forgot your face, Mr. Wayne. Was Pastor Amos Gaby with you at the time?"

"Yes, he sure was."

"I've known Amos for years. You were in the immediate front line, so I had no time to stop and lecture you. The enemy was only eight hundred yards up that hill."

"No wonder Pastor Amos prayed so hard," Larry whistled.

"As a rule, all vehicles are harassed," Neil went on. "Would you please pass more of those rolls, and the butter?"

I noticed that little Georgie wasn't enjoying the food nearly as much as his father. Abigail kept urging him to eat, but he just pushed it around on his plate.

"Where are you from, Neil?" Wayne asked.

"I was born and raised a few blocks from this very house, so I am a Liberian citizen by birth."

"Tell us about your father," I urged, sensing that he must have been a prominent figure in Neil's life.

Neil's eyes clouded over, and he finished the last bit of salad before he spoke. "My father was a very wealthy, prominent Greek businessman who never believed in God," he began. "My mother was a Brazilian dancer by the name of Yolanda Felix, whom my father met in a bar one night—just one of the many women who came into his life. When he grew tired of one woman, there was always another to take her place."

"That's okay, you don't have to go into detail," Wayne said gently.

"I *want* you to know, Mr. Wayne. I remember all the booze and the parties we hosted. You may find it hard to imagine, but my father loved me and wanted me to make something of my life. He sent me to an American school here in Monrovia till I was twelve, then to Switzerland to a boarding school. I can speak five languages. My father spoke seven, fluently."

"Wow, that must be handy!" Willie exclaimed.

"In Switzerland I began taking drugs, Mr. Wayne—and it's

been a losing battle ever since. Even though I toured all over the world, including the United States, I always wanted to live here with my father. Let me just start from the beginning."

We passed around the pie and Neil's father was temporarily forgotten. "My favorite dessert!" he exclaimed in sheer delight. "Coconut cream pie—with real whipped cream! Mrs. Wayne, this brings back such memories. I never dreamed there was such food in all the city."

"Glad you're enjoying it."

"You are the first normal people I have seen since the war," he continued, eating the pie with great gusto. "People around here are not normal anymore. They need jobs and education desperately, yet they are contentious and lazy and pitifully ignorant."

"Not all of them," we disagreed. He seemed surprised.

"I know these people," he insisted. "I was born here. The good ones are few and far between."

"We know *lots* of good people," Julie answered.

"Let's go find a softer chair," Wayne suggested, and they all retired to the living room. I came in about three minutes later, and Neil was sound asleep, leaning against Abigail.

He slept until Solomon and Abigail decided it was time to leave. Meanwhile, they told us all about Neil's chaotic life. I felt sorry for the man.

"I want to be your friend," said Abigail, putting her arm around me. "Would you just call me 'Abi'?"

"Certainly," I said warmly. "I'd love that."

"Dad, was Neil really a commander in Taylor's army?" Larry asked when they had left. "Do you think it's true that he killed lots of people? Even Elijah and Harris are scared of him, but I'm not."

"I'm sure they don't need to make up stories," Wayne told him. "The truth is bad enough. I sure hope they keep coming to church."

There was no service this evening, so we all walked down to the beach. The ocean rolled and tossed its smooth, curling waves, and a little flock of ocean birds flew just above the swell, their feathers glinting in the sunlight as they watched for small fish. It is amazing how they hover just beyond the water, up and down, teasing the breezes.

Bev and Charlotte kept the blankets close around the twins' dear little faces so they wouldn't get too much of a draft. "Remind me to rub Oliver's neck with peppermint oil again," Wayne said. "I just know it's helping that rattle."

"Some days I can hardly hear his breathing," I agreed.

The sun is becoming a reddish blur as it sinks into the mist above the horizon. Another day in Africa is history.

September 3

"Isn't just *being* in Africa enough schooling for this year?" Larry pleaded as we were deciding on his daily goals in the Christian Light school books. "It isn't every day a fellow gets a chance to buy a baby chimpanzee at his own gate."

"Don't we have enough pets?" I asked.

"All the chimpanzees around here love me," he continued, "but you should have seen how this little guy clung to me and screeched when they pulled him off. I think he likes my white skin—though it's not a bit white anymore. He even wore a diaper—you change him just like a baby."

"Are you kidding? Don't even *think* of buying it!" Charlotte said in dismay. "As if we don't have enough babies to change around here."

I am feeling a leanness of wisdom when it comes to making school interesting for Larry. I simply cannot compete with the outside world.

Late this evening, Jalline Francis, one of the girls in our Bible study class, came to the gate. "I have searched all afternoon for Sis Dorcas's house on Twelfth Street," she said despairingly. "I could not find the place, so I decided to come here."

I gave her money for a taxi to take her back home. "We'll take you to Dorcas's house tomorrow," Julie promised. "It's not hard to find. Are you coming to Bible study?"

"I will be here," Jalline said. "Thank you very much."

September 4

Jalline Francis came to the girls' class today, but we could see she was frightened out of her wits. She looked around at us with terrified eyes and suddenly burst into tears.

"Oh, please, no!" Cleo cried.

"Sit down," Esther said softly, drawing the distraught girl onto a chair.

"When I left here last night I could not find a taxi," she gulped. "Finally I got one with three men in it. They would not put me off when I asked them to. I started reading my Bible and praying desperately, but they took me to Old Road and held a knife in my face. They told me they would kill me. But one of the men in the back seat said, 'Let the girl go!' They shoved me hard out the door and threw my bag out with me. I do not know Old Road. God sent a woman who took me in for the night and gave me water to drink."

We all breathed a sigh of relief. "Let us pray right now to thank Almighty God," Cleo said huskily.

Then and there our little circle of women and girls bowed our heads and thanked God most fervently for protecting Jalline.

God is a shield and a buckler to those who trust in Him.

September 6

God is a God of miracles. A whole pallet of ready-to-feed Similac arrived on the container! We are instructed to use it as soon as possible because it is nearing the expiration date. It is a direct answer to prayer, and we are so thrilled and thankful.

We were bathing the children this morning when Matta and Dennis Johnson arrived with an elderly man who claimed to be Princess's grandfather.

Julie was overjoyed. "You must be Arthur Karnque," she said. "I am."

Charlotte brought Princess out to the living room. Instantly, she detected a very familiar smell—the smell of home and her people and the orphanage. It triggered a lot of memories in her small brain. She shrank against Julie.

"Whyayeh," the old man said softly, making no move toward her.

Princess stood still as a statue, clinging to Julie. She didn't attempt to explore their faces or even go close to them.

"I think she's scared of another change," I said. "Come, Princess, let me hold you."

Dennis spoke up. "We are very sorry to inform you, Julie, but Naomi died in Redemption Hospital las' month. She left a son one-and-a-half years old."

"Naomi died last month?" Julie cried in dismay. "And you're telling me she has a little boy somewhere?"

"I will show you," he replied.

"Who is his father?"

"Junior Ben."

"Can we find him?"

"He lives in Fiama."

"What happened to Naomi? If *only* I could have met her."

"I do not know, Julie."

"I will see you after work," Julie promised. "Meet us at the corner where they sell bread, Dennis."

True to her word, she and Esther slipped down to Fiama Market as soon as they could get away. In a surprisingly short time, they returned to Residence, along with Dennis and a small boy.

"Mom, isn't he the sweetest thing? His name is Secret."

The child gazed at us with great, dark eyes. "When they brought him to me, he sat on my lap as solemn as a judge and didn't make a peep," she continued. "Do you think he looks like Princess?"

"I sure do," said Charlotte. "He's really cute."

"Has he smiled for you yet?" Bev wondered, studying the child with great interest.

"Not yet, but he will."

"Let me hold him!" Bev exclaimed. "He's absolutely adorable."

"We have to hurry if we want to get back before your curfew," Esther reminded Julie.

I just had to hug that little boy before they left. The memory of his dear, sober face tugs at my heart. What will become of this baby?

And what will become of Oliver and Alosious and dear blind Princess and thousands of others like them?

September 8

Neil, Abi, and little Georgie came for the sermon this morning, but left immediately afterward. They had plans to visit her mother, who lives somewhere in Monrovia.

I glanced over at them once during the sermon and saw that Neil's eyes were swimming with tears. His thick bush of brown hair makes him look paler than ever.

Garlic Grace and little Shadrach came to services today. They no longer eat rice once a day at our place since she started a small business selling ice water, thanks to a CAM loan.

"Oh, Muttah!" she said excitedly. "Ah am able to eat wi'out begging fro' you. My Shadrach is gettin' *fat*. Ah am so happy, Muttah. Praise God fo' Christian Aid."

Pastor George Wonlon and his family came for a delightful visit. It was rather late when they got up to leave, so Wayne and I took them home to the Doe Community.

It was pitch dark when we stopped to drop them off, having gone as far as we could. The black sewer puddles gleamed in the headlights. "The truck cannot go where we need to go," George smiled. "We mus' take off our shoes and make our way through. Too much rain."

"Imagine wading through those deep puddles to get home," I said despairingly. "Think of all the filth and the creepy crawlies in that sludge."

Bev was rocking Oliver when we got home. Wayne took him and gently rubbed peppermint oil all over the back and front of his neck.

"It is definitely making him breathe easier," Bev observed. "Why don't we take him to Doctor Brisbane in Firestone to see if there's anything he can do?"

"We should probably wait until someone goes out there and hitch a ride," Wayne said.

September 15

The rain started gently during morning service, bringing with it the most beautiful scent in the world.

I was beginning to wonder where all the people would fit. They just kept coming and coming, moving closer together to make room. Every available space was full.

Pastor Mervin's sermon was on the tongue. "Words, words, *words*," he said. "How they can hurt—and how they can heal."

We appreciate the way pastor Mervin preaches. He doesn't scream or gesture, but speaks quietly and forcefully. He certainly doesn't mince words.

Agutta and Amos came to me after church. "You are growing big," I said to Amos, noticing how his arms and cheeks have filled out. Agutta jerked up his shirt and revealed his angry-looking scar. It was red and puffy, and his whole stomach looked distended.

"Whatever is wrong?" I asked with concern.

"I do not know what the problem is," she said quietly. "I jus' pray and pray that God Almighty will heal Amos. He will help me."

Anthony Reeves, Moses Massawalla, Merci Evans, and Dorcas Johnson were among our dinner guests today. Since we feed Security anyway, we like to be prepared on Sunday.

"I am thinking about your request, Sis Ruth," Moses reminded me. "When the time is right, I will write it out for you."

September 17

More news on Princess's family. Even though it is raining heavily, Tumba, Esther, and Julie visited Redemption Hospital to see if Naomi had died there.

"They went through the death records for the last month and

found a Naomi Ban, but it was misspelled," Julie explained. "They meant Naomi Ben, which was her boyfriend's name, so we knew it was the same girl. She was only twenty-one years old. She died from anemia and malnourishment, which simply means she starved to death. The hospital said no one came when she died, so after four days they buried her."

"Where was Junior Ben?" I asked. The picture of that discarded young girl dying alone and unloved was certainly not a pretty one.

"We went to Fiama and talked to him too. I guess he lost interest pretty quickly when Naomi got sick. But he did tell us that she told him she had taken Princess to her aunt. At least that matches all the other accounts we've heard."

"Tell her about the uncle," prompted Esther.

"Oh yes. A man approached us and said he was Princess's uncle. He had been gathering coal in the bush for a month. I asked him a long list of questions, and he told me exactly what Matta and Dennis had. Then I asked him how Princess's eyes looked. I knew he would have no way of knowing unless he had seen her. He said there was some kind of bubble or knot or something on it."

"He knew her," we agreed.

I gave Princess a hug, and she giggled with delight.

"It is too bad her mother died," Julie said wistfully. "She was so close, and so sick, and we never knew it. I wish we could have told her we'll do everything possible for her children."

"Who takes care of little Secret?" Charlotte wondered.

"He lives with Mr. Borbor, Naomi's father," Julie said.

Tonight the rain is drumming on the roof again with a steady roar that becomes louder and louder, fades a bit, then returns with greater intensity then ever. My mind goes to the poverty-stricken locals who have to wade to their beds and then lie there in the black night wondering if the flimsy roof will hold up under the deluge.

September 19

Curt and Evelyn Kauffman are back from furlough, and they brought us twelve jars of peppermint oil. I'm sure Dr. Lamin will be delighted. We use it for everything from toothaches to insect bites.

Larry had the last two Fridays off from school; this one because David Holder, a truck driver for CAM, brought him a jungle parrot, and last Friday because he and Elijah were building a cage for the anticipated newcomer. Elijah bought an armful of assorted sticks and we had some wire in the warehouse, so the cage looks good.

"He's a beauty!" Larry exclaimed when Holder took off the cloth covering the little bamboo cage. "I'm calling him Pirate."

Pirate was a brilliant green, with beady black eyes and a sharp curved beak. When anyone's fingers came too close, he tried to peck through the flimsy cage walls.

"Let Elijah put him in the new cage," I suggested after Holder left.

Pirate's exploring beak soon discovered that the door of the cage was not tight. He pushed hard against it. Elijah and Larry both grabbed at the same time, but it was too late—Pirate was free! He flew gracefully up among the plum tree branches, a bright spot of color against the darker foliage.

Elijah groaned. Larry stood looking up into the tree. "It is of no use, Larry," Elijah said quietly. "Ah am sorry."

"It's not your fault. Maybe we can trick him somehow."

But Pirate was gone for good.

A somber Larry trailed into the house and sat down, but not for long. "Sierra Fox One," barked my radio.

"Go ahead, Sierra Fox Four."

"They just killed a king cobra behind the CAM office."

"Let's go, Mom, please?" begged Larry.

We left the children with Charlotte and drove down to the office, where people had gathered at the welding shop along the CAM wall.

Willie joined us. "They shook the snake out of an iron pipe they brought from Jamaica Road three days ago," he said. "First a snake skin fell out, then a mad cobra. They went after it with iron bars, and it reared its head back and swelled out its hood. When it was dead, they burned the head in the incinerator. They measured it first—it was six feet, five inches."

"Let's not go too close," I said nervously.

The men lifted the black serpent out of the brown paper bag where they were keeping it for supper. It dangled awkwardly on the long stick.

Suddenly I felt a strange scratching on my ankle. I screamed wildly. Willie backed away, holding a little branch in his hand.

"William Wayne Stelfox!"

The group of elderly people waiting at the CAM gate broke out into chortles of laughter. They swayed back and forth, slapping their thighs and grinning delightedly. I felt so sappy.

"Sorry, Mom," said Willie. "I can see why it would bug you to think of a snake like this living near the office. He was wicked."

Wayne met us at the office and wondered if Larry and I could come along with him and Esther to assess some new CAM Self-Help business prospects. "I'll call Charlotte and tell her," I said happily. "We'd love to come along." In no time we were bumping back into a small alley.

Lena wants to expand her restaurant, which consists of one low table partitioned off by a shabby curtain. She would continue to cook in the house, but could CAM help? One table was just not enough.

Grace wants to sew for people, so she needs a machine. Her place is a dingy room in a huge old concrete monster of a building rising above a swamp. The walls are crumbling and filthy and full of blackened mold. The steps are thin concrete slabs with no braces. The huge windows stand wide open.

"Don't fall," Wayne cautioned. "This is dangerous."

Grace scratched her hair continuously. "When the rains come, ah can see the trash more an' more," she complained, indicating the swampy area that stretched out below. It had indeed been a trash heap—worked into the ground to provide more "land" to build upon.

"My man caught a snake in the swamp for food—big snake. Lots of meat," she informed us.

"At least they can't crawl up these steps." I told Esther.

Marie lives in a rusted out shipping container. She, too, would like a sewing machine. I pitied her desperately. How could you sew inside a metal oven? How could you sleep?

God, forgive me when I whine—I have a home, the world is mine.

Driving toward the boulevard to go home, we saw a police car approaching at high speed down the center of the road with its siren wailing. "Uh-oh," said Wayne. "The president's moving—let's park right here."

Vehicles scattered off the road like leaves before a Nor'wester. Even though we were squeezed off to the side, the officers in the next vehicle leaned out the windows and angrily motioned us to move off further. The taxis next to us skidded over the sidewalks and into the grass before the next loaded truck screamed by.

The next set of vehicles came three abreast—a sports car flanked by two Jeeps with black windows. Presently, the third set came flying by—also two Jeeps with a car in between. Several camouflaged trucks full of armed soldiers were next in line, their guns held ready. One truck had a rocket launcher mounted on the hood.

"Someone told me those guns can spew out forty-seven bullets per minute," Wayne told us. "They have hair triggers with no safety clips. Can you imagine?"

No one could.

Police sirens drowned out our voices as their cars screamed along behind the soldiers. Then a lone Cruiser sailed by.

"That's it," Wayne said. "I counted twenty vehicles."

Cars edged back onto the boulevard, humping over sidewalks and curbs and manholes to get back into the mainstream, pushing their noses impatiently out and forcing others to stop and let them in.

September 22

Pastor Mervin continued his sermon on the tongue this morning. The church was overflowing; some of the children had to sit on chairs upstairs to make room for the adults.

We had a crowd for lunch today, including Neil, Abi, and Georgie. They insisted Wayne and I come see their place this evening and eat rice with them.

Our whole family, including the babies, slept most of the afternoon. If company came to the gate, Elijah must have told them to come back some other time. He has been such a blessing to us, especially to Larry.

Around five o'clock, Wayne and I walked down an alley to Neil and Abi's place, where little Georgie met us. He smiled shyly and held out his brown hand.

Neil and Abi live in a tiny borrowed room along an inlet of the Mesurado River, right across from Shanty Town. The land is so built up with trash that the river no longer comes up to the dwellings. The steady lapping of the water has deposited sand over much of the trash.

"Welcome, welcome, Mr. and Mrs. Wayne!" Neil exclaimed warmly. "Sit down right here."

Abi greeted me with a hug and immediately began dishing out generous bowls of rice topped with dried fish. The chickens jumped up onto the table where she was cooking and pecked around for any bits of food. Abi chased them off.

When we bowed our heads to pray I sent a private prayer heavenward. *"Lord, just in case . . . I may need help."*

"We don't always have such good food," Abi explained happily. "It just so happened we had something special on hand for you."

The food was so spicy that I thought I would faint. My throat burned as if I were inhaling fire. I tried to keep the tears from coursing down my cheeks as I picked carefully through the thin, sharp bones and the skin of the pungent fish. Wayne swallowed hard a few times, but he can stand much more zest than I.

There was no water available besides bags of warm street

water. Now I know how people feel when they eat at our table for the first time and pick at the bland food as if it has no taste. It all depends on what you're used to eating.

"Abi takes turns cooking with all the other women who live in the adjoining rooms," Neil informed us. "It's simply a version of communal living, a way of coping with the lack of basic necessities."

A fierce, red-faced goose patrolled the banks of the river. "He's the major security around here because he chases all the kids," Neil laughed.

He didn't seem to bother Georgie, who sat on the banks and threw stones into the river.

A wooden, crescent-shaped fishing boat swiftly approached the inlet, full of swarthy men with breechcloths tied around their waists. They all stood upright, holding their oars and paddling with long, powerful strokes. "That thing must be forty feet long!" Wayne exclaimed.

"That boat was built in Ghana and sailed over here three weeks on the high seas," Neil answered.

"It looks just like a Viking ship with all those paintings and the sharp bow," I observed. "Are they fishermen?"

"They are almost fish," smiled Neil. "Those tribes are such incredible ocean people that you can't drown them—they just act like corks in the water. Every boat goes for a certain kind of fish. Someday I'll have to take you to see what they catch in a day."

"Like what?" Wayne asked.

"I've seen tremendous catches of herring, cassava fish, barracuda up to six feet long, great blue marlin, hammerhead sharks, and tuna. Of course, there are many varieties of smaller ones. I tell you, this place has superb fishing."

"Would you like to see an abandoned baby?" Abi asked, changing the subject.

"Of course. What happened to her mother?"

Abi hurried to get the baby while Neil explained. "In this country there is no justice. The child's mother had a jealous rival who poisoned her. No one knew what was happening to her because she would get sick, and then seem to improve. The witch doctor performed all kinds of questionable methods of healing, but as we both know, he is useless. She finally died in agony—and now there's another Liberian orphan. The woman later confessed."

Abi arrived with the woman who cares for the baby. The child is three months old, and very thin and listless. "What do you feed her?" I asked.

"Fufu," she answered, referring to a starchy white product made from fermented cassava roots.

"A baby can't digest fufu," I said.

"That's all we have," the woman said quietly.

"We have milk for her," I said, thinking of the Similac. "I will give it to Abi."

"Thank you very much, Missie," the woman said, her eyes shining with gratitude. "God will bless you."

I could imagine how desperately the poor mother had wanted to live for her infant daughter—how she wondered what was happening to her, never suspecting she was being poisoned.

After the meal, we walked down to the river's shore. From there we could see into the next compound. "That is my father's house," Neil said sadly. "We lived there until he died. There's the swimming pool, and that's the balcony where my father was sitting when he was shot."

"Do you care to share?"

"I want to, Mr. Wayne. In 1990, when the civil war began, all the civilians were hiding from the government soldiers. The different army factions were fighting for the rice stored at Freeport. The rebels overpowered President Doe's forces, who threw off their uniforms and fled along the river. One of them saw my father sitting on the porch and opened fire, wounding him badly. I was terrified, Mr. Wayne. I crept to the gate and looked out the peephole. Directly across the street were the advancing rebels. I decided to take my chances and ran over to them. They were surprised and asked what I wanted. 'Please help . . . my father is wounded,' I pleaded. 'Son, many of our men are wounded and need help,' they replied. 'But be at your gate in exactly five minutes—we'll be there to pick you up.' "

Neil paused, his eyes clouding with the awful memories. "In five minutes, those tired rebel soldiers helped my heavy, obese father into the back of their truck and, not knowing what they would encounter, made for the closest hospital. At eight o'clock that night they reached the hospital across town, and my father's life was saved. Someday I will tell you of his tragic end."

"Then what did you do, Neil?"

"I liked what I saw, Mr. Wayne. Even though these soldiers were unshaved and desperately tired, they remained disciplined and controlled in the face of danger. I was already angry with the government troops, so I joined the rebels. The senseless war that followed destroyed Monrovia. It has never recovered."

"God kept you alive for a reason," Wayne said.

"That's exactly what Pastor Mervin claims," Neil returned. "I am finally able to see a glimmer of light. I want to get my life back on track and live like you do, with a family, a church, and regular meals. You have it so good, Mr. Wayne.

"Now that I'm off drugs, things look so much better. Imagine the wasted years when I could have been a real man. The young soldiers with me would cut out the heart of an enemy soldier, slice it thin, and eat it off the tips of their knives, just to prove to their superiors how brave they were. I know I can never erase such memories, Mr. Wayne."

Wayne encouraged him to keep talking. One Bible subject led to another, and it was past curfew when we rose to leave. "I feel as if I have been around normal people again," Neil said. "It is through terrible poverty and hardship that the Liberians have become what they are. We will see you in church, if not before."

Abi hugged me. "I am so happy at the turn of things in my life," she whispered. "Neil is a different man."

25

Visitors from the States

September 27

Our family was invited to Dr. Lamin's place for supper this evening. We drove to his country home in Chocolate City, bouncing all the way. Dr. Lamin, his wife Gertrude, Moses Jr., Paul, Florence, Mary, and Mema were waiting for us.

We all sat around the little porch and ate delicious potato salad, cold Fanta, street bread, and rice.

Dr. Lamin related a chilling incident that happened not far from Monrovia. "A woman planned to sell her fifteen-year-old niece to society people who aimed to kill the girl for her blood an' other body parts. The taxi driver was suspicious because the woman gave him fifty American dollars to carry her an' the girl to a remote area in the bush an' put them off. He dropped them off an' parked his car, then circled quietly back. The woman had disappeared to call her contact, so he took the girl an' they climbed a tree and waited. Soon the aunt reappeared, an' then a black car with two men. The woman began yelling the girl's name an' ordered her to come. The men became impatient an' nervous, an' just like that they stabbed the woman with a knife, drained all her blood, cut out her heart an' other organs, an' carried the remains to the bush."

We were speechless with horror.

"The driver and the terrified girl were eyewitnesses to the grisly act," Dr. Lamin broke the silence. "He had to calm the girl so she would not cry out. It was a terrible, terrible deed that backfired on the woman. She anticipated much cash, but instead she died."

"Proverbs speaks of a man digging a pit and falling into it himself," Wayne said soberly.

"The elections are coming next year," Gertrude said darkly. "That means human sacrifices will escalate dramatically. Keep close watch on the children before and during the elections, Mrs. Wayne."

I hugged Alosious closer. "No wonder God seems to have turned His face from Liberia," I said.

"There are still enough righteous among us that we are not totally destroyed," said Dr. Lamin. "But it is a sad fact that Satanism is still practiced in this country. It is not uncommon for a woman's dismembered body to be found on the beach over election time. It is not good to walk alone after dark."

"Let's go home right now," said Larry.

October 2

Kathy Kauffman e-mailed today. It seems so long since we've heard from her, but I can imagine how full her days must be. Nathan is slowly improving and even seems to have some good days.

Charlotte and I baked some dinner rolls and peanut butter cookies to take along to Nimba County tomorrow. Jon Stoltzfus, Mark Nolt, and Nelson Sensenig, all from Pennsylvania, are flying in. They want to see some orphanages, agricultural projects, and medical clinics. Wayne wants me along to keep a diary, and I guess I could use a break.

October 3

At eight o'clock this morning we left the CAM base—Dr. Lamin, Iddo, Mark Nolt, and George Flomo in the new Defender and Wayne, Nelson Sensenig, Jon Stoltzfus, Sam Kargbo, and I in the Cruiser. More would have come if we'd had room.

We picked up our second driver, Bundo, near Paynesville. He generally has the privilege of driving the new Defender since he is so careful.

Our first stop was Project New Outlook, where Iddo explained all the details of rice cultivation and production. "If the workers don't scare the birds away, they literally suck the milk out of the tender young plants. This kind of land can yield up to sixty bags of rice per bag of seed, while upland rice only yields twenty," he said.

"I wish we could see a big snake—from the vehicle, of course," Jon said when we were back on the road.

"We just may," Sam answered. "Boss and I saw a large green mamba recently. They are all around the area."

"Here is the first orphanage for the day," Sam announced as Wayne pulled in alongside an old building.

The Gbarnga Orphanage director is a very heavy lady who complained bitterly about the bush children who come at mealtime and just sit and stare while "her" orphans eat.

"Da chil'ren are brought to da police when their parents are killed or taken prisoner—an' da police bring dem here. Wha' shou' ah do? Dey are many! Wha' wou' *you* do? If da chil'ren sit next to you so hungry an' you had food to feed them?"

"I would do the same thing you are," the men told her.

"Ahhh, den we need more food."

"If we send you more food, the word will spread and you will have a thousand stray children here, Mother," Sam explained to her.

"Poor little things," Wayne said. "Imagine not knowing what happened to your parents, or worse yet, seeing them die, and then begging for food to stay alive."

Mother Blessing Orphanage was our next stop. "These children just arrived here and are in bad shape yet," Sam told us. "But now they are on the CAM program, so they will be fine.

There are sixty-five children here."

The children looked ragged, tired, and so dirty. Many of them had great, scaly patches of ringworm that they scratched constantly. Others had scalp fungus, warts, infected eyes, and scabies.

"They will receive medical attention very soon," Sam assured the visitors.

The caretakers sat on the ground, bathing tiny twin girls in a dark brown solution made from the bark of pine trees. One woman lifted the skinniest baby up for us to see her sore little bottom. It was a strange, whitish color. "No skin," she said, pointing. "No skin left." The child cried weakly.

"Get a case of Thick 'n Easy from the back of the truck, Bundo," Wayne said.

I explained to the women how to use the thick, pudding-like nutritional food that CAM received from donors in the States. It is all packaged in small boxes and needs no refrigeration, so it is perfect for such situations.

"Whew! I've never seen anything like this before," Nelson exclaimed as we left. "Those children are in bad shape."

"You'll get a different picture at the next place," Wayne assured him. "It takes time, but you won't recognize these children in a month."

The Golden Rule Orphanage sits on a bit of a rise and thrives with busy children, clean rooms, an airy outdoor kitchen, and a monkey. They have a huge garden for the children to tend, and all their plants must be transplanted to lower ground during the dry season so they don't wither.

The caretaker is sweet and chubby and wears a white winter toque.

"It certainly is different," agreed Nelson. "Looks like the CAM-sponsored orphans are doing well."

At the Kennedy Orphanage near Saclapea the boys were making nice, firm red bricks with prepared soil from the termite hills. "The termites do all the work and the boys use their soil," Sam smiled. "It is a wonderful arrangement."

"What would you like for Christmas?" I asked a cute little fellow with no front teeth.

Immediately some little girls surrounded me. "A daw baby! Please, a daw baby!" they cried, their beautiful dark eyes shining with hope.

"I can't promise, but I'll see what I can do," I told them, squeezing their sweaty little palms in my own.

Finally we reached the village of Saclapea—and Sis Teresa's orphanage. (Teresa is Cleo Hardy's mother and a member of the Liberia Mennonite Church.) She is a buxom, delightful woman with great plans for a new orphanage way back in the bush.

"I want to show you the fruits of my labor," she said happily. "Come along."

We followed her along a narrow, winding jungle path until we came to her new settlement. The girls' dorm is under roof, but the boys' is barely started.

"There is much to do before we can move in," she said cheerfully.

"How do you find your way down here at night?" Mark wanted to know.

"We use a torch," she answered. "It keeps the animals away."

"I think we better go back before it gets dark," Sam suggested, and no one objected.

October 4

A slow drizzly rain greeted us this morning. We had Rice Krispie squares, bananas, and coffee before we hit the road.

"Elijah claims rainy season is over, but it sure doesn't look like it," Wayne commented.

We stopped for fuel in Ghanta. The owners of the little gas station brought several gallon jars of fuel and proceeded to siphon it into our tank with a rubber hose. The man would suck on the end of the hose, get the gas flowing, and quickly transfer it to our tank. Twenty-nine jars later, the tank was full.

Hours later, we reached the small town of Gbedian, where a torrential rain had swept through and caused a rice dam to overflow. We stepped out of the vehicles into the mud among crowds of curious people.

"It is bad," we were told. "Come, we will show you."

They led us back along a muddy road to the rice fields, a younger guide taking the lead and many of the villagers following. The swollen creek gushed over the elevated road, where it had washed away some five hundred bags of seed rice. The water swirled in angry circles, carrying the stalks of rice around and piling them here and there. It was sickening.

The village people looked on with quiet resignation on their faces. Only they knew of the hours they had spent in the scorching African sun, carefully planting and transplanting those fields of rice. Only they knew the hours they had spent guarding it from the birds.

"The hard rain nevah stopped fo' five hours," the village chief explained quietly. "Da watah washed da rice out of the groun' . . . nothing we kin do."

The villagers have decided to try to gather the damaged rice and divide it amongst themselves. The fields that were not damaged will also be divided so every person receives the same amount.

We visited another field where the soil is so rich they cannot use fertilizer. "We plant vegetables and rice every other year," the guide said proudly. "One acre can yield twenty-five bags, an' if we had a tractor, we could triple that."

"What is that black shiny thing?" I asked, noticing a large black blob in the grass.

"That's a snail," Sam answered. "They are excellent in taste, and healthy too. The doctors recommend eating plenty of them for protein and vision improvement."

Our visit came to an abrupt end as red ants living on the rice dikes began swarming aggressively, angry at our intrusion. Even though we hurried back to the Defender, some managed to come aboard and bite us.

Our next stop was at the farm where former President Tubman lived—and where President Taylor keeps his lion pair. George Flomo offered to find the gatekeeper, so we meandered up the paved road to Tubman's mansion.

The gatekeeper opened the gate and we walked up to the lions' cage and looked down on the mangy beasts. George Flomo gasped and backed away. His eyes doubled in size.

The male lion glared up at us with fierce amber eyes. The sunlight glinting through the trees slanted off the bars and caught the wicked gleam of his teeth as his lips pulled back in a snarl. He lifted his head with a primeval roar.

George's eyes bulged in sheer terror. "Oh, let's go! Let's go!"

The lioness gave a short, sharp spring toward us and opened her jaws menacingly. "Look!" yelped George, frozen with fear. "Their eyes turn blue and green and black . . ."

"This woman feeds them an' cleans out their cage every morning," the gatekeeper told us, indicating the black woman who had followed us in. "They eat nothing but boneless beef at all times. She has been doing it ever since they were cubs."

"Can you believe that woman?" George tossed back over his shoulder as he hurried down the path.

"Now," said Wayne once we were on the road again, "I'd like to treat you fellows to some delicious coconut milk. You've got to be hungry. You hardly ate anything the last two days, Nelson."

We soon found a coconut peddler who expertly chipped the top off a coconut and handed it to Nelson. "It's guaranteed sterile and fresh," Wayne advertised. "Really tasty too."

Nelson took a sip. "Oh!" he exclaimed, shaking his head. He swallowed hard, and bravely tried again. "Ugh. I'm sorry, Wayne—it just doesn't want to go down."

At Paynesville Market I waited in the Cruiser while the guests looked around. Darkness was falling, but the market was wildly busy. Soon they were back with a nice, fresh cassava fish.

Nelson looked strangely uncomfortable. "I saw a dead

275

groundhog . . . ready to eat," he managed before lowering his voice just above a whisper. "It looked bloated; I am sure it did."

"It was a bit old," agreed Sam nonchalantly. "But if it had been fresh, I would have had me a good soup tonight."

"That groundhog! It was horrible!" Jon exploded when he opened the door. "But come with me, Sam—I have a question for you," and he led Sam back to the market.

"Oh, yes. Dried monkey is delicious," Sam was saying when they returned. "They skin the animal and dry the meat in strips. Ummm. Delicious!"

Nelson took a deep, quavering breath in an all-too-apparent effort to settle his stomach.

"You people waste meat in the States," Sam continued. "Every time I saw a road kill when I was in the States I wanted to stop and pick it up, but the lady whose car I was using told me, 'Keep going, Sam. We don't eat that around here.' I would have gone for it right quick."

"I will think of you every time I see a road kill," Jon laughed.

We arrived home at six thirty this evening. "We want to hear *everything*," the children told us. We visited long into the night, holding the twins and Princess, who said so sweetly, "I love you, Muttah."

October 10

This morning, Larry and I were fortunate enough to be with Wayne and the Americans on a distribution of Support-A-Widow and Aid-for-the-Aged parcels in the bush near Kakata.

We met Akin and George Wonlon at the CAM base at seven. We picked up Bundo again in Paynesville so he could drive the Defender. He wasted no time, driving at speeds of 75 to 80 miles per hour so we could finish the distribution and have the guests back in time for their afternoon flight out.

After several hours, we reached a huge, ruined bridge that arched at a frightening angle down into a swift, brown river. "A transport truck was overloaded," Akin explained. "It plunged down right through the bridge—and there is no money to fix it. We must cross the river by canoe."

I stared in dismay at the wide, brown, seething water with swirling currents everywhere. It looked deadly.

"How deep is it?" I asked Bundo.

"*Too* deep," he answered.

"Really," I asked again, "about how deep is it?"

"I would say around two hundred and fifty feet," George put in. "In the dry season we have a wide shore below us, but now there is nothing but the river. The Farmington and Bolo rivers merge at this point."

"Is that the boat coming across?" Larry asked, a note of apprehension in his voice.

"Yes," Bundo answered. "It is the only method of crossing the river. Did you know my people live in that village?" He pointed across the river.

"Then you know the place!" exclaimed Wayne.

"I know it well," said Bundo with satisfaction.

"What makes all those whirlpools on top of the water?" Larry asked.

"The undercurrent is very strong," Bundo told him.

Soon the hollowed-out log arrived, guided by an older man with two oars. "Let us pray for safety before we go," Akin said solemnly.

"I *can't* ride in that thing!" I said desperately.

"It is not safe for you to remain here alone," Bundo said emphatically. "You must come."

The Americans were very sober. "You go first with your wife," they told Wayne. "Hang onto the canoe if it tips."

Larry climbed in carefully, then Wayne. He turned to give me an unsteady hand. I told myself that many others had crossed, including our girls, so I bravely stepped into the two inches of water in the bottom of the canoe. It swayed easily.

"Does it leak?" Wayne asked.

"Naw much—jus' a little," the man said.

The load limit was four people, but since Larry is not heavy, Akin came with us too. The canoe stood about ten inches out of the water.

We headed upstream so we would arrive at the other shore just right. I will never forget the sensation of gliding over that dangerous African river. I stared at the murky water, afraid to hold onto the sides lest something come up out of the water. What if one of those awful currents would catch us?

I forced thoughts of snakes and crocodiles out of my mind. Larry shifted position and the boat swayed. "Don't move," I begged.

Relief flooded through me as we glided under the overhanging trees along the opposite shore and the canoe came to a gentle, grinding halt. We stepped clumsily out into shallow water and on up the bank, where the entire village waited.

"Praise God!" Akin said happily. "These are the villages we like to reach, where the most vulnerable and neediest people live."

We have seen a lot of ragged clothing, but this was the worst. Some garments were so threadbare they hung in strips over various parts of the body. The children were basically naked except for a strip around their middle. "We came to the right place," Wayne said.

We waited for the next group, who had to come without Mark. "When he got in, the canoe began to sink," Jon explained.

Mark came over last. "I took a picture of the tip of the boat, because no one will ever believe I was in that thing," he commented dryly.

Back in the village, the people were quickly lined up outside an old shack while Akin organized a system of distribution. Wayne and George filled out forms and questioned the people, then sent them over to where Akin, Larry, and I would give them the parcels.

Each older person received ten U.S. dollars and a parcel with canned chicken, soap, shampoo, a toothbrush, and more.

I couldn't resist unrolling some of those lovely blankets before I handed them over. The people couldn't believe their eyes. Bundo stood and watched approvingly.

Presently, a blind old man was directed toward us. "He is my brother," Bundo said, happy to see him receive a lovely creation of deep purple, lavender, white, and lilac.

"Too bad he can't see it," Larry said sadly.

Toward the end of our supplies, the people got so impatient they began to push and shove, regardless of Akin's shouting. "It is time to go," he decided, emptying the last bag and dividing the contents among several people. "We are out of resources."

It was so hard to see the remainder of the villagers leave empty-handed. They lingered, just in case. "We will come back," Akin promised.

We almost missed the opposite bank when we went back across the river. The oarsman began to paddle hard and fast to keep us from being swept downstream.

"Now that was too close," Wayne admitted when we were finally safe. "I thought for sure we'd end up in the ocean."

When everyone was back, we headed for home with much to think about.

"Another story to tell," Nelson said, shaking his head.

"We'll never forget Liberia," Jon added with feeling.

26

A World Apart

Marie came at eight o'clock to clean house as usual. She leaned unsteadily against the counter and looked at me with glazed eyes. Beads of sweat stood on her face and trickled down her neck.

"Marie! What's wrong?"

"Ah have malaria, Muttah."

"You aren't cleaning today, my dear girl," I told her firmly.

"Ah will clean," she returned weakly. She pushed her bandanna back with a trembling hand.

"Marie, it is not necessary," I said. "It would spoil my day watching you try to wash these floors. Bev will take you home. She's driving down to Fiama anyway."

Without further protest, she agreed. I gave her a small bottle of Tylenol and a box of apple juice. I felt the stark contrast of our lives when I watched her climb slowly into the Cruiser and shut the door with effort.

When one of us is sick we receive the best of care—soft pillows, cold juices, hot baths, neck massages, and twenty-four hour maid service. It is actually enjoyable being sick sometimes if one doesn't feel too bad.

Marie will go home to her little room, lie there shivering and aching all over, and try to keep Freddie occupied. It isn't fair.

October 17

Wonderful news from a far country today! Julie got an official letter stating that an eye specialist in Hershey, Pennsylvania, is willing to perform surgery on Princess's eye free of charge.

Julie immediately attempted to get her passport, but the embassy refused, so we hope Wayne can get some of the needed information from the States since there is no way we can estimate the amount of the hospital bill.

I feel that God is working a plan for Princess's life. It's so thrilling to hear good news after so much waiting. Meanwhile, Princess keeps this household full of her lively chatter. She is so gentle and loving with the twins that we let her help us feed them when she wants to.

We had visits from Garlic Grace, Agutta, and Abi today. They all wanted to stop and see how the twins and Princess are faring. Grace and Agutta asked for some baby formula, but I told them firmly that it is for starving babies only. I hope I didn't sound too stern.

Since I prefer not to take time out when Larry and Charlotte are working on their lessons, I explain our situation and continue working. The ladies don't mind. They are perfectly content to sit on the couch and relax for an hour or two.

Larry's buddies urge him to finish his schoolwork so he can play soccer. No matter how I scold them, they keep sending whistle signals. This morning, the signals began much too early. I marched outside, through the open gate, and down the street to the almond tree where several boys sat on the branches.

"Boys, if you don't stop calling Larry, I won't let him play at all today," I told them.

They looked down at me, grinning. "Aw righ', O'Ma—we will naw call him," Darling Boy said.

Wayne is working overtime at the office since he is scheduled to go back to the States to represent Liberia at CAM's Open

House on November 1 and 2.

He must have known I was lonesome already, so today he came home early. We drove to Hotel Africa and sat at an oceanside table sipping ice-cold Fanta and watching the fishing boats fight the waves. In one sturdy vessel stood seven men, their oars glinting above the dark water as they dipped and pulled. They would meet each wave squarely, bob way up on a crest and plunge gracefully into the slough until we could barely see them.

Across the ocean, American men were revving up their speedboat motors for a day of fast fun in the sun. What a world apart.

October 18

One of the church sisters told me about Malise, a shy thirteen-year-old thrown out of her home onto the streets. Wicked men waiting for that very occasion descended on her like vultures, and soon she was pregnant, terrified, and discarded like an old rag.

An evil adviser directed her to one of the hideous back-alley shanties where a witch doctor performed a gruesome abortion. Malise developed a severe infection and died in agony several days later.

"This happens to countless others," the sister told me. "They have no one to help them and it's either get rid of the baby so they can get back on the streets or die of starvation. The witch doctors thrive on such practices."

I listened to the story with horror. Those poor little girls!

October 24

Wayne, Dr. Lamin, and Mr. Nimley, a CAM driver, left for the States today. There is a gnawing emptiness around here, so I plan to keep busier than ever to make the time go faster. Willie is the man of the house now.

Dr. Lamin, all dressed up in a new, close-fitting, light brown suit, shook our hands and said gravely, "Well, Ruth Ann, I am ready for your country," but he couldn't hide the sparkle in his eyes.

"You better not try too many American foods, or you won't be able to wear that new suit for very long," I warned. "How will you ever survive without your daily rice?"

"I will eat American rice," he chuckled.

Neil came over to say good-bye. "You're looking much better," Wayne observed.

"I'm off the heroin, Mr. Wayne!" he answered jubilantly. "I've been such a slave till now—but by God's grace that's over. Pray for me, Mr. Wayne. I will miss you."

"I'll miss you, too, Neil."

Dave Waines brought his family here this evening and asked if they could sleep upstairs. Their beach house in Elwa was looted and their home in Ghanta is unsafe because of advancing rebels.

"If we could stay for a day or two, I would appreciate it very much," he said. "I just don't feel comfortable going back yet."

"We will try our best not to be a bother," Audrey said wearily.

"Don't worry for a minute—we just might keep you awake," Julie said. "Nights aren't very relaxing in this house."

"Have you ever thought of the possibility of putting these children you're caring for up for adoption?" Dave commented.

"We have thought about it," I said slowly. "I just can't imagine living without them."

"If you ever need help," Dave continued, "I know just the man to do it—a man by the name of Mitchel Clemmer. I'll give you his number right now, just in case."

I wasn't too interested, but I took the number and tossed it into a drawer.

Bev showed our guests upstairs. "We never know what might happen around here," she told Audrey. "I'm just glad we have extra room for you."

Elijah came in to announce the arrival of yet another baby ma just as we finished helping the Waines family get settled. "Muttah, da woma' needs you," he said simply.

"She must be desperate to come at night like this. Let her come in, Elijah. You come along with her, okay?"

As soon as the woman saw us, she began making all kinds of

gestures and signs, waving her arms in all directions and pointing to us, then to the baby on her back. Her hair was a matted tangle of dreadlocks, and her eyes were wild and worried. There were small open sores all over her hands and legs where she had clawed at her scabies infestation. Her lapa was filthy and torn. A terrible odor surrounded her.

"Is she out of her mind?" I asked Elijah.

"She canno' speak English. She comes fro' the bush," he said apologetically.

The woman turned, still jabbering, and let us see the baby. It lay listlessly against her skinny back. It turned feebly, but did not lift its head. Its eyes were half closed in sunken sockets. Little legs dangled like two large wooden spoon handles.

"Girls, this doesn't look good. Put the twins back in their beds, just in case," I said.

"The baby's dying!" Charlotte cried.

"It's starving," I muttered. "Please hurry and get the milk and a bottle. Is it a girl, Elijah?"

"Ah don' know, Muttah. Ah canno' speak her language."

We gave her a lovely layette with snow-white diapers, rubber panties, diaper pins, powder, lotion, washcloths, baby soap, two sleepers, two T-shirts, two bottles, and a small toy. She knew what they were. She grabbed the soap and made circular motions on her chest, smiling and clucking. She ran her hands over the soft cotton blanket and held it to her face. She unscrewed the lotion and smelled it. She held up the sleepers and looked at them with hungry eyes.

Julie gave her two new pieces of fabric for a lapa. She instantly held them high and danced in a circle. "She's happy," Elijah smiled.

When her excitement died down, we showed her how to open the milk and pour it into the bottle. She unwrapped the infant and inserted the bottle in its mouth. The baby gave a start of surprise, tasted the heavy, warm milk, and began to suck.

"Thank God!" I breathed.

Three ounces later, the child fell asleep. We tried hard to tell the mother to feed the baby whenever it cries, and to come back in two days. I hope we got through to her. What an incredible barrier language can be.

"Where do you think she lives?" I asked Elijah when the woman had gone.

"In da bush, Muttah. She has no home."

When the house was finally quiet, I opened the computer to read our e-mails. There was a letter for the girls, and one from Kurt and Marilyn Shores, a couple in Wisconsin that has e-mailed us once or twice. They have five adopted children of their own, and they heard from Curt's folks that twin boys were available.

> Dear Ruth Ann,
>
> There is a young couple in our church named Craig and Jewel Carter. They are very interested in Oliver and Alosious. I gave them your address and they will be contacting you very soon. Also, we know a wonderful Christian family that may be interested in adopting Princess. They are Richard and Sue Kauffman from Ulster, Pennsylvania. I gave them your e-mail address too.
>
> Lord bless,
> Marilyn Shores

I was stunned. I sat there a long time, trying to absorb this new and unexpected news. How could we exist without the twins and Princess?

I thought about the adoption agent Dave Waines had mentioned. Maybe God was preparing us for the inevitable.

> Dear Marilyn,
>
> We are trying to get Princess's visa so she can visit the States, but we are waiting for more information concerning the hospital fees. This is incredible news. Let's keep praying.
>
> Ruth Ann

October 26

At 1:30 a.m. I heard strange noises coming out of the bathroom, so I hurried to investigate. There was Princess, standing in the tub in several inches of water with both taps turned on high and the white rubber plug perfectly in place. She held the open shampoo in one hand and the soap in the other, and she hummed a little tune of anticipation as she prepared her bath. Her clothes lay in a neat little pile on the floor.

"Muttah!" she cried when I opened the door.

"How did you find the light?" I asked in amazement. She can't begin to reach it unless she climbs up the side of the tub and balances on the edge. *Could she see that the light was on?*

"Muttah, come bath wi' me," she ordered.

"You were really going to have a party, weren't you?" I laughed. "No one to turn off the water or regulate the shampoo— you funny little thing."

"Funny," she repeated, her sweet little face wreathed in smiles.

I woke Julie, who gave Princess a quick bath, toweled her off, and tucked her back in bed. She didn't protest. We found it very humorous, but Princess must have been disappointed.

"Why don't we just feed the twins?" Julie asked. "They'll soon be up anyway."

So we gently shook them and patted their cheeks and rubbed the bottoms of their feet. Alosious opened his eyes just a crack and shut them quickly. Oliver stretched his arms way above his head and groaned a little. Then they both resumed their sleep.

"They're more tired than hungry, I guess."

We couldn't put them down. Their round little cheeks felt as soft as pure velvet. They slept, relaxed and secure in our arms. I told Julie about the e-mail, and we wondered and marveled and even cried a bit.

"I dread changes," Julie said, summing it all up. "We have it so good right now, I wish it didn't have to end."

At 2 a.m. Wayne called from his dad's place in Pennsylvania and said the flight was one of the best he'd ever had. Praise God they are all safe.

Minutes later, Larry woke up, feeling miserable. His sheet was damp with sweat.

"My head hurts," he moaned. I shut the window slats and gave him Tylenol and two tablets of Meladox. It was a while before he fell asleep again.

Larry lay in bed all day long today, alternately getting hotter and then colder, despite cool sponges and hot drinks. I finally radioed Bev to take him to the clinic, and since it would be dark when they came home, I asked Elijah to go along.

It was late when they returned. "Elijah had to carry Larry into the clinic," Bev said. "While we waited, Larry threw up twice. They said he has malaria and 'low blood,' whatever that is. They gave the poor boy two big shots for malaria, and all these pills to take."

She handed me three little envelopes with several pills in each. I had to do a thorough study of the writing to decipher that they were iron, pain reliever, and more Meladox tablets. The required dosage was impossible to read.

Evelyn called and said there's a bad flu going around. Some of the CAM staff is off work because of it. She wondered if that might be Larry's problem.

Tonight I feel so discouraged. I see the pile of unopened letters waiting for Wayne, and then the pile addressed to me. I know what they say is true. I see the deplorable conditions the people live in. I see starving babies almost every day—and it seems so hopeless.

I can't let my mind go to the "thousand millions." I have to focus on the little bit we can do. That's the only way I find peace.

God doesn't call the qualified—He qualifies the called.

October 29

A mother and daughter brought breakfast for Julie around eight o'clock. It was a big bowl of rice with a dark, pungent meat topping.

I had never met them before, but when Julie introduced them they smiled brightly and said, "Dis is fo' Julie . . . fo' Julie."

"I won't fight about it," I assured them. "Sure is nice of you ladies to think about her."

"Ahhh, Julie is a fine girl. She helps my daughter all da' time.

She's a fine girl."

"Julie, you shouldn't eat it," I advised her when they left. "You know how they cook, right out there with the dogs and chickens."

"I have to taste it so I can tell them how good it was," she answered, examining the food with a fork. "Is this a . . . *clump of hair?*"

Marie came out at that moment to get the broom from the pantry closet. "Marie, what's this?" Julie asked.

"Tha' is dog meat. Very good."

"Would you like to have it, Marie?" Julie asked in a strange voice. "You're welcome."

"Freddie will love it. Thank you very much," Marie said listlessly.

I could tell there was something wrong. Her usual sunny smile was gone, her face was drawn and worried, and she avoided meeting my eyes.

"What's wrong, dear?" I asked.

"It is nothing, Muttah," she said softly, her eyes filling with tears.

"Doesn't look like 'nothing' to me."

"My Freddie los' his shoe, an' he canno' go to school fo' a week now," she said forlornly.

"But Freddie is only three. Is he in school?"

"Oh, yes!"

I rummaged around in a box and found a pair of black Sunday shoes. "Will these fit?"

Her eyes shone like two stars. "They will fit," she said.

I wish my nephew could see little Freddie wearing his outgrown Sunday shoes. I wish, too, that every small boy in the U.S. could realize what a privilege it is to go to school.

During lunch, we discussed the startling news from Marilyn Shores. We decided it would be a miracle straight from heaven if our beloved black children could be adopted into Christian homes.

"What about Princess's little brother?" Bev wanted to know. "I just can't forget that little fellow."

"Matta said the grandfather doesn't want to keep him anymore," Julie answered. "Wouldn't it be something if this family would want him too?"

"It's all in the Lord's hands," I reminded them.

Larry slept most of the day, and when he woke he was hungry. I made him scrambled eggs and toast with jam. "Can I go play soccer?" he wondered.

"I don't think so. I'll tell Charlie Boy and the other boys to come in for popcorn. They've been hanging around like flies all day."

We also popped a huge bowl for the Waines family and took it upstairs. Maybe the delicious smell of popcorn wafted out into the street, because soon Harris, Georgie, and Toney joined us. The house rang with laughter and happy voices.

Elijah is very particular about asking us who can come in the gate, or who we would rather not see at that particular moment, so I was surprised to see Neil, Abi, and little Georgie at the kitchen door. It was almost dark outside.

"Do you ever have trouble at the gate?" I asked curiously.

"No, they open it immediately," Neil replied.

We popped more corn and poured ice water and sat around the table munching. Neil wanted to know all about Wayne's trip and when he is coming back. We visited comfortably. My original fear of the man has disappeared since I met his family and heard his sad story. He is just another lost soul, searching desperately for his Saviour.

I spotted Elijah slowly walking by the big dining room window. He stood there motionless for several minutes before he moved on. I had to suppress a smile. I can tell when he's worried about us; he can't relax for a minute.

"You never told us what happened to your father," Willie said.

Neil paused and a faraway look came into his eyes. "I want you to know, Willie, that he really did want the best for me, but there was no God in our lives. He was coming home from having a drink one evening and when he crossed the road, a taxi hit him and killed him instantly."

"That's too bad."

"Oh, I'm sorry."

"Yes, I'm sorry too," Neil said sadly. "When I think of how he tried in his own way to make something of me—like seeing to it that I could play guitar, and Mozart and Bach on the piano, and sending me all over the world to school—it's just too sad."

"Didn't you have any sisters or brothers?" Larry asked.

The pain in Neil's face intensified. "I had a big brother. Tom was four years older than I. We had different mothers, so we only saw each other on vacations. Tom intentionally overdosed on his birthday and died instantly."

No one spoke. We grieved for Neil and his lost childhood years—for the violent deaths of his father and brother, and the absence of his mother. It was ineffibly sad.

"Remember that Bible you and Wayne gave me, Mrs. Stelfox?" Neil said huskily. "Back on September 23?"

"I remember the Bible, but I can't say I remember the exact date," I answered.

"It has been my lifeline, Mrs. Stelfox. I never even knew there was another way till I met you folks and came to church. Subconsciously, I had always wanted to come out of the darkness, but I never knew how. I never knew Jesus Christ. All my life I never knew it was possible to be at peace."

"Jesus is the answer," I said happily.

"He is a different man," Abi said softly.

"You know we don't live together anymore, don't you?" Neil asked. "We live separately now because we know it is sin to live together unmarried."

"Praise the Lord."

"It was only by God's grace that I saw you folks in Monrovia when I came back from the bush to visit Abi and the children," Neil went on.

"You have more than one child?" Larry asked in surprise.

"We have an eight-year-old boy living in the Phoebe Grey Orphanage. His name is John, but we call him Chico."

"Wow!" said Larry. "I'd like to see him."

Neil jumped to his feet. "I didn't mean to take so much of your time," he apologized. "It's ten o'clock already. I will come back when Mr. Wayne returns. Thank you so much for the refreshments. *Au revoir!*"

Wayne called soon after our guests went home. "I can't sleep, so I decided to call you," he explained. "Today I took Dr. Lamin to Ryan's Smorgasbord, Wal-Mart, Lowe's, Gettysburg, and Hershey Chocolate World. So far he hasn't said much."

"I can't imagine him being quiet for too long," I answered.

Wayne laughed. "He's quiet now. He's positively speechless. I also got in contact with the doctor in Hershey who will operate on Princess."

"You *did?*"

"He said that the surgery, all examinations, and the cornea will be free. The only cost will be the room, and that can be anywhere from three to six thousand dollars. He wants to see her as soon as possible, in case the eye is deteriorating. He can arrange a surgery as quickly as we can bring her over. Tell that to Julie."

"Oh, I will."

"I got a really nice study Bible for Neil. Has he been around?"

"They just left. We'll tell you all about it."

We didn't talk long because of the expense.

Another day has slipped away on the wings of time. Years may come and years may go, but one thing is certain, Jesus is still the answer.

27

The Spirit Is Willing

November 3

I held Oliver this morning during church. Pastor Mervin preached on 1 Corinthians 11, and it was wonderful.

Neil brought his family and sat on the side front bench, drinking in every word like a tree in the desert. We haven't seen Solomon for a while, though.

Halfway through church it began to rain—great driving drops that beat a steady rhythm on the roof and forced Pastor Mervin to raise his voice.

After the sermon, we stood around and waited for the rain to stop, but it was no use.

Agutta jerked up Amos's shirt to show me his stomach.

"Amos needs more surgery," she told me. "Amos's stomach is big again."

"It's just as big as it was before," I said hopelessly. "Maybe he grew another spleen."

Willie brought the Cruiser right up to the door. We covered the twins' faces and ran, but got wet anyway. On the way home, we stopped at the office to get the e-mails. We have been communicating with Kurt and Marilyn Shores and were expecting to hear from the Carters, who Marilyn says are interested in the twins. Sure enough, the Wisconsin couple had written.

> Dear Friends,
>
>   You don't know us and we don't know you, but just maybe we'll get to know each other soon. We would like to begin adoption procedures for those baby boys if that is all right with you. We have already picked out some names for them. If things go as planned, maybe we can come pick them up before Christmas yet. Let us know right away, please.
>
>   Love,
>   Craig and Jewel Carter

"I can just imagine how anxious they are," Bev said.

"They're brave, that's for sure," Willie added. "How would you like to adopt two babies you've never seen?"

"Maybe they just want to come to Africa," Larry suggested. "Are we really going to give away the babies, Mom?"

"Remember, they're not going just anywhere. They're going to godly homes," I rejoiced.

Evening song service was so cozy with the dim lights of the church and all the dear faces around. It took a long time to sing one song, though, because there was no one to speed things up.

Later this evening I listened to the crashing of the breakers—low, steady music to my ears. Tossing, restless, beautiful—the treacherous ocean. Only God knows what all has transpired on those very beaches just a block from Residence.

God saw every one of those silent, ominous slave ships approaching in the middle of the night. He witnessed the brutal capture of the black people by men of their own race and kin. He saw every deed done in those deadly cargo holds—heard the dying cries of the people chained like dogs in their own filth.

Every act . . . every deed . . . every motive is recorded.

Someday every person will stand before Almighty God, with

no difference in race or color, for our God is a just God.

November 6

My husband is safely home—right here beside me. I am so happy I cannot contain it. I just thank God we're together as a family once again.

While we waited at the airport for Wayne's plane, Larry entertained himself by purchasing two huge rhinoceros beetles and letting them latch onto his trousers. They are about five inches long. The males have jaws; the females do not. They make a grating sound when they move, and they are fascinating to small boys. I kept my distance.

Bev and Julie have been working on obtaining Princess's medical visa in their spare time. Julie pursued the necessary contacts with the Ministry of Health and the U.S. Embassy, and she hopes to have Princess's passport, proof of immunization, and medical visa very soon.

"It will be a double miracle if we can get her visa in time for Princess and me to travel home with someone else," Julie said hopefully.

We were also able to contact Mitchel Clemmer, the adoption agent, who came right over and outlined the requirements for a visa in a foreign adoption. There needs to be a relinquishment of the children, which includes the father signing them off, a medical history to prove they have general good health, proof of immunizations, a passport, a case history of the child done by officials from the Ministry of Health in Monrovia, and the original INS (Immigration Naturalization Services) approval document from the adoptive parents that welcomes the child into the United States. The list seems endless.

November 7

Wayne was busy answering questions about his trip to the States all day long—about the people he met at CAM's open house, about Dr. Lamin and his impressions of beautiful Pennsylvania, and whatever else we could think to ask.

Mitchel came after lunch to begin the twins' papers. He has made an appointment for the photographer to come take passport photos on Tuesday. He claims to know the American Consulate officer, Glenn Carey.

At five o'clock this evening, our first revival meeting began.

Hughdell Ysaguirre has a stentorian voice that never reaches full throttle. I imagine Apostle Paul preaching like he does—deep, dynamic messages that are simple to understand and totally soul-searching. The topic tonight was renewal.

"I wonder where Neil is," Wayne said afterward. "Too bad he missed this sermon."

Cleon Swartzentruber, Conrad's brother, arrived today to help solve some problems we've been encountering with the two-way radios. Wayne asked him to lead singing on Sunday.

November 10

Liberia Mennonite Church was so full there was hardly room—or air—to breathe. It was full on Friday and Saturday evenings, but nothing compared to this. The people kept pouring in—strangers, regulars, and children by the dozens. It was wonderful to see, but I have never seen people packed so close together. They looked like sardines, sitting sideways and overlapping each other with their shoulders.

Brother Hughdell's sermon title was "Wonderful Jesus," and he encouraged the congregation to remain faithful despite their suffering. "We will remember this very day when we are safely in heaven—and sitting at the feet of Jesus!" he said. "I pray that not one of us will be missing."

"Why isn't Neil here?" Wayne asked Abi after church.

"He's playing at the beach."

"Can you come along after dinner and show us where?"

"I will do that."

"Great! Meet us at the CAM gate at three-thirty."

After a delicious fellowship meal at Curt and Evelyn's house, Wayne, Brother Hughdell, Abi, little Georgie, and I went to look for Neil. Abi directed us to a large public beach on the ocean side of

Congo Town. We waited on the elevated shoreline while she walked at least a quarter of a mile among throngs of bathers looking for Neil.

A while later, they emerged from the crowd and made their way to where we waited.

"Mr. Wayne!" cried Neil, both surprised and embarrassed. "You came looking for me?"

"What did you expect?" Wayne asked, slapping him on the back. "You've really been missing out, and I can't stand it. This is Hughdell Ysaguirre from Belize, our evangelist for the week. Hughdell, Neil Dimacopoulos."

The men shook hands. "I'm sorry, Mr. Wayne, Mr. Hughdell . . . I wanted to come, but . . ."

"I understand, Neil. The spirit is willing, but the flesh is weak," Hughdell said.

"Exactly!" cried Neil. "Is that from the Bible?"

"Yes. Those are the words of Jesus in the twenty-sixth chapter of Matthew where He spoke to his disciples about keeping awake."

"Thank you, Mr. Hughdell."

Neil and Hughdell must have felt some common bond, because there was no lack of conversation between them.

"I can't believe you came looking for me," Neil said for the third time. "You actually cared enough to come all the way to the beach to find me."

"Our Good Shepherd left the flock to find the lost sheep," Hughdell said gently.

"But I'm an ex-fighter. You don't know me, Mr. Hughdell."

"God does, though."

Presently, they discovered they could both speak Spanish, so they switched languages for a time. When we got to Residence, Wayne presented Neil with the new study Bible he had purchased in the States.

"Mr. Wayne . . . I have no words," Neil said humbly. "All I can say is thank you from the bottom of my heart."

We visited until it was time for evening services.

Hughdell spoke on the glories of heaven. "It matters not where you came from, but where you are going!" he emphasized. "No matter what you have done in the past, it can be washed away without a trace. We can look at ourselves as Jesus sees us—washed as white as snow. It is not easy to keep looking ahead, but it is possible. Heaven will be worth it all."

Neil's eyes were flooded with tears by the time the sermon was over. Abi, too, was greatly moved. Georgie sat between them, his beautiful eyes fixed on the preacher. I wondered what was going through his mind.

After the service, Wayne invited Isaac and Neil's family for a snack. We served sausage and egg sandwiches with brown dinner rolls, peanut butter cookies, and tea.

I struggle with Isaac's seemingly callous attitude. How can he come and visit and hardly even glance at his own children? Tonight they were so incredibly lovable, cooing and smiling and laughing out loud, but he sat as if his heart had turned to stone.

And what about Neil and Abi, who have another son in an orphanage? Don't they long for him?

Maybe most of the parents in this country have been desensitized by all the corruption. They give their children away to anyone who will take them—relatives, friends, orphanages, or strangers. Another child means another liability. But according to Hughdell's sermon on Saturday, every child is a gift from God, and someone will be accountable for each one. No child is an accident, because God is the giver of life.

One man's loss is another's gain, and though I am thrilled that the Carters will be able to adopt the twins, I cannot understand Isaac's mentality. I decided to ask him.

"Don't you find it hard to give away your own babies?" I asked, a bit sharply.

He looked at me for a long moment. "It is the only way they will ever have a chance," he said simply. "I cannot care for them, and they have no mother. I am thankful to God Almighty for making a way for Oliver and Alosious."

What could I say?

Before leaving, Neil shook all our hands again. "I will be there tomorrow night, and the next," he promised. "Mr. Wayne will come looking for me if I'm not."

"You've got that right," said my husband.

November 12

The seasons are mixed up this year in Liberia. We had a wonderful storm last night, with just as much rain as in the middle of rainy season. The thunder jolted me awake in time to shut the windows in the living room. Princess sat up in bed and whimpered, but Julie was right there. The twins didn't stir. They both lay on their tummies, and Oliver sucked his thumb. I tucked their blankets under them and caressed their lovely curls and kissed their velvet cheeks ever so gently.

Then I stood beside the crib and wept with the falling rain.

It seems so many people have visited this week. They come to see Julie or Bev or they need something done in the mechanic shop or they want to visit privately for some reason or another. Some just like to sit and watch us work.

Needy, lonesome, desperate, hungry people . . . all precious in the sight of God.

Tonight, Brother Hughdell preached a fiery sermon on the horrors of hell. When it was over, a rush of people committed their lives to Christ. Neil Dimacopoulos was among them.

28

Dashed Hopes

November 13

This morning held the promise of an extremely hot day. I had barely taken a pan of fresh buns out of the oven when there was a tremendous banging at the gate. Security Pa Sumo walked over and looked through the sliding peephole, but he didn't open up. Zubah hurried over, looked out, and ran back to where Henry Cole was working in the shop.

Again we heard a banging at the gate—loud and insistent. Henry hurried over and swung open the gate.

Six armed men poured into the yard, two in the green camouflage uniforms of the ATU (Anti-Terrorist Unit) and four in the black uniforms of the SOD (Special Operations Division). The men in black looked very forbidding.

"Where is your husband?" the leader barked to Charlotte, who was standing on the porch.

"He is not here," Henry answered.

"Mom!" Larry gasped, white-faced. "There are ATUs here searching for Dad!"

I rushed out to the porch and leaned on the railing. My glance took in their dark, sweating faces, their shiny assault rifles, and their polished boots. I felt weak all over.

The SOD commander approached with both hands in the air. "We are here to search your home for any guns or ammunition," he said gravely. "Every room—even yours."

We didn't have a choice. Neither did we have anything to hide.

"Zubah, can you come along, please?" I asked.

Zubah was more than willing to assist. When they had thoroughly searched the mechanics' shop, they told us to show them upstairs.

They had us open all the cupboard doors and drawers upstairs; then one noticed the locked pantry where we store the canned meat.

"We will need the key," he ordered, so I ran downstairs and got it.

They must have noticed my trembling hands when I opened the lock because one of them said, "Missie, we won't harm you. No need to be afraid."

Every kitchen cupboard, the pantry, the fridge, and the oven were checked. The leader would gesture with his hand and Zubah and I opened and moved whatever he indicated. Zubah chattered constantly, trying to explain what everything was. Beads of sweat stood on his forehead.

Larry followed us, holding Oliver for moral support. "The baby . . . what happened?" one ATU asked. Zubah explained so fast I didn't have a chance. The men nodded approval.

The same man asked about Princess, who was sitting very still on the sofa listening to her songs. Zubah told her story in a few sentences.

The commander asked if the suitcases stored way up in the hallway and bedroom closets were empty. "Yes, sir," I told him.

In the boys' room, the commander gestured toward the bed and we grabbed Larry's books off so Zubah could raise the mattress. He looked under the beds and behind the laundry basket.

Both bedrooms and the bathroom were next. They paid special attention to boxes of any kind, but ours contained soap, candles, contact solution, scabies cream, sanitizing lotion, and Kleenex.

"We will go now," the commander announced. "Do you want

to be a policeman?" he asked Larry in passing.

"I want to go back to Canada *now*," Larry answered decisively. The men grinned.

They filed outside to the security booth and asked Pa Sumo for water. I got bagged ice water and handed it over the porch wall.

"They mean money," Zubah whispered. "*Watah* means money."

"I have no money to give them," I answered firmly. "I do have fresh bread if they want some."

He went over and conversed with the men. "They will take bread an' water then," he said when he returned. I quickly sliced some fresh rolls, slathered them with peanut butter, and took out more ice water.

They ate silently, bit off a corner of the water bags, and drank deeply. The commander nodded at us as they left.

"They remind me of the Indian bands who ate at the settlers' tables and left with an 'Ugh'," Larry said, relieved they were gone. "Don't those SODs look wicked? Did you see those guns? Are they searching every house? It scared me so bad when they asked for Dad."

Zubah came in. "They made a big X on the wall outside wi' chalk. That means we are clear."

"Just a minute, Zubah," I said. "You deserve a special treat. I appreciate your help immensely." I spread more rolls with peanut butter and jam and gave him a can of cold Coke.

"Thank you very much, O'Ma."

There was a flurry of excitement when the rest came home for lunch. Everyone wanted to talk at once.

"We got Princess's visa!" Julie cried, holding up the precious document and grabbing Princess to swing her around. "Now we have every single paper we need."

"The SODs and the ATUs were here this morning!" Larry yelled, and everyone listened excitedly as he told the story.

"I didn't see very many Xs besides the one at Tony Hage's," Wayne observed. "Maybe Taylor is worried about the whites for some reason. That reminds me, Tony thought he could arrange for

Julie and Princess to fly home with Cleon tomorrow, but the plane was overbooked already."

"Cleon changed his flight to next Wednesday so Princess and Julie can fly home with him," Bev announced.

"Miracle after miracle!" I marveled.

Princess senses the excitement. She clings to me more than ever. "I go to 'Merica!" she keeps repeating, not having a clue what it means. I didn't even try to explain flying in a jet.

Julie taught her the song "Jesus in the Family," so now she sings *"Wi' Jesus in the family, happy, happy home, happy, happy home,"* then she repeats it with each of our names plus Merci, Georgie, Harris, and whomever else she can think of. She sings and sings.

Tonight, there was a volleyball game over in the Lantzes' yard. The ladies sat and held babies and caught up on each other's lives while the men and youth played.

It was after dark when we arrived home, and we were surprised to find Neil waiting for Wayne outside the gate. "I have a few questions about the Bible that just can't wait, Mr. Wayne," he explained eagerly.

"Come right on in," Wayne invited. "Have you had supper?"

Neil answered reluctantly. "I can't get food like I used to, Mr. Wayne. I no longer threaten anyone and I have no job. I am ashamed to say I have not eaten for two days."

Out came the leftover hamburger soup, macaroni salad, and brown rolls. Wayne made him a cup of coffee and listened to his questions. They talked quietly so the family could sleep.

"I feel like I have to get everything out in the open before I can get rid of it," Neil said wretchedly. "I keep thinking of the initiation of the boys forced into our army—how they had to drink the water in which floated the heart of an enemy soldier, then eat a slice of it, with the commander watching to make sure it was chewed and swallowed."

"I'll listen if I have to," Wayne said.

"Many of the commanders underwent satanic rituals that have certain strict laws. A man had to kill two people a day or else his 'medicine' would be ineffective and he would be killed. If he followed this personal law, he would be bullet proof. Sometimes, Mr. Wayne, if there were no enemies to kill, the commander would glance around at his own men and actually kill some of them when he got the chance. Or he would drive into enemy territory and put himself in danger to shoot the first two people he saw, whether children, soldiers, or civilians."

"The devil is a hard taskmaster."

"Yes, Mr. Wayne. I'll never really be a free man as far as memories go—*never*."

"Time is a great healer, Neil. Nothing is too hard for God."

"I was a brigadier general, Mr. Wayne—a special aid to the chief of staff of the Armed Forces of Liberia. I was way up there, and it took me twelve years to get there. All for nothing. Even Abi and the children gave up on me."

It was late when the discussion was over and Neil went home. "I am weary of the evil in this country," I told my husband. "Think of it—Satanism, voodoo, witchcraft, child sacrifices, cannibalism, gross immorality, incest, and a host of others. It sounds like Sodom—and the innocent have to suffer with the wicked."

"That's why Jesus came into this world," Wayne reminded me. "Just look at the people coming to the Mennonite church here in Liberia. I'm sure most of those people have been into these practices, but look at them today. It's wonderful, isn't it?"

November 17

We had communion today for the second time since we arrived. It is so special to all of us to be included with the Liberians in their church. They welcome us without question.

It rained wildly during the night—a true monsoon soaker that shaved the remaining leaves off the almond and plum trees and made the windows a dirty mess. Marie will have a big job next Tuesday.

Right after church, Craig Carter called with the news that their paperwork is nearly done. They have plans to arrive here on the fourth of December.

November 20

Julie is nineteen today, and I am also a year older. Many of our friends called to wish us a happy birthday.

I asked Merci to keep Princess for the day since Princess has developed a dry cough. All the rest of us drove to Tony Hage's place in Totota for dinner.

Tony's cooks had arrived before us, and a freshly skinned young goat lay on the table with its head cut off. Beside it lay the "edible innards," the "edible outers," and a lanky rooster.

Presently, the cook hung the goat on a branch and began hacking off pieces for the grill, sampling the raw meat as he carved.

Chop . . . taste. Chop . . . taste.

I had to look away.

When Tony arrived, he tossed some hotdogs on the grill and told the cooks to hurry up. They set the table and piled on the Lebanese bread, french fries, fruit juices, and Danish butter cookies. The goat, the rooster, and the hot dogs were wrapped in heavy foil and brought over. It was a feast fit for a birthday.

As Julie prepared to leave for America with Princess, she expressed her sadness at leaving. "Think of it," she said, "I'll miss seeing the twins' new parents, and I'll miss Christmas in Liberia."

"You won't regret it, Julie," I consoled her. "If you don't do this, you will always wonder why you didn't."

"I know, Mom. It's just that I like Liberia so much."

November 21

The van was filled with people when we took Cleon, Julie, and Princess to the airport on Wednesday. We could have had a caravan with all the people who came to see Julie off and secretly hoped to go along.

November 25

I knew something was terribly wrong when Wayne handed me the phone at six o'clock this morning. Julie was on the line and she was crying.

"The specialist said Princess's retina is completely detached and there is absolutely nothing they can do," she sobbed.

I paused to let this startling fact sink in—and searched for the right words. "Julie, I know this is a dreadful blow, but we can rest in the fact that God makes no mistakes, and for some reason He said, 'No.' "

"I did all I could, Mom, but I never even entertained the thought that it might be too late. Everything seemed to fall into place. Maybe I'm just in shock over the whole thing."

Merci Evans arrived soon after and wondered what the eye specialist had said. "I could wait no longer, Sis Ruth!" she exclaimed, but when she saw my face she added. "It is not good news?"

"No, Merci. Her eye is damaged beyond repair. She may never see again."

"Oh, poor Princess!" she cried. "What does Julie say?"

"She's trying hard to accept it, but it's tough. Stay around a bit, Merci. I love it when you're here."

When Larry woke up, he could not find Rikki anywhere, so there is one worried boy at Residence today. It doesn't help either that Elijah was transferred to Mission for a few months.

"I miss Elijah too much," Larry mourned. "I'm going to ask Stone to let him come back right away. These other security guards don't compare to Elijah."

After breakfast, Agutta and little Amos stopped in on the way home from the hospital. Amos had a second surgery last Wednesday to determine why his belly didn't shrink after the swollen spleen was removed.

"This was the last surgery fo' Amos," Agutta said. "The doctor can do no more."

"Then why is his stomach still so big? Right after the spleen surgery it swelled up again."

"I don' know, Muttah."

They had scarcely left when Pa Sumo came to the door. "There's a young woman and a child at the gate," he informed us. "Should I let them in?"

"If it is a baby ma, then of course I will see her," I answered.

She walked into the living room with the air of a well-bred woman and stood regarding us for a few moments. Her eyes took in everything—the crib where Alosious was napping, the freezer, the curtains, the Liberian furniture. She nodded at Merci.

"My name is Sarah Onrah," she said almost defiantly as she unwound the little girl on her back. "I need help. This child's mother was shot down by the rebels when we fled the recent fighting in Gbarnga. She is almost seven months old now, an' I have no way of supporting her. I watched the mother go down, and the child fell too, so I picked her up and kept running. Her mother bled to death."

The child leaned against Sarah's shoulder, peeking at us from under long, curly lashes. Her hair was plaited in thick, heavy braids around her shapely head. Her features were incredibly small and fine. Although her clothing was thin and ragged, she looked healthy and well fed.

"Someone took excellent care of her," I noted with satisfaction. It was wonderful to see a baby thriving so well.

"What's her name?" Charlotte asked.

"Blessing," Sarah answered.

"May I hold her?" asked Charlotte.

"Yes."

Charlotte took the unresisting child, who regarded her solemnly with unblinking eyes. She reached up a chubby arm and touched Charlotte's cheek.

"Merci, what do you think?" I asked quietly. "Is the woman telling the truth? Could it be her own baby and she just wants to get rid of her?"

Merci proceeded to ask all kinds of questions and soon discovered that she used to live in the same building as one of the uncles that Sarah mentioned.

"I will ask around and let you know," she told me. "Come back on Thursday, Sarah. We will decide what to do."

We gave her some formula and a bottle for Blessing. "Bring the baby along with you when you come back so we can see if she is eating enough," I instructed.

She walked out without a backward glance. "That is a proud one," Merci decided.

Tonight, Mary, Staci, and Angela Lantz took us to Fiama Market, where we walked down a steep, rocky slope to a low-roofed dwelling. "This lady's name is Ruth," Staci said. "Don't be too shocked at her room."

We ducked under a low, crooked doorway into a dark tunnel with a mud floor littered with various articles from old shoes to a glowing hot cooking pot. The walls were constructed of metal pieces, wood strips, plastic bags, old newspapers, cardboard, and clay.

The air was stale, dank, hot, and very disagreeable to the nostrils. Something was stuck in every imaginable crevice and crack—dishes, laundry, shoes, cooking utensils, pieces of wood, food, and trash. The walls were her cupboards and drawers.

Ruth greeted us with outstretched hands and a wide smile. She looked at least forty-five years old, or else she's had a dreadfully hard life. Her eyes are big and hollow and expressive. Her rag of a dress hung in loose folds around her scrawny frame, but she welcomed us like a queen to her palace. No apologies rose to her lips. Instantly, I thought of the immaculate homes I have visited where the hostess apologizes profusely for the mess.

Two new babies lay on a hideous bed covered with tattered blankets. Staci and Angela picked them up and handed them to Charlotte and me. We stared in amazement at the two baby girls.

"What is that rash all over their faces?" Mary whispered.

"Looks like a heat rash of some sort. I see she put some salve on it," I answered. "What are their names?"

"Rose an' Roslyn," Ruth said, smiling.

We visited a few minutes until the air seemed too heavy to breathe.

"Come see me again," she begged, as we prepared to leave.

I paused at the door. "Where is their father?" I asked.

"He came to see them once," she said.

"It seems most of the men have two or three households

running," I said disgustedly to the ladies. "They pop in every once in a while, the woman gets pregnant, then they're gone to the next one. I saw the same pattern in the hospital. Few of the mothers even knew where the father of their child was."

When Charlotte and I arrived back at Residence, workers were unloading two CAM trucks and carrying many boxes and drums of supplies upstairs. Willie was helping them unload. "This is a big project for you, Mom," he said. "These are full of flip-flops and baby bundles and stuff to make health kits for the orphanages."

I rummaged through the wonderful supplies of toothbrushes, toothpaste, washcloths, combs, towels, nail clippers, toys, soap, and thousands of pairs of flip-flops. The plan was for us to make individual Christmas packages wrapped in a towel for as many orphans as possible. The supplies came from many churches, sewing circles, and individual families in the States. It was absolutely heart-warming. My head was full of plans to begin assembling them right away so the children could have a Christmas surprise.

There is still no sign of Rikki. "I just have Ranger left, and he just wants to lie around in the sun all day," said Larry.

"Play with Jillie," Wayne said.

"I like Jillie, but she's not as fun as Rikki," lamented Larry. "If only I could have a baby elephant."

29

The Miracle of Adoption

November 30

What an incredible mixture of miracles, wonderful surprises, and shattered dreams we have experienced of late.

Princess will have a home. A real, true, loving home—and best of all, a godly one. She will have a mother and father and five sisters and brothers and live on a dairy farm in northern Pennsylvania in Bradford County—*if* she is granted a visa.

Julie called today with the news, in such a state of excitement that her words tumbled over each other. "Remember the Richard and Sue Kauffman that Marilyn Shores mentioned in her e-mail? Well, they drove five hours down here to Grandpa's to see Princess. Mother, they have positively decided to pursue her adoption. They are the perfect family for my Princess. They have girls to help, and younger children, and they're so calm and gentle and organized—just what she needs. Oh, I'm so happy!"

When I hung up the phone, my heart was full. I am overjoyed at the way God is working things out. But oh, how we miss Princess's happy chatter around the house! I find myself rejoicing in the fact that she has to come back to Liberia to finish her adoption. We will see her then.

It's another miracle that the Carters will be arriving on the fourth of December. Mitchel has every document required for the twins' adoption except their medical forms.

It's too painful to even think about what we'll do when they leave. They get into the funniest little predicaments in that crib. Either Alosious will be kicking Oliver in the face or Oliver will be draped on top of Alosious. They holler until someone rescues them.

The past few days have been a flurry of assembling bundles. Merci Evans did much of the work since she is presently unemployed. We have great piles of bundles sorted into specific age brackets, ready to be delivered. There are still a lot more to make.

On Thursday morning, Merci arrived at the door with Sarah Onrah and little Blessing. Charlotte took the child and hugged her close.

"She tells the truth," Merci said. "The child's mother was killed by rebels. Sarah is just taking care of her. I inquired of the people, and the story is true."

"Sarah, we cannot keep Blessing here, but we will give you formula and baby cereal for her for a few months. Will that be all right?" I asked.

"That will be good," Sarah agreed. "I will feed the baby and come to you when it is finished."

"Take good care of her, Sarah—she's doing so well. Pretend she's your own child."

"I will take good care of her."

Blessing smiled at us—and what a smile! It crinkled her tiny nose in the dearest way, and narrowed her beautiful eyes into slits. Her whole face beamed.

"I don't think you have to worry, Sis Ruth," Merci assured us after the regal Sarah left. "Any woman willing to care for a child who is not her own can be trusted."

December 1

The sermon this morning on moral purity was so frank and bold that it kept everyone awake. The word "vague" is not in

Pastor's vocabulary when it comes to preaching.

Pastor Mervin announced that Nathan Kauffman is definitely improving. "If things improve as they have been, they just may be able to come back to Liberia," he said. There was a murmur of praise through the crowd. "We need to keep praying for his full recovery."

When the security guards changed around three this afternoon, Larry started screaming at the top of his lungs, "Elijah! Elijah!" and sure enough, faithful Elijah walked into the compound with his slate in one hand, his old jacket in the other, and a huge grin on his face. Larry took a flying leap right into his arms.

No other security guard has received such a welcome. "I *knew* Stone would let you come back!" Larry announced. "I told him we all want you to come—even my mom."

"Thank you, Larry, *thank you!*" Elijah told him. "Ah wan' to stay righ' heah. Dis is where ah like to be."

This evening, Dr. Lamin gave a report of his trip to America. "I looked for it everywhere, an' I didn't see it," he began. "I felt the love of the people wherever I went. I was among four hundred men at Deeper Life Ministries in Ohio, an' they treated me jus' like one of them. Wayne's parents an' Conrad, Mark Yoder an' Pastor Reuben took me into their homes an' treated me fine. At one point Wayne and I went to eat where all the gluttons eat for about seven dollars. I could not believe it. I said to Wayne, 'Here she comes for another round. She does not need it—she is fat enough!' It was a place where there was so much food of so many kinds that you could eat however much you wanted. I said, 'Let me bring five hundred Liberians here to eat this food!' "

He went on to explain in great detail how the taxing of the citizens works in America, and how a man can buy gas with a small plastic card and not pay until later. "If you do not pay at the end of the month you are cut off quick," he said.

"At Mark Yoder's I had a buggy ride with a horse in front an' a wagon about as big as a freezer. These people have no cars. They have no current. They *choose* to live this way in America," and he shook his head in disbelief.

"Money is a great detriment in America. When you have so much that you don't need more, what will make you cry out to God? What will make you witness to the lost? On the other hand, these brothers an' sisters in America are the ones who lift our children from dying of starvation."

When he was finished, he gave time for questions. "What was it tha' you looked fo' an' didn't see?" Alfred Gibson asked immediately.

"Racism!" Dr. Lamin answered loudly. "I saw nary a sign of it. Praise the Lord!"

"Praise the Lord!" the people agreed jubilantly.

December 4

The excitement level in our home this morning was at an all-time high. Craig and Jewel Carter were scheduled to arrive around six o'clock this evening.

Larry and Charlotte finished their schoolwork in record time. Larry cleaned out Rikki's cage just in case he comes home. "I think someone stole him," he said. "Rikki would never just run away when he had it so good. If Elijah would have been around, no one could have taken him."

Charlotte bathed and powdered and oiled the twins until they looked shiny clean and became rather impatient. She combed their curls and clipped their nails; she dressed them in soft white sleepers and dabbed baby lotion behind their ears and under their chins. Finally, when she had them all tired out, she warmed some milk and put them both to sleep.

"This suspense is too much," she sighed. "What if Craig and Jewel are cold and unaffectionate? What if they're really shy and won't talk unless we do?"

"Stop worrying," I chided. "They are fine people if they are willing to adopt two babies from Liberia without ever seeing them."

"Muttah, do you know Mr. Borbor?" Elijah asked from the porch.

"Yes. He's Secret's grandfather. Let him in."

Old Grandfather Borbor walked slowly up to the front door and into the living room, leading little Secret by the hand. He sat down on the couch and nodded at us.

"I wan' to talk wi' you, Missie," he began, looking at me steadily. "Naomi died. No one is lef' to take care of da chil'. I'm old an' hungry. I have no food. Shou' I put the child in a home fo' children? No. *You* keep him."

Charlotte and I exchanged glances. "Where is the baby's father?" she asked.

"The father does naw wan' the child . . . he's sick," he explained quietly.

He sat there, an old man with white hair and shaking, shriveled hands. "You keep him," he repeated. "He's Whyayeh's brother—you keep him."

Secret understood. His beautiful dark eyes filled with fear. He grabbed his grandfather by the arm and wiggled up beside him on the couch.

We saw a dreadful, silver-dollar-sized burn on his knee, his distended stomach, his scarred little legs, and his whitish scalp.

"Mom, let's take him and just clean him up a bit," Charlotte said. "Look how infected his knee is." She indicated the sore knee. "What happened?"

"He fell on a cook pot," Mr. Borbor said. He stood slowly but determinedly. "I'll go now."

Secret began to cry frantically and clung to the old man's hand, but he shook him off impatiently. "Don' cry," he said sourly. "You mus' stay."

Secret stayed right by the couch and watched the old man shuffle out the door. His mouth was wide open in a silent sob, and his eyes begged the old man to come back. His tears made crooked little stains down his dusty cheeks. He held out his small arms toward the retreating figure.

"Charlotte, just hold him," I told my willing daughter. "We'll figure out what to do, but it's plain that poor old man can't take care of him any longer. That burn needs attention."

I knelt down and inspected it. Little bits of dirt and string and grass were imbedded in the wound. Charlotte sang and rocked and soothed until the child calmed down. "He thinks I'm Julie," she said. "I'm going to bathe him really good. We still have some of that fungal cream."

"Plus de-worming pills," I said.

"And scabies salve."

A half hour later, Secret emerged, smelling like shampoo and body wash and baby oil. Charlotte put some Silvadene salve on the burn and bound it lightly with a clean white rag.

"He can sleep in that spare bed in the boys' room," I decided. I crushed some parasite medication and gave it to him in a spoon of applesauce. Then we warmed some rice and pumpkin soup and let him finish the whole bowl.

He clung to Charlotte like a baby monkey. "I wonder how often he's been abandoned," she said.

Wayne and the others were surprised to see Secret, but when they heard the story they agreed that we had no choice. "We'll soon have an orphanage right here," Wayne said.

Bev was especially delighted. "I just couldn't forget this little fellow," she said. "Look at those eyes."

Secret looked at Bev—and for the first time, a hint of a smile played about his lips. It completely won her heart. "You little darling!" she exclaimed.

Curt and Evelyn went to the airport this evening to meet Craig and Jewel Carter. We were all assembled in the living room when Curt called and said they would be here in a few minutes. I was a bundle of nerves. I hugged Alosious close and smiled at Wayne, who was holding Oliver.

There was a honk at the gate. It swung open and shut. Curt's truck stopped on the gravel. They came to the front door and knocked before coming in.

They're so young! was my first impression. Jewel came into the living room and hugged Alosious and me together. Her eyes shone like stars when she took him from my arms.

Craig took Oliver and they both stood and just looked at their babies. The twins gazed back, unaffected by the excitement they were causing.

What a sacred moment.

After a few minutes, we were introduced all around. We laughed easily and talked comfortably right from the start.

"You don't like to be called O'Ma, right?" Craig asked me.

"For sure not!" I said.

"Well, I thought that's what I would call you while we are here," he said mischievously.

Right then I knew we would get along just fine. I appreciate a sense of humor. Jewel looked at him fondly and laughed right along.

"We have names for them," she said happily. "Brady Oliver and Brett Alosious."

"Beautiful," we all agreed. "They fit."

Craig and Jewel are both fair-skinned, with reddish-blond hair and blue eyes. The twins' dark heads contrasted sharply against them.

Jewel is small and slim. "You look too young!" Larry chirped suddenly, and we all laughed.

Much later, when the Carters were sleeping upstairs and their babies snuggled in the crib, Wayne and I discussed the miracle of adoption. "It's just like us being adopted into the family of God," he said. "No matter where we come from and where we are going, we can be part of His family."

"I've never understood it more clearly than tonight," I agreed. "What a splendid picture."

December 7

Wayne, Larry, and I were in Waterside early this morning when we heard the unmistakable sound of a rifle shot. People began running in all directions. "Stay put right here," a man told us. "Armed men are fighting."

Just then a police car careened down the street with its lights flashing. Up ahead we saw ATU soldiers running. One pumped bullets into his gun as he ran.

"What's going on?" Wayne asked.

"Just ATU boys shooting at each other," he was told.

We waited a few minutes, then made our way out of Waterside. "I wonder what would happen in Canada if all the young people had access to AK 47 rifles and could just shoot whenever they wanted to," I said. "It's like they're playing cops and robbers with real rifles."

"If some die, they just throw them in the swamp," Wayne answered. "There's no such thing as a hearing or investigation. People say many of these young boys join the very group of soldiers that killed their parents. They have nowhere else to go."

When we arrived at Residence, Zubah was holding a black-crowned night heron when he opened the gate. "A gift fo' Larry," he smiled. "Someone gave it to Harris fo' you."

"There's no way that bird will survive in captivity," I objected, noting the long, sharp beak and the lovely gray, white, and black plumage. Several long white feathers protruded gracefully from the back of its head. Its legs were long, gangly, and bright yellow.

Larry wasn't too happy, either. "This kind eats fresh fish, and where will I get that?" he worried.

Zubah carried the poor bird back to the cage and carefully put it through the wire gate. He wasn't taking any chances with that beak. The heron ruffled its feathers and hopped to the back of the cage where it shrank down dejectedly.

Jewel was busily bathing the twins when I came into the house. She was laughing so hard at their worried faces that I worried they would slip right out of her hands. Brett Alosious's mouth turned upside down in that adorable habit of his, and he hung on to her sleeve with a desperate grip.

Brady Oliver growled low in his throat and Jewel was trying to keep his thumb in his mouth while she bathed him. It didn't work. Whenever it popped out he would growl again. Jewel was overcome with mirth.

"Tell me a bit about Kurt and Marilyn Shores and their adopted children," I suggested.

"Oh, that reminds me!" Jewel exclaimed. "Marilyn said I

should find her a baby girl here in Liberia. She was serious, too. She said she talked to Kurt and they decided they would love to adopt another one. That would make six adopted children in their family."

"Wow! We'll sure keep our eyes open."

Craig and Jewel are so excited about taking the twins home for Christmas to meet their families. They don't know it, but someone from their church is planning a baby shower for them and asked us what all they need. We sent a whole list.

Dear little Secret still hasn't really laughed, but he has lost the fear in his eyes. He has adopted Bev for his very own, and she loves him, so things are going well.

Just before dark, Larry and I checked on the heron. Its eyes were dull and glazed, and the fish Larry had bought for it lay untouched at its feet.

"It's a goner," Larry said.

December 11

That magnificent heron was dead in the cage this morning. Zubah wasn't smiling when I asked him to dispose of it. "Please don't accept any more wildlife without specific permission," I requested. "I can't stand to see them suffer."

The youth retreat for the CAM-sponsored orphanages began today and ends tomorrow at the Baptist Compound. I was given a topic for the young girls: *Growing Up to Be Young Women of Value*. Charlotte took care of the children while Jewel came along for moral support.

Everyone seems to be having a wonderful time. The grounds are close to the ocean and you can hear the surf, although a strip of heavy mangrove woodland hides it from view. Yellow-billed egrets are so plentiful they look like big white polka dots against the green.

Jewel and I walked down to the nearby lagoon—a shallow body of water formed by salt mudflats and full of fresh water. It is several hundred feet across, about four feet deep, and surrounded by trees with arched aerial roots.

"This is a perfect place to swim," Jewel said.

"They tell me the alligators like it too," I said. "Maybe some of those gnarled branches are really alligator snouts."

Greenshanks and sandpipers teetered along in the shallow waters near shore. There was a flash of color and a loud, fluted cry as a blue-breasted kingfisher dove from the branches of a tree and came up with a small fish. On the opposite shore of the lagoon we could see three herons. They were too far away to see their markings, but there was no mistaking those snake-like necks and long beaks.

"A small spot of unspoiled paradise," I marveled.

30

Left to Die

Right after breakfast, Craig, Jewel, Willie, Larry, Georgie, Isaac, Wayne, and I picked up Bundo near Paynesville and headed for River Cess, the twins' birthplace. River Cess County is about four hours south of Monrovia, past Harbel and Buchanan and many miles into the bush country. Much of the road lies parallel to the ocean.

The boys and Isaac squeezed into the back of the Defender, which was full of supplies for the orphanages in Buchanan.

The road to Buchanan was so full of potholes that Bundo hardly dared avert his eyes. He drove swiftly and expertly. We stopped at the Good Samaritan Orphanage and unloaded half the supplies. Isaac and the boys were covered with red dust.

After Buchanan, the road improved dramatically. "President Taylor had this road fixed to make it easy for his trucks to haul the timber out," Bundo explained. "Here comes one."

He dodged to the side as a huge truck bore down upon us, throwing up a cloud of such thick red dust that it was impossible to see for a few seconds. The truck was hauling a load of thick, reddish-colored logs.

"Is that mahogany?" I asked, fascinated by the rich color tones.

"Mahogany or teak," Bundo answered sadly. "The trucks never stop. Night and day—seven days a week."

"I've read about the vanishing rain forests," Craig offered. "Nothing is being done to replant them."

"These logs are worth a fortune," Wayne said. "They're being shipped out to America and England and wherever there's a market. Can you imagine how rich the president is by now?"

Another truck roared past with two logs so huge that there wasn't room for another one. Bundo slowed to a crawl until he could see again.

Truck after speeding truck met us on that hilly, backwoods road. Every time one passed, Isaac and the boys buried their faces in the single pillow we had happened to bring along.

"I wish I had counted all the trucks that have passed us," I said regretfully. "In two hours' time, how many do you estimate?"

"At least ten, maybe twelve," said Craig. "Look at the one coming now."

The truck held a single, magnificent log, that was a medium shade of reddish brown. "Some fancy home will have gorgeous paneling," I mourned. "Or a dining room suite with twelve chairs, a hutch, a matching floor, and a set of cabinets, all from that one tree."

"This is the town where Isaac's home is," Bundo said finally. He slowed and pulled into a small village right beside the road. We welcomed a chance to stretch our tired legs. The boys and Isaac slapped the dust out of their clothes and wiped their faces with Wet Ones we had brought along.

Isaac's former girlfriend, Bonita, came out to meet us, with their little Susan clinging to her hand. Naomi, Bonita's other child, followed.

"This is my home," Isaac said, leading us to a small thatch-roofed hut with sturdy mud walls and rough little benches. Everything was dusty.

"The dust is bad," Bonita said. "The trucks go and go all day. We sleep in the dust. We eat in the dust. We cook in the dust."

Several miles later, we finally arrived at the village where the twins were born. "My heart is beating way too fast," Jewel whispered.

"Mine too," I replied.

The villagers crowded around us, staring unashamedly at the white woman who has Eva's babies. "Go get Musu," Isaac instructed, and a young girl ran to do his bidding.

"This is the lady who took the twins all the way to Monrovia," I reminded Jewel. "She has a warm, compassionate heart."

Musu's pretty face was wreathed in smiles as she hurried toward us. She hugged us both. She looked calm and clean in her colorful wrap, with her hair done up in loose curls and her big eyes shining. "I am happy!" she cried. "The 'twin ma' has come to see me."

She pointed out her family from the crowd. Her sisters looked just like any other African tribeswomen. "What makes you so different, Musu?" I asked frankly.

"I am a Christian—like you," she said in low tones. "Come. Let us see where Eva bore Alosious and Oliver."

"We named them Brady Oliver and Brett Alosious," Jewel informed her, but she just nodded.

The entire village was at our heels as we walked down to the mud block hut where the twins took their first breaths. There was a low doorway into the bedroom where poor little Oliver had lain for eleven hours until Alosious was born.

I can't begin to describe the feelings that chased each other through my mind as we gazed at that little room. A mother had died here in agony as she gave birth to her two little boys. The frightened, superstitious people of the village had laid the crying babies at their dead mother's feet and bolted the door.

Jewel's eyes mirrored what I felt. "Look how small that window is," she said softly. "I wonder if I could even crawl through there."

"Thank God for Musu!" Craig exclaimed.

Musu turned to us and spoke what was uppermost on her mind. "There is a baby in the next village with no ma," she began. "The child's mother has been dead four days and the child has not been fed since. She cries and cries."

"Why won't they feed her?" asked Jewel. "Are they afraid of a curse?"

"Yes," Musu answered. "The child caused the mother to die."

"You don't believe that, do you, Musu?"

"No, that's why I want you to come see. *Please?*"

I didn't know what to think. We have three children in the house already. Was I willing to get up at night for another one? On the other hand, how could I ever sleep again if I knew a baby was starving to death and I didn't help?

We drove a few miles to the neighboring village. We had to park the truck and walk a short distance, then climb a steep embankment to the village huts.

The grieving family was sitting in the shade of the porch. Three women sat on a bench, leaning back against the walls of the hut and nursing their babies. The starving baby was nowhere to be seen.

"Where is Marte?" Musu asked one of the men.

The man reached back behind the corner of the wall and fished up a baby girl, holding her by one small wrist. He put her in my arms and Jewel and I looked down into a sweet little face with huge, solemn eyes and chubby cheeks. The child gave a weak cry and turned her head. She was soft and cuddly and clean, and altogether adorable.

"We *have* to take her, Wayne—we just have to. She's starving," I heard myself say. "How old is she?"

"Two months today," I was told.

Two months. It could take weeks for her to die of starvation.

"They must have given her water," Jewel said.

"Who is the father?" Craig asked.

"Ah am," said the man who had lifted her up. "Ah am Sam Teagh." I noticed for the first time how dejected he looked. His eyes were full of misery.

"How old are you?" Craig asked the young man.

"Twenty-four."

"Is her mother really dead?" Wayne asked Sam.

"Yes, I'll show you," another man answered for him. They led him and Craig out behind the hut where they had erected a tiny hut of twigs.

"Can I see her?" Wayne asked.

Reluctantly, the man pulled open the small thatched door. Wayne and Craig leaned down to see the still form swathed in white cloths.

"She's dead all right," Wayne said when they came back.

Willie, Georgie, Larry, and Isaac sat with Bundo on a carved bench, watching the scene unfold.

"The baby hasn't eaten for four days," Musu reminded me. I looked around at the circle of nursing mothers—two of whom were the dead mother's sisters.

"Why don't you nurse this baby?" I burst out angrily.

I was met with silence. They gazed back at me without a speck of pity in their smoldering eyes. I realized it was fear in its darkest form that kept these mothers from feeding their own sister's baby. They feared the curse that had befallen her. They had listened to the baby's desperate cries all day and all night for four days and not one of them had been moved to feed her.

Someone had bathed her and dressed her in a pretty little cotton dress. I couldn't understand it. "Maybe this was to be her burial dress," I told Jewel. "They probably want to bury her with her mother. Why else would they wait with the body?"

Jewel's eyes were big and half scared. "It's positively creepy," she shuddered.

"Well, it looks like she comes with us," Wayne decided. "Do you want us to take her, Sam?"

"Yes, ah agree," Sam said clearly. *Did I actually see tears in his eyes?*

"Do you have other children?" Jewel wondered.

One of the women brought two toddlers. The girl screamed with fright, but the boy let Jewel hold him as long as she wanted, staring at her the whole time. He was a cute little fellow.

Sam's eyes went to little Marte, and this time I was sure his jaw was working. The baby's beautiful dark eyes fastened on her father's face. He reached out and touched her hand. Only God knows what was in that man's heart, but there was love in his eyes. What a tumultuous mixture of superstition and agony and relief must have churned in his breast!

I heard Bundo's sigh of relief when we headed for the truck. "I was afraid you would not take her," he said to me. "That's a fine little Bassa girl!"

The natives can tell by looking at a child which tribe it comes from. The Bassa tribe is one of the more prominent of the many Liberian tribes.

"Whew! That man looked about sixteen," Craig whistled. "I would have never believed he was the father."

Musu glowed with satisfaction. "This baby is related to Oliver and Alosious," she confided. "Praise God for you people!"

"We already know who will adopt her," I said.

"Who . . . Kurt and Marilyn Shores?" asked Jewel.

"Of course. Imagine the twins having a cousin in the same area."

We dropped Musu off near her home. She hugged us fiercely and looked at the baby for a long moment. "God be praised," she murmured again. "One day I will come to visit you."

"Musu, you are welcome to visit us any time," we told her.

For some reason, I had taken along a few boxes of Thick 'N Easy nutritional formula. "That's perfect—just what we need!" Jewel said when I told her. "Bundo, could you ask for a spoon, please?"

Bundo soon came hurrying out of one of the huts with a spoon, and we were finally on our way. Jewel opened a box of milk immediately, and I began feeding the baby. Her little mouth opened eagerly, but she wouldn't eat more than a few spoonfuls.

We tried about an hour later with the same results. After dropping off Isaac at his village, we drove off the main road to have a picnic in the shade of some African ash trees.

Willie wanted to hold the baby while we prepared the sandwiches on the tailgate. "What's this thing around her waist?"

he asked, revealing a bright red, twisted cord with a bone charm hanging from it.

"Cut it off!" Georgie said in disgust. I cut the offending cord free with the paring knife and tossed it unceremoniously into the bushes, regardless of how many evil spirits I was offending.

Bundo tenderly took the clamps out of her pierced ears. "This child would have had no chance if you had not taken her," he said soberly.

Three hours and many bumpy feedings later, we came to Paynesville, where Bundo got off. He paused to smile at the baby. "How's my girl?" he said softly. "Little Bassa woman."

"He's absolutely smitten with her," I said in surprise. "Who would have guessed?"

"I can't believe she hasn't cried yet," Jewel said.

Bev and Charlotte were incredulous when we arrived home. "Another baby, Mom? I can't believe it. Why . . . where . . . ?"

After a brief explanation, little Marte was whisked away and bathed, powdered, dressed, and cuddled to sleep with a bottle of warm formula.

We were all tired and hungry, but after a bowl of rice and a hot bath everyone felt better. We sat around the living room after devotions and discussed the new baby.

"I think I'll name her Kayla," Charlotte mused. "I just wonder how that mother felt when she knew she was dying—and she knew too, what would happen to her baby. She was a real good mother by the looks of this little one."

The fruit bats of the night were barking in the plum tree when I sat down at the computer to write to Kurt and Marilyn Shores. Some things just can't wait.

Dear Friends,

We have the loveliest baby girl right here on the couch. She's two months old today, and since her mother is dead she was left to starve. She needs a good home. Please respond as soon as possible. Charlotte named her Kayla, but of course you can pick whatever name you want. Her African name is Marte. God Bless.

The Stelfoxes in Liberia

Then I typed another letter to Sue and Richard Kauffman.

Dear Friends,

Is there a chance you might be interested in adopting Princess's brother Secret? He is almost two years old according to the relatives. His father is sick and you know poor Naomi's story. I will add that he is a fine little fellow. He's starting to giggle and laugh now, and has the cutest habit of shaking his finger at you. This is not to pressure you, but to let you know Princess does have a brother. God bless.

The Stelfoxes in Liberia

December 14

Kayla started screaming last night when Charlotte was dressing her for bed. It was as if she suddenly realized that her whole life had turned upside down. She screamed so hard I thought she would faint. She would look wildly around at our concerned, pale faces and just shriek.

"She's got a tremendous voice," Wayne said ruefully. "She'll wake all the neighbors plus Security."

"She's terrified," Charlotte said pityingly.

That baby screamed until she was worn out. We took turns holding her and tried every trick we could think of—from food to toys. Her cries became hoarse and croaky, but she could not stop. When she finally fell asleep from pure exhaustion, Bev gently put her in her bed, which is the couch turned against the wall. Her whole body was damp with sweat, and she took great gasping breaths until they finally subsided to normal breathing. She lay face down, with her chubby little knees pulled up under her. I covered her with a warm baby blanket.

At three-thirty she was up again, but so drowsy that she took the bottle with no protest, then fell back to sleep. *Poor little darling.*

When Henry Cole came this morning, he was carrying two very skinny gray roosters. "Could I let them run in the yard to preserve them fo' Christmas?" he asked. "If I let them go at home they will disappear quick."

"You'll have to ask Wayne," I told him, thinking of our last rooster. "Are they normal or do they crow all night long?"

"They are just regular roosters," he answered, a bit flustered at my question.

After supper, Bev and Willie went to the office for e-mails. There was a letter from the Shores.

Dear Stelfoxes of Liberia,

What an incredible answer to prayer! Yes! We want her. A two-month-old baby girl would be perfect, although we don't like to specify what we want when it comes to a child. (I was secretly in my heart of hearts hoping for a girl this time, though.)

Please, can you tell us more about her? We have decided to call her Angela Naomi. It should not be too hard to proceed with the adoption because we already have the INS approval for the adoption of another child.

We are so excited! Praise the Lord for His marvelous goodness.

Kurt, Marilyn, and family

"Hey, that's your middle name," Larry said to Charlotte.

"I know—and I like it just as much as Kayla."

I am so thrilled I can hardly accept the good news. God has a purpose for each child born under heaven. This dear little one will go from deep in the River Cess bush to a loving home in Wisconsin. She is of infinite worth to her Creator—a precious, living soul whom He loves.

Angela Naomi had another screaming session tonight, so I was still wide awake at eleven thirty when a man called from Zion (the church's radio code) to Mike Charlie (Pastor Mervin).

"There is a baby in a carton on the church step. Please advise."

"Did I hear right?" Wayne asked. "That's Moses Massawalla calling!"

Minutes later there was a honk at the gate, and Mary and Staci Lantz came hurrying in. "We need some formula," they explained. "Moses felt led to go downstairs at church—he doesn't even know why—and there he found a baby girl crying her eyes out in a cardboard box on the steps. Stone and Curt came over, and they decided to call the police. We need to go right now. I think she's hungry and cold."

I called Mary when my curiosity became unbearable. "I am feeding a baby girl," she marveled. "The police came and took her to the station, but it didn't take long, and they called back and asked us to come get the baby. They have no place to keep her, let alone feed her. So, Ruth Ann, what do you think?"

"I wonder if someone was watching from the darkness till Moses came and got the baby," I answered. "Maybe some young girl couldn't handle the thought of raising a child—or maybe the mother is dead."

"There's a whole list of possibilities," she agreed. "Meanwhile, we'll just take care of her. Do you know of anyone who wants to adopt a little girl?"

"I'm sure we could find someone."

"You'll probably see her tomorrow," Mary said. "Have a good night—I mean morning."

December 15

At four o'clock this morning, Henry's roosters started trying to outdo each other with their lusty crowing.

"They must be roosting right above us on the porch," Wayne said sleepily. "It's surely not time to get up."

Every long, drawn-out crow made me cringe. I knew Angela would hear and wake up, and maybe Brett and Brady too.

I dressed quickly and went in search of Sam. "Could you please make those roosters shut up?" I asked softly.

Sam shone the beam of his flashlight to the top of the upper porch wall where the offending birds were winding up for another neck-stretching crowing session. "Hurry!" I urged, and went back inside.

The noises Sam made were worse than the roosters. What a bumping and banging and squawking and flapping of wings! "What is going on up there?" Wayne asked in astonishment.

I was laughing too hard to answer right away. "I have no idea. Sam must be tying up the roosters' beaks."

"He shocked them right out of their socks," he chuckled. "Now maybe a man can get some sleep in this place."

We didn't hear another sound until the cooing of the red-billed wood doves began at dawn.

I was much too sleepy during church this morning. I know Pastor Mervin started a series on the Sermon on the Mount, but I'm ashamed to say I nodded over Angela's curly head lying on my shoulder. It was exceptionally warm. Not a breeze stirred. Wayne's shirt was so wet it stuck to his back when he got up to lead songs, and right behind me, Dr. Lamin's towel never stopped spinning.

Pastor Mervin began to wilt, and stopped preaching five minutes early. Mary had stayed home with the little girl found on the church house doorsteps.

I was surrounded immediately after church and peppered with many questions about the Bassa baby I was holding. I answered them politely, edging my way outside. Some of the women wanted to hold her, but little Angela turned away. The air outside was fresher, but just as warm. The heat waves shimmered in the distance above the undulating ocean.

This evening, we headed out to Elwa beach for a staff picnic. We all arrived about the same time. It was different seeing Mary with a tiny bundle in her arms. She took off the blanket so we could all see the baby.

"How could anyone abandon her?" asked Bev.

"She can't be more than two weeks old!" I exclaimed.

"She's adorable," said Jewel. "Does she eat well for you?"

"Oh, yes. She loves that formula."

The baby has a heart-shaped face with wide-set eyes and a perfect rosebud mouth. She was dressed in a dear little dress of pink and white, with tiny white socks to match.

"Don't you think she's cute?" Pastor Mervin asked, smiling broadly.

"The hard part is thinking about giving her up some day," Staci declared. "I don't like mysteries. I wish we knew where she came from."

Staci's unanswered question is on my mind, too.

December 16

Everyone here is heartsick today. Craig and Jewel visited the Embassy and the American Consular officer, Glenn Carey, told them he would not even review their paperwork unless he had the original documents in front of him.

Jewel called their adoption agency and they said this is a different procedure than any other country they have ever worked with. They will do what they can to send the originals as soon as possible.

"We're not leaving without Brett and Brady," Craig declared. "They belong to us, and we're not leaving until they can come."

"I sure admire your attitude," I said. "That's what I call faith."

"It's hard to give up all our Christmas plans," said Jewel with a quiver in her voice.

Just before supper, Sarah Onrah stopped by for more milk. "Blessing is fine," she reported. "Blessing loves the milk."

"Bring her along next time, would you?" Charlotte asked. "I'd love to see her again."

"I will bring her."

When the children were all taken care of and the house was finally quiet, I took time to check the e-mails. The Kauffmans had written a brief note.

Dear Ruth Ann and all,

We have decided as a family that we are more than willing to adopt Faith Princess's brother also. We have room in the boys' bedroom, so that won't pose a problem. We will begin adoption procedures from this side immediately. Please keep us informed.

Sincerely,

Richard, Sue, and family

P.S. We decided on Faith Princess for her name. We'll let you know about Secret's too, but we're leaning toward Timothy.

December 18

Just before lunch today, Mitchel Clemmer came for all the available information about Secret and Angela. He has arranged for passport photos tomorrow. I appreciate that we have an adoption agent right here in Monrovia, but I wonder how he got his training and authority. I checked some of the work he has done on the twins' important documents and it concerns me, to say the least. On the relinquishment form, their birthdates were different. Fortunately, we were able to change that information. I was appalled by all the spelling errors in the child case history. I sincerely hope this does not affect the final adoption proceedings.

When Bev and Secret came home from the office today, she handed me a Christmas card from the Lantzes. Mary had signed it *Mary, Mervin, Staci, Angela, and "Zion's Angel."*

"They're not going to be able to give that baby up," Charlotte said.

"I know I couldn't," agreed Jewel.

Wayne's brother Dan and his wife Joanne arrived around nine-thirty tonight. They were so tired they went right to sleep upstairs in the other bedroom. They have been in Europe, and this is their last week of vacation. I'm sure they miss their four children.

Joanne gave us a fat pack of letters from our friends at home. There were several for the girls and lots of Christmas cards and letters for all of us. How delightful to browse through them!

31

Christmas in Liberia

December 21

Today was Orphanage Christmas! Charlotte babysat all four children while we distributed those delightful bundles of goodies from the donors in America. Dan and Joanne went with us.

We started with the local C.O. Smythe Orphanage. As soon as the children saw our trucks, they came running from all directions. We pulled up in a little cloud of dust and backed through the gate for easy access. Merci had the packages for every orphanage separated and counted.

After a song and prayer, the caretakers lined the children up according to age and height. The men unloaded the bundles and Jewel, Joanne, and I handed them out while Merci kept track. The children murmured a shy, "Thank you!" and scurried away to see what was inside.

One little girl received a soft white doll wrapped in a tiny baby blanket. She stared at the doll for a few seconds, then looked up at Jewel and back at the doll. Recognition dawned in her eyes.

"A whi' man doll baby!" she cried with glee, hugging it tightly.

We heard cries of joy all around as the children compared the contents of their parcels. They tried on their flip-flops and smelled the soap and ran the combs through their hair. They held the towels against their cheeks to feel the softness and smell the cleanliness.

The toys were the main attraction. Little tractors, books, dolls, plastic sand buckets with spades, balls, toy mirrors, jacks, plastic farm animal sets, and colored pencils were among the treasures.

The older children received a pen with a lined tablet, and the ones over fifteen received a brand new Bible. Dan took charge of handing them out.

"I got the very bes' gift of all!" a young man exclaimed joyfully as he wrote his name in a bold scrawl in his Bible. "*Gold* could naw make me happier."

The next orphanage was the Hannah B. Williams Home, where Faith Princess was staying when Julie found her. Nothing had changed. The pig stench and the flies were worse than ever, and the poor children looked extremely unkempt.

"You can be glad you took Princess away from here!" Dan exclaimed, voicing my thoughts.

Old Hannah B. stared at me for a few seconds. "Are you the one with Whyayeh?" she asked sullenly.

"Whyayeh is in America," I answered sweetly.

Her face registered shock and surprise. "Whyayeh belongs to me!" she snapped.

"Oh? But we found her family," I said evenly. "Your name is nowhere among the papers."

"I will show you." She fished around in the pocket of her floppy African kimono and pulled out a "legal" Liberian passport.

"*Whyayeh B. Williams*," I read aloud. "*Mother of child, Hannah B. Williams*."

"How much did this cost you?" I asked, amused.

"Twenty dollars."

"Well, you'll have to change it again. Her real name is Whyayeh Karnque and her real mother's name is Naomi Borbor."

Hannah B. slowly returned the passport to her pocket. Anger smoldered in her eyes as she turned and walked away. Somehow, she had hoped to profit by the child.

It took a long time to distribute all those packages. The sun burned with such fierce intensity that we sought the shelter of shade trees or buildings whenever possible. We worked more and more slowly.

At My Brother's Keeper, we ran out of parcels before all the children were served. Merci noted their ages and names and promised to send them with the next delivery truck.

It was well past suppertime when we finally arrived home to the table all set and soup warming on the stove. Dan ate three bowls of hamburger soup with three slices of bread.

"I'm sorry, I just didn't enjoy that bean topping we had for dinner," he said apologetically. "I wouldn't make a very good African. I like my meat and potatoes too much."

"You'd get used to it, Uncle Dan," Bev told him. "We all eat cassava and pumpkin soup and palm butter and fried rice. They're delicious. It took Mom a while to find that out, but we children all love African food."

"Why is everything so oily?" Joanne asked.

"Oil is a staple in their diet. They can't eat without large amounts of it," I said. "When Security thinks Sis Bea doesn't use enough oil, they ask for some and douse their food with it. I guess it slides down easier."

"That's about the only source of fat they get," Wayne added. "Their bodies crave it."

"I sure haven't seen any fat people," Dan said.

"There are a few around, though," said Wayne. "The ones who can afford it eat very well. They're not nearly as fat as Americans, though."

December 25

What a wonderful day to think about Jesus' birth.

I got up as quietly as I could, stuffed the two huge turkeys from the UN supermarket, and put them in the upstairs oven to roast. Angela was awake when I came down—all smiles and coos and kicks.

I fed and changed her and decided to rock her while I read the latest *Seed of Truth*. I will look back on these moments someday, and I feel I should treasure them now. I reveled in the softness of her curly head and the feel of her smooth, dimpled arms on my shoulder.

I couldn't shake the thought that she would be dead by now if merciful Jesus had not intervened.

My thoughts were interrupted by a strange bird flying into the branches of the ash tree above the security shed. I caught a glimpse of reddish-brown through the window slats and heard such a melodious, clear warble that I had to investigate. With Angela under my arm, I eased open the front door and peered eagerly into the foliage.

A plain little bird about six inches long sat on the first branch. It was singing so enthusiastically it looked like it would burst with joy. Short bursts of low, rollicking notes were followed by a high crescendo of pure liquid ones. It could only be one thing.

"A nightingale!" I squeaked, causing Angela to stop kicking and look at me for a moment. Once more, those incredibly pure, liquid notes filled the air, and then he was gone. Probably because the new shift of guards was banging on the gate.

I feel as if I have been handed a precious gift. Nightingales are shy birds, so I know this is something I may never see again.

Christmas morning services began at ten o'clock and lasted an hour. After the service the Lantz family came to Residence and we all feasted on turkey and some of the trimmings. We even had a chocolate cheesecake, thanks to Joanne, who had brought along some cream cheese.

"Zion's Angel" is thriving on all the care and attention she has received.

"Have you decided on a name?" Bev asked Mary.

"We just call her Angel for now," Mary said. "We're actually thinking about keeping her, you know."

Our faces must have registered surprise, because Mary laughed and said, "We have to convince Mervin, but I don't think that will be too hard. He loves holding her already."

"That's incredible news!" I said in astonishment. "I don't know why it never entered my mind."

"It didn't enter mine either," Mary said frankly. "But when it comes down to letting her go . . . well . . . it's not that easy."

"I'm sure glad we have the twins," Jewel said, giving little Brady a hug. "It's hard to describe, but it feels like they've been ours all along."

December 31

I always feel a bit melancholy on the last day of the year. There is something ineffably sad about the fact that another year is coming to a close. It's like the last chapter of a delicious book.

Glenn Carey said there has been so much fraud and corruption in Liberia that he will not even make an appointment with Craig and Jewel until the originals arrive. So we can do nothing but wait. Meanwhile, the twins are a constant source of delight to all of us.

This evening we were invited to the Lantzes to sing in the New Year. It was a lovely evening, with the stars hanging low and brilliant. We played a few games of volleyball and then sang until the clock struck twelve. Staci served brownies and Kool-Aid for snack.

I looked around the circle at Craig and Jewel holding Brett and Brady, then at Bev with Secret beside her and Charlotte holding Angela. Little Angel lay in the crook of Pastor Mervin's arm with Mary, Staci, and Angela sitting beside them. Wayne, Willie, and Larry sat next to me.

A warm feeling of contentment filled my heart to see how our numbers had swelled. Who would have dreamed what 2002 would hold?

Now a fresh new 2003 is here. God has taken us safely through another year—praise His holy, blessed name.

32

Victory Over Evil

January 1, 2003

The New Year came in on the wings of the loveliest morning, with the ocean crashing, the gentle red-eyed doves cooing with steady intensity, and the breezes playing with the wind chimes.

Angela didn't have a good night because of an awful cold in her chest. I've tried everything from peppermint oil to Vick's, but nothing has relieved the congestion. I didn't want to go to a clinic today, so I made sure she had lots of liquids and hoped for the best.

We were all up in time for a brunch of sausage breakfast casserole and orange juice.

Craig and Jewel are a real inspiration for all of us. They have taken the startling turn of events in stride and are making the most of their time in Liberia. We laughed and visited and prayed and had a wonderful morning.

We soon discovered that it is an African custom to wish people a Happy New Year. One of our first visitors was Isaac. With him were Susan, Auntie Musu, and Elizabeth, another relative.

Elizabeth asked to hold Brady, and Musu turned to us, smiling. "I came from River Cess to see Marte," she said sweetly. "What's her white name?"

"Angela Naomi. It's spelled like Angel with an 'a' on the end."

She asked for a piece of paper and had us write it down. "The baby is doing fine," she said happily, reaching for Angela. Angela twisted around so she could see Musu's face. She stared and stared. Her head whirled around and she looked at us, and back at Musu. There was such intense concentration in her gaze that we all had to laugh.

We didn't laugh long.

Angela let out such a sudden wail that Musu jumped. I knew what was coming. "Let me have her," I said.

I had to take her back to the bedroom to get those desperate sobs quieted. She cried so hard it broke my heart, and I had to cry right along. I was afraid to go back out to the living room, so I carried her around until she finally fell asleep. All that crying had caused her to wheeze and sneeze and carry on worse than ever.

Musu's eyes were moist as she watched me lay Angela on the couch. "The baby is sad," she murmured. "She misses her mother."

"Rather sad than dead," I told her. "We have a family in America that wants the baby, Musu."

Her eyes lit up. "Then she will be safe?"

"She will be safe, Musu dear. Thanks to you."

"I have something to say to you," Isaac began, and the way he looked I had a nasty feeling I wouldn't like it.

"Go ahead," I said.

"As you know, I have no job and no way to support my own children," he said quietly. "I want you to take baby Susan for your own and . . ."

I didn't let him finish. "Don't even ask!" I exclaimed, trying to stay polite. "We are not here to separate families. She has a father and mother, and we will never even consider it."

"How can you give up your child, just like that?" Jewel asked with a spark in her blue eyes. "I can understand with the twins since they are motherless, but this I find hard to grasp."

"It is the only chance she will ever have for a decent life," he explained sadly. "If we keep her she will go the way of all

Liberians and become a very young mother with no husband and no future."

"We understand," I said. "We want the best for our children too, and you can find out from the Bible how to protect her from such a future. You have to protect her, Isaac. You're all she's got."

Sam Teagh, Angela's father, was our next visitor.

Sam came into the house, surprised to see our other guests. He was all dusty and his eyes were bloodshot and tired.

"Mitchel Clemmer said to come, but ah could get no ride," he said. "Ah rode on the top of the van to come from River Cess."

When a man has no money to pay for an inside seat, he has to either ride on top of or on the end gate of a transport van. No wonder his eyes were so sore. Imagine—all the way from River Cess on top of a van in that awful red dust!

"Charlotte, please call Mitchel and tell him Angela's dad is here. Find out if he should come back tomorrow."

"He can't come today," she reported in a few minutes. "Be here at ten tomorrow morning."

Sam stood and looked down at his sleeping daughter. She still gulped occasionally as she slept. He leaned down and picked her up. She threw out her arms in sleepy surprise, opened her eyes a tiny bit, then leaned against him and slept on. He smiled.

Just before Sam left, Angela woke up and lay there, staring at him. He whispered some words we didn't understand. Her face broke out in a sunny smile and she kicked and wiggled vigorously. Sam pulled her up on her sturdy legs and hugged her close.

"Ah will come back," he said as he gently gave her to Charlotte. "Ah have a bed fo' the night wi' Isaac."

I held my breath lest she start crying again.

"He actually showed some emotion!" Charlotte marveled.

Around two o'clock this afternoon we gathered here for New Year's dinner. I took the opportunity to hold little Shawna, which is what the Lantz family decided to name their baby girl.

"She is getting really cuddly," I told a beaming Mary.

"I'm sure enjoying her," Mervin smiled. "It's nice to hold a little one again, and she lets me hold her all I want."

"She's got you all wrapped up," Wayne laughed. "That's good. Have you decided for sure that you want to keep her?"

"Oh, yes!" said Mary, Staci, and Angela together. Mervin smiled.

"You have your answer," he grinned.

Guests continued to drop by. Neil came and informed us that Abi was sleeping out on the sand of the beach since the lady she had borrowed a room from had returned.

"It is dangerous for a woman to sleep on the beach in Liberia," Neil said. "I feel desperate, Mr. Wayne. I have no room of my own, so I cannot give it to her. Mistress Boma did not want to ask Abi to leave, but she had no choice. Georgie sleeps with me.

"I've got a place in mind if you can wait till tomorrow," Wayne offered. "We have to pick up some visitors at the airport this evening, but tomorrow I'll see what we can do."

I was awakened at 11:45 tonight when Angela had a terrible coughing fit. Gasping for air, her tiny hands flailed the air and her face turned a strange bluish color. The veins stood out in her neck and temples and her eyes were wide with terror. She let out a strangled cry that reminded me of the child in St. Joseph's hospital. She could not get any air. In desperation I began to pray aloud for Jesus to help.

Like a miracle before my eyes, the child relaxed and started breathing normally and quietly. Soon she was asleep.

Thrilled and awed by the wonder of it all, I held her for a very long time. She didn't even snore. I repressed the urge to wake the whole house so they could rejoice with me.

Thank you, Jesus! Thank you, Jesus!

January 5

Neil and Abi approached Wayne right after church. "The room you found for me is working out fine," Abi said warmly. "Mr. Wayne, I cannot begin to tell you how I appreciate your help—it is a fine thing to have my own room. Praise God!"

"She is all settled in, Mr. Wayne," Neil affirmed. "No more sleeping on the beach. Her room even has a lock on it."

I noticed Staci waving and motioning for me to come, so I excused myself and hurried over to see what she wanted. "Ruth is here with her twins," she whispered urgently. "You have to come look at them."

I looked at Rose and Roslyn and a shock of dismay ran through me. "They're dying!" I exclaimed. "Ruth, your babies are starving!"

She looked at me, startled. "Ah feed them every day."

I knew it was no use to try and explain. That awful gray pallor, the hollow sunken eyes, and the transparent skin told the story.

"Staci, please find out where Ruth's new room is; we'll take formula down this afternoon," I requested.

"I'll come along," she said. "Do you think they'll make it? She said she's nursing them, but it sure isn't working."

"Look at Angela—she's only a month older," I told Staci.

After lunch, we picked up powdered formula at Residence and the Lantz sisters and Jewel came with us to Ruth's new residence.

Ruth's two sisters had let her move in with them, and this room was a great improvement over the last one, though dreadfully crowded. A low box served as a nightstand, and the mattress lay on the ground. Clothes hung everywhere, and the tiny windows were all but obstructed. I couldn't understand why none of these grown women could see that the twins were severely malnourished.

"The babies will surely die if you do not follow our instructions," I told them all clearly. "They are not eating enough. They will die soon."

They looked at me in horror.

"You will need to feed them every two hours," I continued slowly, holding up two fingers. "Boil the water at least five minutes, then let it cool and mix it like this."

All of us explained and demonstrated until we were absolutely sure at least one of those women understood. "Wake them up if you have to, but *make sure* they eat," I told them.

"I really don't think Ruth understood a thing," Angela commented.

"I hope Sando did," Jewel said. "She showed me the lines on the bottle and seemed to know what to do."

"We'll slip down tomorrow night and check on them," we decided.

We were sitting around the table munching on popcorn for supper when Merci came to visit. I could tell there was something on her mind by the way she stared into space. She didn't say much until we asked her what was wrong.

"One of my friends had a very terrible experience," she began. "May I tell it to you?"

"I guess . . ." Wayne said doubtfully.

"My friend got on a bus one day, and the weirdest feeling settled over him. He found himself unable to speak or move, no matter how hard he tried. The rest of the people could not speak or move, either. Every time he tried to talk, his jaw would sag heavily. The bus soon left the main road and drove a long way into the bush until he had no idea where they were. Fear gripped his very soul, because he realized he was in the hands of Satan worshippers."

Merci paused and swallowed hard. "He tried desperately to pray aloud, but still he could not make a sound. He felt trapped and terrified, and the looks on the others' faces mirrored his own. So he screamed silently to God for mercy, over and over. They came to a clearing in the forest where a small hut stood. There they were lined up and all their heads were shaved. One by one the people before him were taken into the hut and beheaded, and their blood was caught in a huge basin. There was blood everywhere. My friend never stopped crying out to God in his heart. When his turn came, he knelt by the chopping block, but they couldn't chop off his head. They tried several times, growing more desperate all the time. 'What is this? Who are you?' they cried in terror. Just like that his tongue was loosened. 'I am a Christian!' he shouted victoriously. 'You have no power over me!'

"The men panicked and started screaming, 'Go! Go!' They chased him and all the remaining people out of their sight. It took the frightened band of people three days to find their way out of that place."

Merci's dark eyes were shining. "This is true," she said.

"Whew! That's creepy," Craig said soberly. "I'm glad I'm a Christian."

January 6

This evening we picked up Staci and Angela and went to check on Rose and Roslyn. We ducked into the room where Ruth was sitting cross-legged on the bed, smiling as usual. Roslyn lay like a rag doll on her lap.

Sando was holding Rose. "The baby does not wake up," she said quietly.

"When did you last feed them?" we asked.

"We fed them two times."

"Two times! We said every two hours! They've only had four ounces in twelve hours? No wonder they're not moving—they're too weak to suck."

I opened the can of powdered formula. "You haven't used *any*," I rebuked them.

"Ah used one small, small scoop fo' a bottle," Ruth said. "It will las' longer."

I was speechless.

Fortunately, they had a good supply of boiled water, so we mixed up formula and Staci and Charlotte sat down on the mattress to coax the twins to drink.

"It's too late, I'm afraid," Staci whispered. "She's not taking it."

"Take off their shirts and rub the soles of their feet," Jewel suggested, so they did. No response. The milk dribbled out of the sides of their mouth.

"Squirt the milk onto the roof of her mouth," I said a bit desperately.

Seconds later Charlotte gave a cry. "She's sucking!"

"So is this one," Staci laughed with relief.

The soft glow of the kerosene lantern fell on Charlotte and

Staci and cast long shadows as the women moved about. The gentle sound of the babies sucking the bottles was like music to our ears. In no time the four ounces were gone.

This time we showed the women step by step how to mix the formula and what we meant by two-hour feedings.

"Listen, ladies. Wake them up no matter how hard it is. We will be back to spy on you. We will take the babies if we have to."

I could have laughed at their startled faces if I hadn't been so worried.

It was dark when we got home. A man and a woman with a baby girl were waiting for us in the living room. Jewel and I sat and listened to their story.

"I am Kubah," the woman said. "This is Augustine, the baby's father, and this is Joanna. The child's mother died, and I have no way to feed her." On and on she went, with the man nodding and adding little bits of information.

"I can see she is in good hands," I told them. "She is a fine baby. You must keep taking good care of her."

The father leaned toward me. "You do not understand," he said flatly. "I am giving the child up for adoption. Her mother is dead, and I am without a job. We need help."

We instructed them to go talk to Akin at the CAM base. They seemed to be satisfied and left. "I think we'll be seeing more of them," I predicted. "Have you ever seen such a thin man?"

January 9

The highlight of the week was the arrival of Julie and Faith Princess from Ghana this afternoon. Of course, Julie wanted to meet Craig and Jewel and Angela immediately. She hugged all the babies and toured the whole house.

"It's so wonderful to be home," she said as she hugged Secret again.

"You just missed Angela's father," Jewel said. "He was here taking photos and signing the relinquishment for her adoption. He left Monrovia yesterday."

"He cried when he left," Charlotte added. "Angela just smiled at him and had no idea what was going on. Isn't that sad?"

Faith Princess knew us immediately. "Muttah!" she cried, hugging my skirt. She even remembered which twin was which. When Julie showed her Angela, she leaned over and smelled Angela's hair.

"Shampoo," she said.

"This is Angela," Julie explained. "Angela is a baby. You must be very careful with her."

Faith Princess sensed that Angela was not the only stranger in the house. She quietly sidled up to Jewel and felt her skirt, then smelled her hand. No connection.

She stood there, confused. Jewel knelt down to her level and took the child's hand in hers. "I am Jewel," she said clearly.

Faith Princess felt all over her face and hair. "Jewel," she said clearly.

"She'll remember you from now on," Julie assured Jewel. "Princess, come here and meet Secret. See? This is Secret."

Faith Princess felt his face and patted the top of his head. "Secret small-small," she said.

"Uh-oh. This could get interesting," I laughed. "She knows he's smaller."

Merci came hurrying into the house and swept Faith Princess and Julie up in a bear hug. The child laughed in delight. "Merci, where my guitar?" she asked, so Merci took her for a hunt around the house until they found it.

"I like your hair, Princess," Merci told her. "It is coming back so fine. Soon Merci will be able to braid you."

Tonight we had a full house with all the friends Julie had invited. She handed out all her Christmas gifts and watched with pleasure while we opened them.

It was much too late by the time this evening was over. "Oh well, this doesn't happen every day," Wayne said, savoring a piece of pure Belgian chocolate. "I'm just glad she's home."

January 13

Craig and Jewel were delighted when their long-awaited documents finally arrived this morning. They quickly went to the U.S. Embassy to make an appointment with the American Consular officer, but their hopes were dashed when they found a statement posted outside the door:

> The American Embassy has issued a travel warning for West Africa and Liberia in particular. Anyone insisting on staying in the country despite the warning should exercise extreme caution and stay away from demonstrations or crowds. The Embassy is closed due to anti-American demonstrations planned for the twenty-fifth, and will not be issuing American visas or passports until further notice.

Craig hardly flinched. "Oh well," he said cheerfully. "We're not leaving without our babies."

Around eleven o'clock, I had a phone call from Patrick McMahon, a man Wayne met at the CAM open house in November. He is seriously interested in adopting a baby from Liberia and wondered if we knew of any who needed a home.

"What about Joanna?" Jewel asked. "She is motherless and that father is so skinny it's awful. I think he's sick."

"He did say he is giving her up," I answered. "In fact, he said it quite emphatically. Let's look into this. Patrick said his wife's name is Amy, and they have two young boys. They live in Vermontville, New York."

Maybe another child can be helped.

January 19

During lunch today, Mitchel Clemmer arrived with a tall, smiling gentleman whom he introduced as Charles Bassil. "He will help me with the paperwork."

Charles smiled the whole time he was here. There was something about him I felt we could trust. He told us about his wife and children and how happy he was to be of service in such a worthy cause.

"You will be seeing more of me," he promised.

January 21

It was fiercely hot today. Even the noisy weaver birds didn't socialize as heartily as usual. Larry's head leaned over his books in such a dejected manner that I told him to go out for a break. Seconds later he gave a yell from the laundry room. "Mom, come quick! There's something in here!"

It was a scorpion. "Wow! That's a wicked-looking thing," I said.

"I'd hate to feel that sting," Larry said. "It came out from under the clothes on the floor."

I grabbed the broom and swept it out onto the porch, then squished it flat.

Bev and Julie brought Esther Akoi home with them. Esther was in a jolly mood, and very hungry besides.

"You remind me of a storybook character," I told her. "Is there ever a time when you are not smiling?"

Her dimples got deeper as she smiled harder. Her eyes fairly danced with the joy of living. "I was not smiling when I was not a Christian, Muttah. It smells so fine in here."

A person would never guess that this lovely girl had become a mother at the tender age of thirteen, and that she has a very sad history. Jesus has made the difference.

33

Where is Blessing?

January 29

Sarah Onrah was here before Wayne left for the office this morning.

"Where is Blessing?" Charlotte asked politely.

"She's with my mother," Sarah said with a toss of her dark head.

"Sarah, do not come back until you bring Blessing with you," Charlotte said firmly. "We have been giving you food for a long time, and you still haven't brought the girl. Do you understand?"

"Yes, I understand," Sarah replied sullenly.

We gave her a small amount of Thick 'N Easy. "Are you sure you are feeding her?" Charlotte probed.

"Yes, I am," and she hoisted the milk on her head and walked out the door.

"I don't trust that woman!" Charlotte exclaimed. "I'll ask Merci to take me to where she lives. I want to see Blessing."

Later this evening Wayne, Larry, and I started out for Robert's Field to pick up Dave King and his family, who plan to stay in Liberia for six weeks. The police stopped us at Elwa Junction because President Taylor was somewhere near the airport and no one was allowed through until he passed. We were directed to the beginning of the long line of waiting cars and told to wait.

Finally, after waiting for over an hour, the first police car came flying from the direction of Elwa. Another careened around the corner on two wheels, tires screaming in protest. Then came the soldier trucks, the Mercedes, and more police vehicles. Sirens wailed the whole time, and we were allowed to proceed only after the noise faded in the distance.

The King family was just coming out of the airport when we pulled in. I especially enjoyed meeting the children, since they had been in Haiti with Bev and I recognized some of their names and faces from her photos. We had met Dave and Faith in Pennsylvania at CAM's open house, so it was just a matter of renewing acquaintances.

"Welcome to Liberia," my husband smiled.

The ride back to Monrovia was uneventful, and a very tired little family was finally shown upstairs in the CAM office building where they will stay.

"Neil and Abi were here," Craig told us when we got home. "They'd like to start a small baking business if it's possible. We had a real nice time with them. He seems a lot more at peace with himself than he was when we first came."

"I think he'll do all right," Wayne agreed.

Angela slept all night for the first time last night. I'm hoping for the same tonight. I still marvel at the miracle during that frightening New Year's night when God showed Himself strong in her behalf. When I feel discouraged, I just relive that miracle.

February 5

Kathy Kauffman wrote and said that Nathan has a reoccurrence of cancer. Gone are all the fond hopes of coming back to Liberia.

We were looking forward to them so much. The only thing that matters in a time like this is the absolute knowledge that God is in control.

Christians have heaven to look forward to, but how awful it must be to face death without knowing the Saviour.

February 9

This afternoon, Wayne decided he'd like to see how Marie Toe Fanciah, a recipient of the CAM Self-Help program, is making out.

"Did you hear what happened to her husband?" Wayne asked me.

"No."

"I'll let her tell you. It's awful. Let's walk down to her place."

Marie opened the door when we knocked. In her arms was a tiny new baby. Her mother sat on the lone chair next to a small scrap of a table. She was slim and youthful. She rose and held out her hand. "How's da day?" she said in a friendly, personable manner. "I am Helen."

I liked her at once.

The room was orderly and clean and smelled good. I didn't have much time to look around because Marie put the baby in my arms and burst into a frenzy of tears.

"She's in great distress," Helen said, but she made no move toward the weeping woman.

"Marie . . ." I began.

"My husband Isaac took out a loan from Christian Aid," she cried. "He made out good with his first sale of peppers, so he wanted to do more buying and selling. He left me here to wait, and went to do business in the bush." She paused and wiped her eyes before she continued.

"I waited and waited but there was no word. I delivered the child on January 30, but still no word. Then the message came that he was dead. *The man that God gave me is dead!* They made him come over to the bush to sell the peppers, then they jumped on him and killed him."

"Who did?" I asked in horror.

"His brothers! His own brothers! They could not stand that the man was coming up; they only wanted to see him fall down. Oh, it is wicked, it is *so wicked!* His own brothers!" she cried, her face twisted in grief.

"He had a nice sum of money when they attacked him," Helen

said. "All four of them tried to take it from him, but he resisted so strongly that they had to cut him to get it."

"He was big and strong!" Marie cried, wringing her hands. "They brought me his ring, but I would not touch it. 'Take it away!' I told them, because they had put a demon in the ring. Who will take care of us now? God sent me a man, I married him, and now He took him away. I cannot question Almighty God, but . . . why? *Why?*"

I looked at the beautiful, fatherless baby in my arms. So innocent, so pure, and so small—still unmarred from the misery and sin all around him. Perfectly at peace.

It is hard not to feel indignation toward these men and their awful deed. Because of the evil in their hearts, a heartbroken mother and her small son are left to fend for themselves.

February 10

Craig and Jewel have been here for nine weeks. Rumors say the Embassy will be opening again on the twentieth. The anti-American demonstration didn't amount to anything since all of Liberia knows that the Americans are here to help.

David Holder came to speak with Larry this morning. I didn't realize this was another wildlife situation or I would have gone out immediately.

I continued to wash dishes until I heard a strange hissing sound. I hurried out to the porch just in time to see Merci and Zubah tearing the tail and wing feathers out of a baby goshawk.

"What are you doing?" I cried.

"Now he can't fly," Merci answered triumphantly, holding up a handful of tattered brown feathers.

The poor bedraggled bird hopped unsteadily away, looking as if he'd gone through the wringer. His rearranged feathers stuck out in every direction. He stopped and tried to straighten them out, but it was impossible. Larry tried to pick him up but was stopped by his threatening hiss.

"You two ought to work in a chicken factory," I snapped at Merci and Zubah. "I've never seen anyone pluck a bird so fast and furiously."

"They did it before I could even *think*," Larry told me as we went back in the house. "I didn't say I wanted a bird—now I have to feed it!"

"That little guy is easy to feed. Lizards would be perfect, Larry. Now you can hunt again," I told him.

Late this afternoon, the fish lady brought some cassava, crab, and tuna. Merci came down from upstairs where she had been making bundles just as we were trying to decide what to buy.

"I would like to make you some pepper crab soup one time," she offered, so we bought the crab. I wanted to treat the King family to cassava fish, so I took that too.

"Take it all fo' the same price," the fish lady said pleadingly, so we took the tuna as well.

Elijah cleaned all the fish and received the heads and various internal parts. "My Ellen will *love* it," he grinned mischievously. "She likes dem fish eggs fro' da inside parts."

"She's more than welcome," I said generously.

Elijah had caught the fierce little goshawk and put him in the cage. He ate some of the fish entrails with great gusto.

When school was over, Charlotte, Merci, and I went to the Leprosy Market area to find little Blessing. We drove up close to where Sarah lives and walked the rest of the way to her house. Suddenly, Sarah was there in front of us, blocking the way.

"Oh, hi Sarah. We came to see Blessing," Charlotte said.

"Blessing's not here. She's visiting my mother across the field. She won't come here today."

"Across *what* field?" Merci asked. "Tell me just where she is."

"My mother's home. Blessing went with her . . . across the field."

We could get no more information out of her. "Sarah, bring Blessing to the house," Charlotte said evenly. "I don't believe you anymore. We want to see Blessing *now*."

Sarah remained stonily silent. "Let's go away from this area," Merci said. "It is no use to wait for this woman. My soup awaits me at your place."

As soon as we got home, Merci got busy in the kitchen

cleaning, chopping, and pounding. She sent Julie for some strange African seasonings and hot peppers and added them to the brew. Jewel and I watched curiously.

"What is she doing now?" I wondered as she dumped in the tuna fish pieces, bones and all. Merci grinned broadly.

"Jus' wait," she said mysteriously.

It was after five-thirty when the soup was finally done. Merci ladled it carefully out into bowls and set it around the table. Georgie and Harris, Neil, Abi, and little Georgie happened to be around, so they were invited for supper.

Oh, how the native people and Neil's family loved that soup! It turned out hot as fire, and soon the Americans were sputtering and crying and drinking lots of water.

"Eat some, Sis Ruth," Merci coaxed as she cracked a crab leg with her teeth and chewed on it until all the white flesh was gone. "It is delicious!"

I looked at the bones floating in the mushy broth. "I can't handle the heat," I explained. "Thank you so much for making supper, Merci. It was very sweet of you."

"Neil, you have to come see my hawk," Larry said excitedly. "He's so fierce I can't get close to him."

Neil leaned over and looked. The bird hissed softly. "Bring me some gloves, please," Neil said. "That's one fine little bird. You're right, it's a goshawk."

He opened the door of the cage and slowly reached in, talking quietly all the time. The hissing stopped. The little bird hopped onto the gloved fist and Neil withdrew his arm. He put his thumb over the bird's foot and stroked down its puffed-up neck feathers.

"What a fine bird," he said. "I wouldn't mind having him myself if I had a place to keep him."

"You can play with him all you want," Larry offered.

"Thanks, pal."

Later in the evening, Neil and Abi discussed their dream of a baking business. Wayne encouraged them in their endeavor and said he believes CAM could help them get started. The CAM Self-Help program has tremendously encouraged many would-be entrepreneurs. One of these is Garlic Grace, who can provide for herself and her son ever since she was helped with a small freezer so she could sell cold water. Philippine Doe, a widow with four children, also sells cold water.

It's amazing what a small start can do to keep a family from abject poverty.

February 15

Right after breakfast, Mitchel Clemmer arrived in great haste. His eyes were wide and frightened, and he was bursting to talk.

"I just escaped the militia men," he exploded. "I was in a taxi coming this direction when they approached the car. '*Run!*' the taxi driver screamed, so the whole car emptied fast and we ran in all directions. I hid in a trench until they were gone."

When he calmed down, we spent a couple of hours going over the adoption papers and starting new ones for Joanna Sumo, who is now up for adoption. Patrick and Amy McMahon have asked us to go ahead and pursue her case.

Last night after work, the CAM couples—Iddo and Viola, Craig and Jewel, Dave and Faith, Mervin and Mary, and Wayne and I—went to Mamba Point for supper. Seems like we are all so busy there is hardly time for socializing.

We talked about the agricultural project, the sewing center, next week's distributions, the Liberia church, the coming adoptions, and the work load at Christian Aid Ministries. We had a wonderful time.

When we arrived home, we found that two men had been at Residence and brought a baby armadillo all the way from Nimba for Larry.

"It can hang upside down by its tail," Larry told me. "Isn't his tongue a weird-looking thing? Just like a long pink worm. It should live for years in captivity, but it needs a steady diet of ants, grubs, or worms. I'm going to call it Dillo."

"I think it is too small to live and hunt without its mother," I told him. "I really wish they would have left it in the jungle."

February 17

Craig and Jewel came back from the Embassy this morning with the promise of a ten o'clock appointment tomorrow morning with Glenn Carey himself. I am terribly excited for them—they have been so patient.

Larry has been trying to feed that little anteater off of an ant pile, but it's not that easy. "It doesn't really dig around like it should," he said.

"That's because its mother probably does the digging," I suggested.

Kubah brought little Joanna this afternoon and stayed to talk for at least two hours. Joanna is crawling and sitting up by herself.

"Joanna is eight months old now," Kubah told me. "Her birthday is June 15. I will no longer take care of the child. She is not mine. Augustine gives me nothing for her."

"Just keep her until she can find a home," I begged. "If you put her in a children's home she will get worms and scabies and all that stuff. This way she looks so nice and healthy. God will reward you, Kubah, for caring for an orphan."

She looked at me steadily. "I will keep her," she said.

Jewel was already digging through a bag of used clothing. "Will this fit?" she wondered, holding up a little purple dress of crushed velvet with black trim.

Kubah took it eagerly. "It will fit," she said happily. "Have you any diapers?"

We gave her four homemade flannel diapers and a pair of rubber pants. Jewel found a small petticoat and another green dress that fit Joanna perfectly.

"I will keep her," Kubah repeated.

February 18

The excitement is running so high it's hard to function normally. Craig and Jewel came back from the Embassy with huge grins on their faces.

"Tell us quick!" we cried.

"Consular Carey said we can pick up the twins' visas on Friday and book our tickets for Wednesday," Craig said calmly. "We're actually on our way."

What rejoicing burst forth from that little kitchen! The mechanics stopped pounding for a minute and the security guards walked slowly around the house, pretending to check on the warehouse.

Jewel was absolutely aglow. "It is just too good to be true!" she exclaimed with tears of joy in her eyes. "I wonder why Glenn Carey asked to see Isaac before we go."

"He did?"

"Yes," said Craig. "He said he wants us to bring Isaac in on Friday when we pick up the visas. I think that's part of the normal procedure. Bundo is going right past Isaac's house on Wednesday, so I'll ask him to stop and pick him up."

"Perfect idea," Jewel agreed.

"Let's make ice cream tonight to celebrate," Craig said eagerly. "Right now, Jewel and I are going in to S.N. Brussels for four tickets. See ya!"

I hurried to mix up a batch of ice cream. We have been using Mary's custard recipe that uses powdered milk and whipped topping mix. I've added evaporated milk with excellent results.

Craig and Jewel returned an hour later with four envelopes. "There was no problem at all," he said. "The twins fly for half price because we hold them on our laps. That's pretty good!"

His excitement is contagious, but I feel like a wonderful part of our lives is about to end.

We had just finished churning the ice cream when the fish lady arrived with three huge cassava fish. We asked around to see if any of the staff wanted some, and they all did, so Craig and Elijah got busy filleting fish. After a while the whole house smelled like a fish cannery.

Elijah rubbed his hands together with anticipation. "Two fish heads in one month!" he smiled. "My Ellen will be happy."

I soaked the fresh fillets in salt water then froze them in cake pans to deliver later.

Larry threw some entrails into the goshawk's cage and

watched as the bird tore them to pieces.

"Rikki used to love fish guts," Larry said sadly. "I think he thought the fish was still alive, the way he attacked it. I just have to get another baby mongoose, Mom."

A horn sounded at the gate just as he finished talking. It was Edwin Jackson with a tiny baby fawn. Larry was ecstatic.

"I was just longing for a pet," Larry told them. "This is almost as good as a mongoose!"

"All the way from the bush," Edwin smiled, setting the fawn down. It wobbled toward Larry and nudged him gently with a wet black nose.

"He's hungry."

I warmed milk and put it in an old baby bottle. It was magic to see how that baby drank. "His name is Bambi," said Larry. "I'll just let him run around wherever he wants to."

"At least he doesn't crow," I said.

February 21

Craig and Jewel took Isaac to the Embassy at ten o'clock this morning. Consular Glenn Carey talked with Isaac for a while, and then announced he was going to "investigate certain matters further."

"I can't imagine what his problem is," Craig said. "We have another appointment on Tuesday morning at ten o'clock. I sure hope there's no problem."

February 23

"I hate it when this happens," Larry told Zubah this morning when he found Dillo curled in a little ball from which he would never uncurl.

"See what I mean, Zubah?" I said. "All these poor animals aren't meant to be captives. I insist that you don't let any more come in unless you have specific permission."

"That's for sure," Larry agreed. "Come call us if it's a baby elephant or a mongoose—or maybe a lion cub. They are easy to take care of, aren't they, Mom?"

"I don't know, son."

This morning in church, Pastor Mervin continued his character study. It is truly fascinating. I spent some of the time in the church entrance because Angela still has a fever from her immunizations on Thursday and didn't want to sit still for too long.

I can't help but notice how reverently all the people sit during church. I don't see one of them whispering or laughing. The children sit perfectly still. There are no toys or books or little Tupperware containers of Cheerios to keep them happy.

"I wonder where Neil is," Wayne said on the way home. "Maybe he's sick . . . or maybe he's slipping. I'll have to find out."

February 25

Isaac arrived at Residence this morning dressed in the very best clothes he could find. His sneakers were brushed clean and he looked like a rich Liberian. What a drastic change from the usual unkempt, ragged-looking man.

"You look sharp," Larry said. "Where'd you get those new clothes?"

Isaac smiled. "I borrowed the clothes, Larry. I have to look good for the American Embassy."

Craig and Isaac made sure they were at the Embassy by ten o'clock. We waited, and waited, and waited some more, but it was three o'clock when they finally called to say they were coming home.

Wayne, Bev, and Julie came home from the office just before Craig and Isaac pulled into the yard. One look at their faces and we all knew the worst had happened. Craig could hardly speak. We stood around the kitchen, holding the babies and waiting.

"Glenn Carey declared Isaac well able to care for his own babies," he said finally. "He suggests that Isaac give one to an aunt or whoever would take him, and raise one himself. He saw the way Isaac was dressed and talked to him privately for a very long time. This is what he came up with."

"I told him I have no job and no way to eat," Isaac said, with the calmness of despair. "Nothing I could say would change his mind."

"He admitted it was Isaac's choice whether or not to give the boys up for adoption, but he refuses to give their visas. They can't leave the country without them, so he's got us over the barrel. In other words, they belong to us legally, but he won't let them go."

Jewel was pale as chalk. "What now?" she quavered. Her face crumpled and she cried into Brett's curly head.

All of us women cried. We couldn't help it. What a blow after hearing the good news and seeing Craig wave those four tickets in the air.

The gate swung open and the Mervin Lantz and Dave King families joined us. "We came to weep with those who weep," Dave said comfortingly. "We heard Craig say he was coming home."

We all went into the living room and Craig reiterated every detail for their sympathetic ears.

"I wonder if we'll have the same problem," Mervin said soberly. "If babies can be in such a bad situation and still not be allowed to go, then what will happen to Shawna?"

We tried to reason out the consular's decision, looking at it from every angle. It helped just to talk.

Elijah appeared in the living room. "Sarah Onrah is heah. Shou' she come in?"

Charlotte stood up. "Yes! Tell her to come in."

Sarah walked into the living room with her usual stance—head held high and eyes defiant. Charlotte pulled the blanket back and gasped in dismay.

"Is . . . is this *Blessing?*" she cried. "It can't be."

"It is," Sarah answered coolly. "Blessing is fine."

Charlotte gently laid the child on the couch and unwrapped her. We were speechless.

Blessing—beautiful, chubby, smiling little Blessing—was reduced to a fraction of her former self. She was totally limp, and so thin we could count every rib and bone in her body. She could not close her eyes because the skin was so tight over her cheekbones. Her dear little face was pinched and drawn with severe hunger. Her arms and legs were bones without flesh or fat, and her belly protruded dreadfully below her sunken chest.

Dave came over and looked down on the skeletal child.

"We need to keep her," Charlotte said, choking back tears as she rewrapped her and carried her into the bedroom. Blessing lay like a floppy rag doll in her arms.

I'm not sure if it was the strain of the day or our over-wrought nerves, but before long Jewel and the girls and I were all crying together over that suffering child. Charlotte was trying to get her to drink the warm formula and was overjoyed when she made a weak attempt. It was as if she was making one last effort to stay alive.

Suddenly Sarah stood in the doorway. We had forgotten all about her. She looked around at us incredulously. She smiled— and began to shake with silent laughter.

As if on cue, Wayne appeared behind her. "What's so funny?" he demanded.

She whirled around.

"You ought to be in jail!" he said stridently. "You just about killed this baby, and we were giving you food for her all along. What did you do with it?"

Sarah was no longer laughing. She looked at the floor. "I sold it," she said.

"Sold it?" he asked, trying to control his voice. "You let this child slowly die in some filthy corner while you *sold* her food? I think I *will* report you!"

Sarah backed away. "I fed her," she insisted.

"*Lady, go home. Right now!*" Wayne spoke with authority.

Sarah didn't argue. She left without a backward glance.

Slowly—so very slowly—Blessing tried to suck on the bottle. She swallowed. Seconds passed. She sucked again. "Oh, dear God. Please let her suck . . . just a few more times," I prayed aloud.

Every time she swallowed, those wonderful little bubbles came to the top of the milk. It took over an hour for Blessing to drink four ounces of milk. She was exhausted when she finished.

"Feed her again in another hour," Faith instructed. "Just go by demand and let her drink at her own will. Never force her."

"I won't," Charlotte said. "She won't die, will she?"

"I hope not," Faith told her. "When you bathe her, make sure she gets used to the water very slowly so her body doesn't go into shock."

"She can't weigh more than nine or ten pounds," Jewel observed. "She's ten months old already."

We called Dr. Lamin, who arrived in half an hour. He must have sensed the seriousness of our situation. He brought along de-worming medication, scabies cream, scalp fungus treatment, electrolytes, and children's multi-vitamins, all without being told.

"I know the African child, Ruth Ann," he laughed. "The same thing is wrong wi' all of them. What's her name? Blessing? I think she will be all right."

"Thank you so much, Dr. Lamin," we said gratefully.

"It's so wonderful to have friends," I said to Wayne after everyone had gone home. "It's more than wonderful that Blessing isn't lying on a dirt floor somewhere tonight. Isn't God merciful?"

"Her soul is precious in His sight," Wayne agreed.

February 28

Blessing is alive and gaining strength. There is no bed for her to sleep in, so she sleeps on the other couch in the living room. It doesn't seem to bother her when Angela cries during the night.

Craig and Jewel went in to the Embassy, but Mr. Carey refused to see them without an appointment, so it is set for March 5. Meanwhile, we are all praying that God will soften "Pharaoh's" heart so he will let the "little people" go.

We gave Blessing her first dose of de-worming medication last night after a good feeding. Charlotte was rocking her in the living room this morning when a white worm started coming out of her nose.

"Mom! There's a worm in her nose!" Charlotte shrieked, trying to grab it with her fingers. I came out just in time to see it slither back up. Poor Blessing feebly pushed and pulled at her nose with frantic little jerks.

"Next time I'll be ready," Charlotte said shakily, grabbing a diaper.

Nothing happened for a long time. Then Blessing started rubbing her nose—and out came the flailing end of a white worm. Charlotte grabbed it with the diaper and pulled it all the way out.

I gagged. Jewel looked repulsed. But Charlotte took that gruesome thing and flushed it down the commode. "That medicine is working!" she said triumphantly. "I hope that's all there is."

But Blessing began to gag violently, and suddenly another long one came crawling out of her mouth! I simply had to leave the room.

"Got it!" Charlotte yelled, and made another trip to the bathroom.

I stayed in the kitchen and tried to block out the thoughts of those ghastly parasites and how that poor child must be suffering.

Charlotte kept a close watch over Blessing every waking moment. It was as if God had given her special grace for such a dreadful task.

Six more worms were in her diaper this evening. One was as big around as a pencil and just as long.

"Charlotte, you are absolutely *amazing*," I told her. "I could never do what you're doing."

"I love this child," she said, and that explained it all.

"Has she cried yet?" I asked.

"Not once. Maybe her voice is ruined," Charlotte worried. "Or maybe she's just too weak."

"Give her time," Jewel said. "She hasn't cried for so long she doesn't remember how."

Charlotte invited Staci and Angela over for the night, so the boys had to build a makeshift tent in the living room to sleep in. "This reminds me of sleeping outside in Alberta," Larry said.

"The floor is too hard," Willie complained. "We'll be stiff in the morning."

March 1

The girls visited and snacked and had a wonderful time last night. They let Faith Princess stay up with them until almost midnight. I offered to feed Angela and Blessing during the night so they could have a break.

I almost wished I hadn't, I was so tired and dizzy. Around 3 a.m., Angela woke up yelling. She has the strongest voice I've ever heard in a baby. I hurried as fast as I could to pick her up and get her bottle from the kitchen.

Suddenly, I heard a peculiar sound, just like the bleating of a baby lamb.

What on earth?

It came again—and I realized it was Blessing, crying for the first time. I went to the kitchen to prepare her a bottle. It was awkward, holding Angela and pouring water, but I managed.

Something hopped toward me in the semi-darkness of the kitchen, and suddenly the whole situation seemed incredibly funny.

"There's a sheep in the living room and a toad in the kitchen," I told the sleeping girls, who woke up immediately and joined in the laughter. We laughed at a great many things. We laughed until our sides ached and the tension gradually slipped away.

Bev fed Blessing while I finished feeding Angela. They both fell asleep at the same time.

"It's a good old world after all," Julie said. "Things are always desperately funny in the middle of the night."

I woke Willie and he willingly dressed and crawled out of the tent to herd Mr. Toad outside. "I don't want him crawling in with us," he explained.

What a memorable night.

The men had a really busy day checking inventory at the warehouse while we cooked and took care of babies. The day flew by much too fast.

This evening for supper we were enjoying Jewel's delicious pizza when the phone rang. It was Sue Kauffman.

"I just had a call from the INS office in Philadelphia," she said.

"They are ordering an investigation in Liberia concerning Faith Princess. The birth dates didn't line up on her birth certificate and her relinquishment, so they are suspicious about the whole thing."

"Oh, please, no!" I said. "I told Mitchel to double check, and he said he did. I'm sorry."

"She said it could take a long time, Ruth Ann," Sue continued, "so it will have to be a miracle for Princess to come home with your girls in May. Please pray with us."

God is in control . . . He cares . . . He reigns supreme. Praise His holy name!

34

More Disappointments

Mercy comes in many forms.

I think of that whenever I walk along the streets and see how people eke out an existence and the ways they help each other. I think of it when we visit the CAM orphanages and see the transformation of those children, and when we distribute Support-A-Widow or Aid-for-the-Aged parcels. I am reminded of it when I see the long lines of displaced people waiting for the CAM trucks to start their rice distribution and when all the desperate and destitute wait at the CAM gate.

I thought of it this morning after church when Ruth proudly showed us Rose and Roslyn. Both babies can hold up their heads. Both of them have a faint hint of chubbiness in their cheeks. Gone are the horrible, wasted looks and dull eyes.

I think of it when I see the containers of clothing and shoes and the pallets of medicine and food and other supplies that fill the CAM warehouse.

I see the mercy in Charlotte's heart and hands as she tenderly cares for fragile little Blessing, and I feel the mercy all the way from America when I remember that the Kauffman, Shores, and McMahon families are opening their homes to adoption.

I was especially reminded of it recently when a little girl Julie has befriended off the streets came running up to us when we took the children for their walk.

"Where's Julie?" she asked with a quiver in her voice.

She was holding her hands behind her back. Her heavy ropes of hair were full of bits and pieces of dirt from wherever she had spent the night. Her eyes were swollen as if she had cried until she could cry no more.

"What's wrong, Kawah?" Charlotte asked.

The child held out her hands in front of her. Great tears slid out of her eyes and ran down her dusty cheeks. "See?" she said softly.

"Oh my!" Jewel gasped.

"Kawah, what *happened?*" I asked.

Her hands were a mass of open, oozing ulcers, with streaks of blood and filth running amok. Her fingers were so swollen she could not close her hands or even pull them together.

"It hurts bad," she whispered.

"Come with us, Sweetie," Charlotte said sympathetically.

We walked down to the CAM base and asked Dr. Lamin to come take a look. "This is a very bad infection," he said. "She must go to the clinic for injections an' medication immediately."

"I wan' to see Julie," Kawah said shyly.

Julie was just coming out of a meeting, so we had to wait a few minutes. When Julie saw Kawah, she was horrified. After a hurried consultation with Dr. Lamin, she left to take her to the Good Samaritan Clinic.

Mercy comes in many forms. Somewhere, someone donated the funds to make it possible for little Kawah to find relief.

This morning after breakfast, Pa Sumo came unannounced into the kitchen.

"The owl is away!" he said excitedly, with a sweep of his hand.

"What?"

"The owl is gone!"

"The hawk is gone!" Larry guessed, running for the door.

I hurried after him. The gate of the cage was locked, but the baby goshawk was nowhere to be seen. Larry looked everywhere, in case it had escaped and hidden behind something.

"Someone stole it—and probably made goshawk soup," Larry finally decided. "I sure don't have good luck around here."

Tonight we had a wonderful song service. What a joy to hear people sing with such gusto and eagerness!

Anita King, a Mennonite lady from Maryland who runs a private adoption agency, sent us an e-mail asking if we knew of any Liberian babies available for adoption. She knows a family from Michigan that has been trying to adopt from Haiti, and it just hasn't worked out.

I wrote her back immediately and told her about our dear little Blessing. She needs a home desperately.

March 5

Paul Weaver, executive committee member for Christian Aid Ministries, arrived today from Ohio to spend a week with us. He brought each family a nice round chunk of farmer's cheese from Walnut Creek Cheese. We sliced it thin and ate it with brown rolls and jam. What a treat!

Craig and Jewel have had a very hard week so far. They saw Consular Carey today, and he requested to see Isaac once more, so they have another appointment on Monday.

"They took the six hundred and some for the visas, so I still think we have a chance," Craig said. "Why would they take the money and not give us the visas?"

The twins have been sick with earache, fever, and vomiting. Brett also tested positive for malaria and Brady is teething, and neither of them can keep much in his stomach. Dr. Lamin gave us a big bag of electrolytes to feed the babies so they would not dehydrate. Charlotte is giving some to Blessing for good measure. Electrolytes have many important nutrients and vitamins, and the children drink it down eagerly.

We can't understand why all three babies have such terrible diarrhea and discomfort. They pull up their little legs and just scream.

Jewel is worn out with worry and sleeplessness, so we put

school on the back burner and brought the twins downstairs so she could rest.

I am really worried tonight. I don't want to upset Jewel, but I think there is something seriously wrong. I've never seen babies act this way. When Brady threw up there was a trace of blood in the vomit. I talked to Craig and we're planning an early morning trip to Dr. Brisbane in Firestone.

Great Physician, please heal our babies.

We heard from the Michigan family today. They are Jonas and Elva Yoder and they have five children—and best of all, they definitely want Blessing.

"I need to tell you something special, Ruth Ann," Elva said in her soft voice. "Two days before Anita called me about Blessing, God really spoke to me through Psalms 84:11, where he speaks about withholding no good thing from they that walk uprightly. As soon as Anita called, I knew why God had given me that verse. He was giving us Blessing."

Charlotte is sad and excited all at once. "These children have a way of getting into your heart and not letting go," she said. "I think it's because they're so helpless and they suffer so much."

March 6

I made a dreadful discovery this morning. I woke up before the sun rose because all four babies were crying. The girls came out to help change and feed them all, and the noise woke Jewel, who was downstairs in a minute.

Brady was extremely listless, and his eyes had that sunken look. I was terrified.

I mixed up some of the powdered electrolytes and, just on a whim, began to read the side panel information on the package.

"*Girls!*" I shrieked when the information sank in. "This stuff is for pre-op *adult* patients who have to have surgery and can't have even a trace of matter in their bowels. It's horribly strong—it warns about overdosing—and we've been feeding it to the babies!"

We stood and stared at each other in horror. Jewel's blue eyes filled with tears. "Those poor babies!" she exclaimed. "No wonder!"

Never have we fixed formula and baby cereal so fast. Each of us fed a baby and kept at it until their food was gone.

"Praise the Lord they're eating," I said thankfully. "I was afraid Brady was too weak to eat."

Brady gave a huge burp and settled down almost immediately. Brett smiled for the first time in days. Blessing actually squawked for more. Angela just cooed and kicked and grabbed for the empty dish. Praise the Lord we didn't think it necessary to give *her* an extra boost.

"How will I ever forgive myself?" I groaned, thinking about the last two days. "That package looks exactly like those other electrolytes. Even the name sounds the same. Why, oh, why didn't I read it first?"

"It didn't enter my mind either," Jewel said, cuddling Brady close. "I think Brady suffered the worst. He drank that stuff so eagerly, and finally he just couldn't scream and cry much anymore. He just gave up."

"How do you think I feel about Blessing?" Charlotte said dismally. "Here I want to fatten her up and I feed her this."

"The Lord showed it to us in time," I said.

"I drank some of it," Bev informed us. "It tastes kinda bitter-sweet."

She came home an hour later with severe cramps. "Mother, I cannot *believe* this!" she groaned. "If those babies felt half as bad as I do, they were really suffering. I feel just awful—and I only drank about half a cup!"

March 8

Bev and Jewel finally had to take Brady to the Providence Clinic, where they put him on IV for severe dehydration. The rest of the children are fine.

Tonight after supper, Abi arrived at our door. She was crying and so upset she could hardly speak.

"Neil came over an' picked a fight with me," she sobbed. "He pushed me back over the wall and I hurt my arm bad."

Jewel and I had a long visit with Abi while Wayne and Craig went to talk with Neil. She said he is becoming very frustrated and violent when he doesn't get his own way. "I am frightened of him sometimes," she confided. "He goes from happy to mad so fast."

When Wayne returned he was in a somber mood. "We couldn't find him anywhere," he said. "I sure hope he isn't slipping away from God."

"He asks for my money and gets so angry at me when I don't want to give it," Abi complained.

Abi has been doing well with her little "Abilicious Baking" business. She applied for and was granted a small donation from the Self-Help program, and now she bakes up to five dozen cupcakes every day. Neil sells them for her.

"It is very difficult selling cake," he told us frankly during one of their visits. "I am ashamed to ask around and beg people to buy from me. It is a different experience. Some of my old friends laugh at me, but they sure like the cakes."

"Some of the profit belongs to him," Wayne told Abi.

"He wants it all," she replied. "I have to go now—Georgie is home alone."

"Tell Neil I want to see him," Wayne called after her. "The sooner the better."

March 9

Isaac arrived after church and wondered why Craig had sent for him. "We may just have a chance yet," Craig told him. "Make sure you don't borrow any new clothes so Mr. Carey doesn't get the false impression you are rich. Just wear what you have."

"I wanted to dress up for the Embassy visit," Isaac explained again.

"I know, but now he thinks you're rich."

Brady is so much better. Jewel has lost that anxious look, but I think she's losing weight too. She is the best little mother those twins could ever have.

This evening, we had a house full as usual. Georgie, Harris,

Toney and his family, Moses, Anthony, Pastor George and his family, and Esther Akoi came to visit and eat popcorn with us. We had a wonderful time.

"These memories will never die," I told Wayne later. "I don't even think of the people as Liberians anymore. They're friends."

March 10

Craig came home after five hours at the Embassy with the same verdict: separate the twins and give them to someone else to care for.

"Isaac didn't even want to stop here—he went straight home," Craig said. "We have another option, though."

"What is it?" Jewel asked quickly.

"If we stay here for two years we come under a whole different category. We can do that and reapply for a visa. What do you think?"

"We'd have to go home and make arrangements for our house and stuff," Jewel said slowly.

"I'd have to get someone to look after the business."

"The twins are ours, Craig."

"I know, Dear. Like I said, we're not leaving without them."

"What about the money for the visas?"

"That money is absolutely non-refundable. I asked for it and they refused to give one cent back."

I saw the pain in their faces as they took their two little boys and went upstairs to be alone.

March 14

Paul Weaver and Dave King's family flew back home on Wednesday. We invited them all for supper Tuesday night and had such an encouraging visit.

Angela's father happened to be here, too, since he had to sign another messed-up relinquishment.

"What is in your diet?" Paul asked him innocently.

"Ah hunt rats an' cobra an' cassava snake," Sam answered.

There was a long pause. "Well, maybe you could cook some

good cobra soup for Ruth Ann here—after all she has done for you," Paul said with a twinkle in his eye.

"Ah will do dat," Sam told him seriously. "Ah will brin' it nex' time ah come."

I could only sputter.

"I can see there is a great need for a baby program of some kind," Paul told us. "Maybe we can look at possibilities for the future. Somehow I didn't realize the suffering the abandoned babies of Liberia must endure."

"Tell the sponsors how greatly we appreciate all their efforts," I requested.

"And tell them we're just about out of baby clothes and layettes," Julie added.

"I'll try and remember all this," Paul said. "The whole week has been an eye-opener for me."

"Especially when you saw the maggots all over the dried fish," Wayne laughed. "I'll never forget your face when you asked me if you would be required to eat at the pastor's dinner."

"The cook said she just boils the fish till the maggots rise to the top, then she skims them off," Paul replied. "I suppose there is plenty of protein in boiled maggots!"

The time just flew until all our visitors left. Iddo's brother Harvey is here now. He is doing research for a book he plans to write about Liberia's orphans.

A container came in today with eighteen boxes for us to distribute. There are all kinds of baby clothes, diapers, bottles, formula, children's clothes, stuffed animals, new baby blankets, and food. Wayne and Craig called us upstairs and showed us four trunks of new girls' dresses, from small to size twelve.

"Pastor Mervin wants us to pass these out after church on Sunday," Wayne said. "Why shouldn't the members' children get some nice dresses once in a while?"

"That will be wonderful," I agreed. "There are *hundreds* of new dresses here. I wonder who sent them? There's no note or anything that I can see."

"It's certainly a labor of love," Jewel remarked. "What's that huge box for the Kennedy Orphanage?"

"I can guess!" I cried with delight. "It's dolls for the girls and something else for the boys."

Sure enough. Someone had sent each girl a doll and each boy a toy. "They'll have the best belated Christmas ever!" I said. "Can you imagine how thrilled those little girls will be?"

"Someone will be going to Saclepea next week sometime," Wayne said. "Let's make sure they take these along to the Kennedy Orphanage."

"I'll see to it," promised Craig.

What a thrill to be a channel of mercy!

March 15

Neil was at the gate again. He and Abi had another nasty fight, and he wanted advice.

"We have such a frightening past to forget and work through," Neil agonized. "So many things come back to haunt me. Abi was just sixteen when we first became involved. How does a couple build up mutual respect when you've never really been married? We never had the money for a wedding in the first place. I just have so many questions, Mr. Wayne."

Wayne counseled with him on the porch until late into the tropical night.

March 18

We invited Iddo's family and his brother Harvey for supper on Monday evening. I'm sure the Lord planned that Neil, Abi, and Georgie come here the same night, because before the evening was over, Neil and Harvey had become fast friends.

Neil told the men his whole sad story while the women visited in the dining room. When the meeting was over and the men stood to leave, Neil and Harvey threw their arms around each other in a great bear hug. It was touching to see.

Today, Neil spent almost all day with Harvey over at Iddo's

house. He and Abi have taken their son Chico out of the orphanage and now he's living with them. He sure is a beautiful little boy, with a head of black curls and olive brown skin.

March 19

Mitchel Clemmer has handed the bulk of the adoption work over to Charles Bassil since he is attending school. It is frustrating to sit helplessly by and not be able to speed up the process. We inquired at the Embassy and they deny ever receiving an investigation order for Faith Princess's mismatched paperwork, so we are forced to wait on the mail, on government offices, and on people who don't really care.

Now we are waiting for the American INS office to fax the children's approval here to the U.S. Embassy. The originals need to be couriered here as fast as possible because we are leaving for furlough at the end of May. Bev, Julie, and William plan to leave two weeks earlier.

Neil came after supper and told us that the war is in Gbarnga. "The town was captured four days ago, Mr. Wayne," he said with agitation edging his voice. "I am beginning to feel ill at ease about the whole situation. It is squeezing in on us too closely, Mr. Wayne."

"You don't have to fear if you are ready to meet God," Wayne reminded him. "It is different now, Neil. You're fighting another kind of battle."

"I'm an ex-commander, Mr. Wayne. I am not safe anymore. If I don't fight, they will classify me as a deserter. The rebels know me as a fighter for Taylor's army, and they would have no mercy if they caught me."

"Fear has torment, Neil. Nothing can happen to you unless God allows it. Not a hair of your head can be harmed."

"Oh, to *believe!*" Neil exclaimed passionately, as he paced the floor. "To lose this awful dread that grips my very soul! I know what the rebel forces are capable of doing, Mr. Wayne. You do not."

"Let's pray about it," Wayne suggested, and Neil readily agreed.

March 26

Yesterday, the men had an emergency meeting about the impending war threat.

"I don't want to scare you," Wayne told the family. "Ghanta has been taken by the rebels, and we have to be ready to leave at a moment's notice. It's a serious situation according to the Embassy reports, and according to Neil."

Craig and Jewel have moved upstairs permanently, now that all the orphanage supplies have been distributed. They plan to go home to Wisconsin to set their things in order and then come back for two years for the twins' sake.

35

Please Take My Baby!

March 31

Marie Toe Fanciah, the woman whose husband was killed by his jealous brothers, was at the gate with Benjamin so early that Security Zubah made her wait outside until we were up and around. When he came to ask if she could come in, she followed him and swept past him without a word.

Her face was a picture of abject misery. "Oh, Mama! My mother is *dead!*" she wailed. "She's *dead!* Oh God, why? *Why?*"

She rocked back and forth in an agony of weeping. "First they killed my husband, then my mother died. She was all I had left, an' God took her away. She died on Saturday, an' they never told me till today."

"What happened to her so fast?" Wayne asked. "She seemed fine when we were at your place."

"She was. She was fine. One day she had pain an' pressure so I took her to the hospital. The next day I came in an' they had plastered her face all over wi' hard white plaster. My mother could not talk or move. They had even plastered her eyes shut. I called out to the doctor, 'Why have you plastered my mother's face shut?' They said back to me, 'She had pus running out of her eyes, so we had to plaster them shut.'"

"Is this some weird story?" Wayne asked suspiciously.

"It is *not* a story! It is *not!*" she cried wildly. "I went back in today an' my mother was dead. She was dead, Mama!"

"Who would do such a barbaric thing?" I wondered. "How would a person feel with his face plastered shut? I would panic!"

"Sounds like something demonic to me," Wayne said.

"Yes, it is!" Marie agreed. "Somebody killed my mother! I canno' have her body until I pay twelve hundred dollars or they will take it to the swamp an' dump it for the alligators. Why would they not give it to me for free?"

"What would kill a healthy woman that fast?" I wondered aloud, thinking of how nice and young and slim Helen had looked. I remembered her spotless room, her intelligent speech, and her refined manner.

"They did something to hasten her death . . . I know they did," Marie cried brokenly. "One day she was fine, the next day . . . *dead!*"

"Come to the office, Marie," Wayne told her. "We'll discuss it there and see what we can do."

After he left, Marie turned to me. "Mama, take my baby!" she pleaded. "I have seven brothers an' sisters an' now I must take care of them. Then I have my other two children to feed. There is not enough food. Mama, please take my baby!"

"Your baby is nursing," I said gently. "I can't take him now, Marie. You'll feel better after a while, and then you will want to keep him, okay?"

"I will nurse him for six months. Then you will take him?"

"I can't promise anything like that, Marie. Only God knows what will happen in six months."

She didn't want to leave. I brewed her a strong cup of tea and let her rest on the couch as long as she wanted. She sat and stared into space with brooding dark eyes.

"My mother is dead!" she mourned softly, over and over. She left around ten o'clock with one last plea. "Think about taking Benjamin, Mama."

The episode spoiled my day. I couldn't stop thinking about

how Helen must have felt, dying alone in a hospital bed with her face plastered shut.

"Did they have her arms tied down so she couldn't take it off?" Julie wondered.

"I have no idea. Maybe she was so weak from lack of food that she couldn't get it off," I said.

"That white plaster is used in all kinds of ritualistic things," Jewel remarked. "That really gives me the creeps."

Tonight, I feel weary to the bone. I keep hearing Marie's words in my mind, and it does nothing to cheer me up.

Mama, please take my baby.

April 2

Rainy season swept in during the night with a wild wind and driving rain, sending the dry leaves dancing and the doors banging loudly. We hadn't shut the windows, so the rain drove right in on the living room floor. We grabbed some towels and wiped up the floor, patted the babies back to sleep, and crept back into bed to fall asleep to the familiar sound of the wonderful rain.

This whole adoption process has become rather scary, since it looks like the consular has a problem with Americans adopting Liberians. Craig and Jewel have definitely decided to stay, since abandoning the twins is not an option for them.

Wayne came home this evening too tired to eat. He sat down on the couch and leaned his head back against the cushions. His face was unutterably weary.

He has entered a request to CAM for a different job description when we return from furlough in the middle of June. He loves the hands-on part of the work—the Self-Help program, checking out the orphanage directors, evaluating requests for support, and all the various warehouse jobs including unloading, inventory, and schedule distribution. He enjoys working with the medical director and managing the loan programs for new small businesses. He loves the maintenance jobs, going on distributions, and working with the Liberian pastors, but the office work causes him stress because he is not familiar with it at all.

There is a tremendous amount of bookkeeping involved in the Orphanage Sponsorship program here in Liberia. Christian Aid Ministries demands detailed monthly reports. They need to know where every cent is used. Bev has been Wayne's right-hand girl in the office, and she enjoys it.

"We are responsible before God when we handle other people's money" is CAM's theme.

After resting a bit, Wayne perked up, "CAM is sending another family to Liberia next month," he informed me. "They've been in Ukraine, so the mission field is not new to them. Best of all, the man has consented to be country director, so I can hand all that office work over to him. Won't that be wonderful?"

"It sure will," I agreed. "You'll be able to do the many projects that have been on the back burner for so long. You're going to love it, Wayne."

He was asleep in minutes. The rest of us took all the children and went for a walk around the block and down to the ocean. I was so glad we did. We were walking beside a wall where a wild tangle of vines and shrubbery threatened to overtake the area when a beautiful bird alighted on the branches. It had a copper-colored body with an extremely long tail, a crested black head, and white under parts. It warbled sweetly and dived in among the leaves, looking for insects.

"A flycatcher of some kind," I whispered.

Presently, the exquisite bird flew straight up into the air, over the wall, and on to other hunting grounds. I felt as if we had glimpsed something rare and wonderful.

We came back home to find that Neil had tracked down Wayne and had awakened him from his much-needed sleep. Neil is very concerned about the political situation and claims that this time the danger is very real.

"If they would catch my Chico, he would never get away," he worried. "They would force him to kill and steal, and he would be ruined fast. Mr. Wayne, what can I do?"

Wayne showed him all kinds of Bible verses and encouraged him to memorize them. There is no greater comfort than the comfort of the Scriptures and the Holy Spirit in one's life.

Kathy Kauffman sent an e-mail and said Nathan's health has deteriorated alarmingly. She sent a note of encouragement to all of us, even though she is suffering herself.

April 5

At four this morning, I woke up to Angela's frantic screams. Even though the bedroom door was shut, I could hear her plainly. I raced out to the living room to find she had somehow forced her head through the narrow opening between the hard wooden couch armrest and the firm cushions. She hung face down with her neck pinched so tightly I had a very hard time getting her out.

By the time I worked her out of there I was shaking, and poor little Angela was wet with sweat. She cuddled up against me and gripped my neck tightly. I sat down to regain my composure. There is no doubt in my mind she would have been strangled had I not rescued her.

Angela's father came around nine-thirty to meet Charles Bassil and sign another official form. When Sam saw Angela, his whole face lit up. He took her out to the porch and hugged her and kissed her, then held her away so he could look at her, and hugged her fiercely again.

She stared at him with big, solemn eyes and slowly reached up to touch his cheek. She ran her chubby little fingers in a circular motion over the fabric of his shirt. She felt his hair and his ears.

"Sam, I need to talk to you," I said quietly. "It's not too late."

"Muttah, ah wan' to see her live!" he said simply, sensing the reason for my request.

"I see how you love her, Sam."

"Bu' Muttah, ah cou' naw see her die. She wants to live!" I saw the glisten of tears in his black eyes as he looked at me steadily.

My heart was well nigh bursting. I had to leave the room and warm some rice for him to eat.

Charles Bassil arrived in the meantime, so I gave him some rice too. He had Sam sign the document and then showed me Secret's child case history papers. I read over them quickly, ignoring all the little spelling errors and misuse of words, then he hurried off to collect Angela's medical report.

Charlotte, Jewel, Julie, and I were here when Sam said good-bye for the last time to his baby girl. Her beautiful big eyes fastened on his face, and he tried to smile as he kissed her velvet cheeks. He looked at us and tried to say something, but he had to swallow the lump in his throat. He gravely handed Angela to me.

"Ah . . . Ah thank you, *thank you!*" he whispered, and he turned and left the house.

Angela tilted her face back and gazed at me, and I saw her cheeks were still damp with her father's tears.

Craig came home with tickets for him and Jewel to fly to Wisconsin next Wednesday. "Our plans sure changed," he said. "We're going home without the twins, but we'll be back."

April 6

What a lovely Sunday! Iddo was in charge today since Mervin is in the States for ministerial meetings. He spoke on "Jesus, the Life and the Light."

A lot of people were anxious to give their testimonies, and every one mentioned the coming war. These poor people have seen enough devastation, and they are truly worried. They cried and asked for prayer and exhorted each other to remain faithful.

Craig and Jewel left for home this afternoon. We'll have to give Brett and Brady lots of attention while they're gone.

April 15

Nathan Kauffman went to be with Jesus today. We grieve with Kathy and the children. It seems so unreal to think of how we visited with him the night before they flew out—and now he is gone.

Pastor Mervin is back from the States. Mary and the girls could hardly wait anymore.

David Waines came over this evening and poured out a tale of woe in my husband's sympathetic ears. "We were forced to leave everything we own," he said. "The rebels poured into Ghanta and took over so fast we didn't have time to think. Everything we collected over the years—the pictures, carvings, precious keepsakes, clothing, dishes—it all went up in smoke. Audrey feels horrible. The children feel betrayed, and I am ready to pull out, Wayne. Enough is enough. We're leaving on the nineteenth, heading back to British Columbia."

"I'm sure you did a lot of good that you don't regret."

"That's right. I'll feel better tomorrow, but I need to warn you about something, Wayne."

"Go ahead."

"Don't be under any kind of illusion that just because you are white and American they will give you any special treatment. The rebels will show you no favoritism. Law is non-existent in this country. I really, really think you should all pull out as soon as possible!"

"We're still a ways from Ghanta."

"Right. But looting will start in Monrovia just as quickly as it did in Ghanta—without warning. If you stand in their way, they will not hesitate to do away with you. They're all on drugs, and armed and dangerous. Listen to me, Wayne!"

"I am listening," Wayne replied. "We are prepared to leave at a moment's notice. When Iddo Yoder gets worried, I will too."

April 16

Larry turned twelve today. I gave him the day off and we made ice cream and cake to celebrate.

"I hope I can turn thirteen in Alberta," he sighed. "I like it here, but what about riding my horse, and biking down the country roads? I hate living in a city."

This afternoon, Wayne came into the house with Neil and another man and said to me, "Dear, you have to get this young man's story and send it back to CAM." Then I saw why.

Both of the man's arms were amputated right below the elbow and swathed in fresh white bandages.

Our eyes met for a few seconds—mine full of the horror I felt and his brown ones full of hopeless anguish.

He looked about sixteen or seventeen—a child fighter forced to the front against his will. We sat at the kitchen table while he told his gruesome story. I wrote it down with a trembling hand.

> *Toe Johnson is barely eighteen. The militia soldiers gave him a rifle and ordered him out to fight. On this particular day there were eight young men in his group, some of them even younger than Toe.*
>
> *Between Klay Junction and Rick's Camp they fell into an ambush of dissidents, or LURD (Liberians United for Reconciliation and Democracy) fighters. They were tied extremely tightly, and the deep rope marks are burned into Toe's upper arms. The LURD rebels were smoking drugs and eating pieces of a big white tablet—some kind of drug. They forced all eight men to lie on the pavement and, deaf to their terrified screams and pleas, proceeded to slit their throats or cut them in half with their cutlasses—all except Toe. The screaming and begging can not be described.*
>
> *They held Toe's arms against the pavement and chopped them off without mercy, deaf to his desperate cries. His hands lay there, twitching, while blood spurted wildly from his severed limbs. There was blood everywhere, all over the road, and the LURD soldiers' clothes and the dying men, who thrashed about dreadfully.*

Toe's eyes were pools of anguish at the memory of his buddies' death throes. "O'Ma, ah cried bitterly!" he moaned. "Da pain was bad!"

"How did you escape?" I managed.

"The LURD retreat fo' some reason, an' I escaped in da bush. "Ah bled till three o'clock, when my own commander rushed me to da JFK hospital where dey saved my life. Ah lef' the hospital jus' now."

"Who takes care of you?" I asked.

"My sister an' my brother have to feed me," he said sadly, swinging his stumps back and forth. He looked at them and shook his head, as if he wasn't seeing them right. He turned to Neil. "Tell O'Ma ah mus' go now," he said softly. "I'm naw feelin' alrigh'."

"He wants to go now, Mrs. Wayne. He's dreadfully upset and still very weak," Neil explained. "Mrs. Wayne, there are ex-fighters from Sierra Leone among the LURD forces."

"I understand. They do this for sport, don't they?"

He nodded, and I could see his jaw working. "As you can see, I am upset myself. Things don't look good at all. If this happened on the Monrovia side of Klay, you can see how close they are."

"Neil, keep telling him about Jesus. Please. It's his only hope in the world."

Never again will Toe be able to feed or wash himself, put on his clothes, tie his shoes, or brush his teeth. Never again will he be able to turn the pages of a book properly, or pick a ripe plum.

Wave after wave of nausea washed over me as I saw that boy go out the gate. "Mother, go lie down," Charlotte insisted. "You're as pale as a ghost. I'll watch the children."

I did as she said, still numb from the shock. It just doesn't make sense that human beings can sink into such depths of depravity.

April 17

Craig called from Wisconsin today. "We're coming back!" he said jubilantly. "We'll be in Monrovia the second of May—so please come pick us up. My wife is so lonesome for the twins she can't eat or sleep properly. How are they doing?"

"I think they feel the same as she does," Wayne told him. "They're definitely not the happy little fellows they used to be."

Bev has moved upstairs to sleep close to Brady and Brett so they have some sense of normalcy in their lives. They cry more than usual, and always want to be held and cuddled. We can tell they really miss Jewel.

Blessing is thriving on the cupfuls of cereal that Charlotte feeds her. She acts as if she can't get enough of being fed and cuddled.

Angela is so chubby that we have put her on a schedule to slim her down a bit. Willie has taken a real shine to her, and when she sees him she starts kicking and smiling. We sometimes find them both asleep on the rocker, with Angela resting in the crook of his arm or on his crossed leg. She is so cuddly it is a pleasure to hold her.

Faith Princess and Secret are the very best of friends. He literally leads her around wherever she wants to go.

I would feel desperate if I couldn't cry out to God about her paperwork. Now the INS office said they've contacted the Liberian Embassy three times with no response.

Nothing is too hard for God.

I wrote to Anita King and asked her if she knew of anyone who wanted a baby boy. Little Benjamin is heavy on my heart, and although Marie Toe Fanciah takes good care of him, I think she resents that she has all these children to feed and no income to do it with. She came by again and begged me to find him a home.

I was pleasantly surprised to hear from from Jonas and Elva Yoder, who plan to adopt Blessing. Elva called in response to my note to Anita. "We want Benjamin too!" she cried. "Oh, Ruth Ann, this is an answer to prayer. Blessing and Benjamin! It's just too good to be true!"

"I'm very happy about it too, Elva," I told her. "God moves in mysterious ways."

36

Suffer the Little Children

April 27

Liberia Mennonite Church was overflowing this morning. Six new members were added to the church through baptism.

Every testimony rang with the uncertainty of the near future. Cleo's mother, Teresa, director of the CAM orphanage in Saclepea, described her ordeal of the past few days.

"The dissidents swarmed into the village, shooting their guns and forcing all of us to flee. I took the children out to the bush where they had to sleep on the ground under some branches and leaves. During the black night a poisonous snake came crawling in among the children and they cried out when they felt it moving against them. No one knew what was happening until the snake bit one of the little girls. Finally we found a light and killed the snake. We rushed the child to a nearby village where someone had snake medicine. I am so grateful for Almighty God's divine protection. Praise His name, the child did not die!"

Then Dr. Lamin got to his feet.

"I am moved to speak to the congregation what the Lord has showed me, first in the church service last Sunday, and then in my deep sleep as on a screen. These are the words I encountered. 'I am the Lord; I have seen and have heard the blood of the innocent

Liberians being shed and their crying. I will revisit Liberia and end the senseless war for my own glory, to bring the nation unto myself at my own will and time,' says the Lord. Amen?"

"Amen!" everyone agreed.

We can feel a different atmosphere among the people—as if they are all waiting for something. The security guards hold their radios to their ears all day long. Neil comes often and paces around the house and the yard as if he is in a cage. The mechanics are sober-faced and quiet as they work.

The whole city seems to be on edge. Many of the Lebanese businessmen have closed their shops and left.

"It's like there's a huge lion crouching out there somewhere," I said to Wayne. "Everyone knows it's there, and they know it will spring, but they don't know when."

"They feel trapped," he answered. "There's nowhere to run. We can leave on the next plane, but what about these poor people?"

"It's the children I'm worried about. There hasn't been a word as far as that investigation on Princess goes. Mitchel came about three times this week, but he isn't much further ahead."

Some strange new phenomenon is taking place the last few days. The funniest insects appear right after dark. After landing, they shed their long wings and the main body crawls away. The wings are so thin and filmy that they are hard to sweep. It seems to me there are millions of them.

Our God has a great imagination.

May 1

John Blaney, the American ambassador from the state of Virginia, gave us the honor of his presence for supper this evening. Wayne had attended an NGO security meeting last Friday, and had invited Mr. Blaney for a similar meeting with the CAM staff.

Wayne had ordered fresh lobster tail and cassava fish from the street, and asked Tony Hage if his cook would prepare them. We added corn bread, baked potatoes, and cream pies. It isn't very often that one gets to entertain the U.S. ambassador.

During the meal, Mr. Blaney turned to Wayne. "I see you are caring for local children," he began. "Is there a reason for this?"

We briefly explained the situation of each child, and the pending adoptions. "This is very interesting!" he exclaimed. "If you give me the names of the children, I will talk to Glenn Carey concerning this."

Julie and I looked at each other with hope reviving in our hearts. "Mr. Blaney, this little blind one especially," I said hesitantly. "She is abandoned and motherless, and no one would take good care of her. She has a chance to live in a Christian home in Pennsylvania with people who genuinely want her and her little brother. Please remember Princess and Secret."

"I certainly will," he said heartily.

As we finished dessert, the rest of the CAM staff arrived. We retired to the living room and listened to Mr. Blaney's view of the political situation.

"I feel that this new faction is the most dangerous one yet," he said soberly. "They call themselves *MODEL,* or *Movement for Democracy in Liberia,* and they refuse to enter any peace talks or listen to anyone. They have marines among them who were trained in the U.S., and they know how to fight. We have to be reasonable and not wait until the bullets fly, but go when we can."

"You're saying we are free to make our own choice?" Iddo asked.

"To a certain extent, yes. However, the American Embassy can take no responsibility for those who have been warned to evacuate and choose not to do so. I must warn you that the airlines are among the first to shut down in the face of a political crisis."

It was well past ten o'clock when the meeting was over. "I appreciate your fine hospitality," Mr. Blaney said as he rose to leave. "May God bless you in your work. Good night."

May 2

Craig and Jewel are back upstairs. We picked them up at the airport this evening. Of course we had the twins along—and they looked from Craig to Jewel with the most bewildered expressions. Their eyes were so big and worried that we just had to laugh.

As if a light came on in their little minds, they began to smile and reach for Craig and Jewel.

Jewel's heart was in her eyes. She could hardly quit looking at them and giving them fierce little hugs and kisses.

"I must admit I'm glad to be back," Craig told us. "I don't think my wife could have made it much longer. She didn't even care about what was happening at home—all she could think of was Brady and Brett."

Jewel just laughed, her eyes full of happy tears. "This is where we belong," she said.

"We've really been working on the adoption papers and hope to take at least Princess and Secret and Angela home with us," I told Jewel.

"I know. The Shores family has great hopes too," she said. "What about Blessing? Where will she stay?"

"Harris Kollie's mother has offered to keep her until we get back. Blessing really likes Harris, so I guess that's where we'll put her for now."

"What about that little Joanna?" Jewel wondered. "Her caretaker's name was Kubah?"

"She's doing just fine. Kubah comes now and then, but she basically takes care of Joanna on her own. Patrick and Amy McMahon sound like really nice people, and they're very excited about getting Joanna. Fancy moving from Liberia to New York."

All the way home the rain fell in beautiful rhythm against the flapping windshield wipers, and the blue-white lightning illuminated the magnificent cloud banks along the ocean.

There was a woman in the security booth when we arrived home from the airport. Elijah had refused to let her in the house since we were not at home, but now she literally threw herself against the side of the Cruiser, weeping bitterly.

"Hey, take it easy on the baby!" Wayne exclaimed when he realized a tiny infant was strapped to her back. "Come inside. You're getting soaked."

We dashed inside and held the door open for the woman, who half knelt in front of me.

"Ah beg you, help me!" she cried, with her hands folded in front of her and tears streaming down her face. "Ah have five chil'ren to feed, an' no rice. My husban' died las' week in River Cess, an' ah will die too. See my baby? He's two weeks ol'."

My heart lurched at the sight of that wizened baby. "Oh dear, no . . . is he dead?" I asked.

"Naw dead!" she cried shrilly. "You help! O'Ma, you help me!"

"He'll never make it," I told Julie, who was helping me prepare the formula. "Look at his soft spot." It was deep and dry, and only the faintest heartbeat could be seen.

"Maybe . . . just maybe," she answered softly. "Remember the twins?"

Thus encouraged, we showed the poor, bone-weary woman how to mix the formula and feed the baby. I don't think she had ever seen a baby bottle before.

"You must wash it good," Julie instructed. "That fine baby. You must feed the baby every two hours. Boil the water before you use it. Understand?"

We had Elijah come inside and tell the woman everything we said. She sat on a chair by the table and listened. Her eyes were glazed and dull.

"Mom, she's too tired to think," Julie said, observing how the poor woman slumped down against the table.

"She's going to fall asleep right here," I said. Elijah heard me.

"Go now—you mus' go now," he said to the woman, and helped her to her feet.

We gave what we had left of diapers and clothing, and helped her arrange the small box of formula on her head tie. She used one of the diapers we gave her to cover the baby's face, then she lifted both arms and turned to us. "God will bless you, O'Ma."

"Feed the baby before you go to sleep," Julie told her. "Where will you sleep, anyway?"

"My friend by the beach . . . he'll gi' me a bed."

"But it's pouring!"

"Ah, the rain won' hur' me," and she was gone, out into the black rainy night, widowed and alone with a new baby.

We retired to our soft beds to listen to the pouring rain and try to sleep. *Has the woman found her friend? Has she slipped on the bank somewhere and fallen on the baby? Is he drowned by now? Please, God, be with her. And thank you, God, for a warm bed.*

May 8

Sue Kauffman called and told us that the investigation for Faith Princess has been canceled. "The INS worker said she faxed our approval and other paperwork to Liberia today," Sue said happily. "She has not received an acknowledgement from Liberia and she doesn't want to see the children suffer, so she granted the approval. Praise the Lord!"

"I needed a miracle, Sue," I answered. "Thanks so much for letting us know."

Abi came this morning with a baby girl who was so weak she could not cry. "The baby was born on April 16. She is three weeks old now. The mother is nursing, but she has no milk," she explained. "Sis Ruth, can you take the baby, *please?*"

"We are leaving the end of the month, Abi. I simply cannot take another child now. I really think this poor little thing is dehydrating. Let's try to feed her right now. What's her name?"

"She has no name. She is not wanted, Sis Ruth."

"Mother, we have to take her!" was Charlotte's characteristic comment. "Can I name her?"

I almost took the baby. Starving . . . unwanted . . . not even a month old. But no . . . I was just too busy.

I gave Abi specific instructions about the formula and filled a plastic bag with a warm blanket, diapers, and mini-sleepers.

"Take good care of her, Abi," I said. "Come back when you need more milk."

May 11

Abi came over to me right after church and broke the news that the unnamed baby girl died during the night. "I tried to feed her, Sis Ruth, but she would eat only a little bit . . . then she quit sucking and died."

"It's not your fault, Abi. I'm sure you did your best," I consoled her, but inside I was smitten. I had been suffering such guilt all day I can hardly bear it.

"Maybe she would be alive if I had taken her," I sobbed to Wayne. "She was so tiny and so helpless. I'll never get over this. She didn't even have a name."

"Abi knows how to feed a baby," he comforted. "She was probably too far gone to save."

Tonight I rocked Angela for the longest time. It helped just to feel her dear little body relaxed in my arms—the sweet comforting baby that she is.

Tonight there is another nameless little angel among the multitudes in heaven.

37

Praying for a Miracle

May 13

Mitchel Clemmer was very upset this morning when he and Julie came back from the Embassy. He has asked for an appointment so often that they told him to stop pressuring them. Then suddenly last Friday they singled him out of the crowd and told him they were preparing to address the Kauffman case. Could he be in there at nine o'clock sharp on Tuesday morning?

He and Julie waited a long time until they were called into the back office. After waiting another hour, Mitchel became worried.

"We have been here for a long time. Is there a problem?" he asked.

"You may go now," the woman told him briskly.

"But we have an appointment!" Mitchel protested. "Here is the appointment card. Did you call me in just to look at me?"

"Yes, the consular has seen you now, and besides, today is not immigration day," he was told firmly, and the lady turned her back and resumed her paperwork.

"I am so ashamed," Mitchel mourned. "Why would they treat me so? They dismiss us with no explanation in an unprofessional manner. I will go back and demand an explanation. Someone has told me that since Mr. Carey has come into office, all Liberian adoptions have ceased."

"That's all I need to hear," I told him. "It seems more and more impossible than ever to take Princess and Secret and Angela home with us. It reminds me of the people pouring water on the altar at Mount Carmel. It can't happen unless there is a miracle from God."

"The greater the miracle, the greater the glory to God," Jewel said.

May 15

The house seems so empty without our three oldest children. Bev, Julie, and William flew to Alberta around seven-thirty last evening. The church van was not big enough to hold all the friends who were hoping to come along. The girls were in tears as they said their good-byes. I think the threat of war made the parting a lot more difficult. We just don't know what to expect.

Mitchel waited at the Embassy today until they finally informed him that they had received confirmation of the INS approval for all three children, but were waiting on the original documents.

"Why couldn't they have told me that on Tuesday?" he wondered.

All we need now are the original documents for Faith Princess, Secret, and Angela, and they'll be able to fly home with us on the twenty-ninth. All we need is a miracle.

Hope is aflame again. *Please, dear Lord, let the little people go.*

May 18

Pastor Mervin prayed for all the innocent suffering children of Liberia, and he mentioned all the babies waiting for adoption, including Shawna. It comforted my heart. Time is running out so fast, and we are helpless to do anything more.

The church house was so full that some of the children had to sit in the entrance or outside on the concrete steps. Agutta and her children have been coming faithfully, and Garlic Grace comes with little Shadrach. Ruth brings the twins and Philippine Doe brings her five children. Marie brought baby Benjamin one time. Many baby mas who have been to Residence for assistance come to see what the Mennonite church is all about.

The Word of God is spreading in Liberia!

"I've seen some storms, but never anything like this!" Wayne exclaimed as we stood watching the "fireworks" late this afternoon. "I'm glad we're all home."

The rain hit with a fierce pounding, and when the thunder gave an unexpected, ear-splitting crash, the babies started screaming and crawling toward us as fast as they could.

Jewel scooped up the twins and sat down on the rocker. Charlotte grabbed Angela and I held Blessing. Faith Princess stood with one little hand on Secret's shoulder.

"What's that noise?" asked Faith Princess.

"It's thunder, sweetie. It won't hurt you," Charlotte explained.

CRASH! CRACK! BOOM! It was breathtaking. Suddenly, we heard a sound like the twang of a steel guitar.

The children whimpered with fear. Brett's little mouth was quivering, and Craig took him and held him close.

Larry came streaking into the house from the back porch yelling, "Did you see *that?* It was a flash of fire all along the back yard. Dad, look at Charlie!"

Charlie was hanging in a weird, limp position from the tree branch on the end of his rope. His body looked small and lifeless as he slowly pivoted around with the rain streaming off him and his hair plastered against him.

"Was he hit?" Wayne asked. "Looks like it. He's not moving."

"I don't know . . . yes . . . he's still alive."

Slowly and carefully Charlie opened his eyes and raised his head. He looked around furtively, climbed up on the top of the branch and shook himself, then leaped up farther.

"I'd say we had a direct hit on the lightning reducer," Craig commented.

"For sure," Wayne agreed. "And it's not over yet."

The storm cracked and growled for another hour at least until it moved west. The whole yard is littered with branches and twigs; the front yard is a small lake and the upstairs floor is full of puddles. The rain drove in enough to make the curtains and bed sheets damp, and the window slats are covered with muddy residue.

May 23

Time is winding down fast. This afternoon, Wayne and I were asked to be present at a security meeting at the U.S. Embassy. Ambassador Christopher Data, who is replacing Ambassador Blaney, was the main speaker, with Consular Glenn Carey assisting.

"There was a man living in a huge new house along a river," Mr. Data started out. "It rained so much that the first floor was covered with water, but the man refused to get into the rescue boat, saying the Lord would preserve him. When the second floor was covered, he said he preferred to trust in God and would not accept help. On the rooftop, he sent the helicopter away and subsequently drowned. In heaven he asked the Lord why He had allowed him to drown, since he had such faith. The Lord told him He had sent two boats and a helicopter—what more could He have done?"

He paused to let the words sink in. "That's the situation we are in right now," he said. "It is time to leave Liberia immediately."

He turned to the wall map and showed us where the different factions were situated. "Here are the LURD rebels—here the government forces—and right here is a new and deadly group under the leadership of MODEL, which means *Movement for Democracy in Liberia.* MODEL has made great progress in a short time, taking control of the two ocean ports, Greenville and Harper, plus a lot of other territory. They actually control much of Liberia right now, and the next target will be Buchanan. The U.S. has called on all forces to cease activity until after the peace talks on June 22, but that is no guarantee that they will. If Buchanan falls, they will approach so close to Robert's Field Airport that the airlines will refuse to fly due to insurance risks. Now you still have a permissive environment to leave, but how much longer?" He shrugged. "Maybe two weeks, maybe a month, maybe tomorrow!"

He paused and wiped his brow. "Consider carefully. Do you have to be here at this time? Is the job you're doing so important that you cannot leave? I know you're here on a mission, but at least send your wives and children out. I cannot leave, though my wife would love nothing better. We simply cannot move you out if Monrovia is surrounded. We still hope for a peaceful solution, but I doubt it. I doubt it very much."

Oh, dear God, I begged silently. *Please let us take the children along.*

"Any questions?" Mr. Data asked.

I took a deep breath. "What will happen to children whose papers are just about finalized?" I asked clearly.

"I will let Glenn answer that."

I leaned forward as Mr. Carey spoke. "Since this is a serious situation, we would be willing to review the cases and perhaps take some shortcuts, but if the papers aren't satisfactory, the child will be stuck here. Come see us, and we will see what we can do."

My heart nearly burst with joy, and the spark of hope burst into full flame once again. I know it seems impossible—but not with God!

"Why can't the United States help us?" someone asked.

"There is a never-ending cycle of violence," Mr. Data answered. "First the LURDS, then Taylor, then whoever is next. If Taylor is ousted, he will fight from the bush. The U.S. is not willing to send men here unless the Liberian people themselves decide that things have to change and act accordingly."

Following the meeting, refreshments were served, but my stomach was so full of butterflies I couldn't think of eating. Since we were invited to ask any questions we wanted after the official closing, I approached Mr. Carey, who looked at me kindly enough.

"By shortcuts, do you mean you would accept a cabled or faxed INS approval instead of the original?" I asked.

"Yes, we could. Bring in your paperwork on Tuesday, since we're closed on Monday, and we'll talk to you."

"Oh, thank you!" I breathed, turning away.

"Ah, the folks who want to adopt Princess . . . they are in Canada?" he asked.

"No, they live in Pennsylvania."

"So they are American citizens?"

"Certainly. We're flying out on Thursday and hope to take the children along . . ."

He smiled. "Like I said, come see us."

I resisted the unladylike urge to whoop and holler and walked calmly outside with Wayne. "There's hope!" I said excitedly as we drove home. "What greater satisfaction could there be in the whole world than to take these children home with us?"

"Dear, just calm down," Wayne cautioned. "You know what happened with the twins."

"Mitchel and Charles can continue with Joanna and Benjamin and Blessing's paperwork," I said. "We can't give up in despair. Our miracle is too close! Marilyn Shores said she sent the adoption documents via express delivery, so they should be here by now. The documents for Princess and Secret are in the same package. Oh, I hope they come!"

It was so exciting to tell everyone the news. I tried to be careful so Jewel wouldn't feel bad, but she assured me she would be absolutely thrilled if the adoptions went through.

"It gives me hope that our adoptions will eventually go through too," she said. "Meanwhile, we can be with our boys, however long it takes."

Love is the most powerful force on earth, I thought, looking at her face. She looked so young and vulnerable—and so determined.

This evening, Mervin went to pick up Edwin and Elsie Sommers and their family. Edwin will be the new Liberia country director. We all met at Iddo's house for a get-acquainted supper.

The Sommers are an interesting family with one daughter, Beth, and four sons, Jeffrey, Jerrold, Jeremy, and Jolan.

The men discussed evacuation plans and where to store the CAM vehicles in case of an emergency and how to secure the warehouse supplies and the homes. "There's only so much we can do," Wayne said. "Hungry people don't stop at locks and guards."

Poor Elsie's face became more and more anxious. "I hope we don't have to leave any time soon!" she exclaimed. "We haven't even unpacked!"

"I plan to stick around," Iddo said in his easy, smiling manner. "Maybe I should be scared—but I'm not."

"That makes me feel much better," Elsie said.

"We're leaving one week after Wayne's family," Mervin said. "Staci is flying home with them on the twenty-ninth, and we will leave on the fourth. Looks like our furloughs were timed just right. I certainly hope nothing happens while we're gone; I'd hate to see the church suffer in any way."

May 27

All the native CAM staff have been informed of their responsibilities should the Americans have to leave. Wayne does not even stop to eat these days. Between giving Ed a crash course of country director duties and looking after the distributions, he is stretched very thin.

It has been pouring all day long. The whole world seems dark and dismal and so dreary. Maybe I am weak from lack of food and lack of faith, but things certainly look hopeless. I have learned that uncertainty can be a heavy weight. It would almost be easier to know the children can't go.

Mitchel arrived at nine-thirty and we went in to the express delivery office again. Still no documents! "There is a union strike in Brussels, so your package will remain there for several days," the secretary told us. "I cannot promise you a date because I don't know. Nobody knows."

Another bucket on the altar, I thought wearily. *By now, the altar is under water.*

Mitchel and I waited at the Embassy a long time until the grumpy secretary called us back to talk to Mr. Carey. He flipped through the documents, asking all kinds of questions. I was so nervous I had to fight the tears.

"Where is the adoption medical for Princess?" he asked Mitchel. "And where is the power of attorney? What about the adoption approval for Angela?"

I sensed he was becoming more and more agitated all the time. "I don't foresee them going on Thursday because the Americans will not let them in without the documents I need," he said sharply, looking at Mitchel. "Are you registered with the Liberian government as an adoption agent?"

"Well . . . I . . . ah . . . no, I guess not," Mitchel said lamely. "You see . . . I work for Plan Loving Adoption and . . . "

"Are they registered agents?"

"I don't know . . . you see . . . " but Mr. Carey wasn't in the mood to listen.

"These children have to meet all the requirements of an orphan, so I need to see some of the relatives. As we speak there is a law being drawn up that the children have to be from an orphanage, or there would be babies flying around everywhere. People could be selling these babies right and left if there was no law that kept them from private homes. I appreciate what you have done, Mrs. Stelfox. I know you have no such intention, but from now on there is a new set of rules. I am sorry, but they cannot leave without the papers I need. And you, sir, do not come in again unless you are authorized and licensed properly."

Mitchel didn't answer.

"We're hoping the papers come in today," I managed. "Thank you, sir."

"You told me you were an agent," I said to Mitchel as we left. "Now I find out they don't even recognize you. I'm sure that's why they have been so unpleasant to you, Mitchel. Can you tell me why Princess's adoption medical is not here?"

"Julie said she has a medical," he informed me.

"Only the one for her visit to the States. That's entirely different from an adoption one. Please be here early tomorrow morning, because we have to round up some of the children's relatives. *Please* don't be late. It's really no use, but just in case."

"I will be here at eight o'clock," he promised.

I took Princess to the Elwa Hospital where we requested an interview with Dr. Sacra, who agreed to see her. Could we just wait a few minutes?

Four hours later, Faith Princess and I were called upon. Dr. Sacra examined her thoroughly and filled out the necessary form. "Good luck," he said. "I hope for her sake she can go, Mrs. Stelfox."

I thanked him and we left.

When we arrived home, Charlotte told me there had been a steady stream of visitors stopping by to say good-bye. "Marie stayed a long time, wondering if we were going to take Benjamin with us. I don't think she understands that we need a bunch of legal papers. She thinks we should just take the baby and go."

When Wayne came home he said he had stopped by the express delivery office, but there were still no documents.

May 28

We were all up early and had breakfast over by seven-thirty. Wayne left for the office and Larry started school while Jewel and Charlotte fed the babies and changed them and cleaned up the house.

Secret's uncle George appeared at eight o'clock, and we waited—and waited. Mitchel didn't come. I tried his cell phone but there was no answer.

Charles Bassil arrived at ten. "Where's Mitchel?" he asked immediately.

"He hasn't come."

"But he left his house early and reported to me that he was coming to your place."

"Now I'm really worried," I said. "Where could he be?"

An hour later, we decided Charles should go find Elizabeth, a relative of Angela, then meet us at the Embassy.

Dinner came and went. One o'clock . . . two o'clock, and still no sign of Mitchel. The Embassy would be closing at five and the package hadn't come.

"Why don't you just go in there with Charles?" Wayne

encouraged me. "You have nothing to lose. I'll take you over."

"All right," I agreed, still scared at the thought of approaching the stern Mr. Carey alone.

On the way, we stopped at the express delivery office, and they said the package was on its way from the airport.

Charles and Elizabeth were waiting outside the Embassy. We explained to the guards that Consular Carey had requested that we bring them along for an interview. After checking this out, they let us all come in and sit down.

We waited about forty-five minutes until the secretary called us to the window. She looked through all the papers, then at me. "I still need the other originals," she said, permitting herself a slight smile.

"My husband is bringing them in as soon as they come," I told her.

While she went to consult with Mr. Carey, Charles and I stood at the window and watched. I prayed aloud, oblivious to Charles' amazement.

"We must have faith," he admonished. "God is a God of miracles. He will do this for us."

I looked into his earnest face and saw he meant every word. "Keep talking, Charles, keep talking."

Finally, the secretary came back. "Just wait here, and when the documents come, bring them in," she stated.

I ran out to the Embassy entrance to radio Wayne—and there he was, coming to meet me with the envelope in his hand. I was ecstatic!

Minutes later, the assistant officer motioned for us to come to the window once more. He looked through the papers that had just arrived. "You will need to sign these for me, Mrs. Stelfox. What time do you leave for the airport tomorrow?"

"Around four-thirty," I squeaked, and cleared my throat.

"Would two o'clock be soon enough to pick up the visas?" he asked, and my heart nigh stopped.

"Are you saying you are *giving me their visas?*" I asked in a voice that sounded quite strange.

"Yes, I am," he smiled.

"*Praise the Lord!*" I cried, throwing my arms around Elizabeth in a fierce hug. I will never forget that moment in all my life.

The children are coming home.

Craig and Jewel were thrilled. "Now there's hope for our little teddy bears too," Craig said.

"Did Mitchel ever come?" I asked.

"No, we haven't seen or heard from him."

We spent the evening packing and getting Blessing ready to go with Mamie Kollie. Charlotte had a bag stuffed with food, milk, lotion, powder, and a cloth doll.

"You are making a wise choice, Sis Ruth," Merci told me. She had come to see if there was anything she could do. "I have seen how Blessing has taken a fancy to Harris. She will be fine."

"I'm not worried, Merci—it's just hard leaving that little angel here. I can see how Charlotte feels."

"I know, I know," she said sympathetically. "Charlotte will miss her."

I cannot sleep with so much excitement churning through my mind. Over and over the verses come to me . . . "*For with God nothing shall be impossible. But verily hath God heard me; He hath attended to the voice of my prayer!*"

May 29

All morning long there was a stream of people—all of them saying solemn good-byes and reminding us to come back soon. The women hugged us, then held us by the shoulders at arm's length and gazed into our eyes before hugging us again.

Abi cried softly while Neil paced back and forth or stared moodily out the windows. I felt sorry for her—for all of them—yet I couldn't hide the joy in my heart.

When we arrived at the Embassy, Mr. Carey saw us immediately and waved, but it was a whole hour later when they called us to the window and presented us with the visa packages. What a thrill to hold them in my hand!

When we got back, we loaded and packed and rushed around to

get ready. Faith Princess sensed the great excitement, especially when Merci hugged her and said good-bye.

"Why Sis Merci cry?" she asked, so Merci patiently explained why she was sad.

Secret knew he was going somewhere, and Angela didn't really care what happened as long as she got enough to eat.

Staci was all ready to go along. "You'll be in charge of Secret, if you don't mind," I said to her. "I'll hold Angela, and Charlotte will look after Princess."

"That sounds good," she bubbled.

What a memory—all the dear, sad faces of our African friends surrounding us—all the good wishes and lingering handshakes and tears.

"You will come back?" they cried.

"We will come back," we promised.

Neil Dimacopoulos grabbed Wayne and hugged him fiercely while the tears rolled down his cheeks. "I'll never forget you, Brother," he said brokenly.

"Nor I you," Wayne returned. "Get into that Bible, Neil—it's the only way."

Craig and Jewel took us to the airport. I hugged the twins so much they became impatient with me. How could they understand that it was breaking my heart to leave them?

"I'm glad I could see Brady's first steps," Wayne said. "Brett will be walking before you know it."

"He sure will," Jewel answered, her eyes shining. "Look, he wants you, Ruth Ann."

Brett had reached chubby little arms out to me. I took him and tried to be cheerful, though my heart ached. He snuggled close and patted me with one dear little hand.

I have no regrets when it comes to you, Darling.

38

On Furlough

May 30

As we neared Chicago, I held little Angela as if I would never let her go. It was cold in the jet so I had wrapped her up tightly in a blanket. There in the privacy of the back seat of that huge jet, I wept into her downy curls. She just looked at me with those lovely, big, dark eyes. It was agonizing to think of giving her up.

As we finally made our way through customs, we spotted them immediately—Kurt and Marilyn Shores were waiting with their whole family.

They were all smiles and looked so eager and excited. Marilyn held out her arms and Angela went right to her without a backward glance.

There was something almost sacred about this family meeting their new daughter—and sister—for the first time. I felt the same awe and wonder as I did when Craig and Jewel first held the twins.

When emotions are high, people try to hide them, but I was thinking—*perfect*—*the perfect family for Angela.*

Kurt and Marilyn introduced Bethany, Titus, Delilah, Jonathan, Benjamin, and Jacob. We didn't have much time, so after the introductions we visited a short while and then left to catch our flight. Wayne made sure Staci was at the right place to meet her connecting flight, then we hurried to catch ours.

I was so blinded by tears that Wayne had to guide me through the maze of people. I was glad when we finally found our seats on the jet and could relax for a few hours.

Praise God! Praise God she has such a wonderful, loving family . . . but oh, how I miss her!

Grandpa and Grandma Stelfox and Uncle Jim picked us up in Washington, D.C. As we traveled north into Pennsylvania, my eyes took in everything. Pennsylvania is so beautiful! I feasted my eyes on the clean, manicured lawns and the flowering shrubs and green grass. It was almost a shock to see such beauty after the streets of Monrovia. Everything is so clean—no bubbling sewer coming to meet you or piles of refuse and filth lying along the streets.

Yet I felt strangely alienated.

We were warmly welcomed and fussed over and fed and taken care of as usual, and they thoughtfully allowed us to go to sleep as soon as we wanted to.

Another world, another continent, but the very same God!

June 1

Richard and Sue Kauffman, their daughter Rhoda, and sons Willie and Thomas arrived here at Grandpa Stelfox's around three o'clock yesterday afternoon. Words fail to describe the deep feelings when a parent's yearning is realized. In this case, it was a great miracle that both Faith Princess and Secret were able to be united with their new family.

We went over the details together, marveling at the mighty hand of God. Sue and Rhoda have a calm, quiet way about them that Faith Princess will thrive under.

"We thought it would be easier on the children if we came and got acquainted with them first," Sue explained. "They're not babies anymore. How did Angela react?"

"She . . . went without a problem," I managed.

"It's all right. I understand."

"I've been concerned about how Secret will react, though, because of the way he cried when his grandpa left him," I said presently. "But I think he will be just fine, especially with such dear brothers to play with."

"Thomas is about a year older," Rhoda smiled.

Sue sat down with Faith Princess and explained everything she could. "We will be your family from now on, Faith Princess. You'll never have to move again, if the Lord wills. Do you think you would like to come with us?"

"Co' wi' you," Princess agreed, giggling.

They stayed until this afternoon, and when Rhoda buckled Secret into his car seat, he smiled at her with trust in his eyes. When it was time to say good-bye, he cheerfully waved at us.

"Good-bye, Princess! Good-bye, Secret! We love you!"

"Bye," said Faith Princess.

"I think she'll have a harder time, simply because she's blind," Sue said quietly.

Praise God for another very special family.

June 4

We flew into Alberta on Monday and had a grand reunion with our children, my mother, and all our relatives and friends. Our children had to know all the little details of everything that has happened since they left.

"I can't wait to go back!" Julie said, and Bev agreed heartily.

I have been enjoying the wide fields with the rolling grasses, the meadowlarks, and the flycatchers. I love the clear, fresh air, the western breezes, and the outline of the Rockies. Things look so swept and garnished and clean. The houses seem to have grown in size and they are all so neat and handy with hot running water and hot tubs and telephones.

There's fresh broccoli, California strawberries, and whole milk. No one has scabies or malaria or scalp fungus. There are no disease-ridden mosquitoes or poisonous snakes or boy soldiers with AK-47 rifles. The streets in town are well-designed and controlled by traffic lights and traffic signs. My mother and sisters and brother and many of our friends are close by.

And no one seems to notice all these incredible luxuries!

I cannot get my mind off our friends and the babies waiting in Liberia. Always in the back of my mind is the threat of the war that hangs over them.

I know I need to try to readjust, but just for now, I ache inside.

I miss Liberia.

39

War!

June 5

There's war in Liberia!

Yesterday, six days after we left, the Mervin Lantz family flew to the States, and most of the remaining white staff was evacuated to Accra, Ghana—so the twins spent their first birthday fleeing Liberia.

June 9

Today Iddo, Viola, Jeffrey, and Curt had to be evacuated by helicopter from the U.S. Embassy to a French naval ship lying off the coast because there was a fierce attack from the LURD rebels trying to take the bridge.

The CAM vehicles are safely stored in the compound by the warehouse. Some of the native staff are in charge while we are all gone.

June 20

Our family should be flying back to Liberia this weekend, but no airline is flying into Monrovia from Canada. The war is raging. The newspaper carries quite a few reports of the situation, and

Dave King keeps us informed via e-mail. Our whole family eagerly awaits this daily news.

A ceasefire was declared three days ago. Maybe this will be the beginning of the end.

There are hundreds of thousands of refugees in Monrovia. I'm sure some of them are staying at Residence. At least it has walls that would offer some protection.

We heard today that Reuben Stoltzfus, a brother-in-law to Conrad Swartzentruber and a CAM employee, is in Monrovia now. He does monitoring work for CAM in different countries.

President Bush has demanded that President Taylor resign as the first step toward resolving the war in Liberia, but President Taylor insists he will not leave until a peacekeeping force is actively employed in Liberia.

I almost feel guilty that we could flee so easily and all our friends were forced to remain.

Lord, have mercy on those poor Liberians.

June 26

Reuben Stoltzfus said there were bodies piled outside the Embassy to remind the Americans of what was happening to the populace. People are very upset that the Americans seem indifferent to their plight.

June 27

The LURD rebels broke into the CAM compound and stole the new Defender, the old Defender, the new Pajero, and the van. Then they pulled the doors off the warehouse and ransacked the place before retreating to the St. Paul Bridge on the Poe River.

June 28

Neil Dimacopoulos flew out of danger to Ivory Coast today. Somehow, in trying to find a way out, he became separated from Abi and the boys and has no idea where they are.

July 7

Reuben Stoltzfus was able to leave safely last Wednesday, since things had quieted down for a brief period.

The United States sent an advance team into Monrovia to evaluate the situation, but they are not interested in sending in any troops to fight. President Taylor has not left for the asylum he accepted last week. He hasn't even set an exit date, so there's not much hope of us going back this month.

The LURD rebels are back, fighting with greater intensity than ever, and the casualties are increasing. Monrovia has descended into chaos as the bloody civil war goes on. I can just see our poor friends hiding in terror in their flimsy little shacks—the children screaming with fright and crying with hunger.

Willie is so worried about Georgie. I can only imagine what he must feel like to be in the middle of another bloody war.

Where is our Blessing . . . and Agutta with her children . . . and Elijah, and all the church people? Are Kubah, Joanna, Marie, and little Benjamin still alive?

The questions are tormenting.

July 18

The slaughter of the Liberian people has been compared to chickens on a poultry farm. The dead are being buried in the sandy soil of the beaches or in shallow graves marked with stakes so they can be properly buried later. There are terrible reports of mothers and babies dying in the crossfire and children being separated from their parents.

Abi, Chico, and Georgie were able to fly to Abidjan to be reunited with Neil through a series of miraculous events.

Wayne hopes and prays that Neil will stand firm and true to his new-found faith.

August 7

The people in Monrovia are begging for food. Action Against Hunger estimates that thirty percent of the children suffer from acute malnourishment.

Precious Lord Jesus, have pity.

Dave King was talking to Dr. Lamin on the phone today when it became very noisy. Dr. Lamin explained that the people were all shouting and rejoicing as the first vehicle with African peacekeepers entered Monrovia.

Thousands of people lined the streets chanting, "We want peace. No more war!"

August 11

President Taylor officially handed over his power to Vice President Moses Blah and then flew to Abuja, Nigeria, to accept asylum there. He had to leave—there was no more fuel to run his generators.

In his closing speech he accused the U.S. of forcing him out of office, stating, "I want to be the sacrificial lamb. I will be the whipping boy."

Just before he left, he startled the crowd by stating, "God willing, I will be back."

August 15

Dozens of American troops landed at Robert's Field yesterday, and the rebels began withdrawing from Mesurado Bridge to end their two-month siege.

The peacekeepers tried in vain to keep order as the thronging masses of people pushed across the bridge in search of food. All the food shops and warehouses were raided in a frantic scramble to find rice. Many of the children became hysterical in their unbearable anticipation of a bowl of hot rice to eat.

Lord, watch over all of our friends during this dangerous time.

August 20

Some of the CAM staff in Liberia have been cleaning up the warehouse and tallying the amount of goods that were taken. The rebels stole over two hundred bags of rice, a hundred bags of cornmeal, about fifty bags of beans, Support-A-Widow and Aid-for-the-Aged parcels, canned meat, comforters, oil, shoes, and clothing. CAM was not hit nearly as hard as some of the other NGOs, but there is still no hope of getting the four vehicles back.

August 22

Craig, Jewel, the twins, and Dr. Lamin's sons, Moses and Paul, flew back into Monrovia today. The rest of the displaced staff had returned earlier except for the Sommers family, who spent two weeks in Ghana and plan to return shortly.

40

Back Again

September 3

We arrived in beautiful Berlin, Ohio, on Monday evening with our motor home and one of CAM's vehicles. We are parked in the lovely Scenic Hills Campground right next to the CAM office and plan to relax for a few more days.

Today, when we toured Walnut Creek Cheese and the surrounding area, I found myself, as usual, mentally comparing places, events, and even people with the traumatized Liberians.

We paused to enjoy twenty-cent vanilla custard cones, Walnut Creek Cheese's special of the day. They were so big we could hardly finish them.

Crowds of tourists meandered around, looking at the goodies to eat and licking ice cream. Most of them were definitely overweight.

As we stood in line at the lovely ice cream counter in the air-conditioned store, I pictured the destitute old people lined up at the gate outside the CAM office, waiting in the hot sun for hours for a few cups of rice. Or the tight lines of hungry people in the displaced camps with babies on their backs and faces shining with sweat. I saw the orphans lining up for a mini roll of Life Savers, jumping up and down with excitement.

Somehow, that creamy frozen custard didn't taste as good as usual.

In church last Sunday I marveled at the strong, close-knit, godly families that attended there—grandparents, fathers, mothers, and children who are loved and protected. And babies who are eagerly awaited and cared for lovingly.

In contrast, countless little girls in Liberia just reaching adolescence are forced out on the streets or into the bush to be abused and mutilated. I remembered all the mothers who wanted to give their babies away and the many more infants who are abandoned or neglected.

I looked around the lovely church sanctuary where everyone had a Bible—and more at home—and thought of the thousands of Liberians who have never held a Bible, let alone owned one.

Today we drove past the community laundromat, where the huge dryers hummed and tossed the clothes until they were dry—and I thought of washday in Monrovia, where all the hand-washed clothes were tossed over bushes or spread out on the grass to dry in the sun.

We toured little country shops and huge Mennonite shops and markets where we didn't have to worry about whether they would try to cheat us—and I thought of the tremendous deception and thievery of some of the Monrovian merchants and vendors and street rogues.

We saw many inviting bed-and-breakfasts in the hills and dales of Holmes County—and remembered the pathetic sleeping conditions of people without beds or bedding. No pillows or soft comforters—just the hard, cold floor and their skinny arms folded for a pillow. No pancakes, bacon, eggs, hash browns, orange juice, or coffee for breakfast . . . often no breakfast at all.

In the clothing stores, I remembered the pathetic glee of the villagers who received used clothing—no matter how wrinkled. I pictured the pure joy of all the little girls who received new dresses that one Sunday morning in church, and the rejoicing of the church members when they were able to trade their tattered old shoes for some stout new ones that actually fit.

We marveled at all the magnificent homes—Amish, Mennonite,

or "English"—with their gorgeous ponds and shrubs and healthy livestock, and I couldn't help but compare them with the huts of jagged tin, disintegrating block, paper sacks, and pieces of wood. These were warm and dry against the elements—equipped with cozy wood stoves and in-floor heating or forced air—while the Liberians' homes literally leaked buckets every time it rained.

These have modern kitchens with running water, pull-out cupboards, full pantries, ovens, and fridges—those have an outdoor set of rocks with an old iron pot to cook on and no water unless it is toted from the busy city wells.

At night, when we drove home along the perfect roads and I saw all the pole lights and traffic signals, I thought of all the little candles and kerosene lanterns that sprang up at night along the crumbling streets of Monrovia. I could just picture the soft glow of the candlelight on the women's swarthy faces as they tended their stands and the flash of their white teeth as they smiled.

It all gives me a homesick feeling I don't fully understand. How can I be homesick for Liberia in a paradise like Holmes County, Ohio? I feel a great longing to hold little Brady and Brett and to hug all the church ladies and eat Sis Bea's rice with oil of pumpkin soup. I want to take a long walk along the beach with the wind in my face and the breakers crashing. I want to bake cookies for the mechanics and security guards, listen to the pouring rain in the night, and laugh with Esther Akoi and all our other friends.

I want to go home.

September 22

We received our tickets to Monrovia today. We plan to fly out next Monday on the very first plane SN Brussels sends. Talk about one excited family. We are so ready to go back after waiting and hoping for four whole months.

"Imagine seeing Blessing and the twins in a few days!" exclaimed Charlotte.

"And Esther and Cleo," added Julie.

"Don't forget all the CAM staff!" Bev said.

"What about Georgie and Harris and Toney?" Willie reminded us.

425

"I want to see Kazan and Charlie and all my soccer buddies," Larry said.

"I miss the people, but I also miss the rain and the ocean," I remarked.

"I'm looking forward to my new job," Wayne smiled. "I'm so tired of just sitting around."

Our extended furlough is finally over.

October 1

We're back! After flying to Chicago, where the Lantz family waited for us, we flew from there to Brussels, and finally arrived at Robert's Field Airport here in Monrovia.

As the warm, heavily-scented air enveloped us like a blanket, we took in the wild airport scene and all the familiar sights and sounds. "Some things never change," Wayne said. "Wars may come and wars may go, but the official scene in Liberia is still one mad scramble!"

A smiling Craig Carter greeted us in the baggage claim room and helped carry the luggage.

Finally, we came out into the sunshine where Jewel and those adorable, chubby babies waited. Of course they didn't remember us, but it was enough to coax dear little smiles out of them and hold their little brown hands.

"They have grown so much!" the girls exclaimed. "Oh, they're cute!"

And they are! Their dear little cheeks and tummies have rounded out, and they look so interested in everything around them, smiling and frowning and laughing out loud.

Jewel looked on proudly as we fussed over them. "We looked forward to seeing you adults," I teased, "but we couldn't wait to see the babies."

A mob of people waited for us at Residence. Elijah didn't even try to keep them out of the gate—they just poured in. Already waiting inside the gate were Esther, Cleo, Merci, Dorcas, Harris, Georgie, Agutta and Amos, Charles, our cleaning girl Marie, Benjamin's mother Marie, Grace Allison and Shadrach, and many more friends whom Elijah had recognized and allowed entry. Even Mr. Gurley was here.

We were hugged until our teeth rattled and our smiles hurt.

"Hey, where are Charlie and Kazan and Jillie?" Larry wondered anxiously. "Bambi is here, but not our monkeys and my dog."

Elijah took Larry's hand in his, and tears stood in his dark eyes. "It wa' naw easy, it wa' naw easy," he kept saying. "Ah kep' da deer, bu' da hungry people ate de other animals. Ah am sorry, Larry . . . dere wa' nothin' ah coul' do."

Larry stared at him for a few seconds. "It's not your fault, Elijah. I can get another monkey," he said. "I hope it didn't hurt when they killed them."

"Naw, dey killed 'em fas'. No pain."

"How is my Bassa girl?" Bundo wanted to know.

"She's doing great! Come by someday and we'll give you a picture of her," I said.

"I miss Princess around here," Georgie drawled. "And I haven't had even one tiny cookie for four months, Mom. I am so glad you're all back, especially you, Big Will."

"Harris, please tell us all about Blessing," Charlotte appealed. "We heard that she is in the C.O. Smythe Orphanage, right?"

"Blessing did well with my mother," Harris smiled. "She did not want to leave us; we were pressured to let her go. Now she lives at the orphanage. You must go see her."

"Oh, I will," Charlotte promised. "Jonas Yoder is planning a trip over here to get her and Benjamin."

"How are Princess and Secret and Angela?" Georgie asked.

"We were able to stop in at both places in September on our way home from Ohio," I told him. "They are doing well, with families that love them dearly."

"How are Brother Nathan's widow and the children doing?" Dorcas asked.

"We met them in Pennsylvania at the Kauffman's place," I said. "They are doing well, under the circumstances."

"Thank God," she murmured.

Finally, the excitement died down enough for us to go into the house. "They think they have to hug you really hard to make you feel welcome," I told Wayne breathlessly. "I am shocked at how thin everyone is. Why, their bones feel like sharp sticks along their backs!"

"Elijah looks especially sick," he agreed. "There's more wrong there than just being hungry. I wonder what happened to him, or his family."

The walls have all been repainted, but everything else desperately needs a cleaning. "Let's just wait until Marie comes to help us tomorrow," I told the girls wearily.

I'm not sure what time it is since it is six hours different from Alberta, but we sure need to rest.

Praise God for His protecting hand.

October 2

We're getting used to the constant *chop-chop* of the UN helicopters as they patrol overhead. Sometimes they fly so low and circle so often that it makes us wonder if there's trouble somewhere.

Tony Hage invited the staff and our visitors for a delicious supper tonight. We had been scrubbing and cleaning all day long, so it was wonderful to sit down to a feast of baked cassava fish on rice and steamed shrimp with a tangy sauce and all the trimmings.

Tony was in a jovial mood. "I would not want to experience the last few months again!" he exclaimed. "I am very glad that time period is over and you are all safely back with us. Could you tell me what has happened to the tall white man named Neil?"

"He's married and living in Abidjan," Wayne offered. "He keeps in touch by e-mail, and it sounds like they're doing fine. He's still peddling muffins."

"*He's married?*" Tony asked incredulously.

"Yes, to Abigail Grey. Harvey Yoder married them in September."

"Another miracle," Jewel said to me. "I thought that man would never settle down."

One of the dinner guests was Micah Mast, the new schoolteacher. He plans to begin school on Monday.

"I would like to begin at eight o'clock and end at one, so the children can eat lunch at home," Micah said. "That gives us a cooler time of day, and no lunches to pack."

"Sounds wonderful," we ladies agreed.

It seems so different not to have Iddo's family among us since they terminated their service. The girls flew home from Ghana in August and Iddo and Viola left Liberia in September. The winds of change never die.

When we got home, Elijah followed us to the door. "Ah need a word wi' you." He hesitated.

"Come on in," Wayne invited. "Is something wrong, Elijah?"

"Ah am so embarrassed to tell you," he began. "My Ellen lef' me . . . she wen' away to Redlight an' she won't co' back. Ah feel so bad, bu' wha' can ah do?"

"Who's caring for the children?" Wayne asked.

"Dey take care of demselves, Mr. Wayne."

"I'm real sorry to hear that, Elijah. It looked like you two really got along well. Does she have another man?"

"No . . . no, ah don' think so," he stammered miserably.

No wonder his thin shoulders sag and the happy light has faded from his eyes. He loved Ellen in his own sincere way—and now she is gone, leaving him and five young children to take care of themselves.

Another home in shambles.

October 3

Marie came and we cleaned again today. Now the cupboards, drawers, appliances, and beds are fit to use. The whole house smells like Pine Sol and the windows sparkle in the sun.

At least two hundred refugees lived here in Residence during the war, according to Elijah, Toney, and Dr. Lamin.

This morning, Wayne had to scout around for some vehicle parts, so I went along. We crossed over the bridge and drove toward Freeport and the warehouse.

"It certainly looks like a war zone!" I exclaimed, marveling at the countless bullet holes and pockmarks and damaged buildings all along the way.

Even the signs were shot up as if they had been used for target practice. Jagged pieces of tin hung off some of the ruined buildings and dangled precariously over people's heads as they walked about.

"Look at all the doors of the business places," Wayne said. "They've been yanked off by force. That's why they're all patched up like that."

"It looks like the rebels shot at whatever they wanted to, just for the fun of it," I returned. "Why would you shoot all the windows out of a high building like that?"

"They were drunk—or high on pot. Remember how Neil told us he couldn't remember half the things he did because of the drugs he used?"

Mitchel Clemmer was waiting at the gate when I got home. "Where did *you* disappear to?" I asked, trying to stay composed and calm. "Why didn't you let us know you weren't coming?"

"I told Charles I was leaving for Ghana on a mission for Mr. Wengerd," Mitchel explained. "I am very sorry I did not tell you, Ruth Ann. I will do better from now on."

"I'm sorry, too, but there won't *be* any more chances. I can't be upset because of the wonderful way things worked out, but Maria Luyken from Minnesota will finish the adoptions for us. She's a Liberian citizen, and she's already working on several cases."

He went into a very long tirade of excuses, but I was not interested. "The children are safe, bygones are bygones, and we're starting over," I said finally. "Sit down and let me tell you how the Lord worked things out for us."

October 4

Maria Luyken asked Julie and me to come with her to the Embassy to meet the new consular and give a brief history of what we know about the twins.

We were called in immediately and taken to the office of the new consular. He breezed into the room and began with a list of questions. He was rather pale, with a long ponytail and an uneven complexion, but it didn't take long to realize he was very sharp and determined. He wanted to get all the pending adoptions taken care of and start afresh. He asked where the twins' documents were and why they were refused.

We learned that the only thing we can do now is wait and see if the Ghanian Embassy refuses or accepts the twins' adoption, because all their documents have been sent there for that purpose. The consular thought we should hear the verdict within a month.

Moses Massawalla stopped in today, so we invited him to sit down and eat supper with us.

"The wors' thing by far about the war," he said feelingly, "was the hunger. It stalked the streets an' killed the old an' weak an' the very young. The hunger was a terrible thing."

Moses is not quite ready to give me the story of his brutal experience with the militiamen, since there is still too much danger of him being exposed.

October 6

Jewel and I were having a good visit this afternoon when Elijah announced that Musu was at the gate. She walked in with a slow smile and outstretched arms, her black eyes sparkling. "Sis Ruth! Jewel!" she cried. "You are really back to Liberia! The babies are fine. Thank God!"

We listened as Musu described the terrible events she had encountered during the war. "The mothers would just chuck their babies along the side of the road or in the garbage piles and run when the rebels approached. They had no feeling for their own children. Babies . . . babies everywhere. If no one came along, the red ants would eat the child. Oh yes. Many babies were thrown away."

October 8

One of the guards asked Larry how he liked going to a real school. "With a teacher like Micah? You bet I do," he answered.

I'm not sure what that says about my teaching abilities. I'm just glad for the school. We take turns having Micah for supper so he doesn't have to learn to cook.

Today at eight o'clock, I walked down to the sewing center for my first official day of work and got acquainted with the procedures. Amanda Mathias is the general manager, and I am to open the center at eight-thirty, help supervise the ladies with all their different projects, fix broken or jammed machines, sort and stack new clothing in the supply room, help keep things clean, settle any squabbles, take my turn in daily devotions, unpack new shipments and put them away, check the garments the ladies sew to see if they are acceptable, and whatever else needs to be done.

"This looks like it could be really interesting," I said to Amanda.

She studied me with a slow smile spreading on her pretty face. "We will work well together," she laughed, and I knew I had found another kindred spirit.

Elsie came downstairs now and then to see how we were faring. "There's a list of church ladies who are very eager to learn how to sew," she told me. "Think we could start classes for them in the near future?"

"I'd love to!" I said, visualizing them in lovely cape dresses that they had tailored.

I realize now what a big job Iddo's family did in the sewing center. It all looked so easy when they were in charge.

October 14

There is great excitement in the city today because Gyude Brown was sworn in as the head of the new transitional government. He will be presiding for two years until the promised elections in 2005.

When the news came that he was on his way from the airport, the whole city went wild. Thousands of people lined the streets, waiting for him to drive past. They waved branches and palm leaves and jumped up and down, screaming and chanting, "No more war! We want peace!" There's a feeling of freedom and jubilation everywhere.

Afterward, Charlotte and Wayne went to the C.O. Smythe Orphanage to visit Blessing and came back all discouraged. "She is so skinny and dirty, and there's no one to really care," she sighed. "Her beautiful hair is only about an inch long. Could we take her for a few days before Jonas comes?"

"If we get permission, I don't see a problem," I agreed. "You can clean her up and give her worm tablets and feed her well. Sure, let's do it!"

Craig, Jewel, and the twins came over this evening after prayer meeting for popcorn and lemon iced tea. The twins enjoyed sucking on "Freezies" and walking all over the house.

"Are you feeling okay?" I asked Jewel after noting a listlessness about her.

"I think I might have a touch of the flu," she answered. "It's not bad though; I'll be fine."

"I'll have to admit I'm not on top of the scale either," Craig said suddenly. "Feels like a mild flu of some kind."

October 17

Both Craig and Jewel were so sick this morning that they brought the twins over to our place and went to Providence Clinic, where Jewel promptly fainted in the waiting room.

"We didn't have to wait long then!" Craig said later. "They rushed us in and had that IV in place within minutes. Her blood pressure was much too low, for one thing. We have to go back for treatment every morning till Monday. They think we might have both malaria and typhoid fever."

"I want you to take the twins to get tested tomorrow, Bev," Jewel said weakly. "If we have typhoid, they probably do too."

The new president has certainly won the respect of the people. He offered a long acceptance prayer over the radio, and Elijah let us listen to some of it. He prayed for the brothers and sisters in the bush, that Almighty God would touch their hearts so they would stop terrorizing their fathers, mothers, brothers, and sisters. He asked that the blessing of God the Father, God the Son, and God the Holy Spirit rest upon all the people of Liberia, and he asked it all in the name of Jesus Christ our Lord.

The first thing he did after being sworn in was throw out the rice and fuel monopolies that forced the people to pay outrageous prices. And he abolished the law requiring an exit visa to leave the country.

October 20

Craig, Jewel, and the boys have all been taking treatment for typhoid and malaria since Saturday.

The treatment has helped Craig, and both twins are better, but Jewel is definitely not responding. Tonight, we invited their family for supper since she was still as weak as a kitten and unable to cook. I hadn't seen Jewel for a few days, and was shocked when I saw her. Her skin and eyes are extremely yellow, and her hand shook as she tried to eat the soup. She looked like she was ready to faint.

She's going to die! I thought.

When I got a chance, I asked Craig if he realized what was happening. "Such an extreme color denotes a liver malfunction, Craig. You need to get her to Firestone as soon as you can. You can leave the twins here and leave early in the morning."

"I wonder if we should call her folks," Wayne said after they left. "I've never seen a person so yellow in all my life."

"She looks scary!" said Larry.

"Let's pray," Wayne suggested. "It would be too awful if she'd . . . get sicker."

What a comfort to kneel and pour out our cares to Jesus!

October 21

Dr. Brisbane took one look at Jewel and admitted her to the hospital. Blood tests revealed that she has severe malaria, not typhoid. Her blood pressure is dangerously low and her liver is damaged, hence the yellow color.

October 22

Charlotte and Bev went to the C.O. Smythe Orphanage today to fetch Blessing. The little girl was taller and very thin. Her hair was chopped off real short and looked like it needed a good cleaning, but her smile was as enchanting as ever.

"She definitely remembers this place," Charlotte said with satisfaction.

October 24

Our house is once again full of babies and laughter and fun. Jewel feels so much better that Craig brought her home from the hospital, and they're living with us until she can get back on her feet. The twins have made themselves right at home, since they can always go check to see if Mom is still in the girls' room. They will get up in the middle of playing, trot to her door and look inside, then resume their play. It's a perfect arrangement for the time being.

October 30

Jonas Yoder left for home today with Blessing and Benjamin. He is one brave man. The past three days have been a whirlwind of activity for him—getting all the legal papers finalized, seeing West Africa for the first time, eating cassava leaf and peanut soup, and becoming better acquainted with the children.

When he first held out his arms to Blessing, she went right to him and laid her head on his shoulder. There were tears in the eyes of the onlookers. It was indeed a precious moment.

Benjamin stared at him soberly and allowed himself to be held as well.

Charlotte is having a difficult day, but tears are a balm for the spirit. We are thrilled and thankful that Blessing has a home after all the trauma she endured. Hopefully it won't be too difficult for her to trust another adult and bond to Elva and Jonas and their children.

Little Benjamin will never know his birth father, but he will grow up in a home where love abides and Jesus is the honored guest.

November 1

Wayne came home today with news about the cruelty of former President Taylor. "When the war amputees saw they weren't being paid, they converged on the streets of Congotown and refused to let traffic through. If anyone tried to get by, they broke his windshield, or worse. Many of the amputees were blind, or sitting in wheelchairs, or without limbs—hungry and angry at their fates. Then orders came from the president's mansion that they should all find their way to Salada, and there he would pay them. To make a long story short, he had every one of those men killed and buried in a mass grave."

Oh, the horrors of war!

November 13

We were overjoyed to receive a letter from Neil and Abi today. We sat down together to read it.

> Dear Mr. Wayne and family,
>
> It's us, Neil and Abi. We are wondering about you because we haven't heard for so long. The kids and Abi are doing well. Abi is right beside me. She would like some recipes from Ruth Ann because all was lost in escaping.
>
> Our Saviour continues to pour out His mercy, love, and grace. I always think how the Lord used the war situation in Liberia to get to me. Yes, I'll never forget how we first met in Bomi Hills and then on Randall Street when I tried to get a bag of rice from you and you invited me to church. I want you to know that I love the Lord Jesus and my heart yearns for Him. I love Him. I hope to see you again someday. How wonderful if we could fellowship together and eat some of Ruth Ann's pizza. Yum.
>
> We pray that all goes well with you, for you were and still are an example to us. We, too, want to build our home on Christian principles. When I think of all those things (guns, drugs, fighting, and thousands of other evil spirits) that our Father gave me grace to overcome, I know He is real.
>
> We miss you all. Special love to Larry.
>
> We love you with the love of Jesus Christ.
>
> Neil and Abi

"What a miracle!" Wayne sighed. "The grace of God is sufficient for anyone, no matter what he has done."

41

Forgive Me When I Whine

November 17

The rain came down in an unseasonable torrent all day today. The twins were very upset and cranky since Craig went to visit Jewel at Firestone Hospital and left them with us. She is suffering another case of malaria, so she is very sick.

As if that isn't bad enough, Craig and Jewel received word that the Ghanaian Embassy backed Glenn Carey's decision and will not issue a visa for the twins. They gave six reasons and allowed sixty days for Craig and Jewel to respond and prove those reasons inaccurate.

The news was so depressing and the day so dreary that I wasn't surprised when a woman arrived at the gate with her twin babies. "Probably on their last legs," I muttered to Charlotte as we watched the newcomer hurry past the window.

Elijah held an umbrella over the woman until she reached the porch, but she was still dripping wet.

She hesitated when she saw us. Then she reached out her free hand and smiled. "I am Marpu Anseh," she said softly. "These are my baby girls, Rose and Rachel. Bev sent me from the office to you, Mother."

She handed me the baby in her arms and reached back to

unwrap the second one. We found ourselves looking into the faces of two winsome, adorable babies with the biggest eyes and mops of curly hair.

"They're darling!" Charlotte exclaimed.

"They're much too thin, though," I warned.

"The babies need milk," said Marpu. "They are hungry."

"Yes," I answered. "We can see that they need help. We will show you how to feed them right now. Come into the kitchen. We have one thing you must do, Marpu."

"What that?"

"Every time you come, you must bring the babies along. Every single time."

"I will do that."

"If you don't bring them, there will be no more milk."

"Yes, Mother, I understand."

What a joy to fill those donated bottles with warm formula and watch those dear baby girls drink eight ounces each.

We brewed some tea and sat down with Marpu to chat until the rain subsided. I was drawn by her open, friendly manner and her frank, honest eyes. She reminded me of a princess in rags.

"Tell me, how do you eat?" I asked presently.

"My husband and I ran a small dry goods store until the war," she said simply. "When the soldiers came through they demanded every dollar we had saved, besides taking all the goods. Mother, our savings of ten months is gone. Should I bring a picture?"

"We'd love to see your store," I said. "What will you do now, Marpu?"

"I need to ask Mr. Wayne to help us begin once more. I have no choice but to beg him, Mother."

The babies slept in our arms while Marpu talked. "Mother, it could have been much worse!" she exclaimed passionately. "Some of the little girls and women in our area suffered much. The soldiers have no pity for anyone. It was not easy. God spared me, Mother."

I saw the glitter of tears in her dark eyes.

"You were crying to God, Marpu. That is the answer."

Before we let Marpu go, we packed a bag of diapers and baby clothing and stuck in some powder and lotion and two identical pink baby blankets with small white crocheted edges.

"Bless the name of Jesus!" she cried. "Thanks be to God!"

"That is one nice lady," Charlotte said as Marpu walked out to the gate. "I believe every word she said, Mom, don't you?"

"I sure do. She's got unusual class and good manners."

I think about Marpu and the dreadful things she experienced during the war, the hardships they experience right now, and how ill Jewel is in the hospital. Life can be so sad, yet all things work together for those who love God.

Wayne pulled in after the rain stopped and invited me along to West Point to do an assessment for the Self-Help program. Charlotte was willing to watch the twins, so I eagerly went along. Esther sat in front with us, and Peewee, Harris, and Larry sat in the back of the pickup.

"Why are all these people along?" I asked Wayne.

"They say it's wise to have more people along with you when you descend into West Point because it's so uncivilized," he answered.

"Why do they call it Shantytown?" I wondered.

"You will see!" exclaimed Esther. "It is a place for rogues to live—no law and no policemen. When a thief steals something he can run and hide and no one will find him."

"Who is this assessment for?" I asked.

"Philippine's sister Vivian has given me no peace," Wayne answered patiently. "She says she's nearly starving. We'll see what we can do."

We drove carefully down narrow, crumbling streets until we could drive no further. Harris stayed to watch the truck while we set out on foot. We had to walk a long way. I shudder at the memory, for we have never before encountered such a vile neighborhood.

We ducked into narrow alleys where the stench filled our nostrils and nauseated us. Flies rose up in great black clouds around us like the plague in Egypt. Hundreds of filthy children of all ages peeked out from the doorways and piles of garbage where they played. People were everywhere, sitting and playing cards— or just sitting.

Their eyes—dark, vacant, unsmiling—mirrored the pain of their souls.

Sewage leaked across the streets. Huge old drums blackened from countless fires and filled with drying fish stood in a group, smoking darkly. Toddlers played in the parasite-ridden dirt. Nursing mothers sat in many doorsteps, not bothering to cover up for any passersby. Shacks lined the street, their sagging walls growing with discolored mildew and full of jagged holes. The roofs sloped down into gaping holes where the water had stood too long and rusted out the tin.

At one place the alleyway became very narrow. "I can't get through!" Esther yelped, but she squeezed through somehow.

Finally, we reached the pitiful, tiny room where Vivian dwelt. It was in a huge old building where it was customary for a whole family to live in one room.

Vivian rose slowly from her chair and greeted us. She held out a skeletal hand with not a speck of flesh on the bones. Her clothing hung in a loose sweep over her emaciated body. She walked unsteadily with us out to the front of the building where she wanted to set up a table and sell goods. Her thin toes looked like long claws, especially since the nails were untrimmed and jagged, and painted bright red.

"Ah will sell watah," she croaked. "Ah will. . ." and she stopped in a spasm of coughing that wracked her frame and made her grab for the support of the wall.

"She's dying on her feet," Wayne said quietly, his face etched with pain. "I'll get Philippine to give her a hand. It's very obvious she can't start a business—she can't even stand! Esther, we have to put her on top of the list. The others can wait."

"Yes, Mr. Wayne," Esther agreed. "She will be first."

The waterfront was only a few feet from the entrance to the apartment building. Small boys happily bathed among the flotsam; others fished for supper; and still others pretended they were in a bathroom.

"God forgive me when I whine!" I burst out.

Esther looked at me with concern. For once her chubby, smiling face was very sober. "It is a serious thing," she agreed.

Vivian stood leaning against the door, watching us leave. Sick and in pain. Abandoned and alone. Friendless and helpless.

We made our way through the maze back to the truck where Harris waited. A large group of women danced in a circle, leaning forward and chanting a sad, wailing cry. Some would leave the circle and others would join. As they left they would pass a garland of beads to the next woman in line.

"They are mourning for the dead," Esther said. "They will dance like this all day."

I was glad when those moaning wails could no longer be heard and Shantytown was behind us. Wayne dropped me off at Residence. I walked into the yard and saw Georgie throwing baskets with Craig while the mechanics were fixing a flat tire on Craig's vehicle. Home looked so clean and roomy and inviting and wonderful that I almost felt guilty.

Jewel was reclining on the couch, smiling at the twins' clumsy efforts to pat her face and hug her.

"I'm sure glad to see you home, Jewel," I remarked. "You look a lot better."

"We're going to take malaria preventatives from now on. I felt so bad at one point that I didn't care if I lived or died . . . and that doesn't work."

"I hear the twins have once again been rejected," Merci said. "I think I know why."

Jewel sat up. "Why, Merci?"

"I know the witch doctors can put curses on people, and they really work. I believe the relatives back in River Cess are against this adoption and are taking steps to prevent it."

"That's exactly what Joseph Pawa said," Jewel marveled. "And Isaac said his relatives keep asking him how the twins are— if they're still alive and if they're still healthy. It's weird!"

"They expect something evil to happen to your boys if they keep asking after their health," said Merci. "When people want to destroy another man, they go to the witch doctor and he will put a curse on the person. But these people do not reckon with the power of the blood of Jesus. The Bible says 'they overcame him by the blood of the Lamb,'" she finished triumphantly.

November 22

Larry came home today with a tiny baby monkey he had found tied to a tree in Fiama market.

"I just *knew* this was the one," Larry explained. "Paul Weaver paid for him, so you don't owe me anything."

"That was very considerate of him, " I answered. "Does he have a name?"

"Oh yes, he's Rafiki. Isn't that cute? I need to bathe him, though. He really stinks. Can I do it in the tub?"

"Larry Brandon Stelfox!"

"Naw, I'll use the hose out here," he laughed. "Willie will help me. Then I have to fix Jillie's old house for him and find him some bananas."

Maria, the adoption manager, dropped by this evening and told us she had been scouting around the countryside on her own. "I found that Christian Aid is about the only NGO that actually monitors their food to see that it gets to the desperate and the hungry," she said. "The others just drop it off and leave, and I see it is flooding the market. I am impressed that the CAM orphanages are required to keep their empty cans as proof that it was fed to the children. I also noticed how clean and healthy the children look. Keep up the good work."

November 23

Pastor Mervin preached such a comforting sermon on the Beatitudes this morning. It's wonderful to see how God protected His people during the war. Many of them are extremely thin, but they're all alive.

Tonight after supper Pastor Mervin led a prayer and anointing service for Brady and Brett.

"Now I feel better," Craig said. "It was getting pretty scary how those people always ask Isaac if his boys are still living."

"Greater is He that is in you than he that is in the world," Pastor quoted softly.

December 20

It was extremely warm today. I'm having a hard time capturing the Christmas spirit. Even the leaves on the trees are drooping. The few puffs of air that circulate around are so hot they feel like a microwave fan.

Rafiki comes down to get his food and goes right back up to recline on the big branch in the shade. Bambi sits against the wall and whisks the flies with her long ears.

Grace Allison and Philippine are selling bags of ice and cold water as fast as they can make them. Philippine shares the profit with her sister Vivian.

January 1, 2004

What a wild night of reveling and rejoicing Monrovia just experienced! The music began at midnight, with groups of people walking up and down the streets chanting, "I didn't die. Happy happy New Year. I didn't die. I didn't die. Happy, happy New Year."

The throbbing of the drums added deep, steady rhythm to their chanting. Up and down the streets, over and over they chanted the same lines—rejoicing that they were still alive. They woke us up at one o'clock—then two—then three-thirty. Tirelessly they walked those streets, pounding their drums and yelling until their voices were hoarse.

This morning, I was startled when Charlie Boy and Larry came barging into the kitchen.

"Mother, I've got Rikki back!" Larry shouted, holding out a mongoose for my inspection. "Can I keep him?"

The furry little fellow peered at me with bright, beady eyes, and then stuck his inquisitive nose into Larry's ear. The boys giggled.

"If he stays outside," I said firmly. "You know a mongoose wanders around all night, and I don't want him exploring in our beds."

Some of the sparkle died out of Larry's eyes. "I thought you *liked* Rikki, Mom," he said reproachfully.

"Not enough to live in the same house with him. Now go find him a lizard."

Charlie Boy's eyes darted to the freezer.

"Wait, Charlie Boy. Would you like a cookie?"

"Very much, Missie. Ah thank you very much," he said softly, flashing me a beautiful smile. He scampered outside after Larry, cramming a whole cookie into his mouth. His ragged shirt blew back and revealed the lines of his bony ribs.

I made a bowl of popcorn for Larry and Charlie Boy. Of course, they had to feed some to Rafiki and Rikki, and even Bambi loved the crunchy saltiness.

I peeked out the window as the boys' rollicking laughter reached my ears. There they sat, two small boys, one white and one black, a world of differences between them, oblivious to all barriers of culture and race and enjoying each other's company to the fullest.

Kubah brought little Joanna to let us see how well she was doing. She wondered why we didn't take her home with us.

"You took the blind chil' home—why not Joanna?" she asked, so I had to explain that babies cannot be carried from country to country like goods in a suitcase.

"When can she go?" she wondered.

"You'll just have to be patient, Kubah. Adoptions take a long time. Meanwhile, you are doing a fine job."

Little Joanna looks so clean and healthy that I'm not worried about her at all.

January 8

Emily, Jewel's youngest sister, arrived last evening, so excitement is high at the Carters. She is the first one of the family to see Brady and Brett, and we hope she stays a long time.

January 13

Julie came down with a high fever last night, so we took her to the Providence clinic for a malaria test. It showed negative, but early this morning she became violently ill. Wayne and I took her to the Elwa clinic, where they diagnosed malaria and admitted her immediately.

"Dr. Sacra said she is seriously ill," Wayne told me when we left the hospital. "She has a fever of one hundred and three. She waited too long."

"I wonder if she wasn't sick already last Wednesday," I said, remembering how flushed her cheeks were when she was working in the kitchen.

My mind flashed through all those awful memories of children dying in St. Joseph's Hospital, and of Jewel's close call. I forced myself to think positively.

Later this afternoon when we went back down to the hospital, Julie still felt miserable. "My mouth tastes exceedingly bitter," she moaned. "I can't even keep a sip of water down."

"We brought some cold Sprite," I said. "You need to drink, Julie. Please do."

"They locked me in this room last night," Julie said. "I was horrified and pounded on the wall till the security guard came and opened the door. He thought I had lost my mind."

A peculiar wail rent the air, then another, and another. "Someone is having a baby again," Julie explained. "There must have been lots of babies born last night from all the noise."

"We have to get her home," I begged Wayne. "How can she rest with all this noise?"

"She needs the IV," he reminded me gently, and I knew he was right.

The woman in labor was screaming desperately as we said good-night to Julie and walked out into the warm night.

January 17

Elwa Hospital may not be sterile and modern, but Julie is home and better, and we are so grateful. Many visitors stop by to inquire after her health. If she happens to be sleeping, they sit down and wait patiently until she wakes. The wonderful soup made from CAM canned chicken whetted her appetite and she can rest as long as she wants without worrying about anything.

Jewel and Emily brought the twins over several times and brightened the day for all of us. Craig and Jewel are still patiently waiting for news from the Ghanaian Embassy about the twins' visas.

"I'm sure their papers are buried under a pile on someone's desk," Jewel said. "God knows exactly where they are, though. Meanwhile, we can all be together."

This afternoon, Wayne and I were invited to the engagement ceremony of Anthony Reeves and Sophie Piah. It was held outdoors in a small pavilion created by two tarps thrown over the treetops to shield the guests from the blazing sun. The families of the betrothed couple sat on benches on either side of the clearing, regarding each other respectfully.

During the ceremony, Anthony's father rose slowly to his feet and approached Sophie's elderly father. "We are here to make this official," he stated solemnly, handing Mr. Piah a ten-dollar bill. "I am giving you this as a token of the engagement of my son Anthony to your daughter Sophie."

Everyone clapped.

Mr. Piah smiled broadly. "I appreciate that," he declared, amid more clapping and nodding and cheers.

Anthony's father stood up again. "I don't stop there!" he declared, handing the old man another ten-dollar bill. "I will also give you this to show that they will now marry."

Again Sophie's father thanked him, smiling his widest smile.

Proudly, Anthony's father rose once more, stopping before Sophie's mother. "I have to give something to the woman Sophie pained for nine months. She gets a nanny goat!" and he handed her ten dollars as a substitute for the missing goat.

Everyone was very impressed and clapped loudly after Sophie's mother expressed her thanks.

After the ceremony was over, Anthony's father clarified some of the traditions that have been handed down for generations. "Usually a man's father chooses the bride, but this time Anthony made his own choice," he explained. "He showed me the girl and said this was who he wanted, so I observed her and gave my consent. In days gone by, we would pay a cow or two for a dowry, but now after the war there are none to be found, so we give the value of a cow in dollars. When there is a cow, you give it. The father gets a cow; the mother gets a nanny goat."

"How many cows would you have given my dad for me?" I teased Wayne on the way home.

"A whole herd," he grinned. "Not ten-dollar cows either!"

42

Safe Under the Blood

A surprise was waiting when I arrived home from the sewing center this afternoon. Julie was holding a malnourished baby boy, and by the look on her face, I knew it was no ordinary case. "Look at this angel," she said.

I looked. The child had huge, expressive eyes that didn't quite focus properly. They looked much too big in his wasted little face, but there was an undeniable sweetness about him. I could tell he was freshly bathed and powdered and oiled all over.

"But why do you have him, girls?"

"A young, scruffy-looking man stopped in to get some formula for this little guy," Julie explained excitedly. "Charlotte took the baby and we tried to feed him some warm formula, but he was too weak to suck or else he didn't know how. Finally I got a syringe and fed him that way. He kept spitting it out, so I knew he wasn't getting much. Meanwhile, I tried to get some information out of the baby's father."

"He was strange and fidgety and nervous," Charlotte put in.

"For sure!" Julie agreed. "I asked who the mother was and he said she was a street girl and had left for good."

"We warmed him some rice because he looked so awfully thin,"

Charlotte said. "He ate while Julie kept trying to make the baby take the bottle."

"He ate like a starving wolf!" Julie added. "His clothes were all ripped, and his hair and beard were just horrible. Then he asked if he could smoke and we told him absolutely not in the house."

"He was coughing too," Charlotte offered.

"I thought he was just going outside, but he went on out the gate!" Julie exclaimed. "I wasn't really paying attention, but all of a sudden the thought crossed my mind that he might not come back. Charlotte ran out to the gate, and sure enough, he was nowhere to be seen."

"Elijah thinks he is an ex-fighter," Charlotte said. "Mom, the worst is yet to come."

"What? What happened?" I asked anxiously.

"He stole my cell phone off the fridge on his way out," Julie said. "But look at it this way," she added quickly. "He has the phone, and we have the baby. Quite a trade, isn't it?"

"I'd rather have the baby any day," I agreed heartily. "If the father planned to get rid of him, thank God he came here and didn't throw him in some gully for the ants."

So . . . we have another real, live, darling baby in the house. We will need to find him a home or put him in an orphanage. But meanwhile, he'll be cuddled and pampered.

After supper, our adoption agent did a thorough assessment of baby Ryan, as Julie named our little newcomer. "I wonder if he doesn't have 'shaken baby syndrome.' He is much too languid and unresponsive," she said. "It's too soon to tell, because he may be this way from severe undernourishment, but there's definitely something wrong."

The last of our guests had said good-night, the bats were barking in the almond tree, and the moonlight was casting shimmers of silver thread across the living room floor when the noise started across the street in the Family Planning Center building.

It began with a weird moan that rose higher and higher until it reached a crescendo, then dropped down and began again.

We all heard it, and soon we were standing outside on the front upper porch. The lights were on in the building across the street and we could see people milling about inside.

A low, chanting beat of drums rolled out into the night air. They beat faster and faster until the sounds rolled together in one pulsating throb that seemed to shake the porch.

"Is it some sort of revival meeting or crusade again?" Willie wondered.

"I don't think so," Wayne answered. "This sounds different to me . . . It's awful!"

A man in a long robe with a hood over his head stood in front of the assembly, lifting his arms and motioning wildly. The moaning began again. *Ayeyahayeyahhhh . . . ahhhoooo . . . ahhhoooo.*

Horrible, eerie wails filled the night and made our hair stand on end. We saw people dancing, bent forward, tossing their heads like wild ponies and moaning . . . always moaning.

The robed man moved among them like a specter of evil.

"It's a demonic worship service," I said with conviction. "Listen to those drums!"

"We can't stay out here all night," Wayne decided finally. "We know they'll be at it all night. Let's go to bed."

"Not even a vicious war wakes these people up," I lamented to Wayne. "You would think they would turn to God—not to the devil."

It is hard to sleep with those resonant drums beating in the African night, but there is no fear in my heart. I know the angels encamp round about us, no matter how close the camp of the enemy.

February 4

Baby Ryan has been diagnosed with active AIDS. Although he has begun eating and sleeping, he suffers from a runny stomach and low-grade fever. On Monday, we noticed small white blisters on his skin and sores on his mouth, so Julie took him to Elwa for tests. They refused to give her the test results since she is not a relative of the baby, so she took him to the JFK hospital. They informed her he was definitely positive for HIV.

When Dr. Lamin heard the story, he informed us that the Firestone Hospital cares for such babies, so that is where Julie took Ryan. "They'll take such good care of him, Mom," she said. "I really like the nurses. They gave me a cell number so I can check up on the baby. And the adoption agent said today that she has a family in the States that wants to adopt him as soon as possible. Can you imagine?"

"He's as precious in the sight of God as a healthy child," I said.

Marpu Anseh stopped in this afternoon with Rose tied on her back and Rachel in her arms. She was positively glowing.

"You saved my baby girls," she said joyfully. "Look, Sis Ruth! They are growing strong."

The change in those two babies is truly remarkable. They can lift their heads, and they stared at us anxiously. Charlotte and I thought we saw a glimmer of dimples in their silken cheeks.

"I can see you are feeding the twins plenty," I said happily. "You're a good mother, Marpu."

She had barely walked out the gate when Moses Massawalla entered the house with a large brown envelope. He handed it to me with a smile.

"Your story!" I exclaimed. "Are you *sure* it is safe to expose what happened?"

He nodded. "The danger of war is over. You can tell it now, Ma. An' may God bless you."

"You can't leave without a few cookies, Moses. Let me read it over quickly and see if I have any questions, okay? Sit down and I'll get you some water."

He sat enjoying chocolate chip cookies and ice water while I read his story.

Every year my tribe carries out a festival in which the gods of this world such as rocks, rivers, trees, and mountains are worshipped. Something living and precious needs to be sacrificed so the gods will hear the people's prayers . . . It is an evil, Satanic ritual. When a child is spiritually sacrificed, it eventually must die to add years to the killer's life.

I came in contact with Jesus Christ in July of 2002 when I was contemplating suicide and walked past the church. I heard singing and turned aside to listen. Though it was not easy, I confessed all my sins and renounced the gods of my people. "If we confess our sins He is faithful and just to forgive us our sins and to cleanse us from all unrighteousness," the Bible says.

Then the letter came. It was addressed privately to me, and invited me to come to the family festival in September. It described my role in the festival—as the firstborn son I was to receive the powers of my forefathers. My presence was absolutely essential and my absence would cause Herculean difficulties to the answers of their gods.

The letter haunted me. As a young Christian, I feared death would be my punishment for refusing to attend. I felt nauseated to my very soul. I wept and prayed night after night, but I could find no relief. The only comfort I got was through reading my Bible, and one morning at five-thirty I read the verse in 1 John that says, "Ye are of God, little children, and have overcome them; greater is He that is in you than he that is in the world."

What a wonderful peace flooded my heart as I read it over and over, claiming the promise for my own. I lost the awful fear and anger that had plagued me. Another verse in Matthew 16 became precious to me. "For whosoever shall save his life shall lose it, and whosoever shall lose his life for my sake shall find it."

I felt I was ready to die for Jesus rather than attend the festival.

During my struggles, a thought kept coming back to me: "Escape to an unknown destination for a period of time." I sought the advice of Pastor Mervin and Curt. "It is a good plan, but where will you go?" Pastor wondered.

"What about Ghana?" Curt asked.

I thought about leaving Liberia, and images of my suffering countrymen came to mind. "No, with all the suffering and massacres that my country is going through, I want to go distribute tracts to the believers and unbelievers in Liberia," I told them.

"That's fine with me," Pastor replied. "We can provide you with the necessary funds and the tracts, and you're on your way. May God be with you. Let's pray first, shall we?"

I felt the tears when he talked to me so gently, with so much concern in his voice.

Curt drove me to Totota, which was unknown territory to me. "Keep yourself pure and avoid the lusts of the flesh," he admonished me.

Sorrow filled my heart when he left. I felt like a stranger in a strange land, though the people started to recognize me when I passed out a lot of tracts. I spent the first night in a displaced camp with thousands of other homeless people.

The next day, I left camp and walked to the next village. Immediately, the suspicious citizens began questioning me, thinking I was a spy. After passing out many tracts, I left the village. I had only gone about ten miles when a group of armed militia soldiers roared up beside me and stopped.

"Get in!" the leader commanded.

I didn't waste a moment as I faced the ring of rifles. My knees shook as I climbed onto the back of the old, beaten pick-up truck. They made room for me to sit on the floor.

The truck roared to life, and I glanced apprehensively at the men surrounding me. All nine were about thirty-five or younger. Their hair was either plaited or shaved right off, and they wore ragged head ties and all kinds of African medicinal jewelry to ward off evil spirits. Their clothing was tattered and threadbare, with holes in the knees and gaping rips under the arms. Their rifles were in fairly good shape. Many wore slippers or sandals on bare feet. Most of them were smoking heavily.

Their faces were hard and fierce. Their eyes glittered with unbridled animosity.

"Where are we going?" I asked.

"Bobostown," one young man grunted. "To see our general—Evil Blood."

I felt an icy shiver go up my spine and stop at the roots of my hair. "Jesus! Help me!" I prayed silently. " 'Whosoever shall save his life shall lose it, but whosoever shall lose his life for my sake shall find it' . . . whatever happens, help me."

The truck stopped. Everyone leaped out, and I followed—and found myself face to face with General Evil Blood. I gave a start of horror. The man had fearful red eyes in a gruesome face. He stared at me coldly for a long time.

"Are you a rebel spy?" he asked in an ominous voice.

"No, sir," I answered. "I am on a tract distribution."

"That is impossible," he snorted. He held a tract up and read, "Liberia Mennonite Church . . . there is no such place. Has anyone ever heard of the Liberia Mennonite Church?" He whirled to face his men. No one spoke.

"This man is a spy!" he hissed through clenched teeth. "Here to fin' out wha' we do . . . and go tell it to the enemy. Take all his things an' his money an' prepare him for death."

"Jesus! They can take my money and all my things, but they can't take you!" The thought comforted me greatly. "Almighty God, you can rescue me—I am so afraid! I surrender my life to you, oh God! Help me stand firm, even in the face of a horrible death. I love you, Jesus."

I had no way of knowing how they planned to kill me—I just knew some of the ways they could. Like slowly cutting me to pieces . . . or tying my arms behind my back so tightly that the touch of a knife would split my chest . . . the list was endless.

"Citizens of Bobostown!" shouted the general. "Come an' see how we will play in this man's blood. Come an' see how we will put him to death!"

I heard the sound of flying feet as many people gathered round. I could find no pity in their eyes. Just a morbid curiosity of what was about to happen. Men and women, young girls and babies . . . They all came to see a man die—and that man was me! I knew they would be encouraged to dance and laugh during the execution.

"Our Lord Jesus!" I prayed again. "Give me strength, give me courage. I don't want to die, Lord."

The general turned and faced the crowd. "Who knows this man?" he shouted.

Deathly silence. Did Jesus give an answer?

"Who knows the Liberia Mennonite Church?"

Silence. My heart raced till I could feel it pounding against my ribs. Sweat stood out on my face and ran down my back like a small creek.

"My name is John, an' I know the church, but I do not know the man," someone said clearly.

All eyes turned toward the speaker. "General, I beg you, do not kill the man until I can go to Monrovia and find out whether the church knows him. I beg . . . let me go!"

Time stood still. We waited a whole minute for the general to speak. "I will keep him for two days. If you are not back on the third day, we will kill him. Now go!"

John's eyes met mine. I knew my life was partly in his hands, but wholly in the hands of God. Nevertheless, I watched him go with many feelings running through my heart. Would he come back in time?

"Pastor, would you pray for us before we go into the next town?" the general surprised me by asking. I was moved to pray without fear, asking God to have mercy on these men as they moved toward the battle zone. I knew I could never lift a hand to harm my fellow men, but I was in a situation over which I had no control.

"In Jesus' name . . . AMEN!" we all finished.

Instantly, they raised their weapons and fired into the air. "God has answered!" they cried.

"I feel happy about the zeal of your prayer," the general said, issuing me a rank above all his men. "From now on, you are General Pastor."

"I have overcome evil men through Jesus Christ," I decided, realizing with great joy that all fear was gone.

Later that day they assigned a boy about Larry's size to mind me while they went farther into the bush. He held a big rifle, and the two of us waited and waited.

"You could easily do away with him. Take the gun and escape," the tempter whispered. "Hurry, before they all come back."

"Would that be nonresistant?" the Spirit prompted. "How could you ever kill a child and be responsible for his blood?"

"I don't have a clue where I am," I remembered. "I could never get away from this place alive—so I will stay."

"Eat! Eat!" the soldiers urged me when they returned. I simply could not eat anything but bananas and some cassava. At least I knew what they were.

The sensitive questioning continued. "What are you really doing here? Where are they stationed? Do you know any of the fighters personally? Even if you know one, just call his name. Stop! Come!"

I would leap up and walk toward them. "Stop! Come!" they commanded again, beckoning me to walk toward them. I knew that if a man puts his left foot forward first, they know he has been trained as a soldier and kill him on the spot.

That night I slept on a bamboo bench, fitfully, because the soldiers would periodically fire into the air to scare their enemies.

The next two days are like a living nightmare in my memory. We went deep into enemy territory where the sounds of gunfire were close and frightening. I was to perform the same maneuvers they did whenever a battle would break out.

"Do just as we do," they instructed me. "When we lie down flat, or go behind a tree . . . Do everything we do immediately."

"Dear Lord Jesus!" was my constant prayer. "Please let John come back in time."

I knew their demonic creed demanded one man's blood every week, and if they had no enemy soldiers to butcher, they killed one of their own men. That put me in an awful situation.

The third day we drove back to Bobostown. The men were strangely silent, and they wouldn't look at me directly. General Evil Blood stared moodily with unseeing eyes.

I felt half sick with dread, anticipation, hope, and despair. I could not eat. My heart felt like it was in the grip of a merciless hand, squeezing tighter with every passing mile.

John was among the first people we met. He had just arrived from Monrovia, and in his hand was a letter.

"Please release Moses," the general read. "He is indeed a member of the Liberia Mennonite Church and was in Totota to distribute Bible tracts. Please let the man come back, we beg you." A hint of a smile spread over General Evil Blood's swarthy face.

"Do you really believe this man is from this church?" he asked John. "You saw his pastor? Could you carry me to his pastor right now?"

"If I cannot, you can kill me," John replied bravely. "I tell you the truth."

"If we release this man, an' the soldiers attack us soon, we will know you were part of the spy group—but I need some money for his release."

"Yes, sir," John responded, handing him the funds

"Cut his hair! Give him a sabu!" General Evil Blood ordered his men.

After my hair was cut, my release became official.

Those wicked, murderous soldiers broke out into wild dancing accompanied by Gospel songs. Songs of praise and worship—right there in that remote village. My own heart was so full of praise I could hardly contain myself.

John and I left that day yet, and twenty-four hours later I stood in Pastor Mervin's home. He welcomed me with wide-open arms. So did Brother Wayne, Brother Lamin, and others of my beloved Christian fellowship.

I was home!

I folded the letter with trembling hands, and regarded Moses for a moment. I was looking at a living miracle.

"You will fix any errors?" he asked presently.

"Moses, aside from a few grammatical mistakes, it is perfect," I said sincerely. "You really have a knack for putting your feelings into words. I could just see those soldiers and that general . . . This is one incredible story!"

"Praise be to God Almighty, who took me through the darkness into His marvelous light," he said happily. "I am safe under the blood, Ma."

"I plan to print this some day, Moses."

"To God be the glory!"

43

Tears of the Rain

February 26

Joseph Pawa, James Mast, Bev, and Julie went on an orphanage distribution early this morning. After unloading their supplies at the Good Samaritan Orphanage in Buchanan, they came upon a large group of people milling about in front of a displaced camp. James was driving and, thinking it was just another food distribution, he pulled out to pass the line of parked cars and trucks.

"This isn't a distribution—it's a mob of protestors!" he said, suddenly realizing his mistake. He was alarmed at all the ex-fighters, young children, and ex-fighter girls. Some of them held big clubs, and they had blocked the road with trees and rocks, making it impossible to proceed.

Listening to all the excited explanations, our group was able to decipher the cause of the riot. Three rebels had come to the school and slit the throat of one of the boys. The mob was protesting the boy's death and said they wouldn't let any cars pass until justice was served.

"Now what?" James groaned.

The angry mob swarmed all over the vehicle, sitting on the hood, saying they would spoil the car, and making a frightful amount of noise. They blocked the wheels of the Defender and started a fire right in the middle of the road in front of it.

Joseph and James tried hard to reason with the rioters, but got nowhere. "Christian Aid has helped you plenty," they appealed to the boys in front of the vehicle.

"We cannot get the people in front to let you through," said the boys.

"We need to pray," Bev suggested, and with that the girls began to pray earnestly in the back seat.

A boy came up to the window and demanded James's glasses, then a girl asked for them too. Another boy lifted his shirt and showed off the knife in his belt. James beckoned him to come over so he could talk with him, but the sullen fellow just walked away.

Seeing he made no progress by talking, James bowed his head and joined the girls in prayer, ignoring the people at the window.

Before long, a fellow with some authority approached the window, and the girls convinced him to let them through. He began clearing people and trees out of the way. James drove slowly forward so he wouldn't hit anyone, and got through the first mob right into a second one. Their new friend ordered the boys who were lying across the road to get up and let them drive through.

What a relief when they were finally free to go!

"It is nothing but the protecting hand of God that kept us safe," James said soberly.

Shortly before supper this evening, Esther Tebbs, a lady who has been working at CAM's sewing center, walked slowly through the yard with her baby, Julee, on her back. There was a nervous air of excitement about her, and presently she handed me an official-looking envelope. I slit it open and began to read. *"Dear Mr. and Mrs. Stelfox,"* I read aloud. *"We, Albert Tebbs and my wife Esther, have agreed to give to you our baby Julee . . . "*

The sentence hung in midair as I looked at Esther in astonishment. Charlotte's face registered shocked disapproval and Julie was speechless with surprise.

"Esther . . ."

"Read it," she said quietly, averting her eyes.

" . . . *give you our baby Julee to adopt and keep as your own. Please do this for us, we beg you, as we want the best chance for her. We have both agreed to the arrangement, and we know you will take the best care of Julee. Very respectfully yours, Albert and Esther.*"

For a minute no one spoke. "You know we could never take your baby from you, don't you, Esther?" I asked as gently as I could, trying to stifle the impatient anger that threatened to surface. "You love this baby. I know you do. I see how you take care of her at the sewing center and sing to her and cuddle her. How can you possibly give her away?"

"That's wha' ah tol' my husban'," she explained dolefully. "Ah said to him, she will never take Julee, *never.* But he said you will take her as a gift fo' all you have done fo' us. Ah *tol'* him."

"Well, you were absolutely right. We are not here to separate families and take children away from their parents. Just think how she would miss you!" Julie said.

"It's not the Bible way," I added. "Parents are supposed to raise their own children. What would you think if we gave Larry away as a gift to someone?"

Esther smiled faintly at the absurdity of the thought.

"She's not an orphan either," I reminded her firmly. "She has you and your husband and sisters and brothers. Please don't ever mention this again."

"Ah tol' him," she repeated, taking the offending letter and tucking it into her bag.

She walked outside and past the window. Baby Julee slept, oblivious to the fact that her parents had just tried to give her away.

March 7

Only one more Sunday after this, I thought sadly as I scanned all the dear faces in the crowded church. I wanted to burn the scene forever in my mind. I can hardly imagine where two full years have gone. They flew on the wings of the wind. *Dear Lord, help me to bear the pain of parting . . .*

I thought of all the simple, powerful sermons of the past two years, and Pastor Mervin's genuine way of bringing them across. He minced no words when he spoke, yet the message was unmistakable—*repent and believe, and you will be saved.*

Every week there were new faces in the church. People came to hear what the Liberia Mennonite Church had to offer. Many returned, impressed by the simplicity of the gospel being preached without drums, guitars, dancing, clapping, and shouting.

My gaze wandered to the back right benches where many of the ladies sat. There were Esther Akoi, Cleo Hardy, Sis Bea, Grace Jackson, Merci Evans, Philippine Doe, Esther Tebbs, and many more. Agutta sat between Amos and Jallah, listening intently.

As usual, the children sat wedged tightly, all dressed up and on their best behavior. Some of the smaller ones nodded in sleep. I tried to return their shy smiles, but the lump in my throat kept growing, and it didn't help to swallow.

The Liberian people are dedicated when it comes to farewells. All afternoon long we had visitors. They entered the house with very sorrowful looks, visited with us sadly, and finally left with tears in their eyes. It's wearing me down just a little bit. We still have ten more days to go.

March 11

Sadness enveloped me once more this morning when I turned the key to the sewing center for the last time, slid open the glass doors, and entered the dimly lit rooms. I paused and looked around before turning on the lights. I want to remember everything I can about the place—the scent of fabric, the slightly dusty tables and sewing machines, even the dear little kitten that roams the premises at night and sleeps where she pleases. No doubt she is responsible for the absence of the mice.

After a while, all the other ladies came and started sewing busily. They chattered and laughed and sang as they roared along on the old sewing machines, loving every minute. Choruses poured forth from their lips. "The Old Rugged Cross," African praise songs, and snatches of miscellaneous verse filled the air.

Much of the talk today centered on the recent wave of child abductions. "Elections are coming, so the people running for president go to the witch doctor," one lady told me. "He tells them which body parts he needs for his sacrifices. Usually it's the tongue, the eyes, the private parts, and the blood. Yes, it's true, Sis Ruth! I can see you do not believe. Yet it is true. The candidates believe they will get into office in this manner, so they stop at nothing."

Esther Tebbs spoke up in her gentle way. "Yesterday ah saw wi' my own eyes how dey stuffed a little boy into a rice sack an' put him into da trunk of a car. It was a big sack, abou' so high. Dey slammed the lid an' took off, but da policemen caught dem righ' dere. When dey opened da trunk da chil' had fainted. They would have sacrificed him."

"Another man asked a wheelbarrow boy to deliver a bag of 'fresh meat' for him, and on the way the 'meat' started wiggling," Merci said. "The boy got suspicious and called for help, so the people around the place grabbed the man and held him. When they opened the bag, they found a six-month-old baby girl struggling for breath. The man is now in jail."

"They lure da children wi' biscuits or candy," Dorcas put in. "Then they make them inhale something to put them to sleep."

"The children are still alive when they pluck out their eyes," Merci continued, her eyes staring and serious. "Even Charles Taylor was a member of the Zoe secret society, and Zoe members formed most of his cabinet."

There were affirmative nods all around.

"There is corruption in high places! The leaders consult witches all the time to tell them what body parts are needed for ceremonies that will ensure their continuing power—and they always, *always* require fresh blood."

I felt nauseated. "This is 2004, not ancient Egypt," I managed. "Are you serious, ladies?"

"Everyone knows this, Sis Ruth. It is no secret. Why do you

think Liberia is in such dreadful condition?"

"That is not all," Merci continued. "Most of the young children here in Liberia go through an initiating process—cuttings, genital mutilations and all kinds of wicked ceremonies—and if the family resists, they are put to death." Her eyes flashed with anger and scorn.

"That's why we don' let our chil'ren out of sight. But all we need to do is call on the Blood, an' we will be safe!" Dorcas said triumphantly, with a big smile. "The chil'ren are scared, but they don' need to be."

I smiled back at her, relaxing in the beautiful thought that there is power in the Blood. But Merci wasn't through yet.

"There are many witches operating in Liberia," she said darkly. "If you are not a Christian they will get you. You wouldn't believe what powers the rulers of darkness have on people who allow them."

"Oh yes, I believe it . . . but could we change the subject?" I asked.

It wasn't easy to do. These women live with the horrors of darkness surrounding them. More accounts of kidnappings and mutilations surfaced until I began to wonder if I should walk home alone.

"Greater is He that is in you than he that is in the world," Merci quoted finally.

"Praise God! Thank God!" everyone murmured.

March 12

It was another typical day for my husband—a virtual whirlwind of activity. He is trying to finish all the Self-Help projects he started. That means working steadily from sunup to sundown, then setting up lights to finish. It means keeping the carpenter, welder, mason, electrician, and several others busy. It also means building Philippine Doe a decent wheelbarrow to haul her ice chest around.

At one o'clock this afternoon, the CAM staff held a farewell for us. It was so sad. Some of us could not hold back the tears during all the warm wishes and handshakes.

By four-thirty, twenty-six ladies from the Mennonite church crowded around our kitchen table for another farewell. Merci was in charge of the meeting. We sang several songs and four women led lengthy prayers, then Merci spoke in detail about the qualities of a virtuous woman.

Finally she asked for any volunteers to speak.

Esther Akoi began by reiterating many of her memories of the past two years, then Cleo Hardy followed suit.

When Esther Tebbs began talking, she wept so loudly I wondered uneasily what the other guests were thinking. I soon ceased to care what people thought, however, when I listened to her incredible story of pain and poverty and then answered prayer and power in Jesus.

Everybody was in tears by the time Esther finished. I felt like howling, not just sniffling. As I looked around at all the mournful faces, I realized these ladies are no longer Africans to me, but personal friends. All of us have the same goal of getting to heaven. That bond is closer than any of nationality, race, or culture.

Several of the other ladies spoke, bringing up details about our family that we never dreamed they had noticed, let alone remembered. I realized as never before what a tremendous responsibility Christians have to be an example to the people around them.

March 16

It's hard to believe this is our last full day in Liberia. Many of the church ladies—Dorcas, Esther Akoi, Merci, Grace, Agutta, Cleo, and others—stopped in to say good-bye. They sat and watched mournfully while we zipped up the suitcases and did some last-minute cleaning.

"This reminds me of a funeral," I told Bev in the privacy of the bedroom.

Out in the yard, Wayne had Craig and Willie, and whomever else he could enlist, working on that custom-built wheelbarrow for Philippine Doe. It had to be just wide enough and long enough to accommodate her new cooler. Philippine herself waited in the security booth with great anticipation.

"Ah *knew* God wou' help me!" she crowed over and over. "God has made a way!"

After dark tonight, Wayne strung a light, and he and Craig continued working on the wheelbarrow. I warmed all the leftovers for the night security and took the food and some cold water out to them. I stood looking at the friendly moon shining between the leaves of the plum tree. It gave me a warm, secure feeling. That moon was created and held in place by the God we serve, and it is as predictable as the sunrise.

"*Goodnight, Liberia*," I whispered.

Later on, Harris Kollie, his mother Maima, and sister Fatu came to say good-bye, since Harris will be working early tomorrow morning. They solemnly presented us with a wall hanging and an African gown.

Nothing we could say or do would cheer Harris up. "The friendship and respect I have developed for your family has turned into an unrelenting pain in my heart," he explained.

"I really don't know what I would have done without you, Harris," Wayne said, shaking his hand.

"We will never forget you," he answered.

They walked out into the night—and out of our lives. But, just like all our other African friends, never out of our hearts.

March 17

When the house was finally quiet last night, it was hard for me to sleep. Fantastic dreams kept surfacing about Liberia—huge, unreal problems that no one could solve. Everyone was always sad or something was always wrong. I was relieved when daylight finally broke.

Security Robert and Zubah were kept busy announcing all the people at the gate, but there were just too many to let everyone inside. Elijah came in the morning to help keep things under control.

Larry is having a hard time deciding who gets which of his animals. Finally, Elijah persuaded him to leave them all at Residence, where he can take care of them.

"Elijah, you are the best!" Larry told him. "I wish I could take you home with us."

Elijah's jaw worked. "Larry, you are a fine man . . . a very fine man."

It was sheer agony to go outside and see the crowd of baby mas wanting to show us their children one more time. "What shou' we do now?" they wailed.

It was hard to tell them good-bye, since they all began crying and reaching out their hands to us in the most pitiful way. "O'Ma! Julie! Bev! Charlotte!" they moaned, rocking back and forth.

Lord, this is truly difficult.

Wayne was still grinding on the wheelbarrow when it was time to leave. "I thought he would not even change his clothes," Dr. Lamin chuckled.

In record time, Wayne was ready. He stuffed all his work clothes and boots into a bag. "Here, give this to someone," he said, handing me the bag.

I gave it to Elijah. "No one deserves it more," I said, smiling at him. "You have been a real friend, Elijah. They have to be washed, though."

"Dat's fine, Muttah. Thank you very much!"

Everyone was crying when we shook hands on the way out to the vehicles. Isaac Dixon was there, my dear Marie who cleaned so faithfully for two years, and many other friends.

I tried to get a glimpse of the house one more time, but my eyes were blinded with tears. Outside the gate, all the ladies waved and tried to smile . . . and we were gone.

"Looks like a thunderstorm is brewing," Wayne remarked, trying to cheer me up. I looked at the magnificent white clouds building on the horizon, and the tears came afresh at the thought of never seeing an African thunderstorm again. They have filled my life with wonder.

The ride to Robert's Field Airport was bittersweet. I tried to look everywhere at once and memorize all the sights and smells. Dr. Lamin laughed at his own jokes and tried to cheer us all up, but finally he, too, became quiet.

"Are you sure we have all our tickets and passports?" Wayne wondered.

"All is in order," I assured him.

A light, fragrant rain began to fall as we pulled into the airport and parked.

We lingered as long as possible, holding the twins and kissing them until they squirmed. Then it was good-bye to those who had become so near and dear.

Good-bye, Dr. Lamin, Georgie, Harris, and Elijah. Good-bye, Craig, Jewel, Staci, Angela and Esther. Good-bye, Brady and Brett . . . we love you. And good-bye, Liberia!

The last things we saw before entering the airport terminal were two small, dark, beloved faces and two small black hands waving frantically.

We turned our faces away . . . our tears mingling with the tears of the rain.

Epilogue

May 14, 2004

"Ruth Ann . . . guess what?" Jewel's voice reached all the way across the Atlantic from Liberia.

"You've got the boys' visas!" I fairly shouted.

"We have them right here in our hands!" she marveled. "We're flying home on the nineteenth . . . can you imagine?"

"Oh, Jewel, it was worth it all, wasn't it?"

"A thousand times over!" she replied.

"Did you know the paperwork is through for little Joanna? The McMahon's are all excited about bringing her home."

"Another baby safe," Jewel said happily. "Ryan is going to the States too, even though he has AIDS. The family is determined to give him a good life."

"Hug the twins for me, Jewel. What a miracle that they can come home! Thank God!"

"Did you know Rafiki and the parrot died two days after your family left?" Jewel wondered. "The natives firmly believe they died of a broken heart. Rafiki refused to eat, no matter what they gave her, and the next day she was dead. So was the parrot."

There was a pause as I tried to absorb this startling information. "Do you believe that's what happened?" I asked finally.

"We sure do! Elijah did his best, but there was nothing he could do. They must have known Larry was gone for good."

"I wouldn't be surprised if Larry would go back some day," I

473

said wistfully. "I'll tell him what happened. He wanted to bring Rafiki along home, but that was impossible."

"We hope to see you before too long," she responded. "Have a wonderful day!"

"You too, Jewel. Another chapter of our lives is closing . . . and it was a chapter worth living! Good-bye!"

Afterword

I had no plans of writing a book about our experiences in Liberia, West Africa, until Alvin Mast from Berlin, Ohio, gave me the idea. He urged me to take all the newsletters I had written over the course of twenty-seven months and change them into book form. He said people in America would love to read a book about first-hand experiences on the mission field.

I felt a great burden to portray the triumphs and the suffering of the Liberian people as I experienced it. Many times when I was yearning over some starving baby or suffering child, I felt the need to let others know. My only wish is that God be glorified through my pen.

Of a necessity, I changed a few names, but I stayed as close to the actual facts as it was possible for me to do. Where I was unsure of the order of events, I counseled with others who were in Liberia with me.

If any errors have slipped past me, I fully acknowledge that they are mine.

There would be no book written if people had not given of their time, energy, and encouragement. I am indebted to so many people I cannot possibly name them all. However, I will take this opportunity to express my humble appreciation to:

- My precious Lord Jesus, who gave me strength for each day

- My husband, Wayne Stelfox, and our children, Beverly, Julie Anna, William, Charlotte and Larry who all contributed to life in Liberia

- Alvin Mast, who insisted I could accomplish the task of writing this book and took upon himself the task of editing it

- Paul Weaver, member of the executive committee of Christian Aid Ministries, who was a source of tremendous encouragement

- Mark Yoder, former Country Supervisor for Liberia

- Dave King, Country Supervisor for Liberia, and all the staff at Christian Aid Ministries, who worked with us so patiently

- The generous donors who made it possible to go to Liberia

- Dennis Kline, who painstakingly combed through the manuscript and gave me excellent advice

- Dorothy Yoder, who carefully proofread and made changes where necessary

- Kristy Wadsworth, who expertly combed the final manuscript, and was a pleasure to work with

- My sister, June Hofer, who faithfully copied all my newsletters and kept them filed

- Craig and Jewel Carter, who contributed greatly to the major events in our lives, and kept Brett Alosious and Brady Oliver for their own

- Mervin and Mary Lantz, who helped us over many of the rough spots

- All our black friends in Liberia, for enriching our lives and providing extraordinary material for this writing

- Richard and Sue Kauffman, for opening their home to Faith Princess and Timothy Secret

- Kurt and Marilyn Shores, who gave Angela Naomi a home

- Jonas and Elva Yoder who made room for two more Liberian orphans, Blessing and Benjamin.

Ruth Ann Stelfox
August 2006

About the Author

Ruth Ann Stelfox lives in Raymond, Alberta, Canada, with her husband, Wayne, and three of their five children. Will and Larry work with Wayne building garden sheds for their new family business. Charlotte and Ruth Ann run an in-home daycare, where they care for several preschoolers.

Bev and Julie have been back to Liberia twice to visit their many friends, help in an orphanage, and bring home more orphans. When they aren't in Africa, they are employed by Green Acres Lawn Furniture in Pennsylvania.

The Stelfoxes live on a small farm on the prairie, forty-five minutes from the magnificent Rocky Mountains and forty miles (as the crow flies) from the Montana border. They raise miniature appaloosa horses and keep a flock of eighty laying hens.

They are members of Western Plains Mennonite Church.

Ruth Ann has had many articles and poems published and is a field editor for *Taste of Home* magazine. This is her first book.

L-R: Beverly, Charlotte, Ruth Ann & Wayne, Larry, Willie, and Julie

Christian Aid Ministries

Christian Aid Ministries (CAM) was founded in 1981 as a nonprofit, tax-exempt, 501(c)(3) organization. Our primary purpose is to provide a trustworthy, efficient channel for Amish, Mennonite, and other conservative Anabaptist groups and individuals to minister to physical and spiritual needs around the world.

Annually, CAM distributes 15-20 million pounds of food, clothing, medicines, seeds, Bibles, Favorite Stories from the Bible, and other Christian literature. Most of the aid goes to needy children/orphans and Christian families. The main purposes of giving material aid are to help and encourage God's people and to bring the Gospel to a lost and dying world.

CAM's international headquarters are in Berlin, Ohio. CAM has a 55,000 sq. ft. distribution center in Ephrata, Pennsylvania, where food parcels are packed, and other relief shipments are organized. Next to the distribution center is our meat canning facility. CAM is also associated with seven clothing centers—located in Indiana, Iowa, Illinois, Maryland, Pennsylvania, West Virginia and Ontario, Canada—where clothing, footwear, comforters, and fabric is received, sorted, and prepared for shipment overseas.

CAM has staff, warehouses, and distribution networks in Romania, Moldova, Ukraine, Haiti, Nicaragua, and Liberia. Through our International-Crisis program, we also help victims of famine, war, and natural disasters throughout the world. In the USA, volunteers organized under our Disaster-Response-Services program help rebuild in lower-income communities devastated by natural disasters such as floods, tornadoes, or hurricanes. We operate an orphanage and dairy farm in Romania, medical clinics in Haiti and Nicaragua, and hold Bible-teaching seminars in Eastern Europe and Nicaragua.

CAM's ultimate goal is to glorify God and enlarge His kingdom. ". . . whatsoever ye do, do all to the glory of God." (1 Corinthians 10:31)

CAM is controlled by a 12-member Board of Directors and operated by a 3-member Executive Committee. The organizational structure includes an Audit Review Committee, Executive Council, Ministerial Committee, several Support Committees, and department managers.

Aside from management personnel and secretarial staff, volunteers do most of the work at CAM's warehouses. Each year, volunteers at our warehouses and on Disaster-Response-Services projects donate approximately 100,000 hours.

CAM issues an annual, audited financial statement to its entire mailing list (statements are also available upon request). Fund-raising and non-aid administrative expenses are kept as low as possible. Usually these expenses are about one percent of income, which includes cash and donated items in kind.

For more information or to sign up for CAM's monthly newsletter, please write or call:

Christian Aid Ministries
P.O. Box 360
Berlin, OH 44610
Phone: 330-893-2428
Fax: 330-893-2305

Additional books
from Christian Aid Ministries

God Knows My Size!
by Harvey Yoder

Raised in communist Romania, Silvia Tarniceriu struggled to believe in God. But His direct answer to her earnest prayer convinced Silvia that God is real, and that He knows all about her. This book is excellent for family reading time.

251 pages $10.99

They Would Not Be Silent
by Harvey Yoder

In this book, each of the stories about Christians under communism are unique, yet one mutual thread runs throughout—They Would Not Be Silent concerning their devotion to the Lord Jesus.

231 pages $10.99

They Would Not Be Moved
by Harvey Yoder

A sequel to They Would Not Be Silent, this book contains more true stories about Christians who did not lose courage under the cruel hand of communism. It is our prayer that the moving stories will encourage you, help you to be a little stronger in your faith in the Lord Jesus Christ, and more thankful for the freedoms we enjoy in our country.

208 pages $10.99

Elena—Strengthened Through Trials
by Harvey Yoder

Born into a poor Christian family in communist Romania, harsh treatment at a state boarding school, and harassment from authorities for helping in secret Bible distribution . . . Elena finally decides to flee her home country. Will she make it? A true story.

240 pages $10.99

Where Little Ones Cry

by Harvey Yoder

This is a story about war in Liberia. In the midst of the terror that war brings are the little children. Their stories, a few of which are captured in this book, are not of typical, carefree children. Some of these true accounts have happy endings, but sad trails lead them there. The purpose of this book is not to entertain, but to help you appreciate our blessed country more and create awareness of the pain and spiritual darkness that abound in much of Africa.

168 pages plus 16-page color picture section $10.99

Wang Ping's Sacrifice

by Harvey Yoder

The true stories in this book vividly portray the house church in China and the individuals at its heart. Read how the church—strong, flourishing, and faithful in spite of persecution—is made up of real people with real battles. Witness their heartaches and triumphs, and find your own faith strengthened and refreshed.

191 pages $10.99

A Small Price to Pay

by Harvey Yoder

Living in the Soviet Union under cruel, atheistic communism and growing up during World War II, young Mikhail Khorev saw much suffering and death. Often homeless and near starvation, he struggled to believe in God's love. This inspiring story of how Mikhail grew to be a man of God, willing to suffer prison for the God who loved him, will move you to tears and strengthen your faith. You, too, will come to realize that everything we can give to the Christ who saves us is still . . . A Small Price to Pay.

247 pages $11.99

Tsunami!—From a few that survived

by Harvey Yoder

Just like that, one of the greatest natural disasters in modern history approached the city of Banda Aceh, Indonesia. For most people, the cries of "Water!" reached them too late. But some survived to tell the story.

As you read the accounts in this book, you will experience, in a small degree, a few of the horrors that the people of Banda Aceh faced. Some tell their stories with sorrow and heartbreak, others with joy and hope.

168 pages $11.99

QTY.	ITEM		TOTAL
	Tears of the Rain	Reg. $13.99	
	Tsunami!	Reg. $11.99	
	A Small Price to Pay	Reg. $11.99	
	Wang Ping's Sacrifice	Reg. $10.99	
	Where Little Ones Cry	Reg. $10.99	
	Elena	Reg. $10.99	
	They Would Not Be Moved	Reg. $10.99	
	They Would Not Be Silent	Reg. $10.99	
	God Knows My Size!	Reg. $10.99	

Book total

*Shipping & Handling

Subtotal

OH Residents Add 6.5% Sales Tax, PA Residents Add 6% Sales Tax to subtotal

Grand Total

* Shipping & Handling - USA

$0 to $10. . . . . $3.00 $10.01 to $25.00. . . . . . . $4.00
$25.01 to $55.00. . . . . $6.00 $55.01 and up. . . . . 10% of total
All foreign orders, including Canada please write or call for your postage costs.

Method of Payment:

❑ Check (please make check payable to TGS International)

❑ Visa/Master Card

Name on Card_____

Card #_____ Exp Date___/___

Signature_____

Billing Address:

Name_____

Address_____

City_____ State_____ Zip_____

Phone (_____)_____

Shipping Address (if different from billing address):

Name_____

Address_____

City_____ State_____ Zip_____

TGS International
P.O. Box 355 Berlin, Ohio 44610
*Bookstores and dealers, please
call for quantity discounts.*

To place an order or if you
have any questions, call
Phone: (330) 893-2428
Fax: (330) 893-2305